J

QUANTUM

A survival guide

M

for the new

P

Renaissance

W. R. CLEMENT

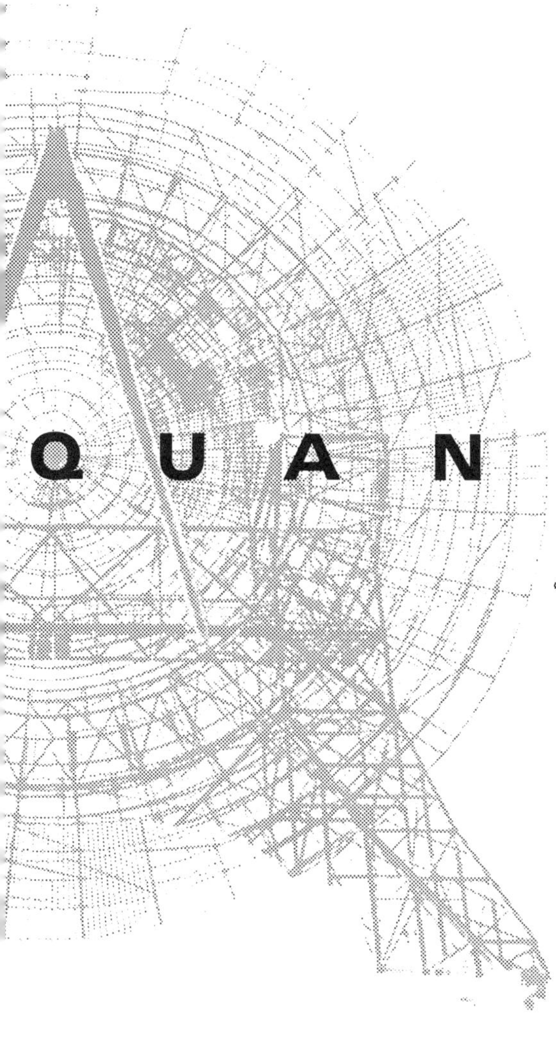

QUANTUM JUMP

A survival guide for the new Renaissance

INSOMNIAC PRESS

Copy edited by Jonathan Blackburn, Kate Harding, Craig Saila, Liz Thorpe
Designed by Mike O'Connor

Canadian Cataloguing in Publication Data

Clement, William, 1928-
  Quantum Jump: a survival guide for the next renaissance

Includes index.
ISBN 1-895837-48-0 (bound) ISBN 1-895837-45-6 (pbk.)

1. Social change. 2. Social history. 3. Twenty-first century. I. Title

HM101.C597 1998   303.4   C98-931827-3

The publisher gratefully acknowledges the support of the Canada Council and the Ontario Arts Council.

Printed and bound in Canada

Insomniac Press, 393 Shaw Street,
Toronto, Ontario, Canada, M6J 2X4
www.insomniacpress.com

The author wishes to acknowledge the following people, who, in no particular order, have encouraged the completion of this work. Without their support, encouragement, wise questioning of tenuous conclusions, and suggestions for vital sources of additional information, this work would never have been completed.

P.C. Mackie, who originally suggested that what had started as an essay should become a book, Dr. Reva Gerstein, David M. Carlisle, Nigel Atkin, Bertram Liffman, Jaan Poldaas, Matt Blajer, Janet Heatherington, Dr. Herbert Tookey.

A special note of appreciation to Cindy Matthews and Sharmain Beddoe for their O/S technical support and maintenance.

A special appreciation must be to my editor, Gregory Boyd Bell, who not only understood the book in its most nascent form in a way that taught me the difference between profound and recondite and that the two words were not irreconcilable. It was he who made the term "editorial query" one that enhanced the excitement and pleasure of the work for the author.

The Author's Perspective: Welcome to Renaissance 2.0

In *The Mechanical Bride*, Marshall McLuhan quotes Henri Bergson's *Time and Free Will*, in which Bergson poses this question: suppose some mischievous genius could so manage things that all the motion in the universe were doubled in speed and everything happened twice as fast as at present? How could we detect this fraud by which we would be deprived of half of our lives?

Bergson's reply was: easily. We could recognize the impoverishment of our conscious lives. The contents of our lives would be reduced.

This book is about a world in which time has not only been speeded up but continues to accelerate. It is a world in which the level of abstraction has become so elevated that many can no longer understand the forces at play. Moreover, the conventional economic stabilities on which we depend for a sense of security against radical change are leaders in the race toward instability.

The author's intent is to uncover the nexus points of this new era in history. This information should elevate the reader's understanding of the multiplicity of decision points every one of us will encounter for the rest of our lives.

One way to approach this is to look at the western European Renaissance, which was a qualitatively similar period, and explore useful commonalities which will help us comprehend our own new time. For, just as in the Renaissance, we face a period when fundamental assumptions about how the universe functions are being reformulated.

RENAISSANCE 1.0

The critical point in the emergence of the Renaissance was the discovery that the residual world-view of the European Middle Ages no longer encompassed the *known and knowable world* of the 15th century.

The Medieval world, before the last quarter of the 15th century, was seen in the light of Aristotle's finite universe, as retrofitted by Thomas

Aquinas and other fathers of the Roman Catholic Church. A finite universe was essential to the belief that God had made the universe perfect and complete. As a result, no evolution or expansion of the cosmos could be considered.

The epistemology (how you know what you know) of the pre-Renaissance Medieval world produced a world-view (collective intellect and psyche) that guided Church and state along a closed, recursive-loop system that only admitted new inputs after rigorous examination by Church theologians.

This system was emphatically negative toward anything which might upset the existing order; that, after all, is what closed-loop systems are supposed to do. The trouble starts when a closed-loop is found to not be closed after all. (It's similar to a computer operating system with undocumented trap doors. Such operating systems are an invitation to improper invasions, whether benign or malign.) That is what happened to the epistemology of the Medieval world.

THE CHALLENGE OF PERSPECTIVE

The Medieval closed-loop was doomed when artists discovered perspective — drawing and painting on a flat plane so that the viewer perceives the picture as if it were in three dimensions.

At the same time a new approach to scholarship emerged called Humanism. Humanistic education called for the study of a contemporary literature of ideas in the context of the great works of the past. It was through Humanism that the Renaissance brought into public discourse the new ideas which destroyed the feudal world and formed the basis of an epistemology for the emerging world of the Renaissance.

Prior to the Renaissance, contemporary ideas were awarded no significance or value. Medieval society was finite and complete. Everything new was simply unrevealed by God and, should God in His ultimate wisdom decide to reveal something new, the fathers of the Church would identify it and prove that it had, in fact, emanated from God. Anything else had already been explained by the classics and interpreted by the Church fathers.

The break-out from this highly structured world came when, in the northern Italian cities of the Lombard League, artists discovered the rules of perspective. It was perspective that cracked open the closed-loop of the Medieval world and brought on what we now call the Renaissance. Knowledge of perspective allows you to navigate on the open ocean. It allows you to build towering cathedrals. It allows your military forces to construct new kinds of fortifications and create new rules of engagement that employ effective battlefield ballistic weaponry.

Perspective was conceptually essential to developing a science of optics and thus telescopes and eventually microscopes. Widespread use of perspective-based art would even result in changes in neural activity among the population (in other words, an evolutionary increase in brain activity) which, in its turn, brought on the most important change of all. Human beings opened themselves to a heretofore unknown level of abstraction. This new level of abstraction brought on a vigorous and profitable series of invention cycles through applications of the new science.

When we talk about "raising the level of abstraction" we refer to a significant leap in our understanding of the forces driving the universe. This "quantum jump" is so profound that it casts doubt upon most, if not all, of our assumptions about how the world is organized.

That this new tier of complexity is real can be empirically shown through the system called the scientific method, which came to us from the Renaissance. This is not to say we regard the scientific method as immutable. There may be something better out there waiting to be discovered. We have tried revealed belief (Zeus came to me in a dream last night and told me to invade Egypt). We have tried classical authority (Ptolemy's great Astronomical System, in which the heavens revolve around the earth, has been accepted for centuries by scholars of all races, so I say let's toast this heretic Galileo). We frequently have tried brute force.

Once we discover the limits of our newly established abstraction frontier, we set about inventing tools that make this knowledge accessible to more people. We begin to see goods and services we were previously unaware of come into common use. Meanwhile, the first steps are being taken to challenge the next stage of complexity.

For example, the concept of "time" and how "time" is experienced underwent a profound shift during the Renaissance. While the first clocks were introduced in the 14th century, there was no idea of "standard time" — that would have to wait until the 19th century and Sir Sanford Fleming. Most clocks would strike the hour but few had a minute hand. They were usually wrong and required frequent resetting. In fact, a whole new trade of clock repairers and installers toured Europe maintaining these clocks.

When a village acquired a clock, the hourly ringing of the bells helped to neurally condition a commonly accepted sense of "time," which allowed work to be organized more effectively and ushered in the new abstractions in a discrete and orderly way.

The effect of the availability of a consensual temporal reference was enormous, with an impact on everything from birth date significance to setting times for the consummation of new commercial transactions which occurred outside the Medieval barter economy. Barter systems are, by their nature, essentially local. Commercial trade, with its attendant bills of exchange, growth in real wealth and overall community well-being, contributed to a new world-view with a heightened and expanded sense of the parameters of the individual's world.

The neural adaptations necessary to accommodate the new level of abstraction resulted in an increase in tangential or non-linear thinking, which is a means of identifying functional relationships between objects, events, and people. When simple cause-and-effect relationships no longer suffice to describe the complex interactions that increasingly make up daily life, tangential thought becomes an essential way to explore new connections — and to simply understand daily life.

This is why the Renaissance is such a good place to begin looking for hints about how to more readily understand our own time. The people of the Renaissance — like ourselves — faced a change-rate of profound proportions. The institutions of their society began collapsing due to their inability to adapt and became increasingly corrupt under assault from an array of new socioeconomic forces. Finally a new world-view, called Humanism, supplanted the world-view of Aristotelian-Thomistic assumptions.

RENAISSANCE SHOCK

In the past 500 years the rate of technological and social change has sped up exponentially. With an ever-quickening pace, new and complex ideas, inventions, and events are foisted on us, while we watch familiar institutions, through which we order our lives, falter and frequently fail to deliver the services we mandated them to provide.

We see our familiar social safety nets collapsing under the shifted economic and political sureties while our institutional leaders no longer demonstrate simple competence, let alone wisdom, in carrying out their responsibilities.

History may very well define the past two or three decades as the "Anaesthetic Age," since we seem to have managed to avoid confronting, or even questioning, what was really going on. This social anaesthesia occurred in spite of, or maybe because of, the introduction into the language of the term "future shock."

In July 1970, Alvin Toffler's book *Future Shock* was published by Random House. "Future shock" was Toffler's term for the impact of the intensification of the rate of technological and resultant social change, which we have experienced since the 1960s. An alternative definition is the sense of bewilderment experienced by those who were not paying attention.

Sadly, Toffler's accomplishment may have been to create a panacea by merely naming the malaise, in the manner of shamans who exorcise demons by chanting their secret names.

In the light of the marketing success of *Future Shock* and the ease with which the term future shock entered the language, one cannot claim that

Toffler erred in his limited message. Having said that, the reader can be assured, without implying denigration of Alvin Toffler, that this book is not another *Future Shock*.

SURVIVAL SKILLS AND ERA SHIFTS

Pictures such as Hogarth's Gin Lane or accurate histories of the wars of the 15th and 16th centuries offer compelling arguments that we could do no worse than our forebears did in managing an era transition.

A major objective of this book is to expose the significant variables which are at play in this era transition and give the reader resources for personal risk management. New eras in history are genuinely risk-intensive, both for individuals and for institutions.

One of the generally accepted aspirations in the wealthy West has been to eliminate or soften the risks we encounter. We have been successful in eliminating risk to the point that most of us have little experience in training our judgment of risk. Our risk-assessment is usually poor. Unless we upgrade these skills we will slip into the category of history which describes those who had it all and gave it away.

In the last quarter of the 20th century it has become increasingly clear that if we don't manage this time-shift better than our forebears did theirs, our own progeny will be justifiably mortified by us. Further, if we don't manage it much better, we probably won't have any progeny to be humiliated.

If the reader agrees with the assumption that we are in the midst of an era transition at least as profound as the Renaissance, then this book should be considered a map of the variables that affect how individuals and whole societies survive an era transition.

Era transitions are often mistakenly termed as new historical "ages," such as the Scholastic Age, the Mercantile Age, the Industrial Age, or the Automobile Age. We'll define a historical "era" as a period of time during which a particular world-view, or level of abstraction which is consensually agreed upon, provides both a description of and a strategy for exploring the known universe.

An age, on the other hand, is derivative of an era. Eras often encompass many ages, such as the Industrial Age and the Automobile Age. But an era has a more profound identity. An age tends toward impetuosities and ill-considered radicalisms. An era has the qualities of a juggernaut. With an age you can negotiate, while an era sets its own terms and conditions. The Computer Age is negotiable, but the era which makes the computer possible comes on with no possible equivocations.

A true era transformation occurs when one or more societies with a high degree of "energy" experience a quantum jump in the level of abstraction, which is then accepted as the norm. When this rise in the level of society-wide abstraction occurs, the world-view of the society changes to accommodate the new insights and resultant discoveries. Then, as new iterations of this world-view take over, significant shifts in the entire society occur.

The Renaissance is still our metaphorical benchmark of burgeoning intellectual, economic, and creative activity. During this time there was little artificial split between the arts, the sciences, government, and business. An individual who exhibited a lack of interest in one or another of these areas was regarded as deviant. Today we look with wonder at the wide ranging yet seamless quality of curiosity people exhibited then, yet we call contemporaries who exhibit these tendencies "unfocused".

In the business community, a person may not readily admit to an interest in the arts for fear of being marked as suspect by peers addicted to "focussing." And an artist may take pride in knowing no science, since science is a "cold and passionless pursuit", apparently unlike whatever artistic media from which the artist derives a sense of passionate engagement.

In this time scientists who abandon the "purity" of their academic search for scholarly truth to explore commercial implementation of their discoveries are usually seen by their academic peers as having become engaged in trivial activities, unworthy of a real scientist.

Obviously the above does not describe all artists, poets, filmmakers, painters, bankers, marketing executives, engineers, prelates, savory salesmen, bungee-cord jumpers, or alchemists who consort with the dead. But our societal commitment to exclusionary specialization is common enough.

Chief executives, when speaking at commencements or talking to university presidents at blue-ribbon panels on "Whither Post-Secondary Education in 2037?" cry out for liberal arts generalists. It's a pity they can't hear their own personnel managers lobby college placement directors for graduates with highly specialized skills.

One thing an era transition demands — as a survival tool — is a degree of perceptual mobility. Perceptual mobility was one of the major distinguishing features of a person who was successful in the Renaissance.

WHEN MONEY WAS INVENTED

Cognitive psychologists in our own time tell us that money is one of the most abstract things most of us ever deal with. As children, we take years to plumb the mysteries of this abstraction and most of us never do get it straight.

If you were an ordinary person living in the earliest years of the Renaissance, you would seldom see money. Subsistence bartering was the principle basis of local economies. If you had been born 100 years earlier in feudal Europe as a serf (and almost everybody was a serf), you would have likely spent your entire life without ever having or seeing money.

In their time, the Renaissance bankers of Sienna, Florence, and the Lombard League acted at a daunting level of abstraction. What they did was to invent money as we know it. They came up with the bill of exchange and, as a means to manage it, the double-entry bookkeeping system. These Italian bankers set in place one of the two key ingredients necessary to move into global trading and set off a new historical era.

In the 12th century, the Knights Templar provided a bill of exchange via their chapter houses throughout the Mediterranean, but these could only be accommodated through the Templars' forts and were really a Templar currency that was only exchangeable within the Mediterranean basin. (They charged a fee of 5 percent for the service.)

In the early 1300s Philip IV (the Fair) of France accused the Templars of heresy, fornicating with snakes and dragons, and all the other charges one laid in the 14th century that resulted in an individual being tortured under an inquisitorial legal system. Philip then grabbed the lands and monies of the Templars, which put them out of the sort-of banking business.

Enter the northern Italian bankers. Traders using their services could carry a bill of exchange into the ports of the Hanse, the trade fairs of Flanders, or the City of London (which is how Lombard Street got its name). The bankers followed trade routes, not the Mediterranean course of the Crusades.

It must have been a tough sell for these bankers to convince merchants to accept a piece of paper in lieu of gold or silver specie — and still tougher for those traders to travel to another country and convince other traders to accept these bills of exchange for goods. After all, these guys carried swords, guns, and knives. The 15th century was not exactly noted for the composed and calm conditions which would encourage the pacific development of international trade. What had happened to encourage people to take these kinds of risks?

OPENING THE MIND'S EYE

By the 15th century artists began to paint pictures using the rules of perspective. The day of flat, linear art was replaced by paintings, drawings, and architecture that exploited a third dimension.

The monasteries of the era taught in their drawing classes (for the monks who were being trained to illustrate sacred texts) a flat, linear technique which responded to the classical abhorrence of a vacuum and justified leaving space, which was "God's space." Fathers of the church argued that this space, in religious illustrations, *proved* that God need not be seen to exist. It was in this space that the Renaissance painters would install perspective.

The monasteries also housed people with a curiosity about the natural and spiritual worlds. Fresh from the "Dark Ages" there was a motley collection of scholars in different monastic order houses who pondered scientific and mathematical problems. To be honest, we might have difficulty recognizing their logic as science or mathematics. They were mostly alchemists whose interests lay in the magical properties of certain numbers. But while seeking the secret codes of the universe, the Church fathers and lay alchemists started to stumble upon mathematical theorems.

With these theorems they began to check the geometry of Euclid. They also began to search for such important things as a proof that centaurs had horns which, when correctly ground up, would cure all the illness to which mankind is prone. Nonetheless a new mathematics was born, which was subject to "proofs," whereby scholars shed their hermetic, closed-loop heritage.

There is plenty of evidence that the discovery of the technique of perspective was not greeted with universally unbounded enthusiasm. Many of the fathers of the Church attacked Giotto, Brunelleschi, fra Luca Pacioli, and fra Angelico, those at the forefront of the perspective movement, for profanity and that catch-all bust of the time, heresy.

Around the same time, Arab numeracy was being incorporated into everyday life. By abandoning Roman numerals and using the more easily manipulated Arabic numerals, a new mathematics evolved for such applications as navigation, ballistics, and architecture. Trade expanded and innovation abounded in daily life.

In fact, things on the innovation front picked up to the extent that, within a couple of hundred years, Isaac Newton could publish his laws without ending up tied to a stake.

WHEN A NEW ERA CALLS

To this day, in tribute to the Renaissance as a period of intellectual and creative flowering, we describe someone who maintains an exceptionally aggressive curiosity about the world and is well-rounded in science and the arts as a "Renaissance person".

The Renaissance was a time when intellectual curiosity was assumed of anyone who presumed to literacy. The urge to improve one's own knowledge of the world was widely spread through the society, which held that acquiring knowledge was in itself both pleasurable and valuable. It was conceivable for an individual to better himself!

After spending some time wallowing in amazement at what those Renaissance people accomplished, the answers to the questions of "Why them?" and "Why didn't they remain in the comforts of feudalism?" become interesting and possibly useful.

After all, in the Medieval feudal world, with its manorial economy, everyone knew who they were, to whom they were obliged, and who was obliged to them. There was no demand for therapy circles for discovering "the real me inside." It wasn't a bad life, especially if you knew of no other options. Only the clergy could read and their reading was rigorously circumscribed. Aside from the occasional plague years, most of Europe was reasonably housed, clothed, and fed. (It was a great time to be a small boy. There was little pressure to bathe and they seldom did.)

The critical variable for a new era is the rise to a new plateau *in the generally accepted level of abstraction*. It was this new level of widely agreed functional abstraction that would necessitate a new world-view. The Renaissance raised up the middle class on the successful commercializations of spin-offs from the new level of abstraction, which in turn expanded democratic politics.

What happened to the establishment, the vested interests? Weren't they miffed? Didn't they try to stop the resultant decline in their revenues and their community status as all-round power managers? Didn't they pull out all the stops to end this pillaging of their "divinely-awarded" rights?

Of course they did. We call this the Reformation. But there was no way the Renaissance bankers were going to stand by while some Church father banned the bill of exchange, which was the basis of the new money. Those who had risked all in the creation of the new money had no intention of giving up their newly bought-and-paid-for status. No matter how any Holy Roman Emperor or Pope felt about it.

BODIES IN MOTION

In 1665, England was in the throes of the pandemic Great Plague. The royal court left London for the country, while Cambridge University was closed down and the students sent home.

Among those students was 23-year-old Isaac Newton, who went to his family's farm at Woolsthorpe, where he discovered his three laws of motion over a 10-month period. It was here at Woolsthorpe that the apocryphal apple came crashing down on his sensitive head. If not for those 10 months of his life, Newton might have been known only to specialist historians. Certainly his unacknowledged debt to Robert Hooke was essential to the full flowering of his work on gravity. In his memoirs, Newton says:

> I began to think of Gravity extending to ye orb of the Moon & ... I deduced that the forces wch keep the planets in their Orbs must [be] reciprocally as the squares of their distances from the centres about wch they revolve & thereby compared the force requisite to keep the Moon in her Orb with the force of gravity at the surface of the earth, & them answer pretty nearly. All this was in the two plague years of 1665-1666. For in those days I was in the prime of my age for invention and minded Mathematics & Philosophy more than at any time since.

There is a holiday celebrated by computer hackers everywhere. It is December 25, the day on which Isaac Newton was born. This is why December 25 is known as Newton's Day.

Newton was a thoroughgoing man of the English Renaissance. The English Renaissance was, among other things, a time unencumbered by conflict-of-interest legislation. Newton's track record, after surviving the plague years and the food at Cambridge, was varied. In 1696 he was appointed warden of the Royal Mint at a time when auditors were unheard of. At the same time, he managed to stay on intimate terms with the royal court. Although the king, William III, had sent along John Locke to make sure that Isaac didn't get too radical in his solutions, there was no doubt about who was really running things.

As the king cheerfully admitted to one of his royal relatives, he really expected that Mr. Newton would solve the problems of the exchequer (buying up the outstanding coinage and replacing it with new) through alchemical transmutation: "although Mr. Newton swore to me that transmuting is beyond any known abilities, I am sure that he carries the secret and will solve the problem by secretly transmuting some easily found base metal into the purest gold."

Newton secured enough royal favour to become the president of the Royal Society (a group dedicated to the advancement of science) in 1703, so he must have been cautious about what stuck to his fingers at the Mint, although he came out quite wealthy. By virtue of his status in the Royal Society, he was able to decide his dispute over priority in the invention of calculus with Gottfried Wilhelm von Leibniz in his own favour, through his power to appoint an "impartial committee" to settle the issue after Leibnitz had foolishly appealed to the Royal Society to arbitrate the dispute.

Never one to take an unnecessary chance, Newton volunteered to write the report for the committee and then reviewed the report, anonymously, for the Society's own journal. This review found that *Leibniz* was guilty of plagiarism!

Newton held the Lucasian Chair in Mathematics at Cambridge (currently held by Stephen Hawking). When the publisher of the second edition of Newton's *Philosophiae Naturalis Principia Mathematica* was preparing the manuscript for the printer, he wrote to Newton, apologetically saying that he had found 20 errors in calculations. Newton replied graciously, telling the younger man not to worry because he knew of an additional 30 errors, but that all the calculations were "close enough."

In his later years, Newton saved the Royal Society from financial ruin. His puritanical personality included a brilliant political mind whose understanding of the body politic of his time allowed him to lead a successful knowledge-for-hire operation that makes the think tanks of our own time seem penny-ante. His political machinations enabled him to establish a scientific community that served his country's commercial and political interests to the detriment of the rest of Europe. Probably the most important immediate result of Newton's work was to provide the, by then, nearly mature new era of history with the basis for a congruent epistemology.

This epistemology included the fundamentals of the scientific method, which he derived from his alchemical experience. His talent for experimental technique and scientific apparatus design and building gave him access to a rigourous empiricism covering fundamental work in mathematics, physics, astronomy, and optics. This commitment to such wide-ranging, world-leading exposure of undiscovered aspects of the universe through what he called "experimental philosophy" still leaves us breathless. The epistemology that began with Newton and was disseminated, argued over, and empirically tested in the pages of the *Transactions of the Royal Society* has served the world for 300 years.

WHEN ORTHODOXY CRUMBLES

In 1900, at the International Congress of Mathematics, David Hilbert posed his 23 problems, which were seminal to the foundations of modern mathematics, and Max Planck reported his quantum theory. In 1915, Einstein published his theory of relativity, which exposed a post-Newtonian universe of demonstrable proportions. Heisenberg's uncertainty principle of 1927 was followed in 1928 by Heisenberg, Schrödinger, and Dirac's reformulation of mechanics and quantum mechanics. Since then, a succession of apparently intractable problems have been solved — sometimes by gifted amateurs and frequently by workers from other disciplines who have challenged the orthodoxy.

Discovery from outside the priesthoods is another sign that an era transition is under way. When the bodies professing concern for the advancement of knowledge try to protect the archives from challenges to their paradoxes, anomalies, and contradictions, outsiders without vested interests in the status quo usually serve as challengers. Outsiders who challenge the conventional wisdom bear a heavy burden of proof. As we will see, humanity has devoted a lot of time to developing legitimate means to challenge historical authority. Since the days of Scholasticism, the number of lives sacrificed to secure a right to free enquiry should give us a clue as to this particular freedom's importance to growth and survival.

Challengers of conventional wisdom must offer rigourous proofs and arguments to support their claims. If a claim attacks the views held by the majority in a discipline, the new knowledge, unblessed by peer support, has the potential to change the lives of millions. It is not the invention — the stirrup, the yoke, the printing press, the astrolabe, the steam engine, electric lights, the automobile, radio, the transistor, antibiotics — which alters the map of the world. It is the idea that changes the level of abstraction.

It comes from the Aristotles, the Ptolemys, the Paciolis, the da Vincis, the Brunos, the Galileos, the Newtons, the Leibnizes, the Keplers, the Darwins, the Plancks, the Hilberts, the Einsteins, and the Heisenbergs, most of whom never invented anything in their lives, but without whom nothing which we see as the icons of progress in our time would have been.

WELCOME TO CYBERSPACE

In the course of writing this book I became more generally optimistic. I also became less optimistic that the corporate and political leaders of the planet have the slightest idea about the nature of the real forces which control the change rate. (This may have been a shedding of the final bit of the innocence with which I entered the world.)

I'm not sure why this should surprise me. After all, politicians — good, bad or indifferent — are no different from the rest of us. They too carry the baggage of the assumptions of their private world-views. The same holds true for corporate executives, professors, and union leaders.

They are all constrained by the rate at which the body politic keeps up with the change rate. When the world-view changes, the signals that it is changing may be hidden in information that is not easily accessible, or is hidden by trivial commercialization. We are all socialized to a culturally defined sense of time and history. During an era transition, history accelerates to the new tempo. Few of us today are untouched by the discomforts of the change rate. Not only is it faster than any historical referents we might have, it is also more profound.

The term "cyberspace," as used here, has gained a wide currency since 1984, when it was coined by William Gibson. Since then it has been appropriated by the computer programming fraternity to describe a "post-industrial" work environment of virtual parallel worlds and potential work spaces. The terms "hyperspace" and "N-space" are used as synonyms in this book for "cyberspace" from time to time. Usually they are used to alert the reader to a slightly different spin on the phenomena of cyberspace.

Another definition of cyberspace is "the space traversed between the third and fourth-plus dimensions." It appears that "cyberspace" has become the accepted term. And so our language evolves and consensus occurs.

The wealthy and powerful are prepared to exert great effort to resist the changes which occur as the entire world tries to bring daily life into some kind of rational congruence with new realities. Fortunately, the rich and powerful usually lack any comprehension about what is really going on.

We are all discomforted by the quality of change and the change rate. When postal employees threaten strikes and Luddite sabotage as their jobs are supplanted by personal fax machines, do they really believe that they are miraculously immune to the change rate? Bicycle couriers had to deal with that one in the 1980s.

Unions are, by and large, as maladaptive to a new world-view as other institutions of society. Union leaders have largely failed to develop or support adaptation programs. Unions are organized on either a craft, corporate, or industry basis. If the craft or industry is to change to meet competitive technological pressures, employees who have no skills to bring to the changed work environment will lose their jobs and no longer pay dues to their union. The union will not benefit from retraining, since the workers will join another union when they are once again employable.

Labor dislocation due to technological change is not unique to our time. When Isaac Newton took over as master of the Royal Mint (on his birthday — December 25, 1699), he found that forgery and counterfeiting were so rampant that England's economic structure was at risk. At that time coins were individually stamped out by hand — the Moneyer's Guild was one of the strongest of the residual Medieval guilds. Newton brought in new mass-production technology that enabled the mint to replace all of the coinage in circulation. The new methods were far more efficient than anyone had anticipated; even though two of the regional mints were closed, there was a five-month period when no coins were minted in England. For the next five years, 75 production days per year were sufficient to meet all of England's coinage needs. (At the time coins formed the major part of the English monetary system.) Many of the members of the once-proud Moneyers were reduced to seeking day-labourer jobs.

For their part, our executives and managers frequently resist implementation of new technologies which they do not understand and which may attack the mythologies a manager has made part of his or her own identity-myth system.

I know a man who sells postal automation equipment. A few years ago, he made a major sale to accompany the implementation of a new postal code system. When asked about the quality of the system, his reply was

---

Lewis Carroll understood how language works:

"When I use a word," Humpty-Dumpty said in a rather scornful tone, "it means just what I choose it to mean — neither more nor less."

"The question is," said Alice, "whether you can make words mean so many different things."

"The question is," said Humpty Dumpty, "which is to be master — that's all."

—Lewis Carroll, *Alice in Wonderland*

instructive. He said: "They bought the highest-level system which both the management and the union officials could understand. That happened to be the lowest-level system we sell."

It is a false argument to suggest that the issue of adaptation to the change-rate is a union/management issue. It is a human issue which sweeps across the entire spectrum of society; ultimately, the responsibility lands on our own shoulders.

LOST LEADERS

When former president George Bush announced his "New World Order," there was a brief period when we thought that he and those whom he led might have some idea about what the world really looked like. No such luck.

The world-views of George Bush and Bill Clinton, Margaret Thatcher, John Major, Tony Blair, Brian Mulroney, and Jean Chrétien are embarrassingly similar to those held by English Social Darwinists circa 1870. Embarrassing because it is difficult to see the value of being led into the 21st century by some of the truly reactionary minds of the 19th century.

The American electorate resolved the anxieties about Bush, but the caveat remains intact for Bill Clinton. For the issues addressed here, those setting his administration's agenda differ from the Bush trendoids only in style.

There is a new world order, but Bush and Clinton and the social elites who form their principal constituency are unlikely to rate more than a footnote in its history. When we consider the power of the president of the United States, it is difficult to realize that Bush or Clinton might in no way be seen as significant a short 250 years from now. Plenty of regimes in history were simply an inconsequential blip in time. Both George Bush, who commanded the most powerful resources on the planet for a brief four years, and the 75-year Communist Soviet Russian experiment will probably not be seen as significant events when this new history's direction is sorted out because they represent the final gasps of an old era.

None of us can count on any government, anywhere, to respond appropriately. Anyone who has ever worked in a government which is even minimally functional will tell you that government's inertia precludes any real action on any problem for which there has been no pre-planning.

What 20th century governments in the industrial world do well is to implement programs designed to deliver services which are general and have strong consensual support from the populace. If the government or the bureaucracy is corrupt or incompetent, the likelihood of achieving a consensus diminishes and the degree of electoral confidence is minimal.

Political accountability, if by no other means than regular elections, seems to be essential. Most politicians in industrial nations seem to become banal very quickly and end up being mouthpieces for their civil servants or the vested interests which brought them into office.

A MATTER OF SURVIVAL

There is no way to avoid being part of the real new world order. Survival appears to be a function of *individual* adaptation to the enhanced level of abstraction. Adaptation seems to be highly influenced by the ability to cast off the historical baggage we all carry. As a society, we will survive only if enough individuals survive. The goal of this book is to help the reader frame some of the right questions which will aid in that survival. That is probably the most we can do right now.

When Christopher Columbus sailed to the Americas, his discovery had a very positive effect back in Europe. By discovering the Americas, Columbus destroyed the assumptions of the feudal society's manorial economy. That economy was based on the idea that land was finite and under the orderly control of the Holy Roman Empire and the Church.

Columbus engaged in a lot of hyperbole as to the amount of land he had found, in order to raise funds for another voyage. Subsequently, other explorers brought back the word that, if anything, Columbus's estimates of the available land were conservative. This idea of infinite land put the Aristotelian-Thomistic belief in a finite universe under a serious cloud and was an unintentional attack on the established order.

The effect on the native societies whom Columbus and subsequent European explorers encountered was less benign. At that time the Native Americans lived in wide-ranging, shame-focused, tribal, largely nomadic, slave-holding societies. These aboriginals met the advance agents of the nation state, whose mathematics allowed them to navigate the Atlantic.

The Europeans were numerically inferior to the point of being almost a token invasion force, compared with the raw numbers of native Americans. But the Europeans were part of culture that was *on the march*. Spain had decided it was an imperial power. Pope Alexander VI, the first Borgia pope, had awarded the Americas to Spain and Portugal. (Did he have the right to do this? Hell no! Ask the French and British.) European weapon systems had been tested on the battlefields of Europe and included horses, which the indigenous people had never seen.

When the Spaniards reached the high cultures, such as the Aztecs, they discovered societies that had independently developed advanced mathematics, which was being used to support religious auguries as part of the control mechanisms to exploit the populace for the benefit of a venal priesthood and nobility. The abstraction of native mathematics had never been allowed to become part of the overall society's epistemology and no technologies, aside from some crowd-pleasing human sacrificial techniques, had evolved from it. The native societies were stable and mature, with no evidence of evolutionary potential.

Similarly, in the first contacts made by the French, Portuguese, and British with aboriginal peoples from mature tribal societies, they were found to have very low levels of abstraction in their epistemologies. When they met these Renaissance greed-freaks from Europe, they fared badly. In simple terms, the American aboriginals were hunting and gathering nomads who had the bad luck to run into a society with all of the energy and power of one at the break-out point of a new era. The meeting was, as we know, no contest.

A NOTE ON STYLE

This book is structured in such a way as to give the reader access to the idea of tangential thought. The central theme is reiterated from time to time in different ways and with different referents in an effort to create the illusion of density, speed and dimensionality — much like the techniques of "cyberpunk" fiction writers.

When we speak of "tangential" or "lateral" thinking, we are talking about the connection of ideas and things getting away from conventionally perceived context-dependency, which is how ordinary "linear" thought is determined.

It isn't surprising that in an era transition we find an increment in tangentially ordered ideas, writing, and the spoken word. The conventional world appears chaotic, while conventional associations no longer fit or indicate the associations they once did. At the same time, people are searching to relate new concepts to familiar ones, for which the language may simply lack familiarity or synonymous terms.

Psychologists have found tangential thought to be highly correlated with creative thinking, but 20 years ago psychiatrists were teaching that tangential thought indicated a disorder.

Another reference point for the book's structure was the model of a neural network. That is, the reading audience is treated as a series of neural network nodes, determining the degree, frequency, and qualitative shifting of reiteration in response to queries from nodes for specialized clarifications. This is the way a neural net learns, through responding to queries from its nodes. This neural network structure was initially set up using the outliner software Think Tank.

Some readers may find the use of irreverence or even humour (?) offensive when applied to some topic they believe to be sacrosanct. It is a device to suggest that we must treat contemporary values as transient events. To assume that future mores will be the same as ours — when the events which determined current mores are either forgotten or seen as amusing anachronisms — is to fly in the face of all recorded history.

In any case, the irreverence is intended in the manner of Erasmus of Rotterdam, who used his high sense of wasp-like irony and satire in the course of *In Praise of Folly*. This book, the most important critique of the period we think of as the Northern Renaissance, was originally written in seven days as a letter to his close friend, Sir Thomas More. *Folly* incorporated biting satire and used a bantering wit he knew More would enjoy.

In a letter to his sometime friend Martin Dorp, a spokesman for theologians who were critical of Erasmus's apparent blasphemy regarding the classical philosophers, Erasmus told Dorp why he kept the material, originally intended for More's eyes only. Firstly, it served to improve accessibility to the main themes. Secondly, it inhibited the reader from attaching too much importance to transient events which are only mentioned because they are markers on an unfamiliar road.

One of the sub-themes of this book is that the idea of simplistic cause-and-effect is dysfunctional in a time of chaos theory-related mathematical models. It is better to place on hold the assignment of true significance to single events, which may be difficult, considering the breadth of the canvas (500 years).

Another sub-theme examines the idea of regional trading blocs, particularly as related to sovereignty. The book is written from the point of view of a single North American economic and political entity because this is the realistic outcome of the Canada-U.S. Free Trade Agreement. The North American Free Trade Agreement merely cements this agreement, although Mexico negotiated a lesser loss of sovereignty than Canada did in the earlier treaty.

PART ONE

Filtering the Background Noise: the Hyperspace Era Begins

CHAPTER ONE

How the World Changes: it all depends on your perspective

In December 1991, the U.S.S.R. formally disintegrated and new governments took over in its former constituent republics. Those who had lived through the Cold War might have expected a day of international rejoicing, but in the former Soviet republics, problems with the infrastructure (such as the likelihood of starvation) made things a bit too tense for celebration. In the West, the order of the day was relieved self-congratulation on "winning" the Cold War and a subdued sense of salvation from doom-laden scenarios. Few wanted to consider the alternatives.

While humanity had managed to avoid making a thermonuclear blur of itself, the end of the Cold War was the resolution to a problem that no longer meant much. In a post-industrial world, the argument over which industrial system was better had become hardly more than academic.

The U.S.S.R.'s collapse into the Commonwealth of Independent States (C.I.S.) was much like the bankruptcy of a large corporation. Everyone knew that the company could become insolvent, but the accounting was so complicated that it might be years before the auditor's final report.

While most of the world's leaders expressed surprise, no informed observer of the Soviet bureaucracy could have experienced the slightest iota of wonder as the U.S.S.R. crumbled. Since the earliest years of the Brezhnev regime in 1964, corruption had been rampant. Kremlin insiders ripped off everything not nailed down — even the term "mafia," to describe the new syndicates of organized crime. We have been treated to many lurid reports of massive social and economic shifts in Russia. Crime rates are beyond anything the Russians, or for that matter we have ever imagined, let alone experienced. Some Russian entrepreneurs have become seriously wealthy in brief months, while pensioners starve. Western business people visiting Russia carry boil-in-a-bag meals, since food supplies are spotty in those provincial cities where, thanks to wider latitudes in which to manoeuvre, the opportunity to become wealthy on a single deal happens with tantalizing frequency.

In the midst of this litany of chaos, some events do stick out as new benchmarks in bizarreness. In December 1994, the British press reported that two Russian journalists had placed deposits of £10,000 for the hot new DB7 Aston Martin sports coupe. The final price for the car was £79,000. The cheeky Brits suggested that *Izvestia* was paying better than usual, but it's more likely the Russian reporters had acquired hard currency through crime, or were moonlighting on a hazardous project for a Western news agency or intelligence service. They also might have done an ordinary (or as ordinary as things get these days in Russia) commercial deal.

The U.S.S.R. had been defeated. With the infrastructures of the residual C.I.S. republics in complete disintegration, citizens of the world's second most powerful nation found themselves in the Third World with little prospect for a better life for the foreseeable future. The U.S.S.R. was bankrupt in a way no one had seen since Germany in the 1930s. The ruble dropped from about U.S.$1.75 in late 1990 to 0.0008 cents within three years.

One reason the leaders of the U.S.S.R. accepted defeat was that they were aware that a new world order, or an era transition, was taking over. They would be unable to participate in this new world-view unless they disentangled themselves from the Cold War on the best terms possible. As the heads of the second-last major land mass to become industrialized, the Soviet leadership knew all too well the price of failing to participate in a new era.

Yet even though this downfall had been imminently anticipated by all Western intelligence officers outside of the thug branches for the previous 11 years, no one had a coherent answer to the question, "What do we do without an evil empire?"

SORE WINNERS

The United States and western Europe are probably bankrupt too, but each has larger and more efficient revenue streams upon which to base a recovery. The problem facing the West is that none of our conventional economic theories can deal with the emerging world.

As the '90s advanced, we found ourselves asking: why have otherwise astute politicians, regardless of position on the political spectrum, totally failed to understand that there was something terribly wrong, and that all of their forecasts were irreparably flawed? Why did their wise and well-intentioned advisors fail to tell them that their nations were on a perilous and politically unworkable course?

In setting up the European Union (E.U.) and the responding North American Free Trade Agreement (NAFTA), political leaders had taken a course of action which assumed that transnational corporations could, in fact, manage global businesses and that senior civil servants could manage regional, supranational states.

For some years, liberal thought in the West has been focussed on the idea of an internationalized rule of law extending beyond the buttresses which have evolved to support compliance with international treaties. Most of these initiatives stemmed from the International Court of Justice at The Hague, which the United Nations (U.N.) had inherited from the League of Nations. The World Court requires nations that are parties to proceedings there to accept the Court's jurisdiction. As a result, no one goes there if there is a chance they might lose.

In the past few decades a range of treaty conventions have been written, usually supported by the U.N. membership. They include the 1971 Montreal Convention for the Suppression of Unlawful Acts Against the Safety of Civilian Aircraft, the 1987 Treaty on Substances that Deplete the Ozone and the 1988 Convention on Drug Addiction and Illicit Substance Trafficking, which obliges signatories to provide data and assistance in pursuing suspects.

Ever since the Nuremberg war crimes trials after the Second World War, international scholars have speculated about the possibility of extending an internationalized jurisdiction over crimes against humanity such as genocide, institutionalized torture, use of weapons banned under international protocols, mistreatment of prisoners of war, and gratuitous attacks on civilian targets.

There have also been a few ideas about regulating and acquiring jurisdiction over the affairs of transnational corporations, with the notion that those engaging in any of the above by selling poison gas, health-destroying products, et cetera, might be brought to task by a supranational court system. Such scholars might check with taxation authorities as to the likelihood of one of those corporations meekly 'fessing up to its sins, paying its damage claims and promising to become a good global citizen. This same crew also thought they could put a tax on global banking transactions, overlooking the possibility that world-class banks and their transnational customers would arrange things so that the governments would owe *them* money. Transnationals are usually less than forthright when the subject of the location of the "real set of books" is raised.

WHAT ORDER?

It has quickly become apparent that the new world order is not the "New World Order" which President George Bush announced during the Gulf War. What is really happening is a breakdown of the weakest unit of the old industrial world-view, which had its roots in the Mercantile Age of the latter-day Renaissance. A new era is emerging.

While the U.S.S.R. collapsed into a collection of squabbling fiefdoms, the West shifted blithely into an economic depression of a magnitude unseen since the Dirty Thirties. This depression, while forecasted, had a magnitude and pervasiveness which was unforeseen and therefore unprepared for by political leaders.

These same leaders denied its existence every time they were questioned in public. Terms like "economic correction", "market force adjustments", and "global rationalization of peaceful, non-Cold War conditions" spouted from the political and corporate leadership until they could no longer be taken seriously.

The public mood in North America was a sense of profound betrayal. Instead of peace and plenty, the order of the day was layoffs, unemployment, downsized work forces, cuts in living standards, more food banks, and more homelessness. There was a sense that this was all, on some cosmic level, deeply unfair. (The first law of the universe is that nothing is ever really fair.)

When speech-writers for President George Bush put the term "New World Order" in his mouth, the world paid little attention. It caught the attention of analysts in the world's foreign offices, but without further guidance or pressure, the term remained without formal definition. International journalists, by and large, simply quoted the president without comment.

Months later, the term enjoyed wider usage, although there still remained little in the way of specific meaning. We don't know where the president's speech-writers found it. Possibly, one of them had seen the Paddy Chayefsky film *Network* and misunderstood the message.

Never mind. It became instructive to chart who was using the term with authority and what they were saying. As the term began to appear in statements or media query responses of senior U.S. or allied administration officials, a pattern or agenda for the future began to take shape. President Bush did not use the term during the 1992 election campaign. Perhaps his handlers found it pretentious in light of the state of the U.S. economy. At the same time, the street-left turned the term into a metaphor for American and transnational corporate connections to the "military industrial complex," which is so simplistic an explanation as to be valueless.

As we in the West live through the fallout from the "Cold War victory," we find that traditional values are at some risk. After all, when the editors of *Glamour* magazine find it appropriate to publish an article titled "What To Do When Your Bank Fails" (January 1992) the universe may have lost its rosy hue.

Our society has granted special privileges and dispensations to bankers because, we were taught, they could be trusted to conduct their affairs with perspicacity and a sense of public trust for the integrity of our monetary system. Instead, it turns out they have loaned the money entrusted to them to real estate speculators without assets, or made sovereign loans to impoverished countries whose leaders expect to pocket half the money.

Even more central values appear to be crumbling. The work we are offered is increasingly without any kind of meaningful direction; there is less and less concern for integrity in the products or services by which we put food on our tables and pay for the roofs over our heads.

The world-view — that set of assumptions that governs our knowledge of the world — seems to have changed suddenly and drastically. Furthermore, there is a wide divergence of view among mainstream political and economic theories, which have not yet incorporated this new perspective. In other words, the old world-view has been supplanted, but the paradigm shift is still in transit.

One object of this book is to examine what is really going on — why the political establishment has failed so profoundly, why the international corporate world is so set on having a global economy mediated by regional trade zones, and hopefully to explore some options which are not being openly discussed.

To do this we need a historical reference — a common starting point. The best place to find that is 500 years ago, during the Italian Renaissance; qualitatively we are in a new Renaissance, so it may be useful to refresh our memories about such things. In other words, we're going to use the Renaissance as a benchmark to help us understand our own times.

By 1993, most of us had become aware (or started to suspect) that the ways in which we have always managed our lives no longer work very well. New technologies and their social consequences appear at a bewildering pace, dramatically altering our expectations of our peers and society, and society's expectations of us.

Also, it appears that people in government, when they are not being outright venal, have no better comprehension of the direction of events than we do. Political parties are still trying to test how far our credulity can be pushed with the candidates they offer up. The inhabitants of Renaissance Europe had considerable experience with these conditions.

Today, there is a consensus that to approach political or economic issues without scientific and technological literacy is to fly in the face of sanity, since the emerging world-view is being built upon the discoveries of contemporary science and the constructs of resultant technology. If this is true, we can dismiss most political and economic proposals which are offered today. (Lt. Col. Oliver North USMC spent all that time shredding documents, unaware that the word processing package used in the White House automatically did back-ups.)

NEW PERSPECTIVES

We all know today that, while a piece of paper presents only two dimensions (length and breadth), the physical universe is three-dimensional (since it incorporates depth). But 500 years ago, no one really understood that. Paintings and drawings were two-dimensional. They were flat and linear, without the illusory appearance of depth.

A three-dimensional universe may be graphically displayed in a two-dimensional format by using perspective. Incidentally, a mathematical "proof" that the universe is three-dimensional is a difficult problem. Strange though it may now seem, it is difficult to "prove" the third dimension which we can all "see" around us and in paintings or line drawings which use perspective.

The discovery of perspective, or the third dimension, profoundly altered the way people between 1400 and 1500 saw themselves and the world.

In the early part of the 15th century, the rules governing the use of perspective in painting or drawing were formulated by such men as fra Angelico, Giotto and Paolo Uccello — of whom his wife complained that "he loved perspective better than he loved her." (Uccello's sketches of objects in three dimensions bear a startling resemblance to contemporary computer-assisted design renditions.)

This change in the perception of space was of great significance in the *Quattrocento*. We can see the perceptual changes as they affected the lives of the wealthy, whose new *pallazi* and renos of the old *pallazi* show reapportionments of interiors and regrouping of furniture and design with an awareness of perspective.

Francesco di Giorgio Martini (1439-1502) was a Sienese engineer, architect, painter, sculptor, and writer who was probably the first to urge that houses built for minor tradesmen and merchants have clear demarcations between areas of the home for family use and those for the conduct of business or work. Francesco was a working architect. He did not speak with the voice of a small businessman, but from the viewpoint of a leader of society who, in his career as a writer, could influence the decision-makers in town.

Francesco moved to beautiful downtown Urbino, where he hung out with fra Luca Pacioli (see below). While in Urbino, he was employed as an architect and all-round Renaissance guy at the court of Gonzaga of Mantua, Duke of Urbino.

There he wrote his treatise *Trattato di architettura civil e milittare* in the 1470s. Of course, the middle classes and the poor continued live as they had always lived. Spatial arrangements had more to do with the fecundity of the family and the number of clerks, journeymen, and apprentices for whom space had to be found.

In any case, it didn't matter to Francesco, who wasn't about to build anything for the poor anyway. He was only writing theory. The rich and famous read the treatise and commissioned him to build pricey new and renovated *pallazos* for them, incorporating his swell ideas for the lower classes. Soon he was a trendy, self-employed professional; he was the in architect in town.

Filippo Brunelleschi, another 15th century architect, used the mathematical tools developed for perspective-based paintings to solve the problem of building a dome. Brunelleschi is principally known today for building the dome of Florence cathedral, but his true importance is probably as a proselytizer for painters, such as his close friend Donatello, who were exploring the world of perspective.

Art historians largely accept that the mathematics of 3-D imagery came from monasteries in northern and central Italy. Fra Luca Pacioli, a Franciscan monk whose order house was in Urbino, was perhaps the major source.

If you are looking for a smoking gun to show who pulled the trigger on the Renaissance, you could do a lot worse than fra Luca. His influence was enormous and largely unrecognized. It was he who tried to persuade Leonardo da Vinci to publish his famous 3-D sketches; Leonardo resisted on the grounds that they were merely sketches, just experiments really. So Pacioli asked if he might have them to illustrate his book, *On Divine Proportion*, and so those wonderful sketches, which Leonardo would have otherwise thrown out, are reproduced in history and art texts worldwide.

We know that *On Divine Proportion* addresses problems in perspective and was widely read. Pacioli was in the right part of Italy, at the right time, travelling in the right social and intellectual circles to influence artists experimenting with the use of perspective. Pacioli's book travelled well and his influence continues to amaze us. For example, Newton's law of inverse squares seems inspired by (one might even say appropriated from) a section of *On Divine Proportion*.

Fra Luca was a friend of Cimabue, who was Giotto's teacher. He was also in frequent contact with the soon-to-be-burned Giordano Bruno. In other words, Pacioli was a prime example of the Renaissance Man.

Pacioli enjoys cachet among historians of business for his invention and publication of a double-entry bookkeeping system. This system was of critical importance to the Renaissance business world, since it accommodated use of a bill of exchange and gave bankers books upon which they could base loan decisions. It is interesting to consider that a bookkeeping system in use by accountants worldwide today was invented by this Franciscan monk. Pacioli was also involved in the management consulting business. In one essay he sounds like a moderate liberal who could be working for

Andersen Consulting or KPMG: "It is the purpose of every merchant to make a lawful and reasonable profit so as to keep up his business." Not bad for someone who had lived in a monastery since the age of 14.

The school of painters working with perspective was based in north and central Italy; it took nearly 200 years to extend perspective all over north-western Europe and Britain. British military and naval sketches, even as late as the end of the 18th century and first quarter of the 19th century, are still two-dimensional.

Pacioli's book on perspective was a breath of fresh air for a number of reasons. At the time, numeracy was not widely accepted and numerate people were not all that common. For some unknown reason, merchants, artisans, masons, and bookkeepers still held on to Roman numerals. No wonder historians expect and see lots of simple arithmetic errors in accounting books of the period. Roger Doucet, editor of the records of the French Crown for 1523, found errors of a magnitude of several hundred thousand *livres*, and that was when a *livre* was still a *livre*.

Pacioli was the prototypical Renaissance Man. He was a mathematician of considerable repute. His book *On Divine Proportion*, which is largely about perspective, was filled with original work at a time when submission to the classical authorities was still considered academic good taste. He had a wide circle of friends ranging from some very weird artists and their friends to the most exciting architects of the day, the heads of trading houses, political leaders, and bankers. When we examine letters of the time that speak of him in passing, we find that in an age when jealousy and back-stabbing (literal and metaphorical) were the social norm, fra Luca was held in universal respect and affection by scholars, political officials, the nobility, artists, *condottieri*, and fathers of the Church as well as members of the Curia and those ubiquitous monsignors who make up the bureaucracy of the Vatican.

If we leave the problems of our own time and go back to the 13th century, we might find Frederick II and his court at Palermo, in Sicily. Here was a Holy Roman Emperor who might easily be mistaken for a Renaissance prince.

Frederick II introduced a legal system based on the Justinian Code, patronized the arts, kept an astrologer, and dabbled in alchemy. The efficiency of his administration, the active exploration of other nations by his diplomacy, his delight in literature and philosophy, and his open-minded approach to all ideas, regardless of the source — Muslim, Christian, Jewish or pagan — was impressive for a man of his time. He was the patron of Lorenzo da Pisa, better known as Fibonacci.

So why didn't Frederick II trigger the Renaissance?

For all his accomplishments, he was more a barbarian than a Renaissance prince. Frederick was much extolled for the exotic nature of his mistresses, said to rival the

There is a painting hanging in the Galleria Nazionale in Naples simply entitled Pacioli by (the painter's name is indistinct) Jaco... Bar... which shows Pacioli and a young male student. The student is believed to be Guidobaldo, the young Duke of Urbino. Men's clothing, for the nobility and the well-to-do in the last quarter of the 15th century, was rich and colourful and the young Duke's outfit is smashing. Pacioli is garbed in the simple gray habit of a Franciscan monk, which is not exactly a fashion statement, but what can you expect from a Franciscan?

THE BURNING OF BRUNO

The shadow is not subject to time but to the time of time, not to space but to the space of space, not to movement but to the movement of movement.
— *Giordano Bruno*

Giordano Bruno (1548-1600), a Dominican monk from Nola, near Naples, was probably one of the most advanced thinkers in history. A close friend of fra Luca's, he was probably the principal mathematical influence on Michelangelo. Bruno is essential to our understanding of the present.

In 1600 the Holy Inquisition found Bruno guilty of heresy, declared him excommunicated, ordered his books to be burned, and directed that he be turned over to the civil authorities for execution by burning at the stake.

Bruno was a polymathic character in the best tradition of the Renaissance. What got the attention of his fellow Dominicans in the Inquisition was his work as a cosmologist, author, and Hermetic philosopher in support of Copernicus' heliocentric theory of the solar system and the view that the universe was infinite, plus the critical thesis that the Earth was one of a plurality of worlds.

As for being ahead of his time, Bruno's understanding of perspective resulted in his proposing a cosmology of multiple dimensions, anticipating

---

exotic creatures of his private zoo. There is in him the sensual quality of a barbarian — the exploitation for immediate gratification of ideas, people, violence, and art, all the marks of someone unwilling to look to long-term consequences. He lacked a reflective quality essential to meaningful exploitation. This was one of the two skills the Renaissance developed, along with tangential thinking. Instead of triggering a new era, Frederick was only a sign of its imminence.

The willingness to take a long-range view is one of the marks of someone who believes that his age will have a long period of influence, and that impulsive self-gratification is not the mark of a civilized person.

Had Frederick been confronted with perspective-based painting, he would have seen it as a toy.

Planck, Einstein, and Heisenberg et al. by more than 300 years.

Bruno's trial and subsequent conviction made his work a resource for specialists, while his place as a source of breakthrough ideas has been denigrated by conservative historical scholars who, to this day, are more comfortable with Aristotelian and Thomistic finitism.

Bruno's geocentric cosmology, however, was not the most threatening aspect of his thought. Bruno's greatest significance was that he recognized that the times required a new epistemology to account for the new science (knowledge) and the resultant split between science and culture (experience). The inquisitorial Dominicans must have felt particularly betrayed by this member of their own order. (Certainly the vindictiveness of their extant correspondence relating to his trial and burning are notably lacking in Christian charity.)

By recognizing the power shift from religious institutions to secular and state-administered and -supported technology, Bruno perpetrated that most awful offence an inquisitor could imagine. He posed a threat to cre-

---

Frederick II, the Holy Roman Emperor known for his wide-ranging investments in collectibles, also brought fra Lorenzo da Pisa, better known as Leonardo Fibonacci, to his court.

Fibonacci is credited with taking Euclid's "golden ratio" and expressing the series in a numeric form — the Fibonacci series. It was Fibonacci's work which provided a base for Pacioli's On Divine Proportion.

Da Pisa probably changed his name when publishing his studies because they were the sort of thing that could bring on heresy charges. As Islam El-Said and Ayse Parman clearly demonstrate in their 1976 book Geometric Concepts in Islamic Art, Euclid undoubtedly got the golden ratio from Arab sources. The authors include pictures of pre-Islamic rug design and architectural applications (wall decorations, building design, and floor tilings) which exhibit the golden ratio.

The Fibonacci series as expressed by Lorenzo of Pisa is the same as we know today. It is the unending sequence 1, 1, 2, 3, 5, 8, 13, 21, 34... where each term is defined as the sum of its two predecessors.

In nature, Fibonacci's series is represented in some powerful examples of regularity which may at first appear to be about as irregular as possible. For his plant biologist fans, one inevitable question arises: if genetics can (in theory) reproduce a flower with any number of petals it wants or a pine cone, with any sequence of scales, why do petals, pine cones, and all the other sub-sets of plant biology keep ending up in Fibonacci numbers? Imagine how unnerved the plant biologists were as they tried to make sense of this apparently across-the-board phenomenon when

dence of the faithful in the infallible teachings of the Church. It meant that the inquisitors were faced with a supporter of Baconian empiricism and that meant trouble-makers like Galileo were right. (Within Roman Catholic canonical circles the matter of Galileo's sinful state was resolved in late 1992.)

All of this must have caused the inquisitors to breathe a sigh of relief when the stake finally burned down and Bruno's ashes, mixed with those of the firewood, could be consigned to unhallowed ground.

Bruno's most serious crime was to call for a new epistemology. *Shadows of Ideas*, Bruno's major book on epistemology, was the principal basis of the charges that brought him before the Inquisition. To question the way in which knowledge is known in the stable society of Medieval Europe was the ultimate civil and religious crime. Bruno was a dangerous man.

Bruno's thought lived on, providing stimulation to the cultural entrances of Schelling, Joyce, Beckett, and Calvino, as well as the knowledge systems of cyberspace, and another example of the need for vigilance against the inquisitors of our own time.

---

they discovered that their colleagues the marine biologists had discovered that ridges on clams, oysters, and indeed all of the mollusks are ordered in a Fibonacci series.

The quick-and-dirty answer was that the Fibonacci series was in the genes. Then someone asked: how? A passing evolutionist asked: why? And added: what's the survival value? (In other words, the ultimate question driving all science as well as other forms on earth: what's in it for me?)

While the number theorists got busy, the astronomers who had taken to calling themselves cosmologists reported that the deep mathematical regularities represented by the Fibonacci series are also present in the parabolas of planets around suns and other stellar objects.

Finally, it was discovered that if you paid some attention to the geometry of the arrangements, instead of being obsessive about the dynamic causalities, you would discover that using the Fibonacci series is the most efficient way of packing petals, fish scales, and mollusk ridges, or keeping planetary objects in parabolas that avoid collisions. And as if to demonstrate how perverse things can get when the Lords of the Universe are having a bad hair day, currency traders started using Fibonacci to discover some representation of what they laughingly call order in their day-to-day trading.

More significantly, Fibonacci's intuition at the beginning of the 13th century means we can abandon the inherent kludginess of binary computers and start to address real problems, like how to characterize a virus and alter the instruction-set of DNA.

The contemporary influences on Bruno are largely covered in this book, but when we look at Bruno's life we see that it was his abilities as a tangential thinker that bring the institution of the Inquisition to a particular and special opprobrium.

"To think is to speculate with images," Bruno wrote. His idea of "images" resulted in his speculations that a new and more powerful epistemology was necessary to explain a universe where space and time were multidimensional. Here is a partial transcript of the proceedings before the inquisitor who sentenced Bruno to death at the stake:

> *Inquisitor*: Give a precise answer. What opinion did you have and presently have of Christ? Since before you said that you were unsure and you also said that you were in doubt about the Incarnation of the Word.
>
> *Bruno*: As far as the doubt I had about the Incarnation is concerned, what happened was that it seemed to me to be theologically untenable to say that the divinity was not with humanity in a form other than by way of assistance, as I have already said; from this I was not inferring something against the divinity of Christ and the supposed divine named of Christ.

That the Inquisition burned Bruno and not Pacioli is probably due to Pacioli being a Franciscan whose order protected him. As well, the laity and nobility of Lombardy understood that Pacioli was a genius whose ideas were making many of them rich. It is possible to make a case that Pacioli was far more in need of burning than Bruno. This is not to say that Bruno did not richly deserve what he got. Unfortunately, you probably have to be a Dominican to follow this argument.

Then again, we may be premature in judging the Inquisition's loyal Dominican servants harshly. Evidence recently uncovered by scholars offers

---

While Dante Alighieri lived in the Middle Ages (1265-1321), he was, like Fibonacci and unlike Frederick II, a true precursor of the imminent Renaissance. His poetic invention of the terza rima (aba, bcb, cdc, ad infinitum), the interlocking rhyme scheme of The Divine Comedy, enables him to treat each canto as an interrelated, yet separate event in a spatial unity of three dimensions. Italian is a language with far more rhyming words than are found in English, although English has a wider vocabulary and a more flexible grammar.

Harold Bloom, in The Western Canon, agrees that Dante, like Petrarch, was aware his poem was prophecy in the same sense as the biblical Isaiah. Through his invention of the terza rima, Alighieri anticipates the horizon on which looms the Renaissance.

convincing proof that Bruno was also dabbling in that almost universal Northern and English Renaissance pastime of being an "intelligencer," or spy. The place where these activities took place was the French embassy in London. Bruno's code name was, somewhat presciently for a person destined for the stake, Henry Faggot.

A great deal of our knowledge of Bruno comes to us via the good offices of that ultimate Renaissance Man, Dr. John Dee. Dee had put together, in his personal library, the most complete collection of Bruno's works to survive the burning of all books, manuscripts, and other writings as ordered by the Inquisition.

WELCOME TO THE FOURTH LEVEL

Mathematicians have postulated the fourth dimension for some time, but until Einstein published his General Theory of Relativity in 1915 the fourth dimension was little more than an idea. Einstein made it real and showed how events in the fourth dimension affected everyone's reality.

With the fourth dimension, gravity could be managed by viewing it as curvature in space and time. This meant that Newton's seminal work was incomplete and that the Newtonian prohibitions, at least as they affected gravity, could be circumvented. When Einstein introduced a space-time continuum in which space was bent as a function of a fourth dimension, time, the philosophic constraints imposed by Newtonian physics were effectively broken. Throughout this book, we will explore the implications of the fourth dimension — which are as significant to us as was the discovery of perspective to the Renaissance.

A French scientist, the Marquis de Laplace, had, early in the 19th century, argued that the universe was deterministic. He reasoned that, if we had complete knowledge of the universe, we could use Newton's laws to predict the events of the solar system at any specified time.

Laplace went even further and assumed that similar (undiscovered) "laws" ruled everything else. He believed this extrapolative predictive capacity could be expanded to all events in the universe. Once the "laws" governing their categories were discovered, a science which was universally predictive was possible. He included human behaviour in his system, which

---

Most of us have trouble with the idea of "time" as it is used in expressions like "time-space continuum." The reason is that our daily usage of the two words "time" and "space" is pretty primitive.

The word "eternity" literally means no time, or the absence of time. Most of us can imagine infinity, such as being in the middle of a large ocean without obstruction, or in the limitless sky. The "time" of "time-space" is a modifier of the infinity of space without time.

has resulted in a lot of bad sociology, anthropology, and psychology up to the present day.

Laplace's work was attractive to many people because it offered the potential to cover a wide spectrum of phenomena with the basic causality of determinism. In other circles, Laplace's determinism was seriously unpopular.

On one hand, the "free thinkers," fresh from the triumphs of the American and French Revolutions, were committed to "free will," which underlay much of their libertarian political ideals. On the other hand, the Christian church needed a God unfettered by a deterministic universe. If God were bound by the same rules which shackled everyone and everything else, it would mean that God could not intervene in the affairs of man. Such an idea would return everyone to oriental fatalism! In any case, Laplace was soon to be placed in the limbo of scientists whom history deems to have been on a false scent.

In 1900, the German physicist Max Planck put forward a hypothesis that light, X-rays, and other waves could not be emitted in an arbitrary way. Instead, light and all wave events were discharged in packets or "quanta." The frequency of these waves was always exceeded by the amount of their energy. In this way, for the emission of a single quantum it was obligatory to use more energy. The result is that radiation would be lost in the upper frequencies and the rate of energy lost was finite.

In the same direct line of development came the work of Werner Heisenberg, who in 1927 explored the idea that in order to predict the future velocity or position of a particle or wave, you have to measure its present position and speed accurately. Essentially Heisenberg found that in the *act of measurement*, the device used for measuring was incorporated into the object being measured. Planck had used light and other wave or particle articulated objects. Heisenberg wanted to predict both the position and velocity of a particle. To do this he had to be able to measure the current position of the particle.

Planck's quantum hypothesis tells us that you cannot use a casually selected nominal amount of light. If you want to obtain precision in your measurements, you have to use at least one quantum more than the light beam you are measuring. That addition of one quantum will disturb the particle and shift the speed in ways which can neither be predicted nor anticipated.

Heisenberg demonstrated that the uncertainty in the position of the particle, times the uncertainty of the speed, times the mass of the particle can never be less than a specific amount. This amount is known as Planck's constant. Heisenberg's uncertainty principle is generalizable across all types of particles and is a lawful property of the known universe.

Heisenberg's work spelled the end of philosophical determinism. A deterministic universe could not exist at discrete mathematical levels. Some disciplines tried to reincarnate determinism, such as stimulus-response psychology and B.F. Skinner's operant conditioning, which use built-in limiting definitions. (Skinner's basic apparatus, the cumulative recorder, displayed data in a flat, linear format. That's why his data showed such clear functional relationships. At least Skinner used the term "functional relationships" and steered clear of attributing results to simple cause-and-effect.) Sociologists, particularly those operating as adjuncts to advertising, are similarly inhibited.

Heisenberg, Erwin Schrödinger, and Paul Dirac set themselves to reformulating mechanics to accommodate Planck and Einstein's findings. In the late 1920s, they produced a new theoretical model called "quantum mechanics," which was built around Heisenberg's uncertainty principal.

Quantum mechanics is used to predict a number of possible outcomes and uses a probabilistic approach to create a hierarchy of these potential outcomes. Einstein was awarded his Nobel Prize for his contributions to the development of quantum theory. But it was this introduction of "chance," or a universe in which randomness played such a profound part, which caused Einstein to reject the idea of quantum mechanics and led to his famous statement: "I cannot believe that God plays dice with the universe." Supporters of Planck and Heisenberg would probably say that God merely runs the house.

In quantum mechanics, every action is qualified in terms of probabilistic values and certainty becomes operationally impossible. Here's one experiment Erwin Schrödinger designed to demonstrate the principles of quantum mechanics:

Take a cat — any cat will do — and put it in a box from which escape is impossible.

Next place a vial of poison gas in a device which, over a period of exactly 60 minutes, has a 50-50 chance of releasing the gas.

Finally, seal the box with the cat, the device, and the vial of poison gas inside. Stand back and wait exactly 60 minutes

Now, Schrödinger asked: is the cat alive or dead? He replied that, according to the principles of quantum mechanics, at the moment just before the box is opened the cat is neither dead nor alive — it is half of both.

Only at that moment when you open the box will the cat become all alive or all dead.

Hey, it was just an idea. Schrödinger didn't hate cats. He didn't even do the experiment.

Most scientists however, accept quantum mechanics because the experimental evidence and the results of its application are too compelling to be dismissed. Modern science, without quantum mechanics, would be without contemporary biology, physics, chemistry, or cosmology. Without quantum mechanics we would have no transistors or integrated circuits and no Boolean-based computers

Einstein addressed problems of apparent incompleteness found in Newtonian physics. Newton's physics are not only incomplete, but there are anomalies, paradoxes, and outright contradictions. The entire body of work, however, makes any critique of Newton a daunting task. By acknowledging these anomalies, paradoxes, and contradictions, Einstein accomplished two things. First, he challenged the intellectual premises of his time. (Other scientists had been laboriously constructing theories that extrapolated from Newton's work.) Second, by openly admitting that his discomfort with Planck's quantum theory was based on a personal distaste for the outcome, Einstein displayed a lack of arrogance which has served as a role-model of honest humility and rectitude in a scientific community that frequently rivals Hollywood for ego theatrics.

A NEW WORLD

Present day science and the technological implementations of that science assume a universe which demonstrably exists in multiple dimensions. At least four dimensions can be shown as discernible planes. Because the fourth and possibly higher planes are not merely discernible, but also provable and not merely illusions, the linearity of perception under which most of us function is inadequate to describe reality.

Yet most of the residents of this planet have not the slightest idea of the forces which drive and control our world. Most of us are truly scientifically and technologically illiterate.

To this known world (our historical world of three dimensions), upon which the previously generally held world-view was constructed, is now added a world that includes the fourth and higher dimensions. It is this multiply-dimensioned universe that is encompassed in the terms cyberspace and N-space, which assume more dimensions beyond the conventional first, second, third and fourth. (That the latter exist remains suspect for most people because these dimensions are unacknowledged by our senses.) Technological implementations of hyperspace paradigms are the basis for most of the "high technologies" under development today.

Our traditional epistemologies fail to account for events that occur and exist beyond the realms of our senses. That these fourth-plus dimensions occur in a continuum of both time and space — not merely space as in dimensions one, two, and three — means that epistemologies constructed to explain events occurring in two or three dimensions are inadequate to handle information emanating from four or more dimensions.

In the computer industry, molecular modelling, 3-D spread sheets, video games, and other applications recently brought to public awareness, such as "virtual realities" and computer simulations, are particularly powerful applications of cyberspace. During the Gulf War, many of the "smart" reconnaissance or attack weaponry deployed by the U.S.-led forces used technologies based on this level of abstraction.

A new world-view that accommodates the time-space continuum is essential, since the reality of cyberspace is being actively exploited — making it increasingly undeniable and unavoidable.

Historically, societies that have failed to accommodate emergent world-views have lost access to the betterments of growth and improved economic and social benefits congruent with their time in history. In fact, their access to the economic benefits decreased as they slipped from the global mainstream. The services they were able to deliver to their citizens deteriorated and their influence on world issues became irrelevant. Societies which do not embrace new world-views do not usually survive. Some slip back to barbarism. Others are subsumed into more adaptive cultures whose intellectual evolution has been more successful.

This new world-view, which is emerging all over the globe, is the territory upon which the New World Order lays claim to leadership. One objective of this book is to evaluate the validity of that claim. Another goal, probably more significant, is to expose the variables which are at play and give the readers resources for personal risk management.

New eras in history are genuinely risk intensive. In the wealthy West we have eliminated the risks we encounter to the point that we have little experience in training our judgment of risk. In fact, as a good rule of thumb, the wealthier a society becomes, the poorer the performance of its members at risk-judgment.

All growth and progress, whether economic, social, philosophical, or technological, has, since the advent of the written word, been the product of increases in the levels of abstraction at which the society operates. These elevations of abstraction have been exploited to harness the forces of the universe. This has not simply been a linear expansion of technologies, which resulted in greater productivities with resultant greater wealth.

The broadly-held current view is built around the products of the Renaissance and supported with the predictive tools of extrapolative analysis. It is shared by economists and political leaders, whether capitalist or Marxist. It is likely to prove fatal to societies which follow it. Yet the necessary adaptations by political leaders are difficult when the body politic is required to respond to increasingly new and assertively abstract levels of analysis while the previously established order circles the wagons, terrified of the potential loss of divinely granted privilege.

It is, perhaps, helpful to briefly consider more of the historical antecedents of this new world-view.

THE QUICK AND THE DEAD

Classical Rome lacked the concept of zero or infinity. Roman numerals were cumbersome, making Roman arithmetic seriously limited. Few Roman ships ventured out of sight of land, and even fewer did it intentionally.

With such a limited mathematical base, it is little wonder that Rome's world-view had a sparse time sense. While contemporary historians claim roots from such Romans as Plutarch and Livy, the truth is that for Romans the past was a cloudy, grey area better left to the Gods. The future was unpredictable and knowledge of it was also limited to the Gods, whose capricious utterances on the subject were mediated by professional oracles.

The Roman view of man was communal and the sense of the world was collective. Roman strategies of government reinforced this view of a common world prospering under the Roman senate and emperor's guidance. The Peace of Rome (Pax Romana) ensured that orderly conquest would benefit the new provinces and Rome herself. Classical art and architecture reflect this view of man-in-the-world, showing the subjects in stark simplicity, without any figure/ground resolution or enhancement.

When its world-view no longer gave it a realistic account of the world as it by then existed, Rome collapsed.

Between the 8th and 16th centuries, the Muslim world became an expansionary force. No writer examining political, economic, social, or military global issues at the beginning of the 21st century can be indifferent the impact of Muslim thought on Europe's development.

No writer can exercise indifference to the fate of Salman Rushdie. Rushdie was, after all, attempting to begin the discussion of the need for a reformation of the verities of the Muslim faith.

When a religious leader can mobilize the resources of a nation to offer a reward for the assassination of one man, living and publishing in another, technically sovereign state, and when that sovereign state places its transitory commercial interests ahead of a defence of freedom of speech and inquiry, its leadership demonstrates worse than cowardice.

They demonstrate indifference to their own economic welfare, since the means of transferring information freely and efficiently were not merely one of the hall-

The classical Muslim world-view is markedly different from that now held in the West. When we are confronted with an unpleasant situation, which would be called "fate" in the Greco-Roman period, we would probably trivialize it to a degree with the term "luck." Should a pattern of "bad luck" appear, we would probably look to a functional relationship rather than a malign deity.

Without a significant technological base, "fate" has a quality of inevitability to it. Most Londoners in the 1880s accepted deaths from cholera as an unalterable fact of life. Then, using statistics, it was found that contamination from outdoor privies was to blame and municipal health codes governing the positions of drains in relation to drinking water sources saved thousands of lives.

The Muslim world has retained an accommodation for ancient fatalism. With fate there are no accidents. Fate is an implementation of God's will. (If you are struck down by a tree that was hit by lightning, God was planning to destroy the tree and you got in the way. Alternatively, God was trying to destroy you and the tree was the agent of God.)

In a relatively short period, as the level of abstraction under which western Europeans functioned expanded exponentially, classical fatalism was cast aside. Without it, man can appeal to forces of intellect and reason to avoid deterministically undesirable outcomes. Further, a malign fate can be avoided by codifying historical precedents.

It is extremely difficult for a 20th century Western mind to be at ease with the traditional Muslim world-view. The Muslim faith is the only major religious force in the world that has not undergone a reformation. When that reformation comes, it will bring with it serious dislocations in countries from the Atlantic tip of North Africa to the southern Indian Ocean and Indonesia. It most certainly will not be peaceful, but there are forces in the Muslim world that assure a reformation will happen in the foreseeable future.

---

marks of the past 500 years, but are one of the critical means of survival in the next 100 years. Before the Renaissance invented the secular state, the Pope could place someone under an anathema, which meant that anyone could kill that person without committing a sin or incurring a civil or religious criminal liability. Entire states could be placed under an anathema, whereupon a rival prince could invade, using the excuse of acting on feudal obligations or just being a pious prince stamping out evil heretics.

No one would deny that all states have, from time to time, sent out killers to remove someone who has offended the government. But today, the only institutional use of hit contracts is found among gangsters.

It was not until it adopted Arabic numeracy and other fruits of Arab scholarship that the West managed to break out of the Medieval world. The level of abstraction associated with the concept of zero or infinity is vastly greater than that of Medieval intellectual achievements. The Renaissance was a period of explosive abstraction-level growth. Humanity's growing ability to modify and control its environment soon weakened the idea of the inevitability of fate. Without the crushingly overpowering quality of fatalism, individual accountability became more congruent with the emergent Renaissance world-view.

IN PERSPECTIVE

Erwin Panofsky has given us some understanding of the rate of social and technological change experienced by those living during the Renaissance. Panofsky recounts the exposure of the German Northern Renaissance artist Dürer who, on his way home from Bologna, stopped off in Venice for a year, where he studied perspective-based painting and undertook formal studies in mathematics.

Dürer wrote to his wife, who had complained that he should be working at his artisan-painter trade, that he expected to "receive instruction in the *secret* (italics added) art of perspective."

Dürer had first travelled to Italy in 1494. He described this trip as a pilgrimage to see "what had been hidden for 1,000 years." After his second trip to Italy, upon his return to Nuremberg, his cronies shifted from painters to Humanist writers and scholars and his income plummeted, to the chagrin of Frau Dürer. He eventually wrote a book on perspective

---

Consider contemporary scientific understanding and applications of evolution. Then consider the problems of discussing with the leaders of an Islamic theocratic state the idea that one might use a genetic modification on a virus and neutralize the specific instruction-set strand of DNA which allows the virus to reproduce. You know, stopping a pandemic plague in its tracks and all that kind of do-gooder stuff.

It would take a really dull mullah not to figure out that we're talking about appropriation of God's divine powers here and he is not interested in a deal that involves going to hell.

He knows that we in the West are already committed to being deal-direct-source-agents on earth of "the Great Satan," a phrase first coined by Egypt's Gamal Abdel Nasser and picked up by every political speech writer in the Middle East as a real crowd-pleaser.

Now we are trying to sell some Islamic politician on an idea that will lead every faithful Muslim religious leader to accuse him of defying God's law by getting into

painting and another book on human proportions in painting which, along with the examples in his own work, revolutionized German art while allowing it to retain its special character.

With perspective readily available to the educated, problems with the mathematics involved in using perspective in architecture appeared. This led to the study of optics, which became the starting point for the scientific Renaissance.

Studies in optics made possible the invention of the telescope. A recent historical find has thrown into question our conventional assumptions about the discovery of the telescope. Colin Ronan, a British historian of science and president of the British Astronomical Society, has contradicted the traditional supposition that the telescope was first developed by the Dutch lensmaker Hans Lippershey. Ronan reports that an Englishman, Leonard Digges, completed work on the principles of the telescope before his death in 1571. His son Thomas used one to look at stars that were otherwise inaccessible to human eyes. Thomas Digges died in 1595; it was not until 1609 that Galileo started using telescopes to make his earth shattering discoveries about the solar system.

Thomas Digges, we find, was a student or apprentice with the estimable Dr. John Dee, Elizabethan England's preeminent alchemist, astronomer, and astrologer. He partially paid for Dee's tutoring in astrology and astronomy by working in Dee's library and assisting him with experiments.

Ronan speculates that the timely warning for Drake, Hawkins, et al. as to the arrival of the Spanish Armada in 1588 may have been because the British picket ships were equipped with telescopes made by either Leonard or Thomas Digges. Neither ever used the word "telescope," but spoke of

---

the life creation business. Most politicians in the Islamic world realize that it isn't hard to get a hunting licence on an Arab politician who signs up with Satan's recruiters.

This failure to incorporate the lessons of the Renaissance by other cultures has given the West a monumental advantage. It means that societies without this acculturation have to leapfrog us if they want to pass us in the life race now running. We have had 500 years to get to the point where we can not merely intellectually know the lessons of the Renaissance, we assume them.

William H. Calvin, author of The Ascent of Man, has pointed out that: "In evolutionary arguments, it is no longer enough to demonstrate that something could have done the job given enough time. By compound-interest reasoning any slight advantage can eventually do the job. There are usually multiple ways to do the job and the one that gets there first on the fast track tends to preempt the niche."

"perspective glasses as a way of seeing things at a distance."

Leonard Digges has long been credited with anticipating the telescope in his book *A Geometrical Practise Named Pantometria*, in which he wrote of the "marvelous conclusions that may be performed by glasses concave and convex of circular and parabolic forms." Digges claimed he had set out his conclusions in another volume, but either it has been lost or was never published. Ronan speculates that Thomas Digges, who served in the Netherlands with English forces, may have told Dutch colleagues of the Digges family's developments.

Until the 15th century, the word "perspective" itself was little used in English. But once the Italian artists had made their discovery and had developed techniques to express perspective, other Renaissance figures, with different agendas, pushed the exploration of three dimensionality far beyond the goals of the painters.

By 1655 British metaphysical poet Henry Vaughn used the word perspective as a metaphor for another dimension populated by those who had died. Vaughn extends the metaphor by using the idea of a telescope to examine the distance between the dead and the speaker (an older man, most of whose friends have died) in his elegiac poem "They Are All Gone into the World of Light":

> They are all gone into the world of light!
> And I alone sit lingering here;
> Their very memory is far and bright,
> And my sad thoughts doth clear
>
> Either disperse these mists, which blot and fill
> My perspective (still) as they pass,
> Or else remove me hence unto that hill,
> Where I shall need no Glass.

Vaughn's equation of the mysteries of death with the third dimension gives us a glimpse of how powerful a tool of abstraction the use of perspective had become. While the poet remained in awe of the concept of perspective he understood that the telescope gave him power to manipulate and extend himself in a 3-D world.

The impact on the Western world-view of Newton's laws and Leibniz's logic and calculus established them as giants. The development of the bill of exchange and navigational tools, derived from Renaissance and Arab mathematics, permitted the commercialization of Renaissance discoveries and inventions. It also created the huge capital base needed to finance the Mercantile and Industrial Ages.

The ideas of the Renaissance undermined the feudal and manorial world-views — those adhering to the conventional world-view of the era found themselves embroiled in the Thirty Years War. Europe was pushed into religious, political, economic, and polemical upheavals which lasted into the 19th century and, arguably, our own.

CHAPTER TWO

A New World-View: The orderly industrial world starts to get creaky

Marcel Duchamp, probably the most significant artist of the 20th century, said it all in the early 1930s: "The third dimension is but a shadow cast by the fourth."

The quantum jump to a new world-view — the era transition addressed by this book — was in full effect by then. In 1900 Planck's quantum theory was reported and in the same year David Hilbert published his challenging 23 problems. The stage was set for a new world-view. In 1905 Albert Einstein published a series of scientific papers that jolted physicists and mathematicians. They realized the young Einstein was capable of discoveries as earthshaking as the findings of Aristotle, Ptolemy, Newton, Leibniz and Pascal. It took a decade before anyone could tell for sure.

That brought things up to 1915, when opposing European claims for colonial resources and international trade boiled over and engulfed the world in war as competing commercial empires set out to beat each other into exhaustion. From wartime Berlin, the pacifist Einstein published a paper called "The Foundations of a General Theory of Relativity," which fulfilled his promise and challenged basic assumptions about the then known universe.

Einstein's theory, simply stated, says that space is bent. To measure space it is necessary to treat it as if it has four dimensions — that fourth dimension occurs in a continuum of both time and space. The shortest distance between two points is not a straight line, rather it is curved to account for the space-time function of N-space. N-space is the assumption that multiple dimensions of space and time exist in different continua, each displayed on a different plane.

With Einstein's theory a new dimension (the fourth) was opened up for exploration. Physicists worldwide struggled to understand this break with the conventions of reality as they had known it.

In the Renaissance the job of articulating the new era was left up to the few painters and architects who began employing perspective. In the new era the level of scientific literacy is higher. The number of scientific workers discussing Planck's quantum theory and Einstein's theory of relativity was about 30 in the 1930s. By the time of the Los Alamos atom-bomb test, there were thousands.

Over the previous 500 years a new model of science had broken away from the magician/alchemist tradition that had created a lot of unprofitable inquiries for early Renaissance mathematicians and others interested in applications of the new post-scholastic learning. It was the artists who were first on the main track of perspective. The painters and architects did not depend on a completed epistemology, rather they brought their *intuition* to the changed view of the universe.

In our own era the bewildering array of thought experiments and particle accelerators of the international mathematics and physics communities have made their findings difficult for lay observers, including artists, to follow. For years the leaps in abstraction left other disciplines behind. For one thing, initially there was no syntax to render speculations about higher dimension space accessible, so the metaphors we now use to describe the abstract principles we're addressing were a long time in appearing.

It is not surprising that in the early days only a few artists allowed their intuition to roam this multi-dimensional universe of space and time. Among these few was Marcel Duchamp, who had perhaps the strongest artistic insight into the visions of Planck, Einstein and Heisenberg. Certainly his works *The Bride Stripped Bare by her Bachelors, Even* and *Nude Descending a Staircase* anticipated Einstein's work. Duchamp explored glass as a canvas, which enabled him to portray both Bride and Nude as moving in a sort of hyperspace. Duchamp's championing of Brancusi was another indication of his understanding of the new reality.

John Cage, who could have been a major painter, preferred the challenge of addressing the new era in music. Cage "proposed an art born of chance and indeterminacy, in which every effort is made to extinguish the artist's own personality; instead of an accumulation of masterpieces, he urged a perpetual process of artistic discovery in our daily life" (italics added). Cage was among the first — and certainly the most influential — in his understanding of the affinity between musicians and electronics. He explored chance as a selector mechanism for the music he wrote and frequently spoke of trying to pierce the layered levels which a composer experiences.

Today we find few artists — outside of those using computers for design or graphics applications — leading the quest for a new epistemology. This is probably unfortunate for all concerned, because their intuitions are needed.

THE NEW ERA TAKES MANHATTAN

For most of the world in 1915, concern with the First World War overrode the momentous scientific event in Berlin. Most of the young European physicists were getting themselves maimed and killed at the front. But once the war was over, Einstein was treated to superstar status as he visited most of the major centres of mathematics and physics — even as his home in Germany became less and less hospitable with the rise of the Nazis.

In 1933, Einstein arrived in the United States. He never returned to Germany. And as Hitler's anti-Semitic policies took hold, more German scientists arrived in the U.S. and the U.K. as refugees.

In 1939, following the now famous letter from Einstein, U.S. President Roosevelt awarded the Manhattan Project top priority. Scientists from America and the U.K., aided by their refugee colleagues, went to work on the secrets of the atom. Initially, the Manhattan Project produced two technological applications — the atomic bomb and a reactor that could harness nuclear power. More importantly, it brought together leading scientists who otherwise would never have spent such significant time together. The outcome was a creative outpouring.

As the Second World War progressed, physicists, mathematicians, and other specialists were uprooted from their conventional, academically ordered homes and resettled around projects such as Manhattan. This resulted a massive disciplinary cross-fertilization.

In the years following the war, the National Aeronautics and Space Administration (NASA) became noted for its strategies of attacking problems requiring cross-disciplinary activity, which in space research are so common as to be normative. Most employed at NASA seldom think of themselves as being part of their original disciplines, rather, they see themselves as part of a work group which is charting the pathways of new disciplines.

Another result of the Manhattan Project was the selection of a language for the new science. With virtually all of the significant figures resident in the U.S. or the U.K., English became the common language for the mega-projects and new definitions. It was the language in which proofs of theorems were discussed.

Communication was also enhanced by the enormous resources of the American domestic economy, which ensured that the scientists, as front-line warriors in the battle against Communism, would want for nothing. Specialty journals, frequent conferences, closed-circuit TV conferences and unlimited long-distance lines all enhanced scientific communication. To clarify a point made by another worker anywhere in the world required only a phone call. With this ease of communication, assertive and free-flowing interdisciplinary consultation and research became a new standard.

For anyone born after 1945, the special quality ascribed to a long-distance phone call is difficult to explain. Older people, who were brought up in a period of minimally automated phone service, can recall being reminded by their parents to "Hurry up! This is long distance." A common stratagem to save on long distance bills was to call home or work and ask for a prearranged codename. In this way there was no impact on anyone's phone bill. This was a common way to advise one's family that one had arrived somewhere safely.

The world-view shift now occurring is the greatest transition ever experienced by the human race. The easiest thing to forecast is that today's conventional wisdoms, which meld society into a functional whole, will increasingly lose their relevance.

Further, we should anticipate an incremental rate of socioeconomic dislocation as leaders, who are not immune to the rigors of the change rate, make adaptive judgment errors or become pointlessly corrupt. Individuals will choose social or economic alliances which fail to support or find support. Businesses will be similarly affected. Governments and corporate institutions will find that they must speed up their decisions as the windows of opportunity become truncated. This will create yet another casualty pool.

This inability or unwillingness to successfully predict economic trends means that we can expect the disappearance of familiar commercial or corporate names. Nations, too, will disappear, as their borders cease to provide rationalities of identity and countries become subsumed into political configurations better adapted to a new and more viable world-view.

Governments will again support emigration as a solution to their own ungovernability. For example, bureaucrats in the Commonwealth of Independent States have talked about declaring redundant to the nations' needs 3 million former members of the armed forces. They are looking to the West to absorb them. When your country is as unstable as the former U.S.S.R., there is no desire to keep around 3 million unemployable guys who know how to use guns.

THE SILICON REVOLUTION

Two crucial stages in the development of a new world-view were part of the Second World War. One was the Manhattan Project. The other event saw major breakthroughs in computer technology, which came on the heels of the code-cracking Enigma project.

There are competing claims for primacy. There was Alan Turing's group in Bletchley. There was the first digital computer, which was built by J.V. Atansoff and Clifford Berry. There was also the ENIAC computer in the U.S., which has a good claim to being first. (Primacy depends on how you define a computer: von Neuman talked about the difference between the "stored program," which he developed, and a "calculator.") Future historians will probably regard 1943 as the benchmark year for the beginning of this new era, much as we regard 1750 as the start of the Industrial Age.

In the late 1940s vacuum tubes were used as switches to handle the zero/one format of machine language, but in 1958 the world of computing was radically altered with the invention of the transistorized integrated circuit.

Then vacuum tube switches were replaced by tiny squares of silicon. The first silicon chips held only a few transistors, but by the 1980s chips holding a million transistors had appeared (see table).

In the 1960s, Gordon Moore, one of the founders of Intel, promulgated a theory of microchip development. Moore's Law held that semiconductor microchip density (capacity) would double every two years. Most of the actors in this new computer world dismissed Moore's prediction as hi-tech hyperbole. Moore was wrong. It turned out that the development rate actually doubled every 18 months.

To put this rate of technological advance into perspective, if automotive technology had advanced at a similar pace over the past 20 years, you would have a car that went 500,000 miles per hour, got a million miles to the gallon and cost only $1,000.

Anyone expecting the change rate to slow down is in for a rude surprise. One hint comes from the cyberspace jockeys who design computers. Computer efficiencies are based on the number of floating point operations the beasts can do in one second (these are called "flops"). It is now

---

The best contender for the first computer is German. Konrad Zuse created the first prototype of a functioning programmable computer, the Z1, in 1938. In 1940 Zuse delivered the Z2 and, in 1941, the Z3. This machine used binary arithmetic for a programmed operating system.

The German electrical industry was by then fully mobilized for war production and any new products were evaluated in terms of their immediate military applications. Germany's evaluators could not see any use for the Zuse device except as a code machine and the rejection noted that to explore potential applications would be a waste of skilled manpower.

It was the opinion of the German technical reviewer that the Enigma would see German coding requirements through the war. In retrospect, it is interesting that in the original technical review documents, neither the critic evaluating Zuse's device, nor Zuse himself, considered the possibility that an Enigma might be captured and reverse engineered, as indeed happened.

Germany continued to use the Enigma machine until the end of the war. Recently the Z3 was reconstructed and placed in a museum in Cologne.

assumed that soon someone will unveil a teraflop computer (todays super-computers, like the Cray Y-MP8, are known as gigaflop machines because they do more than a billion floating point operations per second). A teraflop machine will do a trillion flops. That's a thousand times faster than a Cray Y-MP8 gigaflop machine. Around the year 2000, there will be a petaflop machine. It will do a quadrillion flops. That is, it will go a million times faster than today's state-of the-art machine. As computer designer Gregory Chudnovsky recently said, "once we get a petaflop machine, it will find a way to simulate machines like itself, so that is how we will be able to design some *real* machines."

COMPUTER π, BAKED AND HALF-BAKED

The first reference to π occurs in a 1650 B.C. Egyptian Middle Kingdom papyrus scroll belonging to a scribe named Ahmes. Ahmes begins with the words "the entrance into the knowledge of all existing things" and then takes his reader through a series of math problems and solutions, during which he uses up several feet of papyrus and finds the area of a circle with a rough and ready sort of π.

Though we use a Greek letter for π, the Greeks actually had no word for π and around 200 B.C. Archimedes recorded that π was somewhere between $3^{10}/_{71}$ and $3^{1}/_{7}$ by successively inscribing and circumscribing polygons to a circle. (Not bad — the Greeks didn't use decimals and the fractions are close enough to 3.14.)

Gregory Chudnovsky was discovered by Richard Preston, a writer for *The New Yorker* in the May 2, 1992, issue, in which Preston reported that Chudnovsky knows all about π. With his brother David, Gregory built a gigaflop super computer, from mail-order parts, which performs favourably against computers like the Cray Y-MP8. This supercomputer resided in the living room of the Chudnovsky apartment in Manhattan.

Rate of semiconductor development

1970 1,000 bit memory chip available (1,000 bits = 1 kilobit =1K).

1974 First 4K D-RAM is delivered. It is employed in first personal computers.

1978 16K chips hit the market. They will be used in the first IBM PC.

1981 Japanese chip makers capture the world market with a 64K chip.

1984 Chips with 256K of memory appear.

1987 First commercial release of 1 megabit (1,000K) chips.

1990 4 megabit chips arrive.

1993 16 megabit chips commercially available.

1995 IBM and Seimens deliver a 64 megabit chip.

1999 Seimens and IBM believe they will deliver a 256 megabit chip.

With this do-it-yourself machine the Chudnovsky brothers had pushed π out to well beyond 2 billion numbers past the decimal point. Unfortunately, their research was inhibited by the fear that the building superintendent would discover the source of the drain on the building's power supply. The Chudnovskys have since found work with Sun Microsystems, presumably an environment where the super doesn't whine about excessive power use.

The trouble with two guys in New York developing an algorithmic breakthrough for calculating π is that while the rest of us are still trying to imagine why anyone would want to go a couple of billion numbers beyond 3.14, someone else will want to calculate π even further.

In November of 1995, another pair of brothers did it, this time with name-brand supercomputers. Jonathan and Peter Borwein are mathematicians at Simon Fraser University on the west coast of British Columbia, Canada, where they lead the Centre for Experimental Mathematics. Their algorithm has generated a print-out of 4 billion numbers from a generation of 40 billion extensions after the decimal point of π. They used time on two super-computers, one at NASA and another at the University of Tokyo.

But to what purpose is all of this attention to π? After all, Archimedes had it close enough for all the applications most of us will ever need.

Like most discoveries in pure mathematics the possible uses are not obvious. One use of a robust π algorithm does spring to mind. Nature is not always symmetrical, however much physicists like to pursue pure symmetry. If one were interested in the characterization of viruses, one would find that an accurate description of a new virus is beyond the methods heretofore available to us. If you're not interested in such activities, do words like hemorrhagic fever, AIDS, Ebola, or Mad Cow Disease get your attention? Most attempts at virus characterization are more akin to brute force than elegance. Until now viral characterizations have been, on the whole, strikingly unsuccessful.

Studies using similar mathematics to those found in computer graphics and games are developing robust algorithms on machine platforms that calculate squares and circles in cyberspace and are sought after in environments where the powers that be have a minimal concern for cost. The current Borwein algorithm still shows no repetitive pattern in all those numbers after the decimal point.

Close enough doesn't do the job when you try to insert a neutralized strand of DNA into the reproductive system of a virus; to design that new strand of DNA means molecular modelling at a whole new level of inconvenience.

It would appear that Moore's Law has suffered the fate of most Industrial Age assumptions. It no longer is useful for understanding the real world. The seemingly random way in which these critical quantum orders of magnitude are expanded by the powerful machines that buzz in the next generation of computer designer's heads will change the qualitative order of problems we can address.

A change rate of this kind can only result in massive ripple effects. With the advent of computers powerful enough to run complex simulations, an old discipline — cosmology — went through a complete retrofit, dropped the mystical properties that had hung on from alchemy and drew adherents from physics, mathematics, and computer science. (Cosmologists study the most fundamental processes of the universe — how the universe came about, how stars are formed, galactic evolution, and how Schrödinger's cat always manages to land on its feet.)

In the computer industry itself, memory chip prices fell as Japanese and American semiconductor manufacturers competed for world market share. Because of the computer industry's widely dispersed and fiercely competitive development base, the lag between development and product commercialization is extremely short. The relative ease with which the industry has been financed, particularly in the 1980s, has further pushed the pace with which it has commercialized new products.

The computer has made another seldom noticed (or totally misunderstood) contribution to the evolution of a distinctly new world-view. The evolution of the scientific method and post-war social concerns resulted in a movement among computer scientists and their students which opposed applying Industrial-Age secrecy to computer development.

This ambivalence about industrial secrecy has forced people in the computer industry to think seriously about defining information as property and pushed legal scholars, the judiciary, and practicing lawyers into providing legal definitions for the new industry. Whether these early definitions will prove useful is already in question.

In the 1920s and '30s, a major inhibition to moving the new information about Einstein's relativity to wider audiences was the sheer mathematical elegance of it. It was very easy to lose oneself in a sea of abstractions. Here computer science came to the rescue. Computers are an ideal vehicle to deal with the Einsteinian world-view. The computer's ability to perform complex mathematical functions means that so-called "thought experiments" can be reduced to a lower level of abstraction with a certain amount of ease. With this computational power, it is possible to generate metaphors for many of the concepts which underpin a new world-view. If we speed up the rate of understanding, even an imperfect understanding, the human problems of adaptation to changed conditions are eased. For most of us, understanding a continuum of both time and space is difficult. To abandon our conventional view of temporal events is not a commonplace amendment to our life-learning curve.

SELLING THE COMPUTER

How do you transfer information about computers to a wide public? Experiments with videotex in France have shown that it is difficult to market real applications to home users, while mainframes are capital intensive and really only available to governments, large businesses, and institutions. Software for them is also expensive, relative to personal computer (PC) software.

We might assume that the development of computer applications would have been a major mandate for computer makers and for the computer industry in general. This is not, in fact, the case. Applications pose problems in their own right.

In the real world, a problem has its own environment. But mainframe computer manufacturers attempted to impose the same problem-solving environments on everyone. To empirically work with a problem, you shoehorn it into a test tube or a computer — which is another reality. That is, you organize your data in the way a computer will most effectively deal with it. Once you get the problem in a form that is acceptable to the computer, you have to find or write a program that will process it in a useful way.

The goal of the program developer, however, is to sell as many copies of a program as possible. In the mainframe world, software developers naturally want a one-size-fits-all program. The PC world, however, is a very free marketplace and has developed quickly. When IBM entered the market, personal computers were rigorously defined as a productivity tool. When IBM and Microsoft presented the business community with a standardized operating environment — DOS — a large base of installed PCs came into being. Developers were able to create software for specialty markets and were virtually assured that a large market awaited them.

For example, there are word-processing software packages designed to serve such diverse market niches as film and TV script-writing, or others that support scientific notation and graphics (this book was designed and typeset on a word-processor that is primarily a typesetter). There are equation solvers that address the problems of engineers and architects. Computer-assisted design (CAD) and computer-assisted manufacturing (CAM) programs have changed the efficiency and productivity of entire industries. Personnel people have digitized spreadsheets that generate pay equity and employment equity information. Also, a secondary industry arose which produced one-of-a-kind databases using off-the-shelf software, which speeded up computerization of government, businesses, and institutions. The result was explosive growth in computer literacy and the range of software available.

Early experience gained by Apple and Commodore with the hobby market in the mid-to-late 1970s suggested that the time was right to go for a wider business market. Both Apple and Commodore had found that there was a small market for business usage, mostly transferred from self-taught hobbyists. High schools and some elementary schools began tentatively to take steps into teaching computer applications, based on the skills of teacher-hobbyists.

Critics questioned the availability of programmers to generate software for a PC marketplace — but they failed to foresee the productivity increments. They failed to recognize that Commodore and Apple had created an infrastructure of dealers and support technicians, as well as independent software developers. The early members of the hacker community had matured (somewhat) and were ready to join entrepreneurs and venture capitalists who smelled fortunes in the wind.

Bingo! With personal computers, each user could explore whichever level of abstraction afforded the user the most comfort. The marketing strategies broadly perfected in modern industrial societies suggested that the best plan was to give everyone a personal computer, which would generate software economies of scale unattainable with mainframes — and encourage a level of intellectual exploration unknown since the Renaissance.

On the face of it, the idea of widely distributed personal computers was outlandish. To succeed, you would have to teach everyone to use a computer. Ignorant critics claimed that, if you could not train a huge number of programmers, you would have to teach users to program. That was too weird to contemplate and proved unnecessary.

Marketers of early personal computers assumed that the woodwork was crawling with programmers and software entrepreneurs who were willing to bet their life savings that they could write and sell their software ideas. In 1976 computer kits were sold to hobbyists. Then complete computers designated for "home" use came and fortunes were made under the names Commodore, Atari and Apple.

A fortune was lost by Texas Instruments, which discouraged outside program developers and used software that was unique to its machine and difficult to copy. Texas Instruments's disaster in the personal computer arena was unexpected by corporate America. But the company, a major defence contractor, attempted to apply Industrial-Age standards to a world that had abandoned the Industrial Age.

Texas Instruments should have been number one, but the customers for the first PCs were unwilling to adapt to its military-industrial corporate culture. Commodore and Apple built their companies on the culture of their users. Texas Instruments was whipped by the kind of guys who built Blue Boxes to cheat the phone company.

COMPUTERS GET PERSONAL

In 1981 IBM entered the personal computer market. The corporate world was apparently only waiting for a trusted name to lead the way into mass computerization. The term "user friendly" entered the language as software developers created programs for users who lacked on-site technical support. These developers, recognizing that there were loads of potential users who would never become "friendly" with a computer, wrote software they could affectionately term "idiot-proof." The introduction of idiot-proof software meant a whole constituency who needed a less venturesome learning curve could be brought into the computer generation.

By 1990 PCs could be jury-rigged to compete in power terms with mini-computers and some mainframes. More importantly, software for the PC was competitive with and often challenged the quality of software available for mainframes.

The PC placed the power of the computer in the hands of individuals. A user could define his or her own level of abstraction, depending on their own perceptual vantage point. A secretary could get a letter out on a PC without being in terror that the networked mainframe would "go down." Users realized that mainframes and minis were distant and bureaucratic. Getting a fast PC meant that the computer would never say to you "I can only devote a percentage of my energy to you." With a PC, every user was, in that all pervasive word of the '90s, "empowered."

A second factor rendered the availability of inexpensive, efficient computers critical to the adoption of a new world-view. In the PC industry it soon became clear that the apocryphal "four guys in a garage" could now compete with large corporations in product development. In the PC community, IBM's software, specialty boards and external peripherals were by and large disasters. IBM has been unable to compete. The very size of IBM and clones like DEC, Burroughs, NCR, et cetera, resulted in an inertia that mitigated in favour of the smaller developer.

Personnel policies in large corporations are usually risk-aversive. But independent creators of computer software, add-ons and peripherals have brought about a development innovation rate in which any company becomes at risk unless it maintains its innovation quality and development pace. An entire merger industry lives off one-product companies.

The market for computers is, apparently, insatiable. In this climate, size is no predictor of success, in hardware or software. IBM's PC market share has dropped to a point where its PC division no longer can assume profitability. Outside of its purchase of software developer Lotus, IBM has no software products among the trend-setters. A consortium of PC manufacturers is openly challenging IBM's assumed leadership as the *de facto* standard creator.

Some students of contemporary management now believe that corporate inertia, after a certain size, destroys the capacity for timely development decisions that allow a company to remain competitive. This inertia inhibits the rate of any company's growth and places corporate survival at risk.

The computer industry has been able to cope, and even thrive, amid the dramatic change-rate inherent in a world-view shift. Since about 1960 this rate of technological change and the social consequences have been a matter of impotent concern for social scientists and bewildered educators. By the 1970s there was discussion in most Western governments about a perceived need to inhibit the change rate. The corporate world, which had access to government strategic planners, favoured a slow-down strategy.

IBM AGONISTES

IBM's problems can be traced back to the inability of its management to understand that the Lords of the Universe had decreed that IBM was the best creation of the Industrial Age and as such would have the privilege of ushering in a new era. Yet the reality of that new era was greater than anything IBM's executives and managerial proles could imagine.

IBM was the highest point of the Industrial Age, but it is unlikely that its managers can shed their historic baggage in time to even play a part in the new era.

At IBM, the internal competition for budgets and senior management's mindshare is such that it has been unable to compete at the innovation decision level. As in many other corporations, IBM's top management have become risk-aversive while claiming to be leaders in the era transition.

Part of the IBM corporate myth, a myth in which IBM managers took great pride, was that IBM had never laid off an employee. This policy was a significant part of its success in avoiding unionization. IBM executives set a standard in responsibility for the well-being of their staff.

There may have been a downside to the maintenance of this myth. It has been argued that this policy skewed IBM's recruitment in favour of non-risk-takers. Governments and regulated utilities employ the same skewing, but with them it's up front; prospective employees know there is a trade-off in such employment, between job security and restrictions on internal entrepreneurial competition.

In December 1991, prior to reporting its first-ever loss in the history of the company ($2.8 billion) and its first drop in annual sales since 1946, IBM announced its intention to eliminate 20,000 jobs worldwide. On April 10, 1992, IBM began to notify thousands of employees that they would have to find jobs elsewhere in the company or accept severance packages.

There is no evidence that the change rate is slowing down or likely to become more rational. Even a job at IBM could be at risk! Sure enough, in

December 1992, IBM announced another round of layoffs. This time IBM was being pressured by Wall Street to become more competitive and clear out unproductive staff.

In mid-January 1993, Standard & Poor's, the bond rating service, took away IBM's triple-A rating, which meant the company and its subsidiaries would have to offer higher interest payments when going to the increasingly disenchanted capital markets. Two days later, IBM's fourth-quarter results were due. Traditionally IBM's fourth quarter was when all the great deals of the past year were tallied, the big bonuses paid, and the dividend inevitably raised.

Financial analysts expected the company to announce major losses and it didn't disappoint. In fact, it was the most calamitous report in the 79-year history of the company. CEO John Akers had hopefully suggested that the IBM could come out with break-even numbers. Not even close. $5.4 billion was the loss, including all the charges and sundry expenses associated with layoffs, early retirements, and lousy sales. Even worse, there was a nasty item of $45 million in operating losses. How could IBM, beloved of pension plan managers, widows, and orphans, have rushed into such deconstruction?

The truth is that IBM has been in serious trouble since the late 1950s, when Big Blue set up its product lines — the 7070, 7080, 1401, and so forth. In all, there were 18 different computers in the line-up and every one was incompatible with every other. IBM's customers were not amused. If a business needed to increase its computing capacity it had trouble transferring files from one computer series to another — all the software was model-specific. All files were specific to their host software and computer. The cost of upgrading threatened to drive IBM customers into the arms of competitors.

Of course IBM knew that the company's future lay in "plug compatibility" and the ability to communicate between environments. But how to get there? Gene Amdahl, who later went on to build his own computer company, came up with an answer. Amdahl and a like-minded group recommended that the company proceed with a new series, the 360, and discard the others. The specifications for the 360 were to include full inter-series compatibility.

IBM bit the bullet and bet the farm (it was a time for all those sayings that remind us of a simpler past). Sales of the 360 went off the sales chart into space somewhere and 80 percent of the mainframe market became marked with Big Blue's logo. The 360 stayed in orbit and took IBM into the 1960s when, as that decade ended, a new problem appeared.

There was no IBM communications system software. Ken Olsen, founder of the smaller but still arch-rival DEC, had it — DEC Net — and

IBM's more sophisticated customers were again growing restive while DEC scored some significant gains. IBM's headquarters in Armonk, New York decreed that IBM would develop a new standard for communications.

Over the next three years the company went through a bloodbath as internal fiefdoms fought ideological battles over standards. In the end SNA (System Network Architecture) became the IBM standard. In the process, careers were ruined and friendships destroyed as managers fought over specifications.

After that, IBM's senior managers, and even its blue-ribbon board, decreed that never again would a struggle over such a deeply divisive issue be allowed to happen. Internal wars are simply not IBM's style. The whole company was restructured, with new management systems designed to assure consensus without internal conflict. As a result, there was no longer a place in the company where a decision could be made about the complex issues surrounding the implementation and marketing of advanced technology. The towers of warring Babylon had been muted. Consensus reigned. And IBM had lost its creative edge. Worst of all, the company has lost its ability to make strategic decisions.

INDUSTRIAL STRENGTH SOLUTIONS

As IBM struggled, the investment fund managers who had bought Big Blue's stock searched for a scapegoat. The consensus among the Fund Lords was that CEO John Akers must pay. To be fair, Akers was merely a kid who caught the brass ring when the cam shaft on the merry-go-round broke down.

In January 1996, AT&T decided to eliminate 40,000 jobs. Wall Street promptly booted AT&T's stock up $2.63 per share.

It was IBM all over again, except AT&T wasn't broke. In fact, virtually all its divisions, subsidiaries and operating projects were doing quite nicely, thank you. It was making money hand over fist — $2.82 billion for the first three quarters of 1995 — so the $4 billion after-tax charge for body-bagging 40,000 staffers, 60 percent of them white-collar, didn't cause much blinking in those offices that connected to CEO Robert Allen's suite.

The executives who run the telcos, led by AT&T, have finally figured out what their techies meant when they said satellites aren't distance-sensitive and that basing phone charges on linear lines makes you vulnerable to someone who can buy satellite time. To stay alive, the only place a value-add exists is to charge for each call-related connection.

There is a school of suspicion that says AT&T figured that out when it discovered that there's a price-war for satellite connections. And the queue of weird

To find a new beloved leader, IBM did the unthinkable — it went outside the company. After a few months the search committee announced on March 27, 1993, that they had found their man — at RJR Nabisco. Actually, Louis Gerstner had recently moved there from American Express. At Amex you learn a lot about using computers, if you're at the top of the executive class.

The IBM board's reasoning went something like this: Gerstner may be unfamiliar with the corporate culture of IBM, but IBM needs someone to oversee its reorganization into roughly seven separate, relatively autonomous businesses. The Gerstner solution argued that if IBM were to be healthy, competitive and profitable again, it needed a seasoned CEO who could regain the confidence of investors and major customers. If such a person did not exist within the corporate culture then the searchers had to go elsewhere. IBM's managerial talent pool would field division heads for separate units of the computer business, all reporting to Gerstner.

The board's solution was to treat IBM as a company with a mature product line and give it the kind of executive structure you give a company like Lever Brothers, the soap maker. The problem with this analysis is that no company in the computer industry has a mature product, let alone a mature product line. The scariest thing was that this solution pacified the investment managers.

Those who were scared turned out to be right. In the late spring of 1993, IBM's PC division launched a new product line — the Ambra — to hit back at clone makers. The Ambra was offered internationally with a free three-year, full-service warranty; Gerstner marked the occasion with a

---

investors to get in on putting up even more of the transponder-dense birds is getting longer every day. (Not only does the satellite industry have ready sources of bucks, but the people who launch satellites are even weirder than their investors.)

The key to the AT&T shut-down was how effectively it was done. First a search was done for managers carrying too much intellectual baggage — i.e. "I don't know why the computer made that decision. We didn't have computers when I started here," or "There's an AT&T way to do things and when Mr. Allen tells me that we're changing throughout the company, we will." Once the human resources evaluators find a manager like that, they simply list the manager and the staff who report to that manager as redundant.

The rationale: the manager hasn't learned to get rid of baggage and, by displaying a deep affinity for baggage, has become baggage. The manager's staff have picked up too much of their manager's baggage and retraining them is too problematic and expensive.

warm and fuzzy memo to the 90 percent of IBM employee survivors who had email services.

Three year warranty? On July 29, 1994, after the markets had closed, the Reuters newswire delivered the news that Ambra was toast and 2,000 jobs had been slagged. Louis Gerstner had learned all about tough corporate decisions at Amex and RJR Nabisco.

As if IBM didn't have enough problems back in 1993, events continued to unfold as if some perverse gods had taken over the universe and were not only playing dice with it, but the game was crooked. Two days after IBM had reported the largest corporate loss in history, the company lost its place as the world's largest computer company.

And who was its replacement? Who else but Microsoft, which overtook IBM in total market capitalization as IBM's slumping shares zoomed down past Microsoft's booming ones. At the end of the day on January 21, the market said Microsoft was worth $26.8 billion while IBM, which had been worth $107 billion in 1987, was now worth $26.5 billion. Worse was yet to come. Intel, the maker of the chips that powered the PC, was coming up fast in the passing lane with a market capitalization of close to $24 billion.

IBM had abandoned both Microsoft and Intel in the course of making a deal with Apple. Earlier, Apple had sued Microsoft, IBM and Hewlett Packard for developing software that had same the same "look and feel" as the windowing system Apple had patented. (Windowing was actually devel-

---

If the reader thinks all of this is gratuitous America-bashing, consider two recent changes in the human resources field at Japan Inc.

The first is that, in those companies whose phone numbers are on auto-dial in the deputy minister's office at Ministry of International Trade and Industry, the policy was to give everybody an annual raise on their birthday. This was based on the fact that among the ideas, culture, pictographic script, et cetera the Japanese imported from China over the centuries was veneration of age and ancestors. So it figured that, in your job-for-life, your value to the company would increase year by year. It also helped the sarariman (the Japanese term for salaried employees) keep up with inflation in those post-war years.

Not so, according to what passes in Japan for human resources consultants. Now we've been in an economic depression for five years. It's a warm, fuzzy idea to give the raise on the employee's birthday, but.... You get the idea.

The other item is more profound. North Americans are always unnerved by the paucity of computers in offices of Japan Inc. Now Japanese industry is launching a campaign to make every Japanese senior executive computer literate in two years. One of those spokescreatures that MITI produces in moments of stress said: "the two-year figure was based on the idea that no one in Japan's senior execu-

oped by Xerox at its Palo Alto Research centre, but not commercially exploited). Microsoft's Windows, like Apple's operating system, offers PC users the benefits of graphical user interfaces and ease of use (at a cost of distancing the user from the operating system). IBM's OS/2, which was originally written by Microsoft, was retrofitted yet again by IBM after a problem laden launch and a new version was announced — to be greeted with an even bigger yawn than the previous version.

Part of the IBM-Apple deal was an exchange of patents, whereupon Apple dropped IBM as a defendant in the Windows suit. When IBM and Apple struck an alliance that ostensibly gave Apple access to IBM's systems and patent book, most informed observers agreed that the intent of the deal was to attack Microsoft — the developer of the operating system used in all makes of PC machines.

IBM had extricated itself from the patent dispute, leaving Microsoft to face the music — demonstrating a clear inability to adapt to the change rate. It had abandoned its historic allies, Microsoft and Intel, and betrayed its own corporate culture. When IBM left its two key suppliers to swing in the wind, many in the computer industry saw the act as dishonourable. This charge of *dishonourable* conduct had never been leveled at IBM before. IBM never cheated customers, suppliers, or employees.

The computer industry still attracts idealists who feel they have a chance to make a qualitative difference in the onrushing new era. (We're

---

tive class could hide out for more than two years."

In the meantime they have an upgrade of a Roman-alphabet Kanji and are working hard to produce a Japanese word-processing package. There's a grotesque problem with the literally translated messages coming out from pressing the f1 key. And as for spell checkers, good luck.

There's another point of amusement for those of us who feel better when someone else is suffering. The training of these senior executives has been subcontracted to either computer companies or the multinational consulting slugs. Their training divisions are by and large run by bright, attractive young female University of Tokyo grads or, even worse, the University of Kyoto. Just think of the Japanese concept of "face." And think of all the stupid things you do when you're learning how to propel yourself through cyberspace or a simple two-dimensional spreadsheet.

Remember, Japan is reputed to have the one of the worst sexual harassment records in the industrial world and now Japan Inc.'s senior bosses have been told by the man from MITI that they have to go to a school run by the newest of Japanese women.

using the term "quality" in the way Robert M. Persig, author of *Zen and the Art of Motorcycle Maintenance*, used it to refer to the classical Greek sense of integrity.) To make a qualitative difference to the future is still a powerful vision to many.

A major contribution IBM had made was to set standards for civility and honourable conduct unmatched in most industries. More than one executive wondered, as the market exacted its price for IBM's failure to test its senior managers for comprehension of nature's laws for successful evolution, who would keep the industry honest in the future.

WINDOW ON THE NEW WORLD-VIEW

The rest of the computer industry continues to push the applications envelope. Basic research in mathematics, physics and cosmology is empirically tested in virtual environments of increasing complexity. And applications from these findings reach the marketplace daily. The computer's ability to provide the fast calculation and memory necessary in the exploration of higher dimension space assures that problem solving and the generation of new applications will continue unabated.

The interface between scientists exploring the primal forces of the universe and the computer's capabilities in analysis and dissemination of data has resulted in significant changes in the generally accepted world-view. Some examples of these changes:

- The individual scientist is less dependent on institutional support and control.

On August 9, 1994, Reuters (with bad news experience that dates back to the Napoleonic Wars) reported that IBM CEO Louis Gerstner was going to ask Sotheby's to flog a "significant number" of pieces from IBM's art collection. The collection had been started by IBM mentor/myth figure Thomas Watson Sr. and built up over 30 years. It had its own gallery — The Madison Avenue Gallery in Manhattan.

Thomas Watson Sr.'s collection had fittingly begun with American realists like Edward Hopper and Winslow Homer. Over the years the collection, always overseen by the CEO, shifted to abstract works, including pieces by Robert Motherwell and Helen Frankenthaler. Business Week followed the ravenish Reuters and reported that the reason for the sale was that Gerstner needed cash. The collection was said to be worth something in the vicinity of $45 million.

The business press failed to comment on what the gallery and collection meant to IBM's corporate culture. First and foremost it was a surviving icon of Thomas

• The rate at which information is processed through the development chain — from basic research to technology research to application research to development — is profoundly truncated and the learning curve is reduced by orders of magnitude. The time between basic research and end-use application is shorter today than at any time in history.

   • This results in a change-rate faster than it was even five years ago. It also results in individual, social, economic, and political stress, with significant dislocation as the response to this change rate.

   • With cosmology opening N-space for exploration, the pressures for a change in the world-view are now far in excess of those experienced from the 13th to the first half of the 18th centuries. The key factor appears to be the sophistication, level of abstraction, and availability of information throughout society. For example, it is probable that the TV program *Star Trek: The Next Generation*, with its "holodeck," and all the TV shows about time travel have explained the idea of a fourth dimension to more people than could all the physics professors who have ever lived.

While the assumptions underlying the holodeck on *Star Trek* may be conventional wisdom to a good part of the younger generation, a relativistic view of "time" remains a difficult concept for most of their elders.

Earlier generations have taken hundreds of years to absorb the new levels of abstraction brought on by an era transition. Those early under-

---

Watson Sr., the guy who put the whole thing together in the first place. It made a clear statement of how IBM saw itself. Other high tech outfits commissioned some really interesting contemporary pieces; even IBM's ad agencies did that. IBM, however, built a gallery collection with an acquisitions policy that included American mythic figures like Hopper and Motherwell.

That Gerstner managed to stall the sale as long as he did proves he is one of the few who recognized the internal cultural values involved. If he had sold the pictures in his first week on the job, that might of been excusable. But to do it months later? He probably really did need the bucks. Even on their worst days the Medicis did not throw their collections onto the streets. To make matters worse Bill Gates went out and bought truckloads of World Famous Paintings and original manuscripts to flog with Windows 95. Bill Gates, Encyclopedist? Diderot, get back in your coffin and stop twirling.

standings had to compete in an environment inhibited by superstition and religious/political correctness. One thing we have is a higher degree of communications sophistication. This sophistication, however, is frequently muted by the trivialization of information, by prioritizing entertainment over the transfer of knowledge. Another problem is that our political processes often reward the substitution of short-term gains for long-term benefits.

Some technologies on the verge of wide availability have the potential to cause major disruptions and uncontrollable application spin-offs. One of these is virtual reality (VR). Autodesk, the company that developed the program AutoCAD, is the leader in computer-assisted design (CAD); Autodesk is also the leading force in elegant programs for VR technology. VR was the enabling force behind combat aircraft applications in the Gulf War. Autodesk, which made its reputation in the PC environment, is capable of applying its knowledge and resources in PC programming and consumer marketing to VR.

At George Lucas' Industrial Light and Magic, VR is considered their turf. After all, who put Princess Leia in a simulated VR display in *Star Wars*? Even while they produce special computerized effects for the big screen with Alias Wavefront's software, they are releasing a wide range of video games which test the limits of current VR technology, rendering it familiar to an expanding audience.

Essentially, VR can simulate a 3-D "world" and allow the user to experience this simulation with all senses. The goal of workers in this field is to digitally recreate the actual world. NASA has a database simulating the

---

If you're interested in what it means to have computing power at hand, consider Neil Sloane and David Doehlert. Sloane, whose personal amusement begins with N-space geometries at Lucent Technologies' Murray Hill theme park in New Jersey, and Doehlert, a statistician and the director of the Experimental Strategies Foundation in Seattle, have whistled up a new algorithm for the design of experiments (DOE).

DOE is a way to test experimental designs using statistical modeling that produces a sort of virtual experiment, which at least screens out the more obviously flawed experiments.

The big problem with conventional DOE systems came by way of a Total Quality Management freak named Genichi Taguchi whose process control was pretty good but whose statistics weren't too trustworthy. What was needed was a way to define the virtual test-bed relationships in ways that would produce results that were sufficiently robust and mathematically compliant so that you could do a little more than

planet Mars. The user is provided with interactive stimulation so that the senses experience the virtual "world" within the computer.

Applications appear endless. Simulators are providing an entirely new level of training for pilots, mariners, aircraft controllers, and astronauts. VR will enable a microbiologist to follow a retrovirus through the body and watch its reproduction and mutation cycles.

Such a broadly based development market requires any manager to be prepared to take the necessary prudent steps to bring new and frequently unfamiliar technology into the corporate fold.

Another imminent (to mass availability) technology is the ability to design, model, and simulate molecules. Most computer-assisted design at present is for engineering applications. Almost all of the applications for which engineers use CAD can be done, albeit laboriously, without a computer. Without a computer, molecular modelling cannot be done.

If molecular modelling and manufacturing are viable, so too is nanotechnology, which operates at reduction levels of 1 billion times and assumes that machines the size of molecules can be constructed. These machines are envisioned as engaging in tasks such as gene modification.

If the head of an organization assumes that its computer usage is limited to a secretary's word processor and the bookkeeper's accounting package, then that executive is unprepared to track the evolution of either the emergent world-view or its parallel technology.

As the first multidimensional programs come out, the really interesting thing is the number of people who are jumping into the old swimming hole. The pharmaceutical industry has some sophisticated drugs for tight-fitting

---

simply discard the crap outside a single standard deviation.

Sloane was approached by Doehlert, who is in the business of supporting experimental research models. Doehlert thought that Sloane's passion for N-space exploration might just be the ticket to doing an end-run on conventional DOEs and their kludgy statistics.

In the end they managed to produce an algorithm and a software blackbox that permitted access to and employment of 1,500-dimensional space! That is 120 points in 14 dimensions.

This work guarantees that this era shift is only beginning. Remember, these guys were only interested in the one small problem of efficient DOEs. What happens when the Sloane-Doehlert approach is understood by a global research and development community of say, 100,000? That's when you can assume that "Industrial Age" will show up in dictionaries defined as "a term of derision."

genetic material replacements. The film and TV industries, which have production based employment policies, are demonstrating a very fast learning curve by approving some difficult-to-understand budgeting requests.

You can assume anyone who is involved with chemicals or metallurgy has discovered that their whole industry is now able to do things that people, five years ago, would not believe could happen in their lifetimes. The attrition rate for executives who are imagination-challenged or have failed to understand that the computer represented a quantum cultural shift are going to make the early retirement set a new marketing niche.

WHAT A COMPUTER KNOWS

When Alan Turing (1912-1954) wasn't cracking German codes at Blechey or writing the specifications for the Colossus Computer (the first electronic computer), he amused himself by speculating about a definition for artificial intelligence (AI).

In 1950 Turing published his ideas about AI in the British philosophical journal Mind under the title "Computing Machinery and Intelligence." Turing argued forcefully for a way to define AI and suggested a means to test a computer for AI, which has come to be known as the Turing Test. Turing argued that we would have AI when someone could ask probing questions of both an unseen computer and an unseen person. The interrogator would be allowed no information, outside of that derived by the answers. The human respondent would always answer questions truthfully, while the computer could lie if necessary to avoid detection.

The computer would be deemed to have passed the Turing Test when no interrogator could tell from the answers when the person was responding and when the reply came from the machine.

There are a few quibbles and one real problem with the Turing Test. The real problem is that the machine must be shielded from the human respondent's responses in such a way that the computer cannot copy the person's style, syntax and speed of solving an arithmetic problem.

There is a less formidable definition which says we'll have AI when a computer can address such linguistic ambiguities as telling the difference between "a Venetian blind" and "a blind Venetian." Or, when a computer can address a difference in the form of the words "poles" and "for/four" when we talk about FOUR POLES FROM THE POLISH TELEPHONE COMPANY LOOKING FOR PLACES TO PUT UP NEW TELEPHONE POLES.

Computer scientists have been promising us AI since Ada, Countess of Lovelace and illegitimate daughter of Lord Byron, tried to write a program that would enable Charles Babbage's machine to write better poetry than her father.

Computer scientists have underestimated this task because they didn't know enough formal psychology and neurophysiology to be daunted. They shouldn't feel too bad, however. As the new kids in cognitive studies school, they couldn't be expected to know how iffy the big kids' work really was.

Computer scientists have been spoiled. When they asked for more memory, they got it and the price went down. When they asked for more storage space, not only did they get it, but it was denser and the price went down. When they asked for AI, they expected to get it quickly and cheaply, and like the sillies they are, they went around saying they were almost there.

Neural networking makes totally different kinds of demands on programmers than conventional kinds of programming. And it produces some answers that begin to resemble our definitions of AI.

One criticism of computer system designers and programmers is that they tend to be very tangential in their thought processes. This makes them less than snazzy to party with. Neural networks have the capacity to generate independent associations and form categories. They are able to simulate

---

Charles Babbage was perennially short of cash. In 1842 he addressed his shortage of research and development money with a solution that was, if nothing else, a convincing demonstration that he was well in advance of his times. He applied to the prime minister of the day for a grant. The PM commanded the most efficient civil service since Rome and knew that the watchword for heading such a bureaucracy could be summed up in one word: delegate. So he flipped the file off to the Chancellor of the Exchequer, who sent the file along to the Astronomer Royal with a note that the government was considering asking Parliament to provide funding for the development of Mr. Babbage's "Analytic Engine" and would the Astronomer Royal be kind enough to advise the Chancellor whether or not there was any likelihood that a) the engine might work and b) whether there was a possibility that the thing might improve the economy of Britain, create a few jobs, be of use in record-keeping, et cetera.

On September 15, 1842, Sir George Biddell Airey K.C.B., M.A. (Oxon), LL.D., D.C.L., F.R.S., F.R.A.S., who was accustomed, as astronomers are, to working with big numbers and big ideas, dispatched a letter to the Chancellor with his opinion. (This was long before the Internet — at the time, Londoners received five postal deliveries daily and a letter sent from Greenwich by 10 a.m. would be delivered to Whitehall by 2:30 p.m.)

Sir George's reply was to the point. He viewed the likelihood that the engine could be made to work as "impossible" and the potential for economic benefit to Britain to be "worthless."

simple generalizations about category families. William Allman's book *Apprentices of Wonder — Inside the Neural Network* gives a clear picture of people building a discipline which today can produce a minimally definable intelligent environment. Within very limited parameters, neural networks answer some of our most fundamental questions, which should have been asked long ago, about the nature of intelligence. We should not be surprised if the answers are not what we expected.

Computers work by making millions of tiny yes/no decisions. This is done by turning switches on and off. Inside the computer the yes/no is represented in a language consisting of zeros and ones.

The key to understanding a world of exploitable cyberspace is to fully comprehend the idiot savant quality of the computer and how what most people mistake for intelligence is cunningly disguised through perceptual gerrymandering. Computer developments for the future are focused on moving more complex units of information, more efficiently, from the computer to a display screen. The speed at which the programmer's instructions are implemented (the computing capacity), the amount of memory which the computer has, and the screen where the computer's output is displayed are where the changes become significant.

On the screen, we see the futility of trying to extend the extrapolations of a linear, industrial mindset. The enormity of this historical cycle and the pace with which it is enveloping us emerges with startling clarity when we realize how few of the metaphors we use daily actually describe the new world.

CHAPTER THREE

Meet the New World Order

Is this what the corporate world calls 'a white knight to the rescue?'

To understand the New World Order it would be most profitable first to ask one question: What does the NWO offer? Then it would seem logical to ascertain whether a wise and prudent citizen could believe that the NWO can deliver on its offer.

On the face of it, it would seem that George Bush, his allies in friendly governments, President Bill Clinton and their kitchen door domestic political supporters made the same mistake made by many of the mid-19th century business community in Britain.

Or, as the blessed Niccolo once wrote: "There is nothing more difficult to take in hand, more perilous to conduct, or more uncertain in its success, than to take the lead in the introduction of a new order of things" (Niccolo Machiavelli, *The Prince*).

Suppose you were to ask George Bush, Bill Clinton, or any sufficiently qualified corporate representative of the NWO: "What is this New World Order?" The world-view they hold would lead them to reply something like this:

"The world we live in is very dangerous and some of its inhabitants are positively exothermic. The nation state has become, in many ways, otiose. There are two issues which affect us all, equally. First is the economy, followed closely by the environment. Unless a nation state is self-sufficient, and few truly are, every country must surrender large pieces of its sovereignty to a regional trading bloc. Only the U.S. remains as a superpower."

The sample spokesperson would go on: "In truth, most nation states are too parochial to usefully face the issues. Regional trading groups can manage the global economy. The link between the various trading blocs will be the transnational corporations which, with their global management perspective and their ability to put products into global distribution, are able to avoid the petty jealousies which caused wars in the past."

Modern transnational corporations have evolved standard management strategies to cope with transnational realities. One of these, currently in favour, originated at IBM. The vice-president of manufacturing, located at corporate headquarters, holds a global management mandate. Manufacturing facilities around the world report to that office. This strategy, it is argued, allows global manufacturing to be rationalized in an environment of an increasing rate of product development related to the growth rate of new technologies and the resultant research costs.

Plants are given product mandates with consideration for local labour conditions, national skills development and raw material. Delivery to product shipping centres can be put on a just-in-time basis. Sales and marketing

---

It's instructive to observe how European, American and Japanese transnational corporations actually behave as they attempt to take control of the world's economy. For all of their talk of globalism, they consistently reflect the cultural and geographic determinants of their home offices, although companies may differ from one another significantly.

In all cases, an executive ambitious for promotion must keep to the "main track" of the company.

Following the Industrial Revolution, European firms needed to export in order to keep growing. Since that time, with domestic markets that are too small to generate sufficient economies of scale, European companies have assumed an international marketplace. They opened sales offices in other countries and, without a real communications infrastructure, tended to give the local man lots of autonomy. (This model was in place before international telephone and telegraph cables.) The local man had "President" on his business card. His compensation package was a commission based on the local subsidiary's profit. It was in his interest to begin manufacturing at the first glimmer of a chance to make money locally. With manufacturing materials locally available, or labour rates measured in coolie dollars, he could often do quite well.

The European system tended to give the parent organization a long view and an accounting policy which valued asset acquisition over quarterly results. However, this system also leads to counterproductive and chaotic administrative problems.

The "main track" or route to power in a European transnational corporation is via the product line the company started with. At Lever Brothers it's edible oils and fats. At Hoffman-LaRoche it's chemicals and pharmaceuticals. At Bayer it's over-the-counter drugs. If you are the head of a European subsidiary anywhere but the U.S., your goal is to get back home to the main product line. Otherwise you're out there with the natives. (The U.S. head typically makes so much money for the com-are run out of local national subsidiaries. Because the transnational corporation has separated manufacturing from marketing and technical support, governments are unable to blackmail it into inefficiently manufacturing in their own countries, since the VP Manufacturing is insulated from such internal or external pressures. According to this theory, the metagovernments that administer the trading blocs will keep the transnational corporations honest.

Let's return to our spokesperson for the NWO: "Survival is determined by a country's ability to produce, export, import, and, when necessary, borrow. Countries which have a 19th-century mind set — countries like India, which is monetized with gold — must alter their economies to interface

---

pany, relative to other subsidiaries, that head office defers to him. But he cannot afford to go home and seldom influences corporate policy.)

American transnational corporation are very different. Their local presidents are on much shorter tethers. They "grew up" in a post-World War II communications environment. Their domestic market is huge. Imagine being the managing director of General Motors (U.K.) — the Los Angeles zone manager sells more cars than you do. The U.K. head reports to a VP International Operations and the board hears about him or her for 30 seconds every quarter. Obviously, the U.K. head's goal is to get back to the main track — which, in the case of an American transnational, is the domestic market.

Japanese transnationals search diligently for local executives. Until they get one, they have executives from Japan on three-year tours. The executives' wives accompany them and cluster near families connected to other Japanese companies. That way their children can go to a company sponsored Japanese school. Japanese transnational corporations face a problem recruiting local executives because to run an overseas Japanese subsidiary successfully means being very sensitive to company politics and to the man from MITI at the Japanese embassy.

If it's one of the big trading companies, you have to be sensitive to Japanese domestic politics. It's a very feudal job. You interpret head office policy. You don't manufacture (in some places you may assemble automobiles) and you do no research. You buy product and patent rights on orders from Japan, if the local economy supports innovation.

You travel to and from Japan — a lot — and, if you are Japanese, you plot and scheme to get a job with a future back home. Postings to countries with large product sales are good and you can expect a real promotion on your return. Foreign postings are part of executive development, but they tend to be isolating. The model is based on the trading company and sees any foreign post as not-at-home.

more effectively with global economic realities. In India, gold prices are twice the world price, which results in a huge gray market in goods and a huge black market in smuggled gold. This results in a crushing debt load.

"The environment is a serious issue. The regional trading blocs have to make sure their national members behave — that is, regulate responsibly. Again, we see transnational corporations ensuring the environment is managed to the benefit of all. Most environmental issues are actually about resource allocation. Countries which offer pollution havens fail to understand that pollution results when you lack the trained work force to use the advanced technologies needed to manage industrial pollution. Manufacturers who try to escape to Third World pollution havens are penny-ante players who don't understand that the necessary technologies are not an added cost, but a production enhancement that will make money.

"The transnational corporations, being the largest users of raw resource products, have the management expertise to support metagovernmental units in securing the cooperation of local governments. Real transnational corporations are too powerful to deal with most nation states. Local governments collapse under them too easily. Only the regional trading bloc metagovernments have the clout to keep the playing field level."

How does the NWO see the rest of the world? Back to our spokesperson:

"India is a big question mark, with its religious/semi-tribal disputes of Islamic-Hindu origin, such as the chaos in the northwest Punjab Sikh region and the threat of nuclear confrontation with Pakistan. But perhaps they can deal with their potential for disaster.

"Africa is a disaster. We assume that South Africa will have solved its image problem in six or seven years and can assume responsibility for the burden of the central and southern parts of the continent. Alternatively, the European Union will move in to use the continent as a low wage area."

"In the Middle East there are two problems. One is Israel, but it seems to be coming to an agreement with its neighbours. The other is that the Muslim world is not a trading bloc. A trading bloc has, as its principle function, to deal with other blocs. Countries in which the citizens are predominantly Muslim have to do something about literacy, birth rate, resource management, and stability of local governments.

"Hopefully, when the Israeli-Palestinian question is resolved, the Israelis can bring some attitudes to the region which aren't based in the 7th century. (The contradictions between modern technology and their holy books have never seemed to bother them.) Anyway, those are regional issues and they shouldn't be permitted to infect the rest of the world. It's their problem."

You might well ask, considering the situation in former Yugoslavia, what real clout do trading blocs and metagovernments have?

Both Bush and Clinton would probably answer, "It wouldn't have been reasonable to expect the E.U. to have reacted more effectively in Yugoslavia. The Serbian/Croatian/Bosnian dispute has demonstrated that the international community's will to respond on a regional level is less than effective. If it is ineffective, the U.N.'s peace-keeping mandate will have to be made sufficiently broad to respond at whatever level of force is required. It may well be that the only group that can intervene in the kind of madness we see around the world would be the U.N., but there is little moral-force currency available to the U.N.

"As to the U.N. charter excluding intervention in internal national disputes, historians of the future will probably find that the inviolability of the nation state began to ebb away when the regional trading zone state was voluntarily entered into by its constituent members.

"Two warring states, or a nation state with breakaway provinces, cannot be permitted to interfere with the commercial life-blood of neighbouring states. Nor can such a localized revolution be permitted to shirk the entire globe's commercial discipline. The world's economy is simply too interconnected."

You might then ask, which trading blocs are relatively operational?

BLOC PARTIES

Members of the European Union signed the Treaty of Maastricht on political and monetary union on February 7, 1992, amid pious platitudes as to the landmark qualities of the pact. It declared that 1999 would be the latest date for implementing a single European currency. The treaty also provides for delivery to the European parliament of new powers over security, a common foreign policy, and defence matters (marking the first time the E.U. has had a formal common defense role).

There was however, concern that other members of the E.U. would follow the lead of the Danes, who failed to support a referendum to ratify Maastricht. The Danish electorate were given another chance and ratified Maastricht in 1993. In October 1993, the German federal constitutional court dismissed a number of challenges arguing that Maastricht posed a threat to the German constitution.

At that point, no one was willing to bet on implementation of the treaty, particularly the replacement of national currencies by a single European currency before the year 2000. The European recession had been too savage and only Luxembourg, of the 12 signatory governments, could meet the requirement of a budget deficit not exceeding 3 percent of gross domestic product (GDP) and a total government debt not exceeding 60 percent of GDP.

The treaty of Maastricht locks the 12 signatory nations into the final steps of creating a bloc with a single market, one currency and a unified voice in international affairs. E.U. fans also look forward to the day when the E.U. will exercise a common defense policy. They argue that, with a common currency and a common foreign affairs policy, it only makes sense to bring the armed forces of each member country under a common command and weapons compatibility rubric. Should this goal be achieved, it would give the E.U. powers unimagined until now. The capability of such a military command would give the E.U. superpower status.

Bush and Clinton would agree that the North American Free Trade Agreement (NAFTA) uniting the U.S., Canada, and Mexico is largely on target, although Clinton's political credit has already been stretched to the limit by a Congress resentful of the NAFTA deal in light of poor job stability and employment creation at home.

Just as the ultimate goal for American negotiators of the Canada-U.S. Free Trade Agreement was to create fertile ground for a continental free trade policy, success with NAFTA would make a hemispheric trading bloc feasible throughout South and Central America. America's superpower status would be protected from depredations by Europe, while Japan and China after the year 2000 would be confronted by a single regional trading bloc's economic and foreign policies.

Corporate America argues that Mexico will provide a good buffer to Oriental, African and former East Bloc low-wage areas. It would seem the Canadian and American economies are settling in well and the work of harmonizing their regulatory environments and rationalizing their respective productivity strengths seems to be moving right along without much notice from anyone, in spite of a difficult economic climate. The fact that polls say less than one-third of Canadians support the agreement does not pose a problem.

The game plan of the executive branch in the U.S. took note of the fact that in South America there already exists a limited free trade group comprising Chile, Argentina, Brazil, Uruguay, and Paraguay. With Mexico on line, Bush's "Enterprise for the Americas" is moving forward.

A later administration will, no doubt, change the name to reflect its own contributions. The eventual goal is a free trade zone stretching from the Canadian arctic to Tierra del Fuego, which was called for in President Reagan's first State of the Union address.

In late 1995 the American lead negotiator, Peter Murphy, admitted that the principal goal of the American team at the Canada-U.S. Free Trade Agreement talks was to incorporate a structure that would severely constrain any future government of Canada from engaging in any kind of nationalism. Other American officials have pointed to the energy initiatives of the Trudeau government as unacceptably "nationalistic."

This fear of Canadian nationalism was directly related to the idea that the European Common Market might actually work and become the E.U. that exists today. The U.S. policy was to give up some of its own domestic market to enhance Canada's trade with the U.S. and give Canada economic resources of sufficient size that its businesses could function in the U.S. market. (The rule of thumb is that the U.S. market is 10 times greater than that of Canada.)

The thought that a future Canadian prime minister might go off on a nationalist tangent during a confrontation with Europe was not something the State Department wanted to think about. So increased trade had to be tied to a junior partnership for Canada.

When the Canadian deal was signed, the U.S. approached the Mexican government of President Carlos Salinas de Gortari, which moved with alacrity to close the NAFTA deal. North America was irrevocably set on a regional free trade course which would be difficult to breech after the 10-year set-up time had passed. Whole new trading patterns would have been put in place.

Canada would be vulnerable to another round of separation anxiety from the threatened breakaway of the province of Quebec. The Mulroney government was warned by senior civil servants that the agreements would distort Canadian commerce, with the enhanced North-South patterns of business activity resulting in alienation of the three prairie provinces and British Columbia.

It was also pointed out that there were few, if any, intrinsic benefits in these trade deals for the chronic economic basket cases of the four Maritime provinces. However, Mulroney was by this time so committed, personally and politically, that the deal went through on terms that guaranteed the long term goals of the U.S. were met completely.

No matter how much of a nationalist a future prime minister might be, there would be little that could be done to serve Canadian interests. Only North American interests would count. Quebec nationalists were the governing party in the provincial National Assembly and were preparing for another referendum on sovereignty; part of their platform was that they would "inherit" membership in NAFTA. While Canada had managed to remain technically a sovereign state, it had placed itself at risk of completely breaking apart.

Canadian diplomats, whose mobility as representatives of an independent middle power had enabled them to secure a higher profile, were suddenly turned into a U.S. satrap in the diplomatic world. Mulroney's party went from a massive majority to just two members in Parliament. George Bush was also defeated.

Meanwhile the other anchor of the North American trading alliance, Mexico, had a problem. President Salinas had to retire, since Mexican presidents are constitutionally limited to one term. His chosen successor was assassinated and the new president found himself in a very difficult position. Salinas' brother was accused of murder and the former top leader himself took an extended tour of the fleshpots of Montreal and Cuba. His brother's wife was busted by the Swiss banking cops for trying to clean out an account that wasn't in her name. It does get worse. The ugly "D" word (drugs) started coming up in public.

Mexico's currency, the peso, became an international pariah in the money markets and had to be bailed out by the U.S. and Canada not once but twice. To be fair, the peso had never been a big player, but the NAFTA people had leaned on the currency markets to treat it as if it were real money. After the first peso crash, investigators went looking for the big, bad international money traders. It turned out that most of the outflow was from Mexican citizens and residents who could not believe what the money markets were willing to pay for the stuff. They traded pesos into real currency for as long as dealers would take them.

NAFTA is a pretty sick puppy politically but it has performed well for Canadian and U.S. business. Trade is up. Costs are down. Bitching has been kept low-key. Some obscure products, which involve a lot of money, resist the dispute settlement mechanisms set out in the treaty.

The big question is how long it will continue to work in a time when the global shifts are in other directions. Failure to understand that the New World Order represents the firmly held beliefs and vested interests of the corporate leadership of the industrial world would mean that you believe these people can run a world and that industrial corporatism can and should subcontract the work that governments do to regional metagovernments. Europeans are asking themselves whether they want to tie up their savings in some sort of Eurocurrency and whether they want to have all dealings with foreigners done by Brussels.

The Eurocurrency deal is still not set in stone and some harsh things are being said about this chapter of Maastricht. One of the most kinky stories was hoisted by those who saw the E.U. as a perfidious French plot. It appears that the word "ecu," the name first touted for the Eurocurrency, had been the name of a French (and a Spanish) coin back in the Holy Roman Empire days. The root of the word is the same as that of "ecumenical" and celebrated the universality of that world. Germans and Brits, who were less than enthused about losing their own distinctive currencies and central banks, began to circulate phrases like "Papist conspiracy," "Popish plot," and a new one that gave hope to those of us who expect our conspiracies to have a sense of aesthetics: "Jacobean economic terrorism."

In the Far East, the Japanese parliament, like the German parliament, has authorized the use of Japan's military forces for U.N.-sanctioned peacekeeping ventures. This pleases American politicians, because it suggests that the American taxpayer will no longer be the only one paying the bills for peacekeeping missions.

The Association of Southeast Asian Nations (ASEAN) is settling in to create an effective regional trading group. (Clinton and Bush would probably deny that Japan's agenda was to reincarnate the Japanese Greater East Asia Co-Prosperity Sphere, which was interrupted in 1945 and, it is argued, is back on track with support from ASEAN.) As Japan takes responsibility for the underdeveloped Asian countries, the East will be a full participant in the New World Order as envisioned by the E.U. and NAFTA. It was heartening to see that Japan has been willing, and politically able, to set aside its territorial dispute with Russia and join with the rest of the Group of Seven industrial nations in 1993 to provide crisis aid to the Russian government.

In 1993, when the ASEAN "freer" trade agreement was signed in Singapore, the participants, which included Singapore, Malaysia, Thailand, Indonesia, the Philippines and Brunei, broke with their history of protectionism, based on high tariffs for small manufacturing industries.

Since the oil crisis of the early 1980s, Hong Kong, Japan and Taiwan have invested billions of dollars in the ASEAN countries. Four years ago this massive investment began showing a gratifying average growth rate of 10 percent a year. This regional partnership should benefit Hong Kong, even though it reverted to the People's Republic of China.

The prime minister of Japan sent a message of congratulations to ASEAN members when the January, 1993, trade agreement was signed. Japan had every right to be pleased. Japan Inc.'s investment in ASEAN was so great that it realistically controlled the industrial base of the region. Trade experts expect that it will take 15 years for the agreement to shake out into a full-fledged free trade zone.

However, it would be a mistake to treat ASEAN as a done deal. In mid-November of 1993, the day after Congress met to vote on the ratification of NAFTA, a new group met in Seattle. This was to be called APEC (the Asia-Pacific Economic Cooperation group) and along with the U.S. and Canada includes some of the more active growth countries in the world, such as the People's Republic of China, Taiwan, South Korea, Hong Kong, Singapore, Thailand, Indonesia, Australia and New Zealand, Brunei, the Philippines, and Japan.

Notable for having sent his regrets was the prime minister of Malaysia, Mahathir bin Mohamad. Mahathir had tried to hustle something called the East Asia Economic Group, which would have excluded the U.S., Canada, Australia and New Zealand. Not so fast, said the U.S. and Canada.

The governments of the U.S. and Canada could hardly restrain their glee at the prospects of cutting an export-access deal with all those Asian hordes. A U.S.-Canada sponsored east Asian trade pact offers a powerful disincentive to any plans the E.U. (read France) might have for messing with world trade talks, and if the Japanese got their noses out of joint — so what? Japan Inc.'s financial services industry has, regrettably, capitalized itself with customers' stock at market value.

A final Pacific alliance is the Austroceanic group, which has emerged from the Cairns Group. It is waiting to see where the E.U. and NAFTA have their problems and what solutions work. Very wise of them. They are all small countries and don't have the resources to do original work on metagovernments.

THE POST-SOVIET STEW

President Clinton and other caretakers of the NWO must see the former Soviet bloc countries as one of the truly dark spots on the horizon. The Soviet bloc was not merely outspent during the Cold War. The superficial sacrifices in consumer goods are only the tip of the iceberg.

If the republics of the former U.S.S.R. can avoid collapsing into anarchy it will be a miracle. Should these states manage to escape starvation, create some semblance of political order, and avoid losing any nuclear weapons, they will then come face-to-face with a real mess. This real disaster, left behind by the previous regime, is an imploded economy that lacks any infrastructure to deal with its major, globe-threatening environmental disasters.

In Uzbekistan, the Aral Sea — once the world's fourth largest lake — is expected to disappear by the year 2010. The cause was the diversion of water from two tributary rivers to irrigate an unfertile area that central planners designated as a cotton-growing zone. The old edges of the lake are now salt-encrusted sand. Giant windstorms whip up the sand, creating what looks like a snowstorm and scatters the dried, brine-encrusted former lake bottom on nearby farmland. Neighbouring states complain of huge collective farms being destroyed. Lake Aral was once home to a prosperous and highly productive fishing fleet. The fleet is now nonexistent.

The Soviet nuclear disaster at Chernobyl is now acknowledged to have made hundreds of thousands of hectares of Ukraine's best farming soil uninhabitable. Residents have a cancer rate beyond anything known before. What food is grown is desperately needed by the region, but is too often a grotesque caricature of the previously fertile land's crops. The strain on health services, both human and veterinary, has resulted in an unbearable burden for the Ukrainian health system, never noted for being responsive, beyond the Party elite's needs.

Ufa, a city in the Ural Mountains region of Russia, is little known in the

West, outside of missile and bomber commands in the U.S. and Britain. Ufa, back in the bad old Cold War days, stood high on the priority lists of people who determined which parts of the Soviet Union were most worthy of total annihilation when World War III broke out.

Ufa was a one stop shopping centre and production site for the customers of the Soviet version of the military-industrial complex. It is also the city where the late Rudolf Nureyev was born. Today in Ufa, a photochemical reaction occurs when sunlight interacts with the airborne effluent from the local chemical, nuclear and other weapons system-based industries. Ironically, as East and West are producing accords limiting weapons possession and production, the former KGB (now the FSB, the Russian government's general-purpose truth-digging agency) has advised that the whole area could disappear in an explosive fireball.

In 1987 the explosion of a nuclear waste tank in the southern Urals bathed the air and water systems in radioactivity. The Soviets had to secretly resettle 10,000 people. Two years later, a leak from a faulty gas pipeline exploded and destroyed two passenger trains with a result of 575 dead. This was the second largest death toll in history for a train wreck. No public announcement was made at the time.

The litany of environmental disasters from the Ufa region alone seems endless. It is clear that the region was crucial to Soviet war preparation. It also proves that the U.S.S.R. simply had no way to account for the environmental impacts of all the things that can go wrong in the course of manufacturing contemporary weapons. Today in the area we can see a concentration of ecological marauding unequalled anywhere else (until similar areas of the People's Republic of China are exposed).

If you asked Russian economists how this state of affairs came about, they would tell you that the goals of the industry ministries were clearly targeted at competition with the West. The centralized bureaucracy in Moscow never authorized the budgetary resources necessary to support or train credible environmental experts. There was no institutional infrastructure to provide an ecological "voice at court."

The economic or military ministries did not, under the circumstances, see the environment as their problem. Indeed, you would search in vain for a government ministry of the U.S.S.R which had the environment even mentioned in its mandate. Now the environmental pillaging has come home to roost. It has a demonstrably negative economic impact on the operating economy. Western ecologists who are privy to the actual situations see no way to turn it around. There is not even a means to recover the raw data. It simply doesn't exist!

One of the mega nightmares Bill Clinton has inherited from George Bush (probably something in the White House water supply), a nightmare they share with the NWO's managers, must be the breakup of the mono-lithic forms of the U.S.S.R. When their domestic supporters mouth the anti-communist rhetoric of the Cold War, they must wince at the time warp which limits their response capabilities.

In the pre-collapse days, the official exchange rate of the Soviet ruble was one ruble for $1.80. In early January 1992, *Trud* (*Truth* — the former Soviet trade union paper) quoted Russia's deputy minister of finance as saying that he expected that when the ruble became fully convertible it would start out around 200 to the U.S. dollar and would gradually fall from that point. This, of course, ensured a massive inflation because the Russian government has been pushing the money printing presses, turning out rubles in increasingly large denominations. This course of action has resulted in an even greater inflationary pressure on the ruble (on the order of 30 percent annually). For an ordinary person in the C.I.S. to buy the necessities of life, like food, housing, and clothing, has become a Herculean task.

THE CHINA CARD

The Chinese experience, with failed experiments in polycentrism in the early 1960s, does not suggest that the leadership of the Chinese Communist Party (CCP) will readily abandon the apparatus of centralized state control to which parties of the far left have been committed since the time of Lenin.

The leadership of the CCP have exploited the chaos that followed the breakup of the U.S.S.R., using all the propaganda resources at their disposal to warn the people that only the disciplined Party stands between them and a similar breakdown of public order.

China has had quite enough chaos in the past 150 years to give the Party's argument a sympathetic audience. The Party has always argued that its use of the battle-toughened 27th Route Army, fresh from fighting on the Vietnam border, to suppress the pro-democracy faction during the demonstrations in Tiananmen Square was justified in light of the Russian experience. Since the collapse of the U.S.S.R. and the ensuing breakdown in delivery of government services, which Chinese television has covered widely, the people of China have generally agreed with the way the Party's leadership treated the students and other "radicals" who were seen as at best misguided, but more likely adventurists and counter-revolutionaries.

China's state-controlled press has blamed the collapse of the Soviet Union on Western agitators. The CCP seems to define a "youth problem" as something that affects those under 50. Caught in an ideological struggle between economic reformers and hard-line Party conservatives, its efforts to make China's job allocation system, price structures and state factories more effective and efficient have been stalled by acrimonious disagreements between the two factions.

In one of his last official acts, the then 89-year old retired Party leader (and actual master of the back rooms of the CCP) Deng Xiaoping made a two week tour of southern China's Shanghai region for a ride around the usual new highways, high-tech factories and highrise office buildings. He said: "If China does not carry out reform, it will move into a blind alley. Whoever is not in favour of reform should leave office."

Deng's forces have so far won the fight for control of the real ruling body, the Politburo, but not without leaving out there some very unhappy traditionalist campers. It would appear that China is in for a major power struggle if the reformers lose their grip for an instant. With so many of the leadership aged or in bad health, we are seeing the last of the veterans of the "Long Route March" of 1934-35.

All factions except the pro-democracy group, who are either scattered abroad, in hiding, or in jail, have agreed to mute, for the present, accusations that the West is trying to force China to shift to a Western-style market economy. Citing Marx, who admitted playing the London stock exchange, the CPP has urged the managers of factories to lead the nation to a vibrant free market age.

Western complaints about abuses of human rights have been met by most of China's leadership with unapologetic responses and the Party's view that Western "interventionism" contributed heavily to the Russian Party's collapse.

But as the strains of "The East Is Red" become more and more muted under the economic and cultural influences of Taiwan, Korea, and Singapore, the People's Republic of China seems less and less able to address the rising discontents of a generation to whom the Long March is a distant myth and who have little faith in the chances of an orderly generational leadership succession.

Everywhere in the world the local Communist parties are abandoning their name. (The name which denotes a local party as being in sympathy with the Moscow conservatives is now "The Party of the Democratic Left.")

According to information released by the International Monetary Fund, China may be going through its own Brezhnev-style corruption period. Diplomats and officials of multinational banks ascribe the ongoing currency flight of private funds to corruption among government bureaucrats and Party officials. These funds are following the usual pattern of runaway money. They are being invested by sons and daughters of the Chinese elite, who are studying in the U.S. or Canada. This long-term (multi-generational) investment money usually ends up in North American real estate. Both the U.S. and Canadian governments are concerned that such runaway money is adding to inflation in housing prices.

Better they should worry about the world-view that comes with an extended family (clan) culture running into a nuclear family culture with a short-term outlook. (The author's experience suggests that to undertake actual research into this question is politically impossible.) The millions of dollars that go to support the student offspring of important Party officials are beginning to make an impact on the world's sleazier money marts. The mix of corruption and unofficial transfer of funds abroad is beginning to cause the warning flags set up by international bankers to flutter. The money may start out as the belonging to the State, but after being smuggled from China to Hong Kong as cash, ownership is less recognizable. Approximately 40,000 Chinese students attend foreign universities, according to figures supplied by post-secondary schools.

Diplomatic sources have traced one laundering channel to the now defunct Bank of Credit and Commerce International's (BCCI) branch in Shenzhen, a city in southern China with good connections for points of interest like Shanghai and Hong Kong.

The flow of money, while not yet large enough to impact on China's own strong economy and foreign reserves of $40 billion, is large enough to be noticed by the world's bankers. It is safe to assume that it will require stronger medicine than the government of China can easily produce to slow down this run-off of cash by the country's elite. One recent report says that $14 billion in export earnings never makes it back to China. This kind of information is not heartening to those who wish the Chinese well. One of the side effects of situations like this is that when someone critical to the operation — like BCCI — goes down, its customers have to increase their stealing to recoup their losses. Then they get careless.

Chinese banks are highly specialized by function — national financial management is the prerogative of the Bank Of China and The People's Bank of China. The data suggest that the central authorities have lost much of their control.

The cash drain has not gone unnoticed by the Party leadership. The Party General Secretary (now Party Leader) Jiang Zemin said in Communist officialese on the occasion of the Party's 70th anniversary, "Successors to the socialist cause should not act like landlords, abusing their power to make a fortune. If these decadent phenomena are allowed to continue, the Party will be doomed to self-destruction."

NO WORLD ORDER

The leaders of the New World Order assume that their peers in other regions represent a tradition of success in management. This managerial success criterion is seductive to those in the private sector who view government as incompetent and wasteful.

Ex-Soviet managers have demonstrated the flaws in that assumption. There is realistically little the world's remaining superpower can do in the former East Bloc nations. What would be the point of going to war with a teetering regime in the 11-time-zone ex-Soviet land mass?

When a Canadian businessman became the marketing partner of Chetek, a Moscow-based private company that offered to incinerate toxic waste with underground atomic "burns," a CIA analyst who was evaluating the offer said reflectively: "I wonder if they're trying to tell us something."

Chetek claims that it has no weapons capability, a proposition vigorously rejected by a wide variety of Western Sovietologists. Some optimists in the West point out that the Red Army has always been a highly disciplined force. The "loose nukes" problem probably transcends this discipline when the troops are unpaid and unfed and meet someone willing to pay in hard currency or food.

Meanwhile, as if oblivious to the reaction of a world already concerned about the ability of any successor regime in the former U.S.S.R. to secure nuclear weapons, Chetek added to its toxic garbage offer a willingness to do "whatever a customer wants as long as it is commercial and peaceful."

The former Soviet Union's nuclear stockpile obviously has a new lease on life. Its continued existence in the hands of the leaders of independent republics fills North Americans and Europeans alike with deep concern about the continued welfare and stability of these fragile new states as they teeter on the brink of food and fuel shortages and the potential for flash-fire civil disorder.

The dissolution of the U.S.S.R. and the speed with which events change is forcing intelligence organizations like the CIA to abandon some very comfortable assumptions about the nature of the world. Today's world has little use for Cold Warriors.

Japanese finance ministry officials are the most proactively interested party among those who are considering delivering aid to the former Soviets. However, informed estimates of what is required merely to stabilize the region range from $100 billion to $400 billion. The Japanese want the return of islands forfeited to the U.S.S.R. after the Second World War. The NATO alliance countries are most interested in tying any aid to guarantees of control over nuclear weapons.

When considering the implications of the Japanese interest, one former Russian official, now an emigré in the West, suggested that since the Japanese only wanted territory returned, an eastern region of the C.I.S. could secede, take the money, and run.

As much as ex-President Bush might have enjoyed doing it, and Bill Clinton might wish to, it's not in America's strategic interest to let the

Europeans or the Japanese inherit the former Soviet Bloc market by default. Yet the current calls on U.S. financial resources limit the options. Even less can he accept a breakdown of Soviet hegemony, now referred to as "credit watch heaven."

CHAPTER FOUR

Time Out: What do we mean by a new era in history?

This book is intended to identify and explore the opening phase of a new era in history. One of the central arguments is that this new period has many qualitative similarities to the Renaissance.

New eras tend to be turbulent and messy. There is little that can be done to guide new eras because they have all the subtlety of a bull elephant surrounded by a herd of cow elephants in heat. But, it is argued, new eras can be understood in their own terms.

Before we can understand a new era we have to acknowledge that one is happening… and that is usually difficult to do.

The reason for the difficulty is that new eras require new ways of perceiving the world.

A NEW ERA IS NOT:

• Something we've already experienced in a slightly different form.

• Amenable to outdated analysis. A recession/depression that occurs while an era transition is under way has profoundly different functional relationships. This is why economists steeped in the lore of the 1930s appear unable to understand what is happening to the economy.

• A millennial event heralding the imminent arrival of a messiah and heaven on earth.

• An opportunity for political leaders to heed the siren call to return to the "old virtues."

• A time when science will produce all the wonderful goods and services that unimaginative marketers can conjure up.

• A time for established leaders to use their innate wisdom, personal relationship with the deity of record, deep understanding of the science taught when they were in college 30 years ago, or willingness to adopt the necessary "tough measures" to excise scapegoat problems.

• A good time for societies that have retained their tribalism to take revenge on their ancient enemies in an orgy of ethnic cleansing.

• A time when your religion can offer its version of the one true faith as a refuge from the storms of confusion.

• A time when you can be profligate with your wealth, emotions, or the people with whom you are allied.

• A time when there is much in the way of historical guidance. From immediate history there is none.

• A good time to be part of the established order of your country, industry, institution, or political power establishment.

In this book, it is argued that the early Renaissance is instructive as an example of how an era transition works. The Renaissance is well documented, enabling us to see patterns which, if cautiously selected, may prove beneficial to our survival. We cannot expect one-for-one correlations, but tracking the trends of the Renaissance is probably more useful than the transient offers of the increasing numbers of gurus, direct agents of God, or political candidates bidding for our allegiance.

This book argues that the conditions for a new era in history came about between the years 1900 and 1929.

A NEW ERA IS:

• A time when the level of abstraction (or world-view) for the preceding era can no longer have any more Band-Aids put on it. A new, accepted, consensual world-view needs a new assumptive base.

• A time in which, once this new world-view becomes broadly understood, new institutions emerge which are congruent with the underpinnings of the new era.

• A time when the conventional wisdom of the past is overridden by events.

• A time when issues that generated a great deal of heat previously are found to have been resolved from unexpected sources, or have lost their urgency.

• A time when new causes, problems, and crises emerge over issues which do not surrender to the historical authorities of our ancestors.

• An ineluctable juggernaut. There is little that can be done to modify a new era, since new eras are by definition a time in which the world-view is being radically altered. With this change in the rules under which the universe operates, we are stuck with what is essentially an ahistorical period. That is, a time when we fear to rely on those traditional historical authorities which have guided us in the past because they have begun to fail us so frequently.

This book argues that the Renaissance is a reasonable benchmark by which we can at least be assured that this is not the first time humanity has undergone change of such wrenching proportions.

THE DISCOVERY OF PERSPECTIVE

To this point in the book it is argued that one of the key triggers of the Renaissance was the discovery of perspective, or paintings and drawings representing three static dimensions. By the early 17th century the ideas of perspective had become a metaphor for that period we call the Renaissance.

As we have seen with teachers like fra Luca Pacioli, or the seemingly endless stream of painters such as Giovanni Cimabue, Donatello, fra Angelico and Paolo Uccello, or the architect Brunelleschi, the accessibility of perspective to an ever increasing part of the population resulted in an intellectual ferment and commitment to exploration of the physical and natural world never before equalled.

This metaphorical value served not only the painters of northern Italy, but it travelled well! The metaphor worked for the German artist Dürer, as well as the English poet Henry Vaughn, and supported accessibility to philosophers like Niccolo Machiavelli, Dante Alighieri, Erasmus, and Bruno. The *idea of perspective* was driving the age: In 1610 Galileo called his new invention for viewing the heavens a *perspicillium*. The founder of the academy with which Galileo was affiliated, Prince Cesi, was a more practical Renaissance man — he called it a *telescopium* (distance viewer). The Church fathers called it heresy.

TRADE AND EXPLORATION

The availability of perspective led the nations of Western Europe to devote significant resources to developing trade and exploration to a degree otherwise unknown. The key to this increment in trade and exploration was the application of those mathematical discoveries, including the importation of Arabic numerals and the decline in the use of Roman numerals, which came with perspective to navigation and ballistics. (It is really quite difficult to do long division with Roman numerals.)

With trade expanding because of the new navigation and military technologies, the nations which embraced the Renaissance became ardent explorers as they searched out new intellectual and commercial opportunities.

ECONOMIC REVOLUTION

One of the places where new wealth was created was in the banks of the Lombard League. During the Medieval period, the supply of gold had been centralized or used to bribe invaders from Asia. As a result, little gold was in circulation. The Church banned Christians from usury and part of gold's centralization was in the Jewish ghettos. The solution to this shortage of gold came when the Lombard bankers invented the bill of exchange.

The church's fulminations against usury had little impact in the real world. When Johann Eck of the University of Ingolstat argued in a debate at Bologna that a commercial debt could carry a 5 percent interest rate without incurring either the punishments due for the sin of usury or the social reprimands for venality, Eck's "expenses" were picked up by Joseph Fugger's bank, which was competing forcefully with the Lombard bankers in most Italian and northern European cities. His head office was German-based and culturally German, yet he had succeeded in picking up the confidential banking business of many cardinals and Holy Roman Empire princes.

These banks effectively increased their capitalization through what we know now as the multiplier effect. At the same time, double-entry bookkeeping was invented, which meant that business records would accurately reflect the true state of the company's affairs. The bill of exchange and double-entry bookkeeping are indications of a monumental leap in the level of abstraction from the preceding Medieval period.

Did the bill of exchange result in inflationary pressures? Of course. And this inflation was particularly onerous on the landed nobility. Many early Renaissance wars were based on the economic pressures the new merchant and banking syndicates put on the essentially fixed incomes of the aristocracy.

Naturally these economic developments resulted in massive pressures on governments and exposed the contradictions of the late Medieval and early Renaissance worlds. We frequently find feudal nobility getting into the piracy business or things equally unsavory in order to rebuild family fortunes that were locked into revenue bases that were unproductive in comparison with the assets of traders, navigator/gunners, ship's captains, bankers, and other real Renaissance men.

TECHNOLOGY AND CONSEQUENCES

From the events around the discovery of perspective, a new infrastructure evolved to support the growth of trade and exploration and resulted in the level of abstraction, compared to that of Medieval Europe, being expanded and enhanced.

Perspective in the arts — not just painting but architecture, publishing, navigation, instrument design and manufacture, weapons technology to exploit the three-dimensional mathematics of ballistics, naval architecture and optics, which by the late 16th century brought about Digges' telescope, plus a host of other inventions — meant that new highly paid jobs made severe inroads on the power of the craft guilds and the supply of skilled labor. The guilds adapted to changed circumstances better than did the Church-related institutions of society, which resulted in a speeding up of new technology transfers. The guilds, with lodges all over Europe, were a key link in technology transfers and instruction. The established orders could have no idea how all these innovations fit into a coherent pattern.

CHANGES OF MIND

Not just the way people thought, but the very neural activity of brain function changed with the discovery of perspective. One of the things that seriously altered the whole society was a major increase in tangential thought. It was tangential thinking which made it possible for the "Renaissance Man" to see the connections between heretofore unconnected events and to avoid the specialization of work and identity which marked the Medieval person. People were interested in science, the arts, technology, literature, statecraft, religion, building, manufacturing, metallurgy, military affairs, politics, seamanship, trade, and a host of other activities which were the topics of conversation at the salons of Renaissance Europe. To be functionally and socially mobile in the Renaissance required strong tangential thought processes and skills.

The most significant change in thought processes was the change in neurological activity which permitted people to adapt to a new level of abstraction. The most important thing about a new era is that it follows the collapse in the ability of the level of abstraction of the previous era to explain and accommodate the known and address the unknown. In our own time, it wasn't until the paradoxes and contradictions of Newtonian physics became clearly apparent and unpatchable that it became essential to discover a new physics.

A WORLD ORDER COLLAPSES

Feudal societies are easy to administer because everyone knows where they stand, to whom they are obligated, and the nature of that obligation. Each person knows that this social order has been established by God and that a breach of the order is a sin as well as a crime and may even be heretical, depending on the excuse.

The territorial state was the political entity of the manorial economy and the feudal society. The prince (duke, king et cetera) of the territorial state was a feudal vassal of the Holy Roman Emperor. The Emperor and territorial state princes were crowned and anointed by the pope, or a bishop under the pope's instruction. Thus emperor and prince governed by divine right.

The Church was a civil and religious authority with a secular arm in the Holy Roman Emperor. With the expansion of new wealth, political systems started to show strains from their inability to maintain historic privilege for the aristocracy and to co-opt the emerging middle class.

Some princes realized that a few of the thinkers and monks fleeing heresy charges were actually in the forefront of important scientific and humanist movements. In northern Germany Frederick III of Saxony provided Martin Luther with shelter and assured that the Reformation (as we know it) would happen.

Incidentally, in the first chapter we spoke at length about fra Luca Pacioli, who wrote books on both perspective and the bill of exchange. In 1509 one of the issues that scandalized Luther was his discovery that the Bishop of Brixen, who had just died in Rome, had left no discernible assets except a slip of paper "as long as a finger" squirrelled away in the sleeve of his shirt.

Upon presentation to Joseph Fugger's Rome branch manager of this "slip of paper," the House of Fugger promptly coughed up 300,000 florins. Luther later said that, given the choice of trusting a prince of the Church or the House of Fugger, Fugger won hands down. Apparently at least one bishop agreed with Luther on this point.

Other national leaders quickly understood that their obligations and tithes would cease the day they became Protestants. With the Church in serious political trouble and increasingly unable to extricate itself from theological contradictions with laws of nature, its sway over the secular world began to disintegrate.

The ultimate power to legislate and to allow legislation drifted from papal empowerment to national legislatures, which were often filled with the newly wealthy Protestant merchants and others whom the crown had to tax directly.

The nation state grew as the manorial economy lost its economic advantage. Merchants, contractors, and lawyers with monetary mobility were in a much better position to meet the king's tax collector than was a duke. After all, the merchant could always say "what money?" The local duke could hardly say "what land?"

The pre-Renaissance leadership had no analysis of the phenomena we describe as the Renaissance. Each event, however discomforting, was seen as an isolated incident. The connecting links were not seen. At best a few

— very few — scholars like Erasmus and Bruno had small pieces of the picture. Even the finest minds of the age had no idea of the magnitude of what was happening.

LAW AND ORDERS

Initially, the Church and its loyal territorial state princely allies believed that trouble-makers could be rooted out as heretics and sinners. But discomforting changes were popping up everywhere. The combination of greedy princes in new breakaway nation states and their allies — the inventors, traders, and merchants in combination with the host of tangential thinkers and those commercializing new inventions — were able to outmanoeuvre the leaders of the established society.

Scientists were challenging fundamental matters of dogma. Business people were challenging the right of the impecunious feudal aristocracy to govern and, worse still, to tax. The clergy's authority and ability to order daily life as new lifestyles emerged was being lost. It was not merely the establishment who were outraged at the collapse of values. Many ordinary people saw their most fundamental beliefs shattered. Their status and identity symbols were disintegrating.

To answer these challenges, the law was shifted from the Medieval legal system, with its emphasis on interacting obligations, to an inquisitorial judicial procedure. The key to the efficacy of an inquisitorial system is that it uses church/state terrorism and requires that all suspicions and complaints must be investigated.

While we may regard the Inquisition as an example of a legal system in the hands of S&M perverts, it is useful to realize that this was the response of the established order as it attempted to build a commercial legal system and a new tax base that would address the new world-view.

The papacy sided with the conservative clergy, the manorial aristocracy, and laity to seek out the witches, and since witchcraft could only be practiced in groups, the other members of convicted witches' covens. Not only was torture the principal method of investigation, but the official view became "better a hundred innocents burn than one witch escape." The Dominican order was given the mission of excising the agents of Satan who were causing all these problems.

This response was not limited to the Catholic Church. After the Reformation, Protestant countries vigorously sought out the same scapegoats in the belief that strong national religions would accommodate a world-view which had only required a minor amendment. Literally millions were sent to the stake, with Germany, Scotland and Switzerland being among the leading users of inquisitorial law. The magnitude of the changes in world-view were so great and the lack of comprehension so wide, that the response of our forebears was to institute state-sponsored terrorism as public policy.

In the end the scholastic analysis was wrong. The Medieval church and the territorial state were doomed by a new epistemology which selected the secular state as the powerful institution to mediate the new world-view. We can see why historians place such great importance on the founding, by the English King Charles II, of the Royal Society with its scholarly journal the *Philosophical Transactions of the Royal Society*. The *Transactions* were first edited by a German immigrant to England, who developed a system of peer review. In France, where the royal household was not shy about its divinely awarded absolutist status, the *Journal Royal des Scavans* was published by the *Acadamie Royal des Sciences*. Both publications were relatively unfettered in their publishing policy.

In our own times, the forces of censorship still wear the face of authority claiming the power of "truth." These two journals for scientific communication, as a side effect, reinforced the Baconian ideal of science as a collective undertaking. It was in the pages of the *Transactions* where the first battle between "pure" science and "applied" science was contended by Isaac Newton and Robert Hooke.

THE NEXT LEVEL

There is no generally accepted understanding of the changes we are undergoing. They are usually seen in isolation and few attempts are made to offer a fundamental understanding of the nature and extent to which the shift in our conventional world-view is occurring.

In 1900, Max Planck published his quantum theory. Planck's work made it clear that the continuity our sensory apparatus tells us exists does not in truth exist in nature at its most profound levels.

In 1905, Albert Einstein startled the world's physicists with a theory that disproved much of how classical physics saw light. In 1915 Einstein presented his theory of relativity, which introduced us to a world of planar dimensions incorporating time and space.

In 1927 Werner Heisenberg delivered his uncertainty principle and in 1928 Heisenberg, Schrödinger and Dirac made mechanics compatible with Planck's quantum theory, producing quantum mechanics.

These works established such a new view of the universe that we can be assured that a new era transition is under way.

The social climate of the 1940s — a global war with widespread dislocation — brought about conditions which mitigated in favor of English becoming the *lingua franca* of the international scientific community. A concentration of refugee scientists in English-speaking countries and the decision to proceed with a nuclear weapons program (the Manhattan

Project) created a gigantic laboratory for the seminal theories of the period. Because there were no computers, these implementers of the work of Einstein and Planck were all the more centralized, since all computations were done by gifted mathematicians, aided by mechanical calculators.

Following World War II, computers became available, providing the computational power to develop the underlying principles of a new level of abstraction, which in turn would underlie the newly discovered universe. This new level of abstraction supported a steady release of applications and technologies, creating new industries.

THINKING AHEAD

Today we see the more vulnerable nation states collapsing as a post-industrial world begins adapting to a new world-view.

The main body of this book has been written as an exercise in tangential (a.k.a. lateral) thinking. As noted above, tangential thought is commonplace during the earlier parts of era transitions. The basis of tangential thought is to call out and identify connections between events under scrutiny and weigh the relationship between events.

In this current era transition it is essential to become comfortable with tangential thought because our new world-view must comply with quantum theory. That means there is no determinism at the micro level and that any determinism we think we perceive is an illusion. In other words, we no longer accept that simple cause-and-effect relationships supply the answers we need.

Further, since 1915, when Einstein described relativity, we have been aware that our universe exists and operates in a time-space continuum. In other words, we have to realize that the events which are part of our day-to-day existence may emanate from four (plus) dimensions, regardless of the linear filters through which we may discern them.

Applications of the discoveries of Planck, Einstein, Heisenberg, Schrödinger, and Dirac are coming into our lives in forms and at a rate which we can barely recognize.

Another goal of this book is to help the reader develop skills in dealing with events which have been and will be coming from a wide variety of space-time continua and require a wide variety of adaptive responses, with few historical authorities of much relevance.

The reason for writing most of the book as an exercise in tangentialism is to help the reader experience a visit to a simulated cyberspace where information arrives from widely disparate levels of time and space. Just as in real life, some of the information arrives too soon and some too late. Some will be too uncomfortable to ingest and some will be enjoyable.

A word of caution: Be prudent in what you dismiss as intellectually suspect. The theory guiding most successful cyberspace explorers is that the more preposterous something is, the more likely it is to be a profitable consideration.

More and more people are coming to the conclusion that the world isn't working right any more. Frequently solutions that are offered are out of date or irrelevant to the problems. Too often these solutions end up serving vested interests instead of helping everyone survive.

This new era is driven by the products of mathematics and physics. It is essential to understand the degree to which computing power and an understanding of the way computers operate controls the rate at which the abstraction level of the new era, articulated in the equations of the scholarly papers of mathematicians, physicists and cosmologists, is translated into fourth and fifth order applications which radically alter our worldview and our lives.

Suddenly it takes on a new meaning when we read of more powerful chips coming online to add further power to the computational resources of those who are on the point of discovering further expanses of the cyberspace universe. The fact that computing power is doubled every 18 months gives us a small insight into the change rate that fuels the juggernaut of era transition.

Throughout the book, the qualities of a juggernaut are assigned to the phenomenon of an era transition. Some early pre-publication readers suggested that "Renaissance 2.0" was a "sexier" term than "era transition." It was rejected because the term "Renaissance" has acquired undeserved positive connotations.

While this is not a self-help book it is hoped that it will raise questions in the reader's mind which make the journey into cyberspace safer and more pleasurable.

This book is not friendly to the New World Order announced by U.S. President George Bush. The author believes that those who identify with that New World Order are taking on the role of the papacy and the secular princes of the Holy Roman Empire.

In some ways the NWO is quite accurate in its analysis. The flaws come from pre-Einsteinian, 19th-century assumptions about the relationship between the rate of scientific progress, the rate of technological change, and the resultant social fallout.

The belief that the managerial elite of transnational corporations have a capacity to control innovation has a ring that would have sounded familiar to the mathematicians, physicists, and chemists of England in the 1850s. A Manchester social Darwinist would have felt quite at home in the corridors of corporate power in 1998.

The Renaissance was obviously over in the 1850s, when we see scientists no longer as Renaissance men but hiding in their laboratories doing "pure" research and avoiding the day-to-day events of their times. The business community had abandoned any pretense that scientific or cultural literacy had any tangible benefits.

In 1963, a graduate student in the history of science was looking at the original laboratory notes of the British neurophysiologist Sir Charles Sherrington. He discovered that in 1898 Sherrington had done all of the steps, *except the last ones*, which Pavlov independently completed in 1911. At the bottom of the lab book page, in Sherrington's handwriting, was a note: "This experiment is an unprofitable line of enquiry. Experiment terminated and animals sacrificed."

Would relativity have been discovered had an individual named Albert Einstein not been born? As physicist Richard Feynman said, while commenting on whether individual geniuses were essential to major discoveries in science: "We [the major scientists] are all pretty much the same." Feynman believed that achievement in science came about when there was a widely agreed consensus about the direction science should be going. Within that consensual direction, experimental priorities were selected by individual scientists.

Feynman's biographer, James Gleick, reminds us that this is why primacy of discovery is so important to the scientific community. Once the directions for a generation have been agreed, it is a highly competitive race to see who will solve specific problems first. It is, after all, these solutions which set the directions for the future and establish the individual in the pantheon of "greats" which future generations see as mentors. It is the only standard by which the scientific community judges itself.

We find a clue that the values that fueled the Renaissance were finally gone in a letter written by the eminent Victorian scientist Lord Kelvin to a friend, in a moment of ennui: "There's nothing for the next generation of physicists to do, except measure the next decimal place." This scholarly gentleman could not be accused of prescience. In the next generation Planck, Heisenberg and Neils Bohr completed the precursor work for a new and functional cosmology. Another member of that "next generation," Einstein, offered the equations underpinning the theory of relativity. Some decimal place!

OUT OF ORDER

Unsurprisingly, the NWO addresses economic issues and issues of big government. The neo-governmental model of regional trade zones, when looked at on a global scale, has the appearance of something cobbled together by an investment banker of the early 1980s.

The NWO's view of the nation state is probably accurate. Trade issues are politically volatile because trade is about domestic jobs. It is hard for a politician to remain aloof from tough employment issues and act as a statesman.

The regional trade zone offers businesses, which had been tied to a limited national market, access to the benefits of larger populations and markets. If it can be made to work, even minimally, NWO supporters argue that it will be feasible to build a transportation infrastructure to support this new trade, making goods and services cheaper. Whether this will be true in practice, and whether it will offer improvements in living standards, is dubious. It assumes stability and universality of management philosophies among the transnational corporations — which isn't one of those ideas worth betting the family farm on.

Few nation states can offer much resistance to a transnational corporation resource manager and developer. The idea that the region can agree on how to rationalize the regulation of environmental controls and resource management is unlikely to work because of cross-border impacts on member states. Countries that are not party to the deal between the host state and a transnational corporation do not have the domestic pressures of the host country. The disagreement over agricultural tariffs between the E.U. and the rest of the world has been going on since the founding disputes of the European Common Market. Further, that such ground rules are sufficiently portable to oversee development of underdeveloped countries is an idea of dubious merit. Finally, the argument that regional trade zones are less likely to be awed by or enthralled to a transnational runs up against the management techniques of transnational corporation in places where they are highly successful.

The faith that regional trade zones can control competition between economic models is another questionable idea. Experimentation with economic models is usually pointless. The truth is that most economic experiments are sold to economically illiterate governments by people who are impressed with model building rather then getting down to the hard work of delivering some viable level of goods and services.

The most highly valued characteristic of managers in NWO enterprises is to be a *bricoleur*. *Bricolage* is a term like "the right stuff" and refers to an ability build on the ruins of others. A *bricoleur* is the person who takes charge after a leveraged buyout. It takes a special kind of person to have, as their goal, making ruins bloom.

When we talk about the discomfort that everyone experiences with the impact of the rate of change, we often forget that major changes are no longer predictable as straight, linear, conventional extrapolations. The N-space assumptions that underlie the new event may be totally opaque to the ordinary observer, who may see new products, information packages, industrial techniques, et cetera leaping out at us from some apparent "nowhere" and disappearing into the great wherever. All of this appears to happen randomly or chaotically and certainly not in an orderly, linear extrapolation from a known, historically authentic base.

These days, neo-Luddites who want to slow the rate of technological change can find plenty of bewildered allies in the boardrooms of the nation, in the seats of government and in the council chambers of the trade union federations.

SINGING THE BIG BLUES

Supporters of the NWO persistently ignore the implications of the products of their own labs. The great example is IBM.

IBM's labs are the best, filled with Nobel laureates and Nobel aspirants. Unfortunately, few IBM executives use the information generated there as an early warning system. IBM has consistently sold five-to-10-year-old technology to people who don't understand it, which is referred to as "controlling the customer." When IBM decided to enter the PC market it subcontracted the development of the operating system to Microsoft, which then acquired DOS from a small software company. IBM has spent its corporate life trying to find a "mature" product.

There is much to criticize about IBM — its size, its monolithic qualities, which make it difficult for middle managers to secure the necessary consensus to commercialize a new product, and its adherence to an Industrial Age mind set while jousting with smaller, more innovatively efficient competitors. These days IBM is like a bear in a pit. It need have no fear of any one of its competitors singly, but it is being attacked by hungry pit bulls on every side.

A few years ago the Federal Bureau of Investigation tripped over a corporate espionage case. It certainly looked like the real thing. The target was IBM. Someone was trying to rip off a new chip. A sting was carefully set up and, as so seldom happens in the real espionage world, they got a hit. The line jerked and there on the end was a genuine spy.

Triumphant, the IBM security staff and the FBI hauled in their catch. It wasn't the East Germans. It wasn't the slugs from the GRU. It wasn't the Dutch. It wasn't the always ambivalently opaque, yet ubiquitous Greek service. The spies had been dispatched by Hitachi, one of Japan's leading computer makers.

The event unfolded in the dreary way these things do — the Japanese offered to slit their bellies, the IBMers said "not on our rug," et cetera, so we'll press the fast forward button to December 27, 1991.

The financial press reported that Hitachi and IBM had agreed that Hitachi would sell a 32-bit notebook through its computer distribution channels. (The lack of attribution and the date suggest that business editors had just reprinted a press

IBM is a good corporate citizen, maybe the best in North America. For example, it maintains a number of experts who source devices that help people with handicaps use computers. If you call this office, even though there is little in it for IBM, they are unfailingly helpful. IBM may be the best employer in North America. IBM competitors look at its compensation packages, both formal and informal, and shake their heads wondering how Big Blue can afford it.

The answer is that IBM management procedures are geared to maximizing individual employee effectiveness. For example, a few years ago a number of American states and Canadian provinces created pay equity legislation. At about this time, a vendor of the best software then available for generating a complete pay equity employment program, geared to the jurisdiction in which the purchaser operated, called on IBM, anticipating an easy sale — if anyone could see the value of the program, it would be a computer company.

IBM's competitive products people gave the program the highest marks. Easy sale, right? Wrong. IBM had put its own system in place years earlier, which guaranteed both pay and employment equity and was integral to the company's personnel operations. When the software developer saw the personnel control system he knew that IBM had no need of his wares.

But the IBM personnel executive disagreed. He pointed out that IBM's marketing and tech-support teams prided themselves on their ability to solve customers' problems before the customer was aware of the problem. The personnel executive called in a marketing colleague who, within two weeks, had his sales staff briefed, equipped with a demo of the product and

---

release, since the editorial staff were still recovering from the holiday.) The computer was the IBM Flora series, which had been introduced to a hardly panting world in May 1991. The computer was to be supplied by IBM Japan.

A Hitachi official, speaking on condition of anonymity, said the deal was part of Hitachi's recently announced plans to establish cooperative ties with foreign companies, which would boost foreign sales to Japan and reduce Japan's trade frictions. One unkind wit suggested the headline should have been "Burglar gives aging victim charity." The anonymous Hitachi official reported that Hitachi's links with IBM already included production and sales of printers and development of an operating system for small computers.

Why all the anonymity for the "Hitachi official?" Could it be that the person who had made the announcement was really an official from MITI (Japan's ministry of trade and just about everything else) and that the press release was timed to get the unvarnished news across without having reporters phoning up to ask rude questions?

out selling it for the software developer. IBM is sufficiently well integrated that a personnel executive *saw it as his job* to respond to the accurately perceived needs of IBM marketing.

IBM is probably the best company the Industrial Age produced. In the post-industrial period, the company's industrial strengths mitigate against it in competitive positions where innovations in products is what counts.

In the PC market, IBM discovered that external software developers could bring a product to market in less time than IBM could decide to clear a new product for development. Its "control" of customers fell apart.

As IBM announced further layoffs, business journalists began for the first time to ask what no fan of corporate North America wanted to: was IBM's corporate culture no longer viable? If the answer was in the affirmative, the crack in the confidence of those who believed that global corporations were the answer had just become gaping.

The truth is that IBM people are comfortable wearing suits and having, as their colleagues, people who are comfortable wearing suits. Their cause-and-effect world is highly deterministic. Managers of some of IBM's competitors work in much more complexity-aggressive corporate cultures, cultures more attuned to Heisenberg's uncertainties as a fact of life. For the IBMs of this world to survive in a non-deterministic universe, they will have to get rid of a great deal of baggage.

PART TWO

What's Wrong with this Picture? Fault lines in the New World Order

CHAPTER FIVE

Flaws in the New World Order: Some fatal and others just tacky.

We can be sure that those monster corporate entities whose leaders were at the helm of the New World Order will soon trade their preference for giantism for smaller, more manageable units. General Motors and IBM are already moving vigorously in this direction and the gurus of the business press are already hyping this attempt to accommodate the new era.

M.M. Stuckey, CEO of something called Fourth Shift Inc., is one such trend apostle. He has authored the book *Demass: Transforming the Dinosaur Corporation*, in which he calls for the demassing of megacorporations. Stuckey believes that these large, apparently successful companies are like the dinosaurs which, the captain of H.M.S. *Beagle* and his companion Mr. Darwin believed, grew so large they couldn't fit on the Ark and thus fell victim to the Flood. Alternatively, these dinosaurs grew so large that they couldn't eat enough to support their huge bodies. In any case, you'll be hearing the metaphor "dinosaur" for these megacorps as they lose their trendoid quality.

Inevitably, another such pop term is, what else, "the virtual company," where management of a larger body establishes a relatively autonomous subsidiary to take advantage of a specific opportunity, whether in marketing or production.

The real problem is that there aren't enough people around who can grasp the essence of the widely-based activities these outfits get into to actually manage one. Think of a dinosaur eating like mad and eventually running out of other animals or plants or whatever they ate. Then think about a "market-driven" company like Coke, Pepsi, GM, et cetera, and think about them running out of markets. They thrash around, make some acquisitions and crush the success-generating identity and quality factors out of the acquisitions as they absorb them into the parent's "corporate culture" (a.k.a. "doing things our way even if they don't make sense in this environment") and then divest them because they didn't fit with the acquisitor's "core business." Oddly, the divestiture results in a rise in value of the stock of the parent instead of the board firing management for having done the deal in the first place.

An era transition moves the whole population of the planet in new directions. And those on the cusp of a new era quickly learn not to notice the casualties as they fall by the wayside. If, for example, you're running a business implementing new technologies based in the fundamental driving force of the era, don't expect too much help from lawyers, ad agencies, accountants, et cetera. This shouldn't surprise you. A society's professionals have more baggage to shuck than others.

Even when you drop a breakthrough announcement on an informed journalist, that reporter will have a tough time with a conventionally-minded editor. And the more advanced the breakthrough, the harder the sell-in.

In other words, the closer you are to the actual quantum jump in the level of abstraction that is pushing the new era, the more difficult it is to relate to those who hold onto the illusory comforts of an outdated mind-set.

The negative aspects of the NWO are reasonably clear. First and foremost, its proponents believe that they can manage the change rate. They fail to understand that the fallout from Planck-Einstein-Heisenberg et al. includes rare and esoteric things like strange attractors — the stuff of fundamental research from which can come applications and agents of profound change.

The folks who lead the NWO have not the slightest idea about how such things can and do change global realities. Unless you understand the implications of real discoveries, you won't understand the initial applications. If your world-view is based on a simplistic, linear, cause-and-effect universe, then you believe that success will come to those who focus their attention on whatever they are told is significant. It doesn't do much good to be briefed by loyal lackeys: even if the lackeys do understand what's going on, they will provide a briefing for a mind-set that mimics the mid-18th century. That's how they got access to the executive suite in the first place.

Hubris is the principle characteristic of those who see themselves as the leaders of the NWO — which places their simplistic world-view low among those most likely to be on the survival track. When the established order of the time attempts to take over a new era it usually fails because, in spite of holding the resources of the time, it cannot jettison the ideological and emotional baggage that is incompatible with the new era.

During the Renaissance, the Church fathers were not merely suspicious of the way perspective in paintings usurped "God's place." They also had deep reservations about the new navigation tools — particularly mathematics, which, because the theologians had no classical references for this tool, they suspected of being a product of the occult. Certainly the maps with which the "learned men" of the day were familiar suggested that, were a navigator to actually arrive at his destination, it must be the result of an unnatural force at work. The wheel maps, such as the *mappa-mundi*, showed Jerusalem in the centre of the world surrounded by angels, saints and various other religious icons confronting dragons gamboling around symbolic and totally imaginary continents.

The Scholastic authorities were, of course, familiar with Ptolemy. There was also a Portolan chart of the Atlantic coasts. These "maps," though accepted as accurate by the schoolmen, were so useless that working ships' captains used "rutters." Rutters were books recording piloting information such as bearings, descriptions of currents, soundings, winds, and port information as reported by captains who had actually been there. The information in these rutters was considered so priceless that to sell one or allow it to be copied could lead to charges of espionage and treason.

Then there were real maps. Waldseemuller, a Strasbourg printer, published a copy of Ptolemy in 1513 using woodcuts. Later, in 1550, Waldseemuller published the *Cosmographiae Introductio*, in which he abandoned the 15 centuries between his time and the life of Ptolemy. He also, for the first time anywhere, referred to America as "America."

It is not enough to be told of new insights into the universe. You have to be able to understand the new world-view, even if imperfectly — and for all of us it *is* imperfectly at the beginning. New eras are peremptory in their demand that we adapt to their definition of reality. Those who have too much historical baggage, the new era casts aside with alacrity, as the Renaissance did the schoolmen, Church Fathers, feudal aristocracy, and Holy Roman Emperors.

HUBRIS AND OTHER FASHION STATEMENTS

The lack of intellectual literacy among the NWO's supporters exacerbates the implosive characteristics of their hubris. A second flaw is that the NWO is not a historical force. If anything, the NWO is ahistorical. Its supporters appear to hold onto assumptions of the 19th century Industrial Age. Reminiscent of the Club of Rome's claims to an absence of self-interest, the direction of the Bush administration indicated a desire to deliver the benefits of industrial corporatism on some sort of global basis. However, the NWO proponents' major claim to fame is a touching faith in the ability of transnational corporations to successfully manage anything.

The NWO is concerned with the stability of existing management structures in governments, corporations, and other institutions. In this way, the people who seem to speak for the NWO assume that they can control the rate of technological and institutional change. There's an implied assumption that the social change rate will take care of itself once the technological and institutional shifts are stabilized. This is one of the specious conjectures upon which they believe the NWO can be implemented. It is specious because it is anti-evolutionary. Preservation of the status quo may be a laudable goal — from the point of view of someone who is an executive in a large transnational corporation and has an independently vested golden parachute attached to a handsome compensation package.

One of the clearest messages from the NWO is a fashion statement. This corporate chic calls for the wearing of blinders by senior executives (and aspirants to the executive suite) to anything likely to upset the belief that the business community should be unhampered by the government. Government should not address issues such as income redistribution. Government should minimize its intrusions on the private sector except to act as a purchaser of military and other technologies with built-in obsolescence. Government should not secure any positions of minimal social equity. Government should not intrude in the health-care insurance field (to do so is a "non-tariff subsidy" that endangers the market forces, which global trade and free markets require). Government should legislate ways to limit technological change rates so that the economies of product maturity can be achieved.

In this *haute-couture* world-view there is no such thing as an irresistible historical force. Control of historical forces is achieved when technology is recognized as a patentable application or invention. "Historical forces", as defined by historians, are viewed as rationales for post hoc taxation policies that rob corporations of their fair and just return on capital and intrude on corporate growth and the private sector's ability to create jobs. Government employees have a vested interest in maintaining high taxation levels and government agencies should be reviewed periodically to ascertain their continuing necessity. Universities should be evaluated according to their contribution to the economy through such measures as the number and quality of cooperative research programs they share with private sector sources.

Implicit in such NWO positions is the unabashed willingness to use coercion in dealing with adventurist Third World leaders — whether or not the local leader actually poses a problem. Past operations in Grenada, Panama, and Iraq lead to the obvious question, who's next? Will it be Cuba? Or Libya? How about North Korea? It is this commitment to uninformed control, without an understanding of the level of abstraction operative today, that is central to the NWO world-view.

Another critical viewpoint in the NWO's agenda is that the establishment of new regional trading blocs effectively transfers significant amounts of sovereignty to a trading bloc's bureaucracy, rendering the "bloated" national bureaucracy redundant. In these supra-bureaucracies the corporate world has a stronger voice, while the costs of lobbying are prohibitive for national and regional companies.

GLOBAL MANAGEMENT, THE ULTIMATE OXYMORON

The real problem the NWO cheerleaders face is that no matter how often they go to worship at the Bohemian Grove, they can't seem to manage global corporations. Those metaphorical entities GM, IBM, Apple, AT&T, Kodak, et cetera, along with everyone's favourite bank, Baring's, continue to give away their franchises.

That original virtual reality, the value of a company's stock, is becoming less real and more virtual. The people who run mutual and pension funds are still swinging weight more appropriate to sumo wrestlers (check out their life spans) and getting into the hubristics of the higher public profiles that come with becoming power brokers (surely not principals) in takeover crapshoots.

The only way anyone is going to succeed in running a global entity is with the resources that computers can bring to the table. And those computer resources are not yet in place.

If licences were required to run a computer in the same way a certain level of competence is needed to get a driver's licence, the number of senior executives with a PC would be minuscule, and that includes executives in the computer industry.

Global commercial ventures are complex, far more complex than existing software and memory can accommodate. So what happens? Someone whips up a spreadsheet with a bundle of close-enough numbers, does a smoke and mirrors presentation, answers all questions with "we've crunched the numbers every way possible and this was our most conservative outcome." Everyone at the table nods sagely. Incidentally, journalists who

---

The money managers are being sucked into showbiz. First they decide that, if the financial press is going to keep mentioning their name, they need a personal spinner. As in: "Plunkit Down Mutual Pension funder admitted he had put up a 'few billion' in Disney Corp.'s latest kazillion dollar acquisition." In an exclusive interview Down stated: "the funds we manage only support deals that are characterized by synergistics that enhance the value of the combined forces. We need real growth, not those old market-share buying sprees."

Then you lose your virginity from being a faceless number-cruncher and anonymous stock-picker to become a star on the press conference circuit. But after the deal has been done and the stock price drops enough to get the merchant banker phoning you about his hourly interest payments, there is no spin doctor alive who can stop the media from calling you Kamikaze Down.

cover inquiries into financial collapses find that the term "nodded sagely" has become synonymous with "due diligence."

The main reason that the Japanese have done so well until now is that the face of Japan is that of a trading company. After World War II, Japan, incapable of ever becoming self-sufficient and thus dependent on trade, decided to become a mixed economy. The Japanese senior civil service called on the remnants of the Zaibatsus — the pre-war cartel of Japan's trading companies — who had survived a short rash of war crimes accusations and got them off the ground.

Trading companies don't tie up their hard-earned cash in making things. They spend most of their time worrying about whether their customers are happy, and even if the customers are happy, whether someone out there can make them happier. You respect that your customers may have different values than you do and you don't try to sell them stuff that is culturally attuned to your values. Doing this leads to your calling them barbarians when you're at home, and having liberal sociologists in the customer's country calling you racists, but when was the last time you heard of someone giving up a brand allegiance because a lib/lefty sociologist said that the people who owned, made, or sold the brand were racists?

It also means that no Japanese executive ever thought of lobbying a Western government to suppress the manufacture of knives and forks because he wanted the country involved to start using his chopsticks. That's not the way a successful trading company executive thinks. When a trading company starts to actually make something, usually because their domestic suppliers don't understand the concept of a "happy customer," the corporate culture of the manufacturing subsidiary is drawn from that of the trading company.

Japan's current problem is that the value of the yen skyrocketed and the financial sector became bogged down when those previously happy customers weren't so happy any more about paying a hefty premium for something carrying the overhead that goes with a global trading company. When the revenue in dollars, deutschmarks, pounds sterling, and francs wasn't enough to pay back the loans for the development and manufacturing of all those TVs, cars, computer monitors, chips, robots, et cetera, Japan's financial sector began to get heartburn for which there was no cure.

Twenty-four-hour planetary money marketeering makes for a lot of phone calls in the wee hours to some very senior executives. At the same time, these global communications forces are pumping out a profusion of news which no government can censor, regardless of the phone calls from the executive suite to the politicians.

Today in many nation states, pluralistic societies have reached overkill proportions. The result is that governments are unable to achieve the consensus needed for decisive political support, since anything a government wants to do offends so many of the constituencies in its domain.

And the corporate world's solution to all these failures in the institutions of the industrial world is a new level of government to run regional trading blocs? The master class of the NWO don't seem to get it. The change rate is such that focussing, the skill this group used to get to the boardrooms, has given way to deep, broad, general knowledge of the world that can be upgraded to deal with new information. How many people in your outfit are sufficiently literate in science to see the implications of a change in the Standard Model of modern physics?

One interesting change in the North American political scene from a decade ago are the forces Newt Gingrich has been trying to dragoon into some sort of cohesion. The one thing they all have in common is a wish to turn the clock back to a time when the American myth was transmitted on the cover of the *Saturday Evening Post* instead of a nerd site on the Internet.

Gingrich's biggest problem is that he likes to think that "Newt's America" might have the same cachet for future historians as Newton's physics has for us. While Newton was a closet puritan, his physics didn't have to accommodate a chaos-driven world. But if Newt is to have an America, he has to build it around chaos models, which aren't what his supporters are excited about.

Raising the level of abstraction to one that was current in 1900 is apparently too confusing for those men who began trooping into the all-purpose stadiums of America for Promise Keeper rallies in 1995. Another part of the phenomenon is what *The Economist* calls the mega-churches, which have been at the forefront of the North American populist right-wing revival and have as their main arm the Christian Coalition.

The supporters of this movement seem to believe that the traditional Norman Rockwell family, which enjoyed its high point in the years 1946 to 1960, could withstand the changes wrought by the extensions and emphasis shifts in entertainment, the effects of the release of effective reproductive technologies, and the economic effects of bringing women into the workplace, which raised middle-class disposable incomes and aspirations and provided the fuel for the shift from war-time production into a consumer product-based economy.

The romanticization of '50s family values should not surprise us, but that we have failed to teach the boomer generation that "for every action there is a reaction" should make us wonder about the school system. After all, that's 17th century Newton. You don't need quantum physics to understand that you can't have the benefits of a two income family if only one person has an income.

KEEPING IT SIMPLE

Among NWO fans there is no attempt to reach out for the profundities in the quantum jump in the level of abstraction. It is in the levels of abstraction, not their metaphors, that you can find the explanations about the nature of the real forces which are at work. But the espousal of non-corporate values or attempts at transcendence have gained little popularity in the circles supporting the NWO thesis.

The NWO's leaders are managers and what they do is manage. Success is determined by the size of the venture under administration and that venture's relationship to the profit and ultimately the survival of its own and parallel ventures.

The NWO myth is not concerned that an individual with power may be too easily open to corruption. They hold that market forces will identify such persons and the market will punish them. There is no perception of, or even lip service to public service.

The rule of business is that successful management will achieve its bottom-line goals. In other words, survival is determined by growth. Profits are a waystation on the road to expansion. Accountability is reserved for annual general meetings. But, increasingly, stockholders are institutional investment managers whose attention spans are limited. One can only assume that the primary reinforcer for NWO management behaviour is the control of power for its own sake. The American savings and loan fiasco does not seem to have been part of the NWO's learning curve.

In the NWO world-view, government has no expectations that civil servants should be committed to excellence. The public is informed that the minimal government services offered are all that stand between the citizen and apocalypse.

On one hand, we have a new world-view which is driven by high-order abstractions. Such abstraction is substantively enhanced by having, as the principal tool of exploration, the computer, in which everything that is entered is abstracted into energy. But the NWO seems singularly attracted to concrete views of the world — toward simplicity. This is a universe where President Reagan's one-page precis is something every NWO manager will instinctively grasp as a desirable tradition. In the real world outside the NWO corporate world-view, such as a leading-edge software company, the world-view abstractions most valued are those vectored to *elegance*.

Esthetics have no place in American contemporary management, whether in statecraft or business. The effects of esthetic events defy quantification. This view has, during negotiations with the E.U., with Canada during the Free Trade Agreement negotiations, and with Mexico during the NAFTA talks, resulted in some of the most difficult table-pounding.

The U.S. defines what Europe and Canada call the "artistic sector" as the "entertainment industry." In negotiations with the E.U. and Canada, discussion became rancorous and was further exacerbated by the fact that "entertainment industry" exports are the Number two foreign exchange earner for the U.S.

What makes the issue difficult is that Europeans and Canadians officially provide large subsidies to their arts sectors because they see the arts as articulating a national identity. Actually, both the E.U. and Canada see themselves as besieged by American culture via motion pictures, TV, and merchandising spin-offs.

Global syndication of TV programming provides a large part of the U.S. entertainment industry's foreign exchange earnings. For a foreign broadcaster, an American syndicated program is still priced significantly lower than a domestically produced original program. There is an economy of size factor working here — a domestic distribution deal will finance costs of the American production. Added to the U.S. dominance in TV and film production is the question of U.S. multinational advertisers, who frequently use U.S.-made TV advertising that is, naturally enough, designed to attract an American customer. Naturally, the commercials frequently identify American values as desirable. American production values for TV, film, and commercials are the highest in the world.

COWBOYS AND DINOSAURS

The NWO has little interest in understanding or taking an active part in the intellectual world. The NWO shares with the 19th century British business community a belief that the link between growth and invention is good management. There are few signs of any understanding of the processes which precede invention, or the events which dictate the broad direction of a country's political and economic performance for the foreseeable future.

In practical terms, the biggest flaw that pervasively infects the NWO is probably that the NWO is terribly provincial. Relationships seem to be based on "what is it you have that we want?" This dependence on transient power forms is a dubious survival characteristic. Essentially, NWO adherents are cowboys. Subtlety is not their hallmark.

There are some people, sitting out there on the global village park benches and listening to the grass grow, who might have the NWO for lunch meat without thinking about it, or worse, without even intending it. How many North Americans or Europeans have ever heard of *Sarvodaya Shramadana*, the Buddhist technological movement? The impact being made by this group on limiting negative ecological outcomes, especially in a high-growth context, is quite impressive. It is very strong in Japan, Indonesia, Singapore, Brunei (even though it is principally a Muslim country), and India. It is supported by a strong grassroots base among Buddhists, including leading Japanese industrialists.

Within the Buddhist faith there is a category called a "bodhisattva." A bodhisattva is one who makes a commitment not to achieve heaven until the entire human race is able to enter heaven. When this level of belief exists around the applications and implications of contemporary technology, it brings a whole different level of abstraction to the table, plus a world-view that we may have a problem adjusting to. Certainly we have had little success in learning to treat with respect and, when possible, learn from other world-views. This is a small example of the kind of thing we have to learn to understand, if only to knowledgeably reject.

We've seen how the fundamental work of Planck, Einstein, Heisenberg, and their successors has made deterministic models of the universe untenable. But, while simple-minded causality has become a casualty of quantum theory, the reverse side of this particular coin is that *no event is ever accidental.* As the new era unfolds, its complexity provides challenges that make chaos theory a particularly timely event. Within the Buddhist technological movement we see chaos systems achieving the highest degree of fit with contemporary problems. In other words, they are posing better questions than Westerners are.

Unfortunately, institutional Western mathematicians and physicists have little access to Buddhist work in this area. It is not that the Buddhists are hiding anything. Rather, it is that the mathematicians and physicists are at the top of an academic hierarchy which has its foundations in 18th century rationalism. The intuitive strategies of the Buddhists are so alien and offensive to the values of Western academia that they are unacceptable for citation and general argument.

The Buddhists have no problem with a universe in which no events are accidental. Neither do we, in an inaccessibly complex chaos model. The problem for us is that our chaos theorists risk being blasted out of their tenured retreats if they use the assumptions of the Buddhists. We can't translate the grammar of Buddhist metaphysics into the grammar of the rationalist scientific method. For us, the dissimilarities between them are too weird to access, let alone blend.

The Buddhists, on the other hand, have no trouble translating the grammar of our math and physics and because of this they are aggressively addressing epistemological problems. Karaoke is virtual reality — that's why it took so long to cross the Pacific.

In summary we can say that the NWO paradigm is already destabilized. It is already a short-term milepost, not the destination. The idea that control of the change rate can be affected through transnational corporations is as unlikely a flyer as you'll be offered. The level of abstraction makes such censorship practically impossible, as does the level of paranoia and distrust among corporate oligarchies.

The least worst possible option for those wishing to avoid the death throes of this dinosaur is to move out of its orbit. As the NWO power bases start collapsing, the thrashing around could be dangerous. When this instability goes critical, the pieces will fly everywhere.

CHAPTER SIX

A Brief History of Conspiracy Theory: Who won the Cold War, and what went wrong

Do you remember Bohemian Grove? The Club of Rome? The
Trilateral Commission? They may have plotted, but where are they now?

In the good old days the only conspiracy game in town centred on the
crowd who hung out at a California club known as the Bohemian Grove.
At the time, America's power elite were stylistically ahead of Iron John,
running around the lavish grounds starkers and doing all those things dead
German psychologists dubbed "homoerotic."

When last heard from, the Club of Rome was still operating, despite the
sloppy computer programming that doomed its 1972 neo-Malthusian book
Limits to Growth, not to mention the problem of its sponsors at Olivetti
being busted in Italy's Mafia purge. *Limits to Growth* was a modest volume
espousing ideas that had their genesis in the works of Thomas Malthus. It
was found to have bad data and kludged programming (it predicted that oil
would run out by 1992). Based on it, the Club's founders (Aurellio Peccei,
head of the Italian auto maker Fiat, and the Scottish chemist Alexander
King) flitted about the planet meeting with kings, presidents, and prime
ministers. Mover and shaker corporate executives vied for membership in
the club. Five years ago the Club of Rome elected the former publisher of
Toronto's *Globe and Mail*, Roy Megarry, as its president. He, in turn, hired
an ex-*Globe and Mail* editor, Cameron Smith, as the executive secretary.
Since then, nada.

For a short while, Trilateral Commission conspiracy buffs crowed over
the election of Jimmy Carter (a member) as the U.S. president. That didn't
work out, and when the accusations began to include charges that the
international Communist conspiracy was headed by the Rockerfellers, this
theory lost some of its zing.

The perennial favourite of conspiracy buffs is, of course, Who Killed
President Kennedy? A veritable cottage industry has arisen around the
Kennedy assassination and the Kennedy presidency years — and every
government in the world learned from the Warren Commission.

There are few remaining believers in the "one lone assassin" theory postulated by the Warren report. To most, the lesson was obvious: if you could get away with killing the president of the U.S., there was nothing you *couldn't* get away with. Another lesson is that governments are domestically judged by what the ordinary citizen is getting from the society. (Things were a bit simpler back in Roman times — just your everyday, low-overhead colosseum for the "bread and circuses.")

Apparently we don't expect government to act from a set of principles. Pragmatism is what counts. A government can get away with virtually anything. The Kennedy killing message is clear: *they*, whoever *they* might be (choose your favourite), will "get you" if you "try to rock the boat." The home base of the New World Order has learned, since 1963, that pragmatism wins out over principles every time. More than three decades after the event, the slaying of John F. Kennedy is thought to be a covered-up assassination by forces within the government, probably aided by allies who contributed personnel and logistics support. The damage done to trust in government has far outweighed the significance of the actual event.

But all is not lost, thanks to Scott Burbage, a copywriter whose way with words would make Jonathan Swift jealous and do credit to his 17th-century theatre-promoting namesake. While working for the ad agency Goodby, Berlin and Silverstein, Burbage was assigned to write copy for a line of designer bottled water. Burbage took the Zapruder film of the Kennedy assassination and added a voice-over saying, "They told you there was one lone gunman. Now, are you going to drink their water? "

One of the conspiracy heavies is L. Fletcher Prouty. Prouty is a retired colonel in the U.S. Air Force and a Pentagon intelligence guru. He was also the advisor to the movie *J.F.K.* and has written a book called, fittingly, *J.F.K.*, which postulates an international "high cabal elite" whose mailing address is the offices of Wall Street lawyers Sullivan & Cromwell. Prouty also speaks of a "National Plan" which might be a viable NWO agenda — if we were into conspiracies. Prouty's candidates for the forces of evil are the Dulles brothers, who led the Central Intelligence Agency and the State Department for so much of the Cold War.

Is Prouty right? Are the NWO backers just another crew of world domination freaks?

HOW THE COLD WAR WAS WON

On March 12, 1947, while proclaiming the "Truman Doctrine," U.S. President Harry S. Truman said, "I believe that it must be the policy of the United States to support free people who are resisting attempted subjugation by armed minorities or outside pressures." According to CIA historical sources, prior to the release of Truman's doctrine there had been no mention of the Soviets in any of the planning papers or directives establishing the intelligence service's mandates.

In April of 1947 the Pentagon's planning group estimated that a Red Army push into Western Europe could reach the English Channel in about three weeks without serious interference. General Lucius Clay, the senior U.S. representative in Berlin, reported that he had a "gut feeling they were about to move" and within a couple of months the Pentagon predicted an invasion of the West as being "imminent."

Obviously this got the White House's attention. This was 1947. The U.S. and its allies had demobilized their armies, mothballed their fleets and sent their airmen home to fly the thousands of tourists that the aircraft manufacturers believed were waiting to ride in their new jets. *The Soviets had not demobilized any of their military formations.*

In view of this state of affairs, a new Western intelligence doctrine was developed, principally in the U.S., by the new CIA. This world-view held that:

• It was unlikely that the U.S. and Soviet agendas could accommodate each other.

• The Soviet military were not making any serious provisions to initiate a hot conventional or nuclear war against the West.

• The Soviet leadership and its planning agencies were convinced that there was no way to avoid, *eventually*, some sort of total war with the West. Lenin and Stalin's post-Marxist theory was very clear on the idea that there was no room for two competing political systems.

• The Soviets intended to create a new type of competition. The strategy was based on an endless campaign of disinformation — *prepyastovat*. This long-range campaign was meant to deny resources necessary for a full-blown capitalist system to compete on its own terms. The Soviet plans did not call for capturing territory, friends, or raw materials for themselves, but only to *deny them to the West*.

• Wherever Western and Soviet interests brought them face-to-face, the intent of Soviet strategy would be to play on Western weaknesses rather than to Soviet strengths.

• Psy-war strategies would play an increasingly vital role. Psy-war is, after all, an easier game for a nation with no tradition of a free or frequently critical press.

• The Soviet doctrine predicted that the outcome of any confrontation involving American military forces would be determined by U.S. domestic political opinion, not the actual confrontation.

This was how the West and the U.S.S.R. entered the Cold War. In 1950 came the early reverses of the Korean War, which the CIA and U.S. military intelligence failed to predict would happen at all, let alone the strength the North Koreans would bring to bear. As a result, U.S. intelligence planners and their allies rethought their assumptions.

The Cold War was to become a war in which the side that managed information best would win. This led in 1955 to one of the first precursor moves to the NWO. In that year, following the Korean War, there was a significant shift in U.S. strategic intelligence doctrine:

• There will be no World War III. The Cold War will continue and it is World War III. Fighting will be limited to surrogate and client states.

• The Soviet Union is an authoritarian state that is inherently unstable. The Soviet bureaucracy cannot indefinitely continue to centrally manage government across 11 time zones and 122 languages. The information technologies coming on stream will internally expose the myths of the Soviet system.

• Neither the U.S.S.R. nor the U.S. have the slightest intention of ever occupying the other's land mass. While the Russians might like access to America's food production and the U.S. might like to get its hands on some rare metals, neither is interested in occupying the other.

• The estimates on technological change for the next two decades indicate major capital investment will be required. Basic research suggests that some interesting weapons options may follow from the proposed technology. The fiscal base of the U.S. will not be overly taxed if the government funds the high technology environment and infrastructure as well as specific weapons elements.

Throughout history, humans have accepted total self-destruction in hopeless causes frequently enough to have made the possibility real during the Cold War. Boadicea and the Romans, the Islamic forces defending Jerusalem from the Crusader's encirclement, the Jewish defenders of Massada, the Highlanders at Culloden, the 1,000-day siege of Leningrad where most of the defenders died from starvation, and Hitler's sacrifice of the German Sixth Army when the Red Army broke out of Stalingrad are just a few.

Total sacrifice of entire military formations has been common throughout history. The concept of mutual assured destruction was accepted, more or less, on both sides.

• The U.S.S.R. will have to compete at these weapons levels. Since they cannot compete economically, the effect will be to place the integrity of the state at risk. Eventually, as the new technologies become essential for state and institutional administration, dissent and bankruptcy in the U.S.S.R. will bring about a collapse of the Soviet state.

• The U.S. will be deeply in debt, but will have accomplished the transition to a high-technology economy. America will be assured of being the leading post-industrial state.

• The plan can be executed from relatively few control points. High-tech industry will cooperate blindly in its own interest. The U.S. military will cooperate, mostly blindly, since it will be guaranteed a large standing military posture.

• When the doctrine becomes known, the anti-Communist Right will be livid. America's democratic Left will be appalled. Still, secrecy of the plan is feasible, since it is virtually impossible for planners in the U.S.S.R. to conceive of the assumptions behind this scenario. If the secret of the real targets can be maintained until 1975, the U.S.S.R. will be irrevocably committed to its own destruction.

It was to this strategy the White House speech-writer alluded in President Eisenhower's farewell address, in which he urged caution toward the U.S. "military-industrial complex."

The plan was certainly audacious. And it worked. In fact, the secret was maintained until 1986, by which time it was all over for the U.S.S.R.

The doctrine's chief failure was that in no place did it look for a moral high ground on which Americans could feel good about themselves. It failed to predict Vietnam and it did not recognize the degree to which U.S. credibility would hemorrhage in a sea of drugs, junk bonds and savings-and-loan losses. Above all, the plan failed to prepare for the exponential growth curve of the nation-state-as-a-weapons-system, which took over more and more of the American economy. By 1988 it was impossible to turn the weapons system off, even after the collapse of the U.S.S.R.

MY COUNTRY, MY WEAPON

The plan's greatest weakness, which should have been foreseen, is that America has become one big weapons system which became, not just redundant, but, with the collapse of the Warsaw Pact, a weapon with no target.

The plan also disregarded a Japan that refurbished its industrial/innovation infrastructure and charged the bill to the U.S., which was fighting an extravagant regional war in Korea.

Nor did it foresee a European Union in which France and Germany, unbonded from the U.S., would include the United Kingdom, despite its "special relationship" with the U.S. The authors could not anticipate an E.U. dedicated to trade supremacy with complete disregard for the Warsaw Pact nations because it assumed that all was lost if conflict with the Warsaw Pact became a military event.

The reindustrialization of the former DDR, plus the market share expected in the late East Bloc countries, guarantees the German economy market exclusivities the Americans have not seen or competed with since the 1920s. Similarly, France's political agencies and the Bank of France are looking forward to two decades of prosperity. Dutch food and electronics traders, Belgians with their special African expertise, and Turin's industrial productivity, all with mercantile traditions reaching back to the 14th century, are unlikely to feel indebted to America. Something about "that was then and this is now." The Europeans after all, have few illusions about such things as the pipelines from the great Russian oil fields, which they financed.

The idea of the weapons-system state is pretty new (Frederick the Great of Prussia had the idea but lacked the technology), so the plan's authors should not be faulted for failing to anticipate it. Such a state isn't easily converted to commercial activity. Its economy is made up of too many short production runs, which are extravagant and not amenable to recovering research and development costs through a rationalized product life. The fruits of R&D must be put on the table at once, since the goal is to incrementally raise the stakes for the other side.

Government security agencies rose to new prominence during the Cold War. With the collapse of the Soviet Union, the Western intelligence services, which, like their East Bloc counterparts, had been functionally defined by their opposite numbers, required a new justification for their budgets.

If you are a conscientious, newly appointed senior bureaucrat whom your country's security services are required to brief, the problem of the service's credibility becomes a major issue. The solution is relatively easy. There is really only one way to evaluate an intelligence service.

Your predecessor will have the earlier briefings archived. Take the briefings of the previous three years and tabulate them as follows:

• The service said that X would happen. Did it happen?

• The service said X would happen in a given time frame. If X happened, did it adhere to the time frame predicted?

The Cold War may be over, but the U.S. seems set to maintain its military-industrial structural base and its standing military establishment. The real problem is what to do with this standing force when a large portion of it leaves Europe (which cannot happen too soon for the E.U.). Actions like those in Somalia or Panama are not technology intensive and require small troop commitments, which isn't going to justify maintaining a large standing force, especially when the folks on the home front don't want to have to deal with ghastly wounds and death scenes at news time.

The Cold War intelligence doctrine failed to plan for the fact that war-based economies tend to fall prey to social, economic and moral corruption.

It also failed to consider the fundamental strengths of America — the redemptive quality that grew out of the "Great Awakening" of the 1870s and the optimism, with its concomitant social mobility, that is inherent in the American national psyche. This optimism has been part of the American world-view since the founding of the Republic. It draws its sustenance from the *individual's* right to liberty and the pursuit of happiness. Enshrined as a right, this optimism has been constantly fuelled and renewed, both generationally and through a selective immigration procedure, since the country's earliest days.

The doctrine's greatest predictive failure was that it did not take into account the domestic social data, particularly the impact of the massive cresting of the baby-boom wave. The authors would have, at the time, been indifferent to these kinds of social data. As a result, the doctrine did not address the idea that the new technologies would not be restricted to military applications — rather, that the upsurge in civilian information tech-

---

- The service predicted that if X happened, Y would be the consequences. Did Y in fact happen?

- How does all of this affect your mandate?

- How often did the briefing officer lie in a way which, had you responded as you might be reasonably expected to respond, would result in some other agenda of the intelligence service being advanced?

Your response to the final item does not necessarily suggest that this anticipated response would be deleterious to you. In fact, a wise and career-conscious briefing officer would avoid a situation where you could be left with egg on your face. Rather, the briefing officer would attempt to steer you in ways which would enhance your career and, of course, his.

nologies would bring a new economy on-stream. Neither did it address the discomfort all would feel as the change rate speeded up.

PILLS, POT AND THE POST-SOVIET WORLD

Probably the most influential invention of the 1950s was the birth control pill. Mass distribution began early in the 1960s and it was widely adopted by consumers. Caveats were expressed in *Reader's Digest*-type publications, principally warning that women could now have a sexual freedom similar to that held since time immemorial by men. Few commentators recognized that what would happen would be an inversion of sexual mores and the tactics of sexual social controls.

By the mid-1960s *The Harrad Experiment* was published. It became the underground book for forward-looking early-teenagers. It was a novel set in a private residential secondary school where none of society's sexual taboos were operative. On entry, everyone was randomly assigned a room-mate of the opposite sex. It was okay to move and change roommates. This experiment went on for the four years of high school. The erotic content was geared to a 14-year-old mind.

The Harrad Experiment reflected the confusion and fantasies everyone experienced with the release of birth control technologies — it became a best-seller as soon as it went into paperback distribution and may well have been the most influential book of the 1960s.

The Pill presaged a massive breakdown of historical authority in Western industrial cultures. Quickly on the heels of the Pill came endemic availability of marijuana, LSD, and the alphabet of illicit drugs from the brew shops of chemists.

No parental generation in history had suffered such a breakdown of its conventional claim to influence. Under this technological assault, the parental culture's attempts to reassert its social control did not exactly cover it in glory. During the mid-1960s, one of the major concerns of drug-law enforcement agencies was what to do if a legitimate use were found for LSD or marijuana! Most enforcement agency officials practised serious levels of denial.

Then, of course, the feared disaster happened. It was discovered that pot ameliorated the nausea side-effects of cancer chemotherapy. Reputable physicians were forced to tell patients suffering the side-effects to ask their children or grandchildren to get them some marijuana. Governments dithered, then refused to allow legitimate medical use of cannabis to aid in fighting the big C.

The first clinical investigation trials were authorized and eventually permission was granted to allow cancer sufferers access to pot. By that time most Western governments agreed to supply THC delta-9 (the active ingredient in marijuana) in a tablet form, which was significantly less effective than the smoked illicit form. Governments lost more of their diminished supply of credibility when compassionate physicians told patients who continued to have trouble controlling their nausea to get the real thing, since the strength of illegal marijuana had already been trebled by some not particularly advanced genetic engineering.

The change rate had struck yet again. The highly democratized underground science community had become interested in genetically engineering dope to increase its potency and bio-availability (the efficiency with which it takes effect). The techniques used to improve the bio-availability of marijuana were recognized as highly significant by scientists interested in mainstream genetic engineering of plants. But no one could formally replicate the procedure since no government would issue an investigational licence to make pot more potent. "Seeds might escape from the research facility" was the official excuse.

In the 1970s, if you wanted to make a lot of money in the movie business, you made a disaster film. Thematically and structurally, disaster movies should have given the nascent NWO pause to consider the level of disrepute to which bureaucrats, public and private, had fallen.

A disaster film consisted of a lot of movie stars doing cameo performances. The movie patrons knew that a lot of the stars would die, but they didn't know which ones. The disaster affected a sheltering environment — a luxury liner, an aircraft, an office building, et cetera — and was caused by the arrogance, malevolence, or stupidity of bureaucrats combined with the hubris, at best, or even criminality of a leader.

In the end, there was redemption for the character who admitted his complicity in allowing, or not speaking out against the conditions that brought about the apocalyptic event. This character, while flawed, could be redeemed. The leader who risked everyone else for self-aggrandizement or greed had to perish with his own creation.

In each disaster movie, the survivors would huddle together and create a non-hierarchical mini-society under a consensually selected, morally strong leader who was able to hold the forces of chaos at bay.

That such apocalyptic films were so popular and came at the same time as the Watergate drama, which brought about the downfall of President Richard Nixon, should have caused U.S. spin doctors to engage in some serious reflection. But as long as the U.S. mass media continued to interpret events in a linear extrapolative fashion and North American schools failed to demand mathematical or language literacy, well-financed political candidates were safe.

At one point U.S. President Nixon employed military helicopters to spray paraquat, a plant poison, on Mexican pot plantations. It was similar in execution to the defoliation operations in Vietnam. As the repressive arms of the state were turned on its own middle class, the public reaction was a difficult one for the administration.

First, many areas of California and other states became major producers of marijuana. Second, when kids became sick from the paraquat, their parents stopped supporting the President in anything and, despite his later protestations, Richard Nixon was increasingly seen as a crook. Third, according to anecdotal data which became perceived truth, availability of heroin and cocaine appeared to increase when the campaign against marijuana was particularly active. Finally, huge profits from the illicit drug trade resulted in many government officials and police being corrupted.

Public policy was held up to be trivial, inept, and dishonest. A drug-dealing criminal infrastructure became well-established and, in time, this crime cartel introduced cocaine and crack. When dishonest police and other government administrators were caught, there was a view that crime against the public trust was increasing disproportionately. And all of this occurred simultaneously with the disastrous last years of the Vietnam War.

It must be remembered that these problems are intrinsic to the afore-mentioned intelligence doctrine. But there has emerged another flaw in the doctrine — that with the collapse of the Soviet Union would come problems which were never considered.

The 1955 intelligence doctrine should have addressed the Pandora's box of age-old competing ethnic-tribal feuds and animosities which would accompany the collapse of the Soviet Bloc and the disintegration of Russian-led Communism. However, to have added a section on "What To Do When We Win" would have been seen as pretension and self-indulgence on the part of the authors. Not a good thing if you're a lieutenant colonel trying to fast-track yourself into the general-grade ranks.

RUSSIA: BACK TO BYZANTIUM

The doctrine's greatest flaw was that no one — economists, military strategists, Marxist scholars, intelligence analysts, dissident Soviet officials, and certainly not Western central bankers — understood the Soviet economy, or the dynamics and assumptions that underlay the whole mess.

With the exception of some minor reform attempts by Peter the Great, Catherine the Great and Alexander II, all of which were sabotaged by the bureaucracy, Russia under the Tsars and indeed Lenin and Stalin or their successors would have appeared to any Ottoman caliph or Byzantine ruler a swell, reasonably well-run place. Our hypothetical Byzantine or Ottoman official would have been confused by the complications of a modern industrial state, but would have done just what the Politburo of the U.S.S.R. did, which was to assume that the complexities were not worthy of a big thinker's time.

Government was quite simple in a Byzantine world-view. Everything belonged to the state. If that was too abstract an idea for you, the state was personified in a leader — Khan, Caliph, Tsar, King, Emperor, Party Secretary, whatever. The leader's authority was absolute, subject only to critical review by God. The leader appointed administrators, sub-administrators and so on, who also possessed absolute power, subject only to non-peer review by the leader.

Their job was the day-to-day running of things and collecting the state's revenues (taking a cut for their trouble). They were also under a mandate to maintain the integrity of the State's borders, the docility of the citizens, and the so-called economy, which was technically primitive and principally land-based. There were a few small-time domestic merchants, who had no more rights than anyone else. The state provided few services to the populace, unless you want to include the various vehicles of repression under the "service" column.

Religion was part of the established order and subsidized by the state for the good and sufficient reasons of the state. The church, whose hierarchy was part of the elite, was seldom at odds with the state or its leader. The church also had a lock on education and charities.

The army was a force of conscripts with a usual term of service of 20 years, served in areas of the country with which they had no ties, leaving no room for second thoughts if some serfs started to whine about the share of crops being taken for taxes. The army was also mandated to take over any neighbouring land-mass. It only makes sense: growth of the territorial state is a good thing when wealth is defined by how much land is being worked by the ever-abundant supply of serfs.

In 1905, after losing a war with Japan, three things started to go weird in Russia's version of this system. First, the court of Tsar Nicholas became *really* corrupt. Its capacity to deliver its mythic services — and the court itself — had become pretty well disorganized. The language of the court had become French as the court tried to become Westernized — but only for its own benefit. Any attempts at real reforms were superficial. Second, the ideas of Western liberalism became generally available to the boyars (the small commercial class noted above) and through that small conduit these ideas got wider distribution. Third, a revolution was attempted and in the general roundup of troublemakers a whole lot of people who would otherwise never have met spent some time in Siberia and Kazakhstan swapping ideas.

In 1914 World War I began and the Russian armies suffered huge casualties and continuous defeats. Finally, in 1917, Russia suffered a collapse of the Imperial virtual government and entered into a separate peace with the Central Powers. This breakdown of the state, personified by the Tsar, was accompanied by all the nasty things that go with state disintegration: food riots, starvation, political riots, and massive inflation. The Tsar accepted a new liberal government led by Alexander Kerensky, which was in turn overthrown by a socialist faction, the Bolsheviks. That government was then replaced by the Communist Party, led by V. I. Lenin.

Lenin replaced the trappings of the Byzantine state with the trappings of the Communist state. He took the Orthodox Church's properties and made atheism part of the new state dogma. He tried to industrialize Russia, reestablished the secret police, fought a war with the remnants of the old established order and began to set up the institutions of Communism.

In 1924 Lenin died and Stalin began to do what you do to become the leader of a Byzantine state in turmoil. You convert the opposition to supporting you. Any who don't want to support you are obviously counter-revolutionaries whom you send to that vacation spa Kazakhstan and then shoot, after a trial in which the accused are proven to be agents of the German High Command, the Wall Street bankers trust, and the King of England. You get a new head of the secret police, change the organ's name, then upgrade the level and randomness of state terror. You organize rural and industrial collectives, establishing real control. Any peasants who hide or otherwise try to avoid shipping their crops are spies and saboteurs. You send the army to collect the rightful property of the state while the secret police deal with the ne'er-do-wells.

In other words, the only revolution Lenin and Stalin could sell was one that retained the Byzantine world-view, which, for all its horrors, was the only structure with which the Russian people were culturally familiar. That world-view called for everything to be owned by the state and a leader to personify the state.

To survive the early stage of a Byzantine despot's reign it is essential to have an active and clinically certifiable level of paranoia. After all, they *are* plotting against you.

This is where the Dear Leader problem kicks in. When the despot begins to experience the inevitable effects of aging, the state undergoes sympathy pains. As the leader experiences the fears and anxieties of the loss of personal, physical, and psychological power, the state experiences a sense of fragility and vulnerability. The usual response is increased randomness in the exercise of state terror. (The Chinese appear to have effectively muted the paranoias of aging in their leaders by institutionalizing it through cultural veneration of the aging process. But in practice the best this strategy can do is create a gerontocracy like the one China got from the later Mao years.)

In 1985 Mikhail Gorbachev found himself the leader of a Russia which had been defeated in the Cold War. The Russia that Gorbachev had inherited still had not absorbed the lessons or the experience of the Renaissance. He frequently proclaimed his faith in Communism in an effort to propitiate the old order's establishment figures. He attempted to institute a market economy that retained the trappings of the Communist state. Instead of ship's captains and navigators he brought in academic consultants to teach the bureaucracy how to run a market economy. What he needed was Cosimo de'Medici (1389-1464), who knew how to run a real mercantile state (Florence) and understood how to exercise real power. Cosimo's tenure as head of the Medici Bank left behind a legacy that survived 300 years of, with a couple of exceptions, flaky heirs. In fact, Cosimo de'Medici's money can still be identified in some Italian and Austrian fortunes.

Cosimo knew you have to work hard to understand a new era. He knew you have to promote people who can select which mental baggage to get rid of and what to replace it with. He knew that the unemployable nobility, who couldn't learn to operate in a new era, were thugs and window-dressing you hired for those inevitable moments when you needed thugs.

Imperial Russia and the U.S.S.R. failed to incorporate the experience and lessons of the Renaissance. They did not and do not have a mercantile system that works sufficiently well to put together a viable industrial infrastructure. But the biggest difference between the West, which absorbed the Renaissance, and the remnants of Byzantium is simple. Byzantine states had no means of self-correction except overthrowing the despotic leader.

The Byzantine legal system was filled with exceptions and lacked the concept of equity — the key focus of Western legal systems. If you have a plan involving major intervention by the state and significant sacrifice by the population, you can emphasize the many benefits accruing to the masses. You can build a semiconductor industry, so long as you put TV sets in every house. In other words, in the West the beloved leader's appeal for public sacrifices won't be accepted unless there is an equity component. And the West had its underpinnings of equity in place after Magna Carta 1215.

It's not that the West *achieves* equitable distribution of the society's goods and services. But such an attempt is a commonly held aspiration of the society. In the old U.S.S.R. the assumptions underlying the concept of equity were as alien to most Russians as their system was and is to us.

The people propping up Boris Yeltsin are like bureaucrats everywhere. They hate innovation that doesn't fit in. But how do you fit the innovations of cyberspace into a world-view that was constructed to deal with the Council of Nicea and a Justinian codex that places above the law the elite, the police and all of the organs of power in the Rodina? How do you allow for the freedom of thought and speech so essential for economic growth, unless you shift your academic system from Scholasticism to Humanism and your dominant religion has undergone a reformation?

That is the real problem facing Boris Yeltsin today. He has stopped shooting political dissidents — and that is not a loss that his Byzantine culture can easily absorb.

THE TRADE BLOC SOLUTION

The decision of the Reagan administration to organize a North American trading bloc, which President Reagan announced in his first State of the Union address, was essentially designed to counter the E.U.

Presently, this continental free trade zone is in a lot of trouble. In the U.S. the unions and the working class have just figured out that they're about to be replaced by Mexican labour, for whom anything which doesn't involve stooping and tugging on plant roots is upscale. Surprisingly, the Democrats did not find this an issue made in heaven for them, once they had discussed the matter with their new Wall Street converts. President Clinton expressed reservations about the North American Free Trade Agreement, but in the end he came around to the fiscally conservative policies inherent in the treaty.

After George Bush, Mexican President Carlos Salinas de Gortari (hereinafter known as Salinas), and Canadian Prime Minister Brian Mulroney signed the NAFTA accord on December 17, 1992, corporate North America saw a green light at the end of the transition tunnel.

In Canada, Quebec's business communities had managed to convince the Quebec electorate that with NAFTA they could afford independence. In the rest of Canada the corporate drum-beaters had been less successful at preaching enthusiasm. At the end of it all, the ruling Canadian conservative party was driven out of office.

Events in Mexico had a sharper edge. Prior to the signing of NAFTA, the Canadian government, the U.S government, and U.S. and Canadian corporate flacks had led us to believe that brother Salinas was one of the greatest political figures of the 20th century. He was innovative, compassionate and so virtuous that he was loyal to his wife. He was, the PR hacks gushed, so honest that Mexicans had found it impossible to bribe him. His clear-eyed view of the future had left Mulroney and Bush breathless and he would bring a profound sense of idealism to the jaded world of North American intercontinental affairs.

"The whole of Mexico a low-cost manufacturing zone, not just a little bit on the border," whispered one gringo free trade negotiator. "No more wetbacks" echoed his immigration expert colleague, while one of their Canadian trade-pact haggling mates, in a glassy-eyed, apparently hypnotic state, kept repeating "there's more middle-class consumers in Mexico than in the whole of Canada." All these analyses would become less attractive in the face of Mexico's less than robust infrastructure.

Things started to go down the tubes for Salinas at Christmas in 1993, when a bunch of political rebels from the state of Chiapas decided that it was time for the people to rise up in their righteous anger and "liberate" the state. When the Mexican army was less than polite in attempting to put down the insurrection, human rights busybodies in the U.S. and Canada wailed about murders and assorted pillaging.

Then the Mexican peso came under pressure. Debt, corruption and low productivity were cited. Now it wasn't just the "landless ones" who were tired of waiting for the NAFTA love boat to come in. It was the world's money traders, so Canada and the U.S. had to rescue the peso. The price was high. In the U.S., the new Republican-controlled Congress, keen to cut government spending in general, had trashed the Clinton health package and was unwilling to rescue the peso. Canada's debt status with the world's money-lenders was wobbly. But they managed to put something together which was basically too little, too late.

In March of 1995 Mexico's new president, Ernesto Zedillo, decided that ex-president Salinas could best serve Mexico's future by moving into exile. Carlos departed for Boston where it was expected that his three university-aged offspring would join Brian Mulroney's daughter at Harvard, from which Salinas earned a Ph.D. in political economy in 1978.

As Salinas was leaving he said he was confident that his brother would ultimately be exonerated on charges of murder and corruption and denied that Mexico's current financial woes should be laid at the door of his administration.

The expectations of the Mexican peasantry, when they are told that NAFTA will benefit them, are at odds with the realities of the implementation. Further, the agendas of anglo North America for cyberspace exploration and exploitation are pretty divorced from people in Chiapas, who are putting their lives on the line in the hope of getting some subsistence farming land.

Chiapas is one of those parts of the world where a few barons control all the land and don't intend to give it up. They are still at the end of the feudal world and have never experienced the Renaissance, let alone industrialization. The political environment of Mexico appears, from what we can see above, to operate on the same level of political and economic sophistication that were the hallmarks of the Borgias, the Medici, or Henry IV of England. Certainly the land barons assume they can hold out until some Mexican government gives them an outrageously high settlement.

Few political commentators during the NAFTA negotiations appeared to be aware of how close Mexico was, outside of a few urban areas, to the feudal mind-set. Whenever government or business negotiators addressed the medieval world-view their answer was that when Mexico became industrialized, Mexican peasants would make the 500-year leap. This was the answer during the Russian and Chinese revolutions from central managers adhering to the party line.

It usually takes about three generations before a people can create the base level of assumptions underlying a new era. It is essential that workers have some sense of what the end-use of their labours will be. When they can't imagine it and are illiterate, they tend to make a lot of mistakes.

CANADA'S MARRIAGE OF UNEQUALS

There is a strong body of opinion in Canada that former prime minister Mulroney sacrificed the sovereignty and identity of Canada in the 1987 Free Trade Agreement. By late 1991 Mulroney had an approval rating of only 14 percent in national polls. By 1992 Canadian anti-continentalists claimed that the FTA had cost some 250,000 Canadian jobs. There is a strong tendency to blame free trade for all problems connected with the 1990-93 depression and virtually anything else that goes wrong. (This scapegoating is a fine old Canadian tradition. For generations Western Canadians have responded to all problems with "Goddamn the CPR!") For

---

The 13-state Caribbean Community (CARICOM) has watched with a degree of uncertainty as the Canada-U.S. Free Trade Agreement resolves itself into a continental trade agreement. The principals of NAFTA haven't given much, if any, thought to the Third World disaster area of the Caribbean. The area's exports to North America are minimal (sunshine and beaches aren't all that easy to package and ship).

CARICOM officials have repeatedly voiced their concern that once NAFTA is functional, the partners will abandon some, or all, of the aid programs of which Community members are now beneficiaries.

CARICOM's concerns are not unfounded sibling rivalries. Third World diplomats have bitterly observed that aid to former Soviet bloc countries has come at the expense of cancelled or truncated aid meant for elsewhere, primarily Africa. They look at the horror shows in Somalia and Rwanda and ask in private if this is what must happen to get the West's attention.

The cases of Bosnia and the Chornobyl nuclear plant in Ukraine were also, the Third Worlders claim, put forward at the expense of aid to the South (to use the North-South metaphor of "developed" and "developing" nations). The Third World fears that its needs will go unanswered as the new regional trading blocs pick up steam and become even more capital intensive.

the first time since the War of 1812, there is an active anti-American political movement.

One of the most prominent defectors was Gordon Ritchie, formerly the senior civil servant on the Canadian free trade negotiating team. Heretofore an uncritical fan of the FTA, Ritchie publicly accused the U.S. administration and Congress of dealing in bad faith in the day-by-day management of the pact. These are harsh words for a former self-effacing civil servant who is accustomed to letting his minister make all political remarks.

For the Canadian government, this was embarrassing. Ritchie's litany of violations, he claimed, came to a boil in 1992, a presidential election year. After his list of grievances he added, "The real threat to Canadian prosperity is not free trade, but the possibility that free trade will not be allowed to work to Canada's advantage."

Canadian commentators were less than kind. Many accused this leading architect of the deal of being naive if he expected America to live up to the agreement without a struggle when it failed to get its way. The idea that the U.S. sees legislative and administrative stalling and bullying as a legitimate means to resist those parts of the treaty which are not in America's best interests is new to the popular Canadian view of the U.S., that "Americans are just like us."

The most serious defection from the ranks was Simon Reisman, Ritchie's boss during the FTA talks. Reisman, a former Canadian deputy minister of finance, is known for the candour with which he presents his often acerbic and iconoclastic views. When he, too, joined the foes of America's management of the FTA, corporate Canada gulped and started to publicly attack the agreement. When Reisman was asked for his comments on his former aide's charges, his usual sense of diplomacy and tact were firmly in place. "Americans are bastards!" was the immediate Reisman quote.

North America isn't Europe. In Europe, even Germany cannot assume that the European parliament will support it on anything. In the North

---

In the spring of 1998, during the Stanley Cup hockey play-offs, Canada's Molson beer company unveiled a new commercial. It represented the governors of the National Hockey League listening to someone with a southern U.S. accent urging the league to use brightly coloured pucks and follow the puck with a computerized trail when a goal is scored.

The southerner (a Turner Broadcasting homeboy?) finishes his pitch and the commercial ends with him being thrown out the door and sliding down a long, lavish hallway. A senior Molson executive told the author how impressed Molson managers were with the enthusiastic response to this commercial across the country. In fact, an American TV executive had proposed the ploy.

American free trade pact, American domestic political pressures guarantee that the playing field must be tilted toward the U.S. and that American interests will dominate.

Today, there is agreement among economists in both the American and Canadian governments that the result of establishing a trading bloc and removing tariff and non-tariff trade barriers is larger, more efficient internal markets. These government economists also believe that a trading bloc will be more effective in negotiations with other trading blocs — i.e. the E.U. and Japan — than individual countries would by themselves.

These are the same economists who supported the trade bloc scheme in the first place. They no longer claim the internal economic gains they did when they were selling the deals to the politicians. Now they say that, once the blocs are working, there will be productivity gains in those industries which haven't departed for Mexico, Taiwan, Singapore, or Korea.

When these economic wizards talk about this latest iteration of the plan, they usually neglect to mention the new level of bureaucracy they have had to create to run the trading blocs. They also anticipate some standstill in the northern U.S., Ontario and Quebec, and an outflow of resources to the low labour cost southern U.S., Latin America and the Orient. There will also be a significant loss of sovereignty, as many European countries have already discovered.

We can expect transnational corporations to act more like sovereign powers. We're not talking about a free-trading international economy with open access for all here. National, regional (within a nation's boundaries), and local businesses don't have the infrastructure to support direct foreign marketing between trading blocs. These national businesses will only act as suppliers to real transnationals.

When economists who are not involved with power politics look at this scenario they are usually aghast. The most polite comment is that the trade blocs are inherently unstable. This is the economic crux of the New World Order: the civil servants of the world have created a group of trading blocs which will break down sooner or later.

Probably sooner, but until that happens the trading bloc bureaucrats will pig out in fat city. And why not — they've earned it. They've managed to convince those who live under the corporate icons of the transnational corporations to support this power exercise with the promise of bigger profits and now there won't be any, except for a new level of government on a global scale.

All this provides even more grist for the conspiracy theorist's mill. But as conspiracy theories become more popular and trust in politicians deteriorates, it doesn't matter if the conspiracy theorists are right now and then. They are easily labelled as paranoids and placed in the new post-Dantean *Inferno* Circle, the Circle of Triviality.

GIVE DILIGENCE ITS DUE

There is an interesting, albeit tangential way to look at regional trading groups such as NAFTA and the E.U. Try thinking about organizing a trade bloc the same way corporate managers think about mergers and acquisitions.

When creating a mega-trading bloc, you know that there will be a loss of sovereignty to varying degrees. The more powerful members of the partnership will lose less sovereignty than is lost by the less powerful members. The trade-off is that all partners get access to the full market without tariff hassles or other impediments. The more powerful members will lose proportionately less sovereignty *because they have more sovereignty than they can use*, but will gain from being able to use larger production runs. The corporate world is pretty indifferent to the loss of sovereignty because sovereignty is a very abstract and expensive concept, compared to the market expansion opportunities.

In a corporate merger or acquisition there is a stage in which the acquisitor conducts "due diligence." This means the organization being acquired opens all its records so that there will be no surprises when the deal closes. In other words, the acquiring party goes in with its eyes wide open and is not allowed to whine if all does not go well. Once the due diligence has been completed, the acquirers go back to the office to plot and scheme the merger of two corporate cultures.

If all goes sour, then we wake up to the news that ABC Corp., having acquired XYZ Inc. a year ago, has put XYZ up for sale again with the statement that "due to changed global conditions ABC intends to return to its core business." (Where, in theory, it has some idea of what it's doing.) There is never any suggestion that the "due diligence" system failed or that the corporate cultures could not be merged, no matter how many people ABC found to be redundant in the restructuring.

Now, wouldn't it be interesting if the diplomats in charge of regional trade zone deals had to undertake some form of due diligence instead of simply responding to policy announcements by political leaders?

Imagine what the U.S. State Department told President Clinton when the Mexican peso's convertibility suddenly disappeared. (First they tried to blame the evil international currency speculators but then it turned out that the money had all been converted into U.S. dollars and shipped out of the country by Mexico's financial elite.)

Imagine what the U.S. State Department told Clinton when Canada survived a referendum on Quebec sovereignty by half a percentage point. A different result would have left the U.S. very exposed, particularly with over three-quarters of the Canadian debt owed to American investors.

It would seem that due diligence, for which the business world has pretty clear rules, might be a useful way to give nations some forewarning about the real cultures of their proposed free trade partners. It would probably be good to have a realistic idea of their strengths and limitations before you decide to bet a major share of your country's economic future on them. But you can't do that when national leaders stake their reputations on closing the deal before the negotiations even start.

CHAPTER SEVEN

Pride and Peril: People who count, and people who think they do

Were we living in the Renaissance, who would we consider as people who count? We would probably think of popes, kings, dukes, and assorted princes. Today we know that the people who mattered were a few thinkers like Erasmus and Bruno, a few artists, a bunch of social activists like Luther, St. Ignatius of Loyola and John Calvin, a gaggle of bankers, some military captains, some captain/traders, and some writers like Pacioli, Machiavelli, and Dante, all of whom exercised the perceptual mobilities available to those who assumed that perspective was accessible and exploitable.

There were no journalists, no media to sell their reports. There were no public relations people, no media consultants, and no spin doctors. (Who says things don't get better?) One of the ways information and news travelled around was through the first institution that was largely and formally in the hands of women.

This institution was the salon, which evolved from the court. In the feudal period all landholders held a court: it was where the feudal leader dispensed justice and met with his vassals. In stable times, the court was the site of entertainments and other social activities, with the landholder bearing the costs. When the court travelled, the great houses where the ruler and his retinue stopped had to bear the costs. By the time of the Renaissance, it was an economic disaster to have a state visit.

In Italy and France the custom arose among wives of wealthy men of holding soirées, sometimes nightly, where information could be exchanged, returning explorers quizzed, the new scientists could discuss their activities, and bankers and merchants could put together deals, all under social conditions. The salon was a way for the new middle class to compete socially with the court circles. Hostesses competed to set the best table, provide the most unique entertainment, and have the most interesting guests. Even in Plague years, the salons of France and Italy offered a place to continue the day's activities under adventitious social conditions. Invitations to the important salons of the period were eagerly sought after.

To search out those who count today we face the same problems we would have in the Renaissance. It is easy to identify those who represent the established order and whom speech writers for George Bush or Bill Clinton would say are the representatives of the New World Order. But if you really are looking for the movers and shakers, then you have to go to the electronic salons of the present.

A friend of the author's, Stephanie Parker, writes charming and interesting allegorical novels. Also she is a vegetarian. (Aside from this one lapse she is amazingly sane.) Her criterion for food she will eat is that the source of her food must not have a central nervous system.

On an Internet chat line that operates for the convenience of people who are on the leading edge of research in artificial and machine intelligence, there is an interesting argument. One group holds that the most useful approach is to try to simulate human neural activity. The alternative view is that it is better to use insects as the benchmark, because it is evolutionarily more effective and less expensive.

This particular "salon" attracts some major investigators in the field but is not particularly accessible to everyone. The theories underpinning the arguments are often less than clear.

Just how wrong is it possible to be when judging whom history will select as significant versus what contemporaries believe?

Giorlamo Cardano was one of the leading astrologers of his time. In 1564 he decided that it was time to publish a book of the horoscopes of the 100 outstanding men of that juncture in history. On that list was only one artist: Dürer.

Twenty years later, France's court historian, Andre Thevet, published his True Portraits and Lives Of Illustrious Men. Renaissance historian John Hale describes it as the "fullest Who's Who and Who Was Who of the 16th century."

Thevet hired a crew of Flemish artists to produce 233 engraved portraits to go along with the short (People magazine-style) biographies. He tells us he left out any pictures he felt failed to deliver a true likeness. There is not one artist on his list. He also took a pass on sculptors, architects, and musicians. He did manage do a little better for writers: Du Bellay and Ronsard each get a line in someone else's life (Flemish portrait not included). He notes that Rabelais is a "man of unusual knowledge" while Thomas More gets the full treatment for his career in administration and diplomacy and his being charged, tried and found "githy" which, Thevet says, means in English "worthy of death." There's no mention of More's Utopia. There's no mention of More's long friendship and correspondence with Erasmus.

Thevet stipulated that inclusion was based on the subject being known for polit-

Most people interested in robotics have tried to develop analogues based on a model of human intelligence. One of the participants on this chat line was arguing for an insect model from a basis of psychobiology. Finally, a glimmer of understanding: his goal is to build an insect robot that Stephanie would eat, if the construction materials were chewable. He wants to evolve a simple central nervous system and not have to deal with non-essential complexities of a more evolved creature with all the, for this purpose, redundancies which accompany a biological life form, at this stage of the state of the art.

This guy uses chips normally associated with calculators sold to primary school kids and mass production weapons. He is trying to build a prototype that will allow him to address some very basic problems you can't get to if you're dealing with chips with a wider potential. One lab following this developmental route is trying to design a warbot hand grenade which would creep toward an enemy. Perhaps Star Wars (SDI) is not on the main track — but maybe Cockroach Wars has a future?

What we have here is the equivalent of overhearing some explorers at a Renaissance salon. The number of people who could use the information for direct pecuniary gain are few and up to their ears in their own hypotheses.

We are all conditioned to think of robots as R2D2 or C3PO saving princesses or working on vast consumer product assembly lines. What you

---

ical, military, theological, or legal achievements. He was also prepared to certify an entry for being knowledgeable in socially useful branches of learning such as navigation, history, cosmography, and medicine.

Thevet was willing to grant that some artisans were, by virtue of their "ingenious labours", worthy of notice because of their contribution to the public good. However, with this lot he was more exclusionary, limiting representation to the inventors and not the then-current practitioners. So the nod for printing went to Gutenberg, the alchemist of record was Jabir ibn Haijan and Pythagoras was chosen as the "father" of mathematics.

While we might be surprised at these choices, given the emphasis we place on the celebrities, the scientific discoveries, and the technologies of the Renaissance, Cardano and Thevet do reflect the values of their time.

There was no general term for "culture" in any European language in the 16th century. The Latin root cultura had a wider meaning and was appropriately used to cover ploughing, manuring, and husbandry. John Hale tells us it was not until the 19th century that "culture" came to have as its principal use the fine arts. Hale also points out that there was no term for the fine arts in the Renaissance.

gain from "overhearing" such a conversation is a better understanding of the way truly creative and original thinkers avoid the stereotypes of the conventional wisdom. It gives us some idea of how difficult it is to explain original research.

Imagine trying to sell this to a typical corporate magnate with no understanding of psychobiology. The tangential connection between Stephanie's vegetarianism and the author's understanding of what was being argued may have not been useful to you. It is only when you are communicating with someone else you have to worry about whether the connection is useful.

The benefit of being a fly on the wall at this type of conversation is that it helps you to choose whether or not to abandon another piece of your own historical baggage. You can decide whether you need the R2D2 image whenever someone mentions a robot. The situation also means that your conventional perceptions are challenged and your abilities to think tangentially may take you to original understandings of your own.

The supporter of the successful model of robotics development — insect or human — *will*, probably, go down in history.

THE NWO ROLL CALL

To identify New World Order supporters in the corporate world isn't all that easy. Faces below the CEO are usually publicly obscure, and in government the faces behind elected officials are equally blurred. Former President Bush is the most obvious figure as the NWO progenitor, but there is probably a galaxy of superstars from the business community whose ability to get the president's attention is the key to their opaque profiles.

George Bush's presidency will certainly be historically marked as the beginning of an era when training for the White House must include a spell at one of the nation's senior intelligence agencies in an executive capacity. If nothing else, the national leader would learn when the intelligence service is merely serving itself. A candidate without this kind of personal experience will make for a pretty skill-free president. Today a national leader needs to have someone who is absolutely and *personally* tied to them heading the CIA and the National Security Council, or their equivalents in other countries.

That the world's intelligence services have become ideologues is not news. Whether Bill Clinton or any other senior power's leaders can trust their intelligence services will be the test of whether democratic institutions are going to survive.

Historians sympathetic to the world-view of the NWO will argue that in the Reagan-Bush White House years a capital collapse was averted and that the economic infrastructure maintained the highest overall standard of living in the world. They will further argue that the national, post-Vietnam ennui was reversed and that America took its rightful place, as predicted by the Manifest Destiny thesis, as the only superpower. Further, these historians will add, the roots were laid for a self-renewing meritocracy to assume a wider power in directing the nation's economic strategies and the rationalization of government services.

The ascendance of this meritocracy was supposed to enable the government of the U.S. to finally achieve the true goals and intentions of the Founding Fathers. Future leaders would be identified among those who proved their competence and integrity within an expansive, social Darwinist corporate America.

The political side of this thesis appeared to fall apart in 1992 when Bill Clinton upset George Bush's bid for re-election. The reason we can say "appeared" is that it is difficult to say that Clinton is not as seamlessly attached to the corporate world as Bush was.

Another major NWO figure whom we can expect to continue to exert power and influence would be the Bush Administration's Secretary of State, James Baker. Baker has all of the requisite credentials: civility, stable independent wealth, managerial competence, and political savvy, coupled with membership in the top echelons of the Texas corporate elite.

The performance of the U.S. State Department under Baker was professionally superb, and its orchestration of Gulf War support did not miss a beat. Further, State was singularly free of leaks. Baker, who went from being President Reagan's Chief of Staff to Secretary of the Treasury for the second Reagan term, has established himself as a team player among those who would establish a New World Order. Baker has only one problem: his management of the disastrous Bush re-election campaign. Still, the *New Republic* once described him as the man who "turned smelling like a rose into a job description." Baker enjoys favourable relations with the press, well honed during his White House days, and is treated with respect by the international media.

In Europe, the British corporate establishment and John Major, successor to Margaret Thatcher, provided a listening post for the NWO. Major's Conservatives were replaced by the Labour Party under Tony Blair, whose technocratic leanings are, if anything, even closer to Baker's.

Brian Mulroney, the Canadian prime minister, was a valued branch manager who never rose above the rank of toady. Interestingly, Mulroney shared one highly prized cachet with James Baker. The government of Canada under Mulroney was singularly leak-free on the origins of the Free Trade Agreement and in most matters involving the U.S. government. Mulroney has been pensioned off to a Montreal law firm and a round of highly-paid, low-profile directorships, including posts with the huge gold miner American Barrick and Archer Daniels Midland, a food processor and frequent defendant with the U.S. government.

In the private sector, James Robinson III, former CEO of American

Express, appeared for some years to be the leading corporate contender for the prototypical NWO counsellor. Since the early Reagan years, Robinson had been selling the "new competition" from which the Canada-U.S. Free Trade Agreement emanated. Robinson was known as an active Republican with a solid record of strong support for the Reagan and Bush presidencies. In addition he has the key to various back doors in the corridors of power on Wall Street and in Washington. He was also the chairman of the blue-ribbon Free Trade Committee that convinced corporate America to endorse the original Canada-U.S. Free Trade Agreement, sight unseen.

Robinson's Canadian connections have been interesting to watch. Robinson and Amex were strong supporters of Prime Minister Brian Mulroney from Mulroney's first run for the leadership of Canada's Progressive Conservative Party. Robinson was heavily involved in the RJR-Nabisco control battle, in which he supported the losing management team of F. Ross Johnson, who is also a Canadian and who, along with his wife, has a close political and social friendship with Mulroney and his wife, Mila.

When Robinson secured a Canadian Schedule B Bank licence for Amex on November 21, 1988 (the same day as the federal election that decided Canada's approval of the Canada-U.S. Free Trade Agreement), in spite of the intense opposition lobbying by all of Canada's chartered banks, many eyebrows were raised. The charter gave Amex access to the Canadian Payments System, which is the vehicle used by the Bank of Canada to manage the M1. The specious rationale for granting the charter and the large amount of regulatory red tape that was waived left little doubt in global financial circles that Robinson was at least the holder of a ducal fiefdom in the NWO.

Make no mistake, however, Amex needed a bank in Canada. While it owned offshore banks and a number of American financial services institutions, it needed a respectable bank in a scrupulously conscientious jurisdiction away from the prying eyes of Congress, if Amex was to be the source of financial services in the NWO. After all, American Express is not the mob and offshore banks are tacky, even if the mob doesn't own them. The last thing anyone who owns a bank wants is to be seen as the equivalent of the now defunct Bank of Credit and Commerce International. That scam gave Pakistani management systems a bad name in some otherwise ethically flexible circles.

All of the above is relatively common knowledge among political observers in the U.S. and Canada. But few of these government and business watchers recognized the one feature that put Robinson head and shoulders above his peers in corporate America. Amex is really in the ID-card business for both "individuals who count" and "businesses that matter." As the ultimate custodian of the American Express database, Robinson held information on millions of individuals worldwide and thousands of global corporations. Amex also controls Shearson-Lehman, the corporate banking house. The idea of gaining access to that database must cause political spin doctors and intelligence agency chiefs to salivate like Pavlov's pups.

Further, Amex's international marketing resources are not inconsequential to anyone considering selling a concept like a style of government. As the guru of today's competition philosophy, James Robinson III is probably one of the most experienced exploiters of information systems in the world.

That Robinson's ambition may have outrun his understanding of what was really going on is not impossible. In the last week of January 1993, Robinson found himself under pressure from major investment managers, who were calling for tougher senior management that would drive up the value of the company's stock. The downturn in Amex's core charge card business was upsetting the fund managers. When the American Express board resisted, the stock dropped 10 percent.

The board had no difficulty understanding that message: Robinson was out, to be replaced by someone whom Wall Street trusted to recover the net worth. It was the same end as that which befell IBM Chief John Akers just weeks before and GM's Stemple in December of 1992.

As more corporate heads opt for the celebrity CEO route and are inevitably crucified when their 15 minutes are up, their friends will see them as having been martyred by an insensitive press. But the martyrdom label doesn't work. They've merely become examples of what happens to those who demonstrate an inability to drop their useless mental baggage.

WHO OWNS THE FUTURE?

Many Canadians opposed the original Free Trade Agreement with the U.S. and the successor NAFTA treaty which incorporated Mexico. Throughout the heated debate around free trade, neither proponents nor opponents ever raised the question of whether Canada or, for that matter, the U.S., had any choice. Jim Robinson would answer "no." And if the NWO needed a Free Trade Agreement, it is doubtful whether a choice did, in fact, exist.

Perhaps the single most meaningful comment on the NWO comes from an allied intelligence officer who has specialized in understanding the U.S. for 35 years. This is what he says:

"I think the American leadership realize that the U.S. cannot succeed to the sole holder of superpower status. There are no more superpowers. A superpower must have worthy targets for its implements of mass destruction.

"What the supporters of the NWO are really after is to write the rule book for the post-Cold War period. Bankers, oil companies, and transnational corporations like rule books. A rule book for the world's trading blocs would cover three major trading transcontinental areas, two minor trading groups and include policies for dealing with the three unstable regions — the former U.S.S.R., the People's Republic of China and Africa. This would leave only the Middle East, which would be controlled with nation-to-nation military and commercial alliances and militarily-induced dependencies."

Then he adds, reflectively, "It's really too bad... these guys have no sense of vision at all. They're power managers and not bad at it. They've never operated anything in their lives. They act as if their mergers and acquisitions people have acquired the U.S. for them and they have to increase profits so they can jack up the dividend and pay off the junk bonds.

"They have no vision beyond immediate, pragmatic, simplistic economics and global political strategies. You have to remember, from the time they were at Choate, they have never had a reflective moment... and never, never a moment of self-doubt. They are the best the American system produces. They really are the first-string team.

"Finally," he concludes, "If they start to feather their own nests, watch out. These guys do know how to cut their losses. If it looks like the stakeholders are turning on them, it will be time to cash in their stock options... and they wrote the book on that one. They are not twits, though they still aren't sure that they're in the fight for their lives. When they figure that out, it will be nasty and they fight dirty.

"Read your Innis — look up Carthage and Carthaginian in the index of *Empire and Communications*."

The Canadian economist and historian Harold Innis (1894-1952) argued that the development of advanced communications forms led to the "growth of trade and trading institutions... and to the development of trading oligarchies such as emerged in Carthage." David Godfrey, an Innis student who has edited and annotated a new edition of *Empire and Communications*, has pointed out that Carthage is a possible historical marker which may prove valuable to North American free-traders.

Carthage was a commercial empire that ran head-on into another empire which also valued trade — from its colonies — but whose agenda went beyond just acquiring more tributary states. Rome was a successful city state that was to become an extended territorial state.

Transnational corporations have expansive powers but no ambitions to control space or time. Rather, they wish to control productivity. The weakness of the Carthaginians was that they were nationless and rootless traders who threatened another power, Rome — which ploughed under the walls of Carthage and salted the land, denying the trading oligarchy its physical base.

With corporate America filling the role of the traders, you have a new twist on the Carthaginian option. In other words, the U.S. provides an oligarchy called corporate America with a secure home base and a temporal historicity. There have been other Carthaginian models in history. The Carthage option bets the family farm with every generation of the oligarchy. Will the rest of the world put up with having these new Carthaginians securing the kind of monopolies that finally drew the full attention of Rome?

Spokespersons for the NWO are always careful to pay lip service to the American Constitution and interpreted American values. In actual practice there is less concern for adherence to constitutional restraints. Over the terms of office of Presidents Reagan, Bush and Clinton the conduct of U.S. policy has vacillated between the amoral and the immoral in relations with other countries.

That George Bush was left as the titular leader of a group of individuals who see themselves as "owning" the focus point of a global information age is not a happy thought. That Bill Clinton has taken over this role brings cosmetic changes of no particular significance to the view that America's corporate leadership is engaged in a last-ditch stand of the Industrial Age mind-set, in a ring of circled wagons.

Since the beginning of the Reagan years, adherents of the NWO have used the power of the U.S. to put in place a view of the world based on 19th-century social Darwinism. Their goal is to make their world-view truly global. The problem is that their strategy is comparable to someone trying to maintain a territorial feudal state in the middle of the 17th century while surrounded by some very aggressive commercial nation states.

There are lots of people out there sitting under celebrity security bubbles who might as well be bag people for all history will say about them. In fact, the way we exploit celebrities speaks loudly about how little we value ourselves, and could become a topic of great interest to historians of the future.

Have you ever thought about who, from our time, will be seen as significant to historians 500 or so years from now? They will evaluate us according to how our accomplishments led to their time. No doubt many will laugh at our naiveties and stupidities. Idealists among them will call us courageous for doing things that are a part of everyday life. And they will honour a few of us by putting us in *their* historical records.

Based on our own standards, we can work out the criterion we have used fairly well. Will they use the same criteria? Will they hold us up to adherence to their transient standards of morality? It is impossible to construct a correct answer but it is interesting to try.

Who gets into history today?

People who manage power with a long-term view.

Both Hitler and Churchill spoke of a 1,000-year period of political suzerainty, although Churchill used it to ennoble and boost the morale of the

British people during a difficult time of World War II — when you read his "finest hour" speech today, you are struck by the daring use of metaphor, since the collapse of the British Empire became unalterable in his lifetime. Hitler, on the other hand, really believed in the 1,000-year Reich.

Historians favour people who discover real knowledge: Planck, Einstein, Heisenberg, Schrödinger, and Dirac are shoe-ins. Also, inventors whose creations change the time in which they live at a fundamental level: Gutenberg yes, Bill Gates no. Inventors whose works are not recognized as profound at the time don't make it.

Losers also make it with historians because historians use them for didactic purposes (see what can happen if you act like this).

It's difficult to make a judgment when it comes to contemporary politicians. Historians are generally leery about politicians for a few hundred years, because it takes that long for political consequences to be clear enough to begin making judgments. Right now, we want to know everything we can about Lenin and Mao, but perhaps Communism appears on the screen of the big historical database as a minor 70-odd-year aberration.

A really big success at business who then becomes a politician can get there, but only if it's up front. If the tycoon simply buys and sells political agents, there is little chance that a historian will recognize that person as significant, except for one writing *Greed Through The Ages*.

Ben Bradlee and/or the *Washington Post*'s coverage of Watergate will probably make it, unless the history is written in an authoritarian time, or when an oligarchy or a tyrant is in power. The fatally flawed Richard Nixon is unlikely to be significant, regardless of his achievements, because Watergate is unique in the annals of corruption. A free press brought down the head of state of a federal republic that had all of the levers of power at its disposal and apparently little compunction about using them. Nixon is a natural subject for revisionist historians — the kind of historians whose litany goes something like this: "Yes, we know all this bad stuff, but not enough attention has been paid to (you fill in the gap here)."

It would seem that the critical basis for getting into the history books is to make a profound break with the conventional wisdom of your time and bring enough other people with you to assure the acceptance of your break.

Religious leaders? Pope John Paul II might as well move to Avignon. His failure to come up with the accommodations needed to have a creditable voice for commenting on science won't give him favoured status with doctoral candidates as a thesis topic.

We might think about our future historians at least enough to wish them well, because they are losing some of their most important tools. Due to the acidic content of paper used to publish most books of the last 150 years, volumes that were so carefully archived are rotting away, being eaten by mice, or used for home building purposes by rats and birds. Only in the past few years has archival quality paper been available, while few libraries have built atmospherically controlled archives.

When Alexander Graham Bell invented the telephone he came close to destroying the art of letter writing. Samuel Morse didn't do the language much good, as people tried to send a message for the least possible cost with the result that various truncated and imprecise linguistic structures became widely accepted. Despite the advent of computerized communications systems like the Internet, we still don't write letters. And if we did, where would they be stored? Just how long will laser print or ink jet remain legible? Letters only get passed down through generations, usually as family curios, until a historian hears about them. The idea of depositing personal "papers" with a library or university is only available to the great and the wealthy, not unlike their peers of 500 years ago who might pay big bucks to be included in a painting of the Last Supper. Usually they appeared as an apostle, although one enterprising Milanese banker who wished to demonstrate his piety and humility had himself painted into a picture washing Christ's feet. But what shape will magnetic storage be in five centuries from now?

One becomes fearful that in a time when we, the residents of this period, are stifled by our information overload, those who would record and evaluate us and our times will be working with a paucity of raw data. Maybe they will decide that the world was so decimated by World War I, the influenza epidemic of 1916-1919, or AIDS, that we lost the ability to write until the 21st century was underway.

There is a final caveat. As we saw in the Renaissance, living systems, whether governments, churches, or academies, make serious efforts to defend themselves, just as other organisms do. This is not necessarily a bad thing.

It means that when they do get overthrown, the force which overthrows them is likely to have been overwhelming and leaves little doubt of the necessity of tossing the former established order out. Also, these established orders usually have the police, death squads, inquisitorial legal systems, the army, and all the resources (stakes, gibbets, et cetera) of state terrorism.

It is important to remember that the veneer of civilization is still pretty thin among humans. That veneer of civilization is precious and we should try to preserve what we can of it in the coming years.

CHAPTER EIGHT

Mismanagement School 101: the NWO and the environment

In 1962 Rachel Carson's seminal work on environmentalism, *Silent Spring*, was published in *The New Yorker* as a special piece taking up the whole issue. *Silent Spring* was published as a book later the same year. Carson charged that the planet was being poisoned by flagrant industrial polluting practices, stating that "the right to make money at whatever cost to others is seldom challenged." Since 1962 every one of Carson's allegations has proven true.

At the time, Carson and *The New Yorker* were the target of an intimidation campaign directed by corporate America. Certainly *Time*, referring to Carson's evidence of the health hazards posed by DDT and other commonly used pesticides of the period, pulled out all the stops when it accused her of "frightening and arousing" her readers. Scientists employed by manufacturers of pesticides challenged Carson's understanding of the topic — a few questioned her intellectual capability (since she was, after all, female), while another spokesman for the scientific community attacked her right, since she was a "spinster," to express concern about unborn generations.

Time's advertising salesmen were reported to be pointing out to *New Yorker* advertisers that *Time* was "on side," while *The New Yorker* was obviously "unfriendly to the business community." Time wasn't the only publisher to use this ploy.

Advertisers put direct pressure on *The New Yorker*, but it was too late. A globe-encircling environmental movement became one of the most enduring issues of the next three decades.

In the spring of 1993 *The Journal of the National Cancer Institute*, probably the most prestigious publication in the field of oncology, reported the startling information, drawn from mortality data from public heath sources, that women with high exposure to DDT face a risk of cancer four to five times that of women with the least exposure. This means that for the past 31 years the incidence rate for breast cancer, which it is believed will affect one out of every eight to nine women in the U.S., could have been effectively minimized for about half the victims. The data had been clear and widely available, but the pesticide industry was able to avoid regulatory limitation by effective lobbying.

Throughout the Reagan years the debates over acid rain were stymied by the lobbying of the NWO's political supporters. Reagan himself insisted that there was insufficient scientific evidence as to whether acid-rain damage actually existed. This was in spite of the efforts of such state officials as the governor of New York and all the northeastern states. Acid rain, because it is airborne and crosses regional and international borders, is an issue best dealt with federally, if not continentally. When local jobs are at risk, heavily industrialized jurisdictions are often indifferent to the concerns of those downwind.

Acid rain brought on international ramifications as both private bodies and the government of Canada made the strongest possible representations to the U.S. government. The Reagan and Bush administrations stalled

---

Pollution is not something new. Classical Roman writers discussed, in lurid detail, the need for sanitation systems. Renaissance Europeans were loath to bathe and opted for perfumes as an alternative. The contents of their chamber pots were habitually thrown out of windows, to the discomfort of those on the sidewalk below.

Popular novels and social science articles of the 19th century abound with appalling descriptions of industrial pollution. The use of Galton's statistics to pinpoint the cause of a cholera outbreak in a contaminated part of London led to more serious consideration of the impacts on the health and safety of latter-day Victorian Londoners. Similarly, in the same period on the east coast of North America, the public health and industrial safety movements gained their legislated status through proofs of deleterious environmental practices.

Even back in the Renaissance, without an understanding of germ theory, it was considered wise by folks still into alchemy, to get out of town to the clean air of the countryside during Plague periods. Remember, Isaac Newton discovered his three laws of motion while spending 10 months away from Cambridge during the Great Plague.

while the industries involved tried to find cheaper clean manufacturing processes and smoke scrubbing technology.

The corporate members of the NWO fan club are caught in an uncomfortable bind. Historically, industries found that no one complained what environmental havoc they might wreak as long as they contributed to overall prosperity. Therefore ecological considerations had no place in designs for plant machinery or choosing materials for manufacturing processes.

Suddenly, from the point of view of industrial managers, a "green" consciousness seemed to sweep the Western industrial world. Initially, environmental issues were a job for the company flak-catcher to "manage" until the "tree huggers" found a new fad. A few companies have gone to the Third World, where they hoped to obtain, at least, a respite. Executives who make these kind of decisions merely demonstrate their lack of contemporary literacy. They are unaware of the global nature of the ecology movement and its ability to focus outraged protest on a single target, whether a company, an industry, or a product, making it vulnerable to boycotts, noisy demonstrations and unfavourable publicity in consuming parts of the First World.

Initially, senior executives reported getting little of this heat from the boardroom or at annual meetings. Then some political activists started making token share purchases, going to annual general meetings and asking rude questions. Next, large pension funds whose equity owners were the clergy, teachers, or health professionals came under fire. Fund managers passed on this unhappiness to corporate executives, but some mutual fund managers sniffed the wind and launched a few environmentally responsible mutual funds. To their joy they discovered that not only were individuals prepared to put their money where their mouths were, but so were a few pension fund officials.

The final wave of assaults came when someone in the supermarket industry decided that lines of eco-friendly products might be worth a few market share points. It was an idea whose time had come. Guys who run supermarkets survive by hopping on bandwagons first and "green" products began to steal market share from those with less environmentally sensitive logos. Some environmental groups were prepared to provide an encomium in return for their expert assessment of the authenticity of claims and use of the organization's label.

For those with no way to get on the eco-bandwagon, it was not a good time. To make matters worse, new environmental issues were being raised daily. The only way most of the major polluters could look good was by comparison with industrial operations in the former Soviet Union or the People's Republic of China.

As those in control of the most powerful nations on the planet, supporters of the NWO have a very big problem when it comes to environmental issues. The administration of George Bush stalled on enforcement, fought back when charged with ecological piracy of the planet, and tore the teeth from the Joint Declaration of the 1992 U.N. Environmental Summit.

THE HOLE IN THE SKY

The world was first alerted to the dangers of ozone depletion in 1974 by Professor F. Sherwood Rowland of the University of California at Irvine. He reported that a category of industrial chemicals called chlorofluorocarbons (CFCs) were being released in sufficient quantities that, by the year 2100, the atmosphere's ozone layer would undergo a 7 percent depletion.

The ozone layer absorbs ultraviolet radiation, which is dangerous to living organisms, including people. UV is part of the total radiation we get from the sun; it comes in short wavelengths that can be absorbed by human DNA. Most UV is screened out by ozone particles, but as ozone is depleted we get more and more UV radiation. The degradation of the ozone layer is caused by CFCs, which are used in refrigeration equipment, dry cleaning processes, and the electronics industry.

An initial industrial survey of CFC use by the U.S. Environmental Protection Agency discovered that the major source of CFCs was products using aerosol spray cans. In 1978, a salutary response time for any government action, the EPA banned aerosol spray cans. Spray-can moguls aren't really able to mount the kind of campaign necessary to thwart a determined U.S. government agency. From this point on, things started to go downhill.

Atmospheric scientists continued to study the phenomena, and in 1985 the world was informed that the ozone layer had developed one large hole and several small holes above Antarctica. Shortly afterward Australia and New Zealand reported a rise in the incidence of skin cancer. An Australian cosmetic maker introduced a new blocking cream, in a range of fluorescent shades, which has shown great potential as an acceptable unisex cosmetic. By the summer of 1992, we in the Northern Hemisphere were quickly learning that the shorter wavelength, UV-B, was dictating the fashion statement for the mid-'90s — long-sleeved T-shirts and slacks, not shorts. Soon we'll be right up there with the Antipodeans, checking ourselves and each other for keratosis lesions.

The 1985 report was sufficiently compelling that, at a 1987 conference in Montreal to address the issue of holes in the ozone layer, 24 nations signed an agreement, known as the Montreal Protocol, to eliminate CFCs and the other compounds, including domestic and industrial refrigerants, which have been shown to cause ozone depletion, by the year 2000. Eventually, 66 countries signed this protocol.

At the Montreal meeting some Third World countries objected that they were just about to move into a development phase where their populations could expect to have refrigeration and that the industrial world was simply trying to keep the Third World down. The data since 1987 appears to have quelled these doubts. That the research can be done by Third World scientists has been useful in securing cooperation from their governments. In fact, UV exposure may be worse in the underdeveloped countries south of the equator.

At another international meeting in London in 1990, 55 countries agreed to amend the Montreal Protocol and called for an outright withdrawal of CFCs. This London protocol permitted less-developed economies a further 10 year period to achieve the total ban.

As the global scientific community reported new research, the confirmations of Rowland's original findings were surpassed in the incremental urgency of new reports. Rowland, whose initial research had been disavowed by some industrial scientists, turned out to be Mr. Probity and the conservative rectitude with which he had couched his report made it impossible for anyone to rebuff his data. The benefits of the struggle for open and free scientific inquiry had never been so clear.

The U.S. EPA announced in 1991 that the depletion was moving twice as fast as had been projected in the original 1985 report and that there could be about 200,000 deaths from skin cancer over the next 50 years. This got people's attention. On February 3, 1992, NASA reported that a massive new ozone hole had appeared over the Northern Hemisphere. The new ozone depletion zone affects the British Isles, Scandinavia, northern Russia, the North Pole, Greenland, New England, and eastern Canada.

The then Canadian Minister of the Environment, Jean Charest, announced on February 7, 1992, that Canada would reach 85 percent of the goal set out in the Montreal Protocol by 1995. He also announced that the government would begin releasing ultraviolet radiation danger advisory bulletins, similar to weather reports. The minister said that a good rule of thumb is for everyone to "avoid the sun as much as possible, especially children aged two to 18 years old, who are very vulnerable."

Hard on the heels of Charest's announcement, the U.N. Environment Program reported that the increase in UV-B radiation coming through the ozone-depleted atmosphere would cause an escalation in the effects of a wide range of infectious and viral diseases, including AIDS and the herpes simplex viruses.

Interestingly, the report was released without consultation with member governments, whose health and environment officials, when contacted for comment by the press, were careful to emphasize that while they had not seen the report, they felt the U.N.E.P. was a completely credible source. Even usually well-informed environmental lobbyists were surprised.

The latest word from this front is that a vibrant black market in CFCs has developed. The Montreal accord assumes that the nation-state signatories will police their own national CFC manufacturers. This has not proven to be the case and now there is a muted hue and cry for amending the Montreal accord to give it some oversight teeth, as in the nuclear weaponry agreements.

The major sources for black market CFCs are the U.S.A., Russia, and India. The principal sources of enabling end-use certificates are various Caribbean states and countries in southeast Asia, where civil services are up for rent. The actual principal end-users are the U.S.A. and China.

A query to a senior Canadian RCMP officer as to the likelihood of actual enforcement of the Montreal agreement gets a less than sanguine response. This officer points out that enforcement of international treaties is not something any police force in the world looks forward to because it is an administrative jungle.

To begin with, give up any hope of getting much help from the local uniformed general-duty police. You will have to set up a special squad and begin by teaching them how to spell chlorofluorocarbon. Identification of CFCs poses a significant problem and the international character of the crime is a multi-jurisdictional nightmare, similar to the narcotics and nuclear crime trails.

After the 1985 reports about ozone holes and skin cancer, there was the expected creative corporate lobbying for exemptions. But as the scientific evidence mounted, the lobbyists found themselves increasingly exposed and isolated.

One transnational corporation, the communications firm Northern Telecom, decided in 1989, without any PR hoopla, to try for zero tolerance of CFCs, which were used to clean the soldered connections that attach computer chips to their boards. Northern Telecom appointed a vice-president responsible for environmental issues, Margaret Kerr, and, despite reservations by many at the company about the technical feasibility of the project, set a goal of three years to complete it.

Kerr directed a research program that sought a way to eliminate CFCs completely without significant impact on product cost or quality. Northern Telecom established a computer bulletin board, OZONET, to share its findings with other transnational corporations and governments. The results are impressive. By reaching its goal early, 9,000 tonnes of CFCs didn't get into the atmosphere — and the company saved $50 million.

As if life were not difficult enough for exemption-seeking lobbyists. It's always difficult when you're trying to avoid legislative restrictions to have someone like Northern Telecom beat the deadline and do it so well.

From a police administration point of view, there is so much money at stake that the probability of police corruption is right up there with the cocaine cartels. This inherent potential for corruption will make any police chief on the planet pause before accepting a mandate to get into this new area.

METHANE AND OTHER HOT AIR

In 1975, *Science*, the journal of the American Association for the Advancement of Science, published a paper by climatologist Wallace Broeker, who warned of impending massive global warming owing to a build-up of "greenhouse gases" like methane and the carbon dioxide created by burning fossil fuels.

When a scientist reports something, two questions are asked by other scientists. One is, does the report predict *accurately* future events of the phenomena under study? The other is, can the scientist's work be replicated by other investigators?

Broeker's 1975 *Science* paper has proven highly accurate in its forecast of global temperature variations. Today, it is difficult to find a climatologist who would question his findings. Scientists worldwide agree that the Greenhouse Effect will happen.

Even if we do everything possible to inhibit greenhouse gases, they are still expected to produce a warming of the Earth. Such a warming effect will have a brutal effect on forests and wildlife. Present projections by the International Panel on Climate and Change (IPCC) say that by 2035 the warming effect will have reached one full degree centigrade above present levels and thereafter we may expect a rise of three degrees centigrade per decade.

Of course there is, as Wall Streeters say, a contrarian view. Richard Lindzen is the Alfred P. Sloan Professor of Meteorology at the Massachusetts Institute of Technology. He came to MIT from Harvard and has credentials as strong as any academic you might care to find. He disagrees with the conventional wisdom. Lindzen doesn't believe that humans are causing the planet to heat up.

Obviously, the major carbon fuel producers and consumers and their political allies find in Professor Lindzen a ray of sunshine in an otherwise bleak world.

Lindzen was originally trained in physics and applied mathematics, which led him into fluid mechanics. From fluid mechanics he began studying the atmosphere and oceans. He says that the global warming models all have the same quality, which is that "none of the models have the physics or numerical accuracy to handle the problem."

He continues: "It sounds like a technical detail. It may sound arcane. But I think most people don't understand that the large warming scenarios all depend on that sort of weakness." Lindzen's view is that any warming will dry out the upper troposphere, the layer of air six to 16 kilometres (four to 10 miles) above the Earth. Lindzen believes that this will stop the warming in its tracks.

But isn't the troposphere where the ozone holes are popping up? Who to believe?

The director of the Centre for Science, Technology and the News, Mark Mills, while not siding with Lindzen, claims that the media deals unfairly with Lindzen when they deal with him at all. Usually he is simply ignored. Mills points out that there is a wide range of support for specifics of Lindzen's assertions among atmospheric scientists.

However, when all the evidence is collected, a compellingly large body of scientific wisdom is solidly behind the global warming hypothesis. That didn't prevent the carbon fuels industry (oil and coal) and the Bush administration from citing Lindzen frequently in their releases on the topic.

Those who argue against the global warming thesis are singularly lacking in both clean hands and a probable theory to support their argument. It remains a good bet to assume lowland flooding and things getting warmer.

The Maldive Islands are a former British protectorate, now independent, in the Indian Ocean. They are sinking. Think about moving everyone out of all the cities which were once principally ports, such as New York, London, Shanghai, and Tokyo.

There is no quick tech fix for either ozone depletion or global warming. We have now learned how fragile the environment has become. When the environment has been put at risk for prolonged periods it can suddenly "go critical" in an irreparable way.

In the summer of 1995, the ozone hole over Antarctica became the size of Europe. There was a significant shift in the reproduction patterns of a host of bugs, such as wasps and cockroaches. It was a summer in which death from health-related causes (primarily among the elderly) in Chicago hit epidemic proportions rivalling spots like New Delhi (until we learned that the Indian government does not collect such medical statistics among the poor).

In France, the cops banned cars from the centre of Paris to prevent the city's outdoor cafe customers from dropping off their seats and raising unpleasant speculation about the coffee. Other northern European cities instituted similar protective measures. In Britain, dogs and cats from the most genteel homes found themselves infested with fleas as the flea population found itself with extra time to breed. Animals without sweat glands or who are otherwise less evolutionarily prepared for weather that requires serious temperature controls were in trouble. Pigs, who fall into this group, found that the wells and boreholes they normally used to shower down had dried up. Finally, the Ministry of Agriculture offered the helpful suggestion that farmers might be well advised to put suntan lotion on their pigs.

The corporate elite's spinners, who had fought the good fight against the idea that atmospheric ozone shredding was real and managed to convince the Reagan and Bush administrations to do nothing without further long-term studies, left their bosses with egg on their faces — which has not been recommended for its UV-B protection qualities.

GERMANY CLEANS UP

The environment is not the strong point of the NWO fan club in North America, its home base. Its geriatric corporate and political supporters are uncomfortable with the issues. This does not bode well for the NWO.

All too often the NWO has a conflict of interest on environmental issues because its supporters are often the problem. Taking away a business will seldom please the owner. But the Greenhouse Effect will be a big enough problem. Anyone who complains about business losses due to environmentalists whining about emissions of greenhouse gases should get into the business of making sunblock or treating skin cancer, both of which appear to be great growth industries and are also probably recession proof.

In simple terms, the global warming process is for real. As the data unfold, it appears that the changes in the next two decades will be abrupt

---

In February 1992, Britain's prestigious magazine The Economist reported that Lawrence Summers, then the chief economist of the World Bank, had written a memo asking whether "the World Bank should encourage more migrations of the dirty industries to less-developed nations." The World Bank's Washington headquarters quickly released a statement that "Mr. Summers deeply regrets the obvious misunderstanding his memo has caused and apologizes for any misconceptions it may have generated." The bank PR hack went on to suggest that Summers had intended his memo to provoke debate and sharpen the analysis in a forthcoming World Bank report on the prospects for the global economy.

The Economist quoted Summers as writing: "I think the economic logic behind dumping a load of toxic waste in the lowest-wage country is impeccable and we should face up to that." He added that, after all, "The demand for a clean environment for esthetic and health reasons rises with income."

It would seem that like all great satirists Summers (now deputy secretary of the U.S. Department of the Treasury) was hoisted on his own petard. Perhaps Summers should have found a venue with a less literal-minded readership than the internal memo readers and leakers of the World Bank.

and drastic. The American administration will have to exert some of its single world power status to organize the necessary global measures. For now, Germany, the force driving the E.U., has become the international leader in environmental matters.

Germany has managed to set up environmental regulatory conditions — with which German industry has complied. (Of course, if the United States had inherited the environmental cesspool that came with East Germany, environmental concerns might be a bit easier to sell.) Former West German cities have banned the cars made in East Germany because of the smoke and noxious fumes they emitted. Factories in the former East German territories are such ecological disaster zones that they have been bulldozed and completely rebuilt.

On January 20, 1992, Reuters reported that Europe's largest garbage sorting plant, at Kerpen, processes 100,000 tonnes of municipal waste annually. The plant is discretely placed behind a screen of trees and emits no noxious odours. Of the 100,000 tonnes of waste handled each year, 60,000 tonnes are recovered for reuse. Trinekens Entsorgung, the company that manages the plant, expects to build between 20 and 25 more in the next few years.

In an even more interesting move on environmental issues, the Reuters report tells of the regulations designed to cut into the amount of packaging materials, which are responsible for about one-third of the 40 million tonnes of garbage Germany produces annually. Under these packaging control rules companies must take back packaging after using it to ship goods. For example, Japanese and Taiwanese electronics manufacturers must recover the plastic foam and cardboard cartons that they ship to Germany with their products. They have to take the waste back or find someone who will dispose of it for them — at a price.

Two of corporate Germany's giants, Bayer and Wella, collaborated on a joint-venture recycling system — Duales System Deutschland — that provides consumers with colour-coded bins for packaging. These are emptied every four weeks without charge to consumers or government. Aside from collecting in separate bins brown, green, and clear glass bottles, Duales also picks up paper.

Duales has its headquarters in Bonn. Bonn is a university and government city and Duales is sensitive to how bureaucratic thinking works. A spokesman for Germany's Environment Ministry has said: "We expect the regulations will change the market in due course. It only makes sense that packages which can be recycled easily will show up in improved profit margins."

Initially worried that the regulations would function as an impediment to the E.U.'s free trade premise, European trade bureaucrats and

Germany's own federal Cartel Office approved the regulations with the proviso that any producer could join the recycling effort. Critics realize that Bayer and Wella probably made a profit off the top from that order.

The environment ministry said that the packaging recycling operation was seen as a pilot program, adding that regulations governing printed matter, electronics, and cars would follow shortly. The rest of the E.U. had no choice but to fall into line.

Wait a minute. Cars? Back to another Reuters dispatch. All of the German car makers — BMW, Daimler-Benz, and Volkswagen — claim they are 95 percent confident that by the year 2000 they will have a car that is 100 percent recyclable. North American manufacturers must ship into the E.U. Doesn't it seem likely that, if these companies are nicer about their garbage over there than they are at home, some young Ralph Nader is going to start saying rude things about them? Much of North America's goods are already flogged in European-designed packages. Check the patent on your juice or milk carton, or a package for over-the-counter drugs.

Europeans have, for years, concentrated on an engineering approach to package development, while in North America packaging designers tend to come from art schools. The problems related to recycling are well within the professional skill-base of an engineer. An artist, on the other hand, may

---

All is not completely wonderful in the bigger, better, reunited Germany. In the former East Germany they made a people's car of their own, called the Trabant. These cars were an excremental blot on the environmentalist's landscape. They were known for the clouds of filthy, black smoke excreted from their (usually) leaking exhaust pipes. When East met West two problems arose around the Trabant Werks.

The first was the ecological disaster of the factory itself. It was discovered that bringing the plant into compliance with German safety and environmental regulations would cost 60 percent more than it would cost to level the place and build anew. Volkswagen, which had been lucky enough to win the bid for the company, had no problem deciding that one.

Volkswagen's other problem was what to do with the junkyards all over the former DDR filled with Trabants. The car was made of a plastic called duroplastic which cannot be recycled or safely burned. With typical Germanic zeal, a neighbourhood genetic engineer offered to brew up a specialty microbe which would eat the disgusting Trabants and then die from starvation when all had been gobbled up. The price for this: $990,000. Does this mass assassination of microbes by starvation give animal rights activists a headache?

become unhinged if you harass him or her with questions about the atomic weight of the particles of yucky stuff in the smoke from the burning packages.

Speaking of yucky smoke, there's good news and bad news which speaks to the complexity of responding to things environmental. Jack Miller, a science journalist, has reported that, for the past 250 years, UV radiation has been screened by a component of industrial coal smoke.

The ingredient is aerosols of sulphur (little particles of sulphur) which comes from sulphur dioxide, the major contaminant of smoke produced by coal and coke burning industry and the main cause of acid rain. The best way to measure this stuff is to estimate how far you can see. Data on this goes back to the beginnings of the Industrial Revolution, when people first noticed the pall hanging over them. So the smoke has been protecting us from UV — which is dangerous stuff.

As Shakespeare said, "There's the rub." We are cleaning up this smoke.

SMOKERS AND SMOKESTACKS

A few years ago the idea that a significant portion of the world's smokers might be convinced that they should give up smoking would have been considered ludicrous. After all, the tobacco industry was very rich and powerful, while its products were among the most addicting substances available.

Then along came Dr. C. Everett Koop, surgeon general of the United States. Koop was a devout Republican, a devout free enterprise fan, a devout Christian, a solid member of the American Medical Association and an honest pediatrician who cared about "his kids," as any pediatrician must. (Otherwise parents make the job a really hard way to make a living.) When Richard Nixon appointed him to the surgeon general post he was initially seen as an insignificant political appointee — the kind of party hack who wouldn't rock any boats.

One day, Koop was given the results of an epidemiological study on the correlations between smoking and a list of illnesses including cancer, bronchial diseases, fetal injury, ill effects on pregnancy, and heart disease. The study's authors suggested that there seemed to be some repulsive outcomes from something called second-hand smoke. The data weren't all that good on the second-hand smoking, but there was no doubt whatsoever about the figures for smokers.

Koop read the report and was outraged. His officials thought a little anti-smoking campaign would get their boss off their backs. After all, they reasoned, who could take on folks like Philip Morris, British American Tobacco, R.J. Reynolds, the mayor of Durham, N.C., the governor of North Carolina, the mayor of Richmond, Va., the governor of Virginia, the secretary of the Treasury of the United States, the Vending Machine Operators of America, and assorted interstate tobacco smugglers?

Even the tobacco industry didn't get upset until Koop's anti-smoking campaign was well under way. Koop released the research findings under the title *The U.S. Surgeon General's Report on the Effects of Smoking*. Graduate students studying statistics when the report was released found themselves running the data from the study and corroborating the findings.

The tobacco companies were banned from television advertising. Then they started to fight back and Koop went public. No one could doubt the integrity of the kids' doctor whose outrage and appearance resembled biblical images of a patriarchal Moses returning from his conversation with the burning bush to find an orgy going on back at camp.

No one could stand up to Koop's sustained offensive. He brought his personal integrity to support the power of his office. And no one could criticize either the data or the findings of the report.

The second-hand smoking data weren't all that clear and the methodology was less than elegant, but Koop had ordered all tobacco product advertising to be labelled with a health warning. Signs in workplaces saying "Thank you for not smoking" proliferated, as did smokers' rights groups.

Social-political activists with skills honed in the civil-rights and anti-war movements of the 1960s began to institute workplace lawsuits and the signs became more strident. Now they read "This is a smoke-free workplace." Hospitals began to ban smoking. The TV newsmagazine show *60 Minutes* discovered that all the early Marlboro Men had died from cancer except one and he had it, as he stated between wracking coughs for the *60 Minutes* crew.

Prominent figures closely identified with smoking, such as Edward R. Murrow, died from cancer. Yul Brynner, star of *The King and I*, did an anti-smoking TV commercial while he was dying and instructed that the tape be released after his death. The tobacco industry was driven to trying to claim that its freedom of speech was impaired, since it was barred from television. Hospitals enforced their ban on smoking and today when we drive past a hospital we often see patients and staff standing outside in medical uniforms, pajamas, and robes smoking, further emphasizing the irrationality of their action. Municipalities have developed boilerplate bylaws banning smoking in public places.

Koop even started his own foreign policy. In the Orient he got nowhere. The government of France found him droll for believing that it would fall for his ploy to "take over French markets for the American tobacco industry." After all, in the former French colonies of the francophonie, Gauloises and Gitanes are sold with old American TV shows in which the actors all smoke heavily. A cigarette salesman shows up with a truck, movie projector, and screen to an African village and dispenses handfuls of samples of his brand. The French marketing geniuses have been gratified to report to Paris market growth where no one had ever smoked before.

Koop's international campaign did have some positive results. In Canada, the former minister of health and welfare, John Munro, was well-known as a four-pack-a-day smoker. One day he got up in the House of Commons and announced that he was so convinced of the deleterious effects on health, as reported by the U.S. surgeon general, that he was giving up smoking right then. His conversion only lasted a few hours, to the discomfort of his aides, who then had to keep an open package of his brand on hand for the next few weeks, until he finally started carrying his own four packs a day again. Munro has since managed to give up smoking completely and his successors (regardless of party) have found it politically possible to run much more aggressive attacks on tobacco product use than has happened in the U.S. For example, the warning message on Canadian cigarette packages is very large and noticeable, with messages that are disease-risk specific.

Until recently, Canadian taxes on tobacco products were raised with each budget. The tax bite in Ontario, for example, was $4.34 per package with the provincial and federal governments splitting the take. In the 1990s the high taxation policy resulted in a major tax revolt, the first such action in living Canadian memory. This grassroots tax rebellion was based on the fact that Native Canadians and Americans have the legal right to import goods and services from one country to the other without paying duty. They proceeded to do so with cigarettes and to a lesser degree alcoholic beverages. The contraband was shipped by the truck-load to border and inland reserves. From there it was shipped into towns and cities more informally. Law enforcement officials grew concerned as the trade took on a return to the 1920s, with guns and all of the corrupting influences that came with prohibition.

All of this came about with the country in the throes of a recession, the worst since the 1930s. At first the smuggling was limited to American brands, but when the American cigarettes began to take serious market share from the Canadian manufacturers, the Canadian tobacco companies were placed in the ludicrous position of having to export their products to U.S. wholesalers so that they could be shipped back into Canada by the Indians and resold by convenience stores and unemployed students with knapsacks.

Even more upsetting were polls showing that one of the reasons that people gave for support of the illicit market was that it was seen as a blow against the Mulroney government. According to the pollsters, respondents would gratuitously point out that it was just another form of free trade and if they were losing their jobs because of free trade then it was only fair that the Conservatives should feel some pain also.

Governments saw revenue dwindle to the point that budgets were being hastily rewritten and eventually they caved in. The next federal government essentially abandoned cigarettes as a revenue base.

AFTER TOBACCO, WHO'S NEXT?

The anti-tobacco campaign may turn out to have been only a pilot, a trial-run for a bigger issue.

The U.N.'s International Panel on Climate Change has no doubt about the build-up of greenhouse gases assuring a devastating environmental collapse. To do as much as possible to avert the damage which is now imminent, first from the warming effect and then from the mini-ice age which has historically followed warming cycles, it is essential to secure a reduction of 20 percent in the worldwide emissions of carbon dioxide, CFCs, methane, and nitrogen oxide. No one is calling for more research.

Any effective reduction plan must start with higher taxes, much higher taxes, much-much higher taxes, for coal, oil, gasoline, and natural gas. The argument goes that such a tax should be based on an assessment of the carbon content of the fossil fuel involved. The coal used in electrical generation would, for example, have the heaviest tax, followed by oil, gasoline, and then natural gas.

The Organization for Economic Cooperation and Development has a report from two economists, Peter Hoeller and Markku Wallin, which shows that taxes on gasoline already act as a sort of carbon tax, but no industrialized country assesses coal or natural gas. The OECD report concludes that a carbon tax applied to all fossil fuels could reduce carbon dioxide emissions by OECD member countries by around 25 percent.

Among fans of country and western music there is a bumper sticker/hat/T-shirt which enjoys great popularity. It says "Don't mess with Texas." As in the case of the tobacco companies, the fossil fuel-based companies have powerful friends. They will be able to point to job losses and reduced income tax revenues should such a program be set up.

The auto industry, the coal and oil lobby's primary ally in the coming battle over carbon taxes, are ready to jump ship. All the automotive companies have major alternative fuel programs nearly ready to kick in. Marine and aircraft engine makers have similar plans. There is a hydrogen-fuelled engine which has been tested and shown internationally.

The oil and gas industry has targeted its American political allies and will be counting on them. The external pressures on Bill Clinton and others will be massively intimidating. But remember second-hand smoke — that's the one which turned the moral pressure on the smokers and made it impossible to hide.

Greenpeace, the toughest of the environmental groups, has just entered this particular fray. Founded in Canada, Greenpeace is as North American as it gets and shares the North American distrust of established authority. It has always prided itself on its willingness to define the edge for its foes. Greenpeace has decided to take a leaf from the anti-tobacco gang's book of tactics. You can now buy a Greenpeace bumper sticker that simulates the health warnings on cigarette packages. It says:

"WARNING: This vehicle emits Carbon Dioxide, Carbon Monoxide, Nitrogen Oxides, Sulphur Dioxide, Hydrocarbons Benzene, Methane, Aldehydes, and VOCs. Causes respiratory diseases and cancer. ESPE-CIALLY HARMFUL TO CHILDREN."

Notice the similarities in the campaigns. The U.N. for credibility. The super scientists for authenticity. And the edge-defining Greenpeace for the shock troops. The coal and petroleum companies have no capabilities to deal with what's coming.

CHAPTER NINE

Lost in Cyberspace: Language, race, and religion on the edge

One of the arguments central to this book is that history is useful in surviving an era transition and even doing well as the new era unfolds. However, history is only of use as a guide. It only lets you know that there is directionality out there, regardless of the apparent chaos. While it is true that those who fail to learn from history are doomed to repeat the lessons, we also know that history on its outer edges never repeats itself, except in macro terms. In other words, the guidelines we can identify are non-specific.

Some of these guidelines are:
- Era transitions precipitate a variety of political collapses.
- They bring a high rate of technological innovation.
- They result in a breakdown of historical authority.
- The hierarchy of social values with which we order our lives gets shuffled.
- Currencies disappear or undergo major devaluations.
- Wars are fought over issues which did not exist 50 years before or which have their roots 1,000 years before.
- True belief groups (religious, economic, ideological, mythic) emerge offering increasingly anachronistic refuges from the change rate.

Marshall McLuhan was right when he said "the medium is the message." McLuhan was just applying Heisenberg's uncertainty principle to information: the medium (e-mail, book, TV, newspaper, film, radio, music, art, play, painting, photograph, et cetera) used to communicate information will colour the message with the inherent strengths, biases, and limitations of the medium. It is easy to forget that language is a medium, too.

We in Renaissance 2.0 share one big advantage with our predecessors in Renaissance 1.0. We have a universal language of exchange, a *lingua franca*. In Renaissance 1.0 the language of universal access was Latin, which was spectacularly unsuited to facilitating a new era. It was the language of the established order and was used to differentiate the intellectually respectable and scholastically trained from the lower orders.

The Humanist cadres of the Renaissance opted to communicate in the local vernaculars — Italian, French, English, et cetera Unfortunately for those who wanted to retain Latin, when the era-shift got under way the printing press and vernacular translations made the new knowledge immediately and widely available. Censorship became difficult.

The vernaculars of the newly emerged nation states were key tools in communicating the vulnerabilities of the waning world-view. Because they used vernacular instead of Latin, participants in the new era were drawn from all walks of life. Not only was involvement more socially extended, but easier knowledge and technology transfers made discoveries and inventions more widely available.

The debate over Latin versus vernacular came about because the crackers who guarded the Church and Empire's exclusive access to truth and knowledge used Latin to maintain their elite status. In the same way, the Aztecs hid their mathematics from non-priests. In Renaissance 1.0, the Humanists needed the political support of the masses to pull off their reforms and used the vernacular to distribute the information that enabled the public to take part in the era shift. It's usually easier to make people literate in their native tongue.

In our time, we also have a universal language — English. For us in North America, this is an amazing stroke of luck. It happened because the roots of the era shift were largely initiated by native German speakers who emigrated to the anglophone world. The discoveries of these German scientists were disseminated through the English language-based scientific and engineering communities, which contributed significantly to the winning of a big war.

We're fortunate in North America that we don't have to translate what a bunch of foreigners are on about. In Renaissance 1.0, there was a strong impetus for the non-Latin speaking community to translate discoveries and innovations into the local vernacular. For us, there is no translation downtime and we whose native language is English have, by and large, an unexcelled window of opportunity on information about potential commercial and cultural implementations of our new era.

Leaders at the ledge of the edge seldom see a benefit in translating their discoveries, which becomes a major activity in me-too parts of the globe. So desperate is the rest of the world for an early fix on knowledge transfers that a lot of our academic research is first reported in Dutch, Japanese, Swiss, British, or German publications. Many of these journals will publish in the author's native language when that language is English, as well as the language of the originating journal. How do we feel about that? Interestingly, such foreign publication is seen as providing special kudos for academics when tenure or promotion is being considered.

EN FRANCAIS, S'IL VOUS PLAIT

The French view is that the French language articulates the highest achievements of European esthetic and intellectual gymnastics. To the French, their culture was the beacon that preserved Europe from the cultural calamity of being overrun by various Germanic tribes during the Dark Ages. The mistake of the *Academie Française* is its identity is all wrapped up in being the guardian of this beacon.

Its attempts to protect the language from external pollution show the French civil service is sadly misinformed about the way living languages grow and influence others. For all their labours, words like "hot dog," "jumbo jet" and the ubiquitous "parking" continue to infiltrate the lan-

---

One easy way to see what the change rate looks like is to look at changes in your own language. First take a list of words which were not commonly used 15 to 20 years ago and that are in common usage today — like dweeb, wuss, meme, condom, homophobic, technophobic. Then see how many the spell-checker on your word processor will recognize.

Next, make another list of words that are combinations of words which any spell-checker will accept. Contemporary usage has led to the merged version, whose meaning differs slightly from the original two words: timeline, cyberpunk, timeframe, marketshare, spreadsheet, database, hardliners, rulebook, stakeholders, dysfunctional — or newer ones like digerati (the digitized version of the literati) and cosmeceuticals (pharmaceutical industry products containing drugs which are used as skin anti-wrinkle agents and sometimes require prescriptions).

Spell-checkers are usually constructed with very sophisticated algorithms. Think about the daunting problems you would face in making a spell-checker for Chinese, Japanese, or other non-alphabetic languages. This lack of office automation capacity could create competition problems. If your language — or some other salient feature of your culture — is not amenable to being incorporated into contemporary technology, you will end up with some tough choices.

Both Japanese and Chinese have been converted into artificial, westernized script languages. The alternative is to reject the technology, which is economically impossible. So you end up tacking a "borrowed" culture onto your own. The French have tried to keep "borrowed" words out of their language by using the Academie Française to rule on the cultural legitimacy of new words — or to create authorized new ones.

guage. As to why the members of the *Academie Française* have gone along with this dubious venture for so long, one can only assume that some sort of virus has attacked their usually powerful logic circuits. In the matter of language the French seem to be quite mad.

Recently the French have been going through an upscale apartment rental scandal that offers some comic relief to concerns about linguistic purity. It seems that France's chronic housing shortage is aggravated by the fact that a lot of posh apartments are privately owned by public bodies and rented out at artificially low rates. The only way to get one of these desirable *domaines privés* is to belong to one of the elites of France, like nuclear bomb makers, politicians, literary trendists, bankers, or fashion panderers. These and similar groups set up private "public" housing venues to which only members of the group may apply.

Once identified as a member of what impudent French journalists have taken to calling France's *keiretsus*, you become eligible for a lease in a *domaine privé* at a price that is less than impactful on your disposable income. Needless to say, there is vicious competition to get your Gallic snout into this trough.

Some French media stylists were saddened and shocked when former prime minister Alain Juppé, who aspired to being thought of as literary person, was found to be living in a domaine *privé* owned by the city of Paris, as were his ex-wife, his son, and his daughter. To the literary persons

---

In April of 1997, Julia Preston of The New York Times found herself in Zacatecas, Mexico, where President Ernesto Zedillo had invited King Juan Carlos of Spain to join him in opening the First International Congress on the Spanish Language.

The briefing is fairly simple: after Pope Alexander VI divided the new lands of the Americas and the East between Spain and Portugal, Spanish (or rather Castilian as it was then known) became the meme for amusing the natives with Spanish culture.

When Mexico's president came up with the congress scheme he was rather tactlessly announcing that, with the world's largest Spanish speaking population, Mexico claimed sovereignty over the language. Linguistically, Spaniards constitute about 10 percent of the 400 million people in the world who speak Spanish as their first language.

It's surprising that Spain's prime minister had not advised Juan Carlos to send his regrets. Madrid is home to a Royal Academy of Language that publishes a dictionary for the purpose of dissing words originating in Latin America or other uncouth philological points of the compass. (Possibly Spain's prime minister was

of the French gutter press, the Juppé clan's troughing cried out for exposure.

Most French word borrowing is from English. But now the *Academie Française* is confronted with *keiretsu*, a Japanese word used to describe the bottom-feeders of Japanese industry, who are ordinarily suppliers to the giants of Japan Inc. Large Japanese corporations usually own a significant part of keiretsus, although they frequently deny such ownership on the grounds that to admit owning assets like most *keiretsus* would cause someone, not just to lose face, but to have their face slither off completely in the middle of the Ginza.

The *keiretsu* concept has the connotation of the parasitical and completely non-independent world-view held by everyone working at such companies. Everyone there scrambles aggressively to retain some recognition of being necessary, right up there with tanners of animal hides and honey wagoneers. "Necessary" is the right word. "Essential" would indicate a lack of humility, which is just about the worst sin possible for a *keiretsu*'s CEO.

While the "K" word is obscure for most French speakers, its very obscurity makes it deliciously elitist. It has been taken up with a vengeance by French media word-wankers to describe the elitist groups. *Keiretsu* was being used as a term of derision, and not just in Paris. It was picked up by daily press and broadcast journalists in both Lyon and Bordeaux, hardly hot spots for trend-watching.

---

sending his king into a lion pit.)

On the third day of the festivities the Royal Academy sent a letter proclaiming its displeasure at not being invited. Preston discovered that when the Academy had issued the latest version of the authoritative dictionary in 1992, it had added about 600 words submitted by Mexico's academics. At the congress, Mexican scholars produced a 561-page list of 69,566 words. In the past the Royal Academy had described as unacceptable "Mexicanisms" such words as chocolate, chili, and tequila.

With three of the world's living Nobel literature laureates writing in Spanish and most of the best Castilian writing coming from Latin America, the obvious scenarios unfolded. Nobelist Gabriel Garcia Marquez spoke about language propagation, reporting that in Ecuador there are 105 words for male genitalia.

The straw that bent most in the winds of change came when the token and only Nobel laureate from Spain said: "The educated men of the 21st century have to be on the alert so that Spanish does not cease to be our common language."

"The educated men?" Not even the Japanese would make that kind of an international faux pas in the 1990s.

All of which tells us everything we want to know about the unlikelihood of the French language having any significance in the real new world order's emerging culture, regardless of the paranoia of members of the *Academie Française* keiretsu.

PANDERING TO THE PANDA

Whoever is in charge of things like linguistic purity in the People's Republic of China follows a view that has been central to Chinese governance for the past 4,500 or so years. To the Chinese, it is all very simple: the superiority of the Middle Kingdom is patently obvious to anyone with an intact central nervous system. This includes the thesis that the Middle Kingdom is the centre of the earth and the earth is the centre of the universe. (Galileo might say, "Eppur, si muove.") The Confucian mind holds that the Chinese culture is innately superior and anything outside the Middle Kingdom is uncultivated and inhabited by barbarians.

China's population is prepared to flex its linguistic muscle. The chauvinism that is so architecturally essential to the culture does, however, accept the need to translate Chinese terms into romance languages.

There are two systems of translation. The first is known as Wade-Giles, after the two committee heads charged with creating a system by which Chinese characters could be expressed in the Roman alphabet. The trouble with Wade-Giles is that it set out a rule structure that permitted simple translations to serve the commercial requirements. It tends to be more accommodating to English and was less congenial to the use by Chinese of sounds not used in Romance tongues.

The second system, *pinyin*, is more congenial to the original Chinese. It was invented in the 1970s in Beijing by a group of Chinese bureaucrats, scholars who had recovered from the depredations of the Red Guard movement, and a motley crew of expatriate/defector communists living in the Foreign Friends Compound of Beijing and who worked at the Foreign Language Publishing Institute as translators. As the handover of Hong Kong by the British on July 1, 1997, came closer, *pinyin* became the official choice.

Hong Kong is a Wade-Giles rendering of a Chinese character that means "fragrant harbour" (which would make anyone who has been to Hong Kong's harbour suspect that Wade, Giles, or both were in the pay of real estate developers). But on July 1, 1997, "Hong Kong" datelines were supposed to miraculously change to "Xianggang" courtesy of an edict from Beijing's (formerly Peking's) *pinyin* council. Similarly, Canton has become Guanchou and Macao is now Macau Aomen. Nanking, which gained fame as the World War II capital of Nationalist China and the site of bad romantic movies about Flying Tiger pilots, is now Nanjing, while Chungking has turned into Chongqing. Sinkiang, where China's border abuts on

Kazakhstan, is now known as Xinjiang — which looks a lot like the new spelling for Hong Kong, but doesn't sound remotely like it. Your local Szechwan restaurant had better rename itself Sichuan if it aspires to gourmet correctness.

Neither *pinyin* nor Wade-Giles has any capacity to change in relation to the development by the target Romance languages to describe technology or linguistic evolutions. Both are merely phonetic caricatures of vibrant languages. How can the Chinese bureaucracy impose its stylistic will on the commercial and technical language? The answer is they can't, but they can define the rules for translators.

There is no domestic political risk for the Chinese. China will notice no difference since no Chinese terms have changed. The number of foreigners trying to pronounce Chinese terms is not a problem for the ordinary Chinese person. Any foreign journalist who persists in datelining dispatches in the old way will get a chance to meet a censor from the Bureau of Public Affairs. (Any translator working for foreign media is an informant for the Bureau.)

The Bank of China will maintain its cachet of putting customers' surnames before given names because that is the way its internal forms work. That's how Jackie Chan's cheques are imprinted. Don't forget, the Bank of China has been demonstrating good taste to the West since its Hong Kong (sorry, Xianggang) head office was sited in such a *feng shui* correct fashion that its shadow cut through the middle of the residence of the British governor like a cleaver slicing through a pork rib.

THE DUTCH DEFENCE

The Dutch, whom we might expect to be more anxious about their language being overrun — given their geographic limits and smaller population — have a very different take on linguistic purity.

Dutch had an infusion of French-borrowed words in the 17th century and in the 18th century it absorbed many German terms, both through mass culture. (Significantly, the Dutch language has limited borrowings from Spanish, even though the Netherlands were technically Spanish territory until 1648.)

Now, just as the French and Chinese complain about, the Dutch language is being influenced by the mass culture of American English at the end of the 20th century. The French and Chinese view is that mass culture is vulgar, brash, and superficial. The Dutch say: that's right! Mass culture is vulgar, brash and superficial. It is also vital, exciting, and inspirational.

The Dutch contend, based on their previous track record of borrowings from transiently dominant mass cultures, that their citizenry can be very efficient in the choices they make about which words to borrow from the mass culture that is, only incidentally, American English and global. Further, this selective adoption appears to make access to a globalized economy less stressful than it is for those who regard a vibrant mass culture from a defensive mode.

Dutch language scholars point out that the biggest borrowers of words from foreign mass culture are the young and those who work in science and technology — those who have less of a vested interest in the conventional wisdoms of Dutch cultural norms. Thus the Dutch have a culturally-evolved role for their budding scientific, cultural, and technological elites — to provide a filter for linguistic borrowings.

GATHERING THE TRIBES

In our time there are two profoundly contradictory political forces. One espouses regional, trade-centred hegemonies, which enhance the efficiencies of the supply, manufacturing, and marketing functions of transnational corporations. The other change agent in play is the movement for polit-ical independence and economic sovereignty among cultural, linguistic, religious, and/or ethnic groups.

The spear carriers for the global traders are the New World Order and the transnational corporations. The tribalists are an equally unattractive col-lection of folks whose interests have an equally low probability of success.

The tribal romantics of the 1990s can be found everywhere. They thrive in some countries that have had the misfortune to have previously been part of a larger political body which has become dysfunctional. Likewise, we have the citizens of countries that have become part of a trading bloc and have lost, in the process, a considerable degree of social independence, sovereignty, and cultural symbolism, leaving behind a lin-gering, no longer real, identity.

Even familiar recreational activities are not immune to changes in language. In chess there is a classic defence strategy known as the Dutch Defence. A variation on the Dutch Defence was brought into the game by a group of young Leningrad players, including the superstar Victor Korchnoi, in the mid-1950s. The Leningrad Defence is considered quite risky, but in the past decade some grandmasters have adopted it as playable, albeit hazardous.

Now a new question has arisen. In 1991, Leningrad, the former Tsarist capital where the Communist Revolution of 1917 was born and where the failed revolu-tion of 1905 had been attempted, has changed its name back to St. Petersburg.

Traditionalists in the Russian chess world insist that the term Leningrad Defence be retained. More radical elements, particularly chess journalists, insist on renaming it the St. Petersburg Defence. Is this the way a language changes?

Then there are those countries which are sufficiently homogeneous, religiously or ethnically, to identify the rest of the world as "unclean", "heretic", or some other "outsider" term. These countries actively search the world's arms bazaars for the cast-off nukes of the U.S.S.R. and for some industrial age corporate idiot who will cook up a witch's brew of biological or chemical weaponry. Japan was the first nation state to discover that it is possible for a small group of the psychically disposed to manufacture nerve gas and hold the nation hostage. (While priding itself on its homogeneity, Japan doesn't fit any of the other categories above and certainly needs to shop no one else's armament souks.)

Finally, there are those of similar racial or otherwise ethnic identities who have been subsumed by a majority drawn from a dissimilar ethnicity. These minority groups perceive the worldwide breakdown of historical authority as an opportunity to express anger about their diminished status relative to the majority. If nothing else, they will frequently resort to various attention-getting devices in an attempt to redress conditions of perceived discrimination. They often attempt to re-acquire lost identities by becoming involved in political causes in those lands where their ethnicity and culture prevails.

The phenomenon is global. Koreans whose parents or grandparents came to Japan as labourers during the Japanese occupation (1905-1945) of Korea, North American Afrocentrists, and Muslims in the U.K. whose parents secured British passports during the colonial period all fall into this category. The Commonwealth of Independent States is honeycombed with such groups. The Far East has a role model in the "overseas Chinese."

The residents of the ancestral homelands that provide such groups with identity are usually confused by sudden profferings of allegiance. The Chinese, who have played this game for centuries, use these groups as a beachhead for tourism and as an opportunity to encourage trade, but the cultural values to which the overseas Chinese aspire usually hearken back to some murky past.

Recently, North American daily papers carried frequent obituaries of young Serbs, Bosnians, and Croatians whose parents emigrated to North America and Australia following World War II. They were killed after returning to their family enclaves in the tribal war which has followed the collapse of Yugoslavia.

All the above manifestations of tribalism are likely to form a core of pseudo-nationalism that will be the nexus around which the economic, social and political unrest of the next hundred years will be focused.

Over the past 40 years, that child of the Cold War, national self-determination, has become an internationally respectable rallying cry. With the Cold War over, there is no conflict between superpowers to make it worth anyone's while to buy off or bribe the various freedom fighters (or fighters-in-the-cause-of-national-liberation, depending on your propaganda orientation).

There are lots of little wars in the offing. There are over 3,500 religious, ethnic, tribal, and cultural groups who aspire to nation status. If the U.N. is to take on the burden of stopping the ethnic cleansing or whatever other atrocity 3,500 ethnic leaders can dream up, the U.N. peacekeeping mandate will need pretty drastic revision.

The world's tribal groupings like to play with infantile ideas about "independence." While their seamstresses sew new national flags, their composers write toe-tapping national anthems, and their lawyers write aspiration-fulfilling constitutions, the countries sink into the kind of problems which attract the attention of UNICEF.

These places are all terribly proud and economically arrogant. Once they obtain independence, predictably, they are at the small-loans counter of the World Bank before the ink is dry on their U.N. membership certificate.

INTEGRATION AND PLURALISM

In North America, there are two theories of how best to integrate displaced ethnic groups. The United States developed the theory of the melting-pot, which was expected to heal and resolve all this alienation. To the cynic, the idea that immigrants might lose and not wish to propagate their ethnocultural heritage is reminiscent of the thinking of popes and holy Roman emperors who declared that defeated barbarian tribes would be converted *en masse* to Christianity when ordered to do so by their chiefs. Or that the mass conversions and baptisms to Christianity by missionaries might make aboriginal North Americans more trustworthy as military allies against other natives and competing European powers.

Canadians have rejected the American melting-pot model. Instead, Canada implemented a political theory known as multiculturalism to address the issues which arise when people wish to maintain the values of ethnically diverse origins.

Multiculturalism was born out of the findings of the Commission on Bilingualism and Biculturalism in the 1960s. Established by the government of Nobel laureate Lester Pearson, the commission was mandated to find a way to establish linguistic and cultural equity in a context of political fairness between francophone and anglophone Canadians.

The final report of the "Bi & Bi Commission" pleased no one except the governing Liberal Party's Quebec federalist wing, whose political sensibilities had been honed during the "quiet revolution" of the 1950s, when political thinking moved from a jesuitical church-based leadership to a secular, non-clerical but still jesuitical world-view.

The report referred to the ancestral anglophones and francophones as "two founding races" — which set the aboriginal communities to muttering that they had been around there for at least 12,000 years prior to the arrival of anyone talking in French or English.

By this time, the immigrant communities who had come to Canada following World War II were citizens, which is spelled V-O-T-I-N-G B-L-O-C-K-S. They, too, muttered something like, "What are we, chopped liver?"

The commission's report was badly flawed. It pleased neither the francophones nor the anglophones in that it failed to address the collectivist (tribalist) values of the Quebecois.

On the other hand, anglophones had internationalist (globalist) values which were founded in the British Commonwealth, where Canada had considerable clout, and the U.N., where the Canadian delegation was seen to represent a politically moderate country without territorial ambitions and frequently acted in an "interpreter" role.

The Canadian compromise, which was hacked out by politicians and senior civil servants, was a 19th century liberal rationalist compromise. They announced that Canada would henceforth be a "multicultural" nation built on the values of freedom, religious tolerance, and racial harmony, as well as peace, order, and good government. To achieve these laudable aims, a Department of Multiculturalism was established to encourage Canadians to become multicultural.

Multicultural or not, Canada has not resolved its constitutional problems, since a minimum of 40 percent of Quebecois wish to separate and form an independent state. Should an accommodation be reached, this percentage will not change significantly unless the myths that make tribalism attractive are demonstrated to be false.

Canadians as a whole have already voted against a constitutional agreement supported by all provincial premiers and the federal parliament, telling Quebeckers that the country wanted its governments addressing economic issues instead of playing constitutional games. Nothing was resolved and a lot of bad feelings were left to simmer. Whether Quebec separates or not is largely out of Canadian hands. To separatist Quebecois, it looks like the best of all times to pull it off. The rest of Canadians, wearied and hurt by Quebec's rejection, are increasingly looking at options which do not include Quebec. The only people with a strong political will to maintain the country appears to be federal civil servants.

In any case, whatever decision Quebec and the rest of Canada work out, it will be a cold day in hell before any other country opts for multiculturalism.

WHO'S WHO IN TRIBALISM

The reversion to tribalism is a major force and all governments are struggling with it, including those nation-states that have given up their mandate to govern to a larger, regional neo-government.

There are the cultural protectionists such as Canada's Quebecois; the Basques, who blow up a police car from time to time in Spain or France; or the Scottish National Party, who believe that a combination of wearing kilts and controlling North Sea oil fields will provide the resources to become a pseudo-country under the protection of the European Union. (The SNP enjoyed improved voter confidence after, with a spark of wit, the party hired Sean Connery, formerly James Bond, Her Majesty's super secret agent 007, to plead its case in television commercials.)

There are also the religious tribalists, such as militant Muslim sects, the Sikhs, or the Christian Armenians, whose relations with their Turkic host countries have not gone well for centuries and who maintain that the whole world needs to know how oppressed they are.

Others claim that their separatism is grounded on more practical ideas — as in Italy, where the Lombard League, a.k.a. the Northern League, argues that the Mafia and political corruption can be eliminated by reverting to the Medieval city state.

Another place where this is happening is Brazil. After 1945, a lot of Germans recognized that the good life in the late Third Reich would be pretty limited for the foreseeable future and decided to emigrate. Many found their way to Argentina and Brazil, neither of which were interested in asking or investigating questions of possible war crimes. This emigration worked out well for everyone concerned. Argentina and Brazil got a white, industrially sophisticated, disciplined immigrant population, some of

---

Virtually all ethnic communities have discovered the urge to assert their distinctiveness, regardless of how many hundreds of years the ethnic group has shared political union and common "national" currency, nation-building goals, language, political cohesion and land-mass contiguity.

The current trend of separatism is often attributed to the persecution which has been the historic lot of the separatist group. It is seldom seen as the inability on the part of the government of the country being separated from to deliver satisfactory government. But as social pluralism increases, the ability of governments to mediate the conflicting desires of the competing pluralistic sectors diminishes.

In North America, Hawaii, Quebec, and Puerto Rico aspire to independence. Aboriginal people in Canada are using the Canadian constitutional confusion to secure a stronger self-governing political identity. They, of course, risk being seen as non-allies when things cool down.

whom had money. The Germans, for their part, got out of Germany. In Brazil they settled largely in the three southern states, which in the 1890s and early 1900s had been settled by Italian and German immigrants. Fast forward to the present.

In southern Brazil, in the capital of the state of Rio Grande do Sul, Santa Cruz do Sol, you'll find the headquarters of yet another separatist movement called the National Pro Pampas Movement. The Pro Pampas Movement is committed to separating the three southernmost states from Brazil and is led by Irton Marx, the son of a German immigrant. The Movement has issued identity cards and presented the region with a new flag (a blue speckled orb embossed on a gold and black cross on a red banner).

This separatist cause differs from the independentist mainstream in that it is based on the Germanic majority in Brazil's industrial heartland. There are no shanty towns, no killing of orphan street urchins. *Oktoberfest* is celebrated and the towns of the region are squeaky-clean, as if they had been lifted from a postcard of modern Bavaria.

In the three southern states the Movement claims a membership of 750,000. It claims the region is under represented in the legislature and overtaxed to support the less efficient, overpopulated northeast and under-populated Amazon basin. Rio Grande do Sul furnishes 15 percent of the national economic output and receives 9 percent of the federal government's investment.

In the former U.S.S.R., the newly independent states have stepped forth on the world stage, their U.N. application in one hand and their E.U. application in the other. One might ask, isn't this contradictory behaviour, to become economically sovereign and politically autonomous and then immediately sign away these new freedoms to become part of the E.U.? They reply that they cannot turn back the forces of the global economy any more than King Canute could stop the sea.

Similarly, Canada's Quebec separatists assume that they will automatically inherit full participant rights in NAFTA.

It will be interesting to see what happens when a group like the Basques of France and Spain, or the Welsh and the Scots in Britain, or the Northern League in Italy decides to exercise its distinctiveness by becoming politically independent. What might the historically unionist state do when confronted by a separatist entity unilaterally declaring itself independent and starting its own army?

The regional trading blocs are less than effective at delivering government. For a very short time, everyone will be willing to give their constituent states the benefit of the doubt, until they make a real faux pas like nuking someone (militarily, or by having a power plant go crazy because they can't afford the maintenance contract), or getting into a war which inconveniences everyone else.

With the exception of the southern Brazilians, who have been called fascist, racist, and loony, independence movements usually are devoid of economic realities and the romantic view that they could manage their own affairs is usually based on wistful thinking.

Globally, the list of tribal revisionists is pretty well endless. For Americans, the designation of "oppressors" comes from native Hawaiians, who can justly point to an armed invasion. History records that a force of 162 U.S. Marines backed up a largely white, civilian *coup d'etat* in 1893 against the incumbent Queen Liliuokalani.

The agenda of native Hawaiians is economically focussed on two land trusts covering about 800,000 hectares (1.9 million acres). Native Hawaiian groups argue that the American government has transferred these trust lands illegally, for purposes other than those authorized under the trusteeship. When the native Hawaiians received support from U.S. Senator Daniel Inouye, who promised to introduce legislation to create an independent Hawaii, representatives of the U.S. Interior and Justice departments testified before a congressional hearing that there had never been any federal obligation to the land trusts in the past, in the present or in the future. At stake is 41 percent of the islands.

As an immediate tactic, native Hawaiian leaders proposed bringing a lawsuit against the federal government claiming mismanagement and asking for compensation for past claims. The government has refused to give the natives anything, citing constitutional principles against government actions favouring one racial group over another. Hawaiian leaders have pointed to the exclusivity features of the reserve lands system which benefits native Americans.

As this argument heats up it attacks two fundamental features of the American myth. One is the desirability of American citizenship. The other, a consequence of the American Civil War, is that no state may secede from the union, once admitted. An attack of such proportions on the fundamental principles of a nation state's myth structure is usually disregarded and denied. This attitude is then met with an increment in rhetoric from the dissident group —and frequently violence.

Current rhetoric from native Hawaiian leaders shows their anger is rising. The usual denial attitude of the rest of Americans will dissuade Congress from dealing with the issue (no one in Peoria will harass their representative or senator) and then it will blow up, since the Hawaiians are serious. The issue is not money, it is tribal feelings against the overgroup. Never mind that mental picture you hold of a native Hawaiian as a bronzed god or goddess lolling about on a pristine beach, a surfboard close at hand. The native leaders only have to change that image and they're in business. A picture of armed-to-the-teeth Hawaiians standing in an open truck in front of a burning dock full of Dole pineapples and holding up a sign saying "this time we're fucking serious" should do the trick.

TRIBALISM IN THE RAW

For five months in 1992, Expo '92 in Seville, Spain, celebrated "The Age of Discoveries" as its theme. Five hundred years earlier, Columbus had set out from Seville with his three ships, the *Nina*, *Pinta*, and flagship *Santa Maria*, so it is not surprising that Expo focussed on Columbus' visit to Central America and the Caribbean.

However, folks who run expositions in the '90s have a clear picture about the need to be sensitive to a variety of view-points. In the Age of Navigation pavilion, one display carried these words from Captain James Cook, the British global circumnavigator. In referring to the many primitive societies he came into contact with, Cook wrote: "It would have been much better for these people not to have known of our superiority. They will never be able to return to the state in which they lived when we discovered them."

The problem of what to do with primitive societies who come into contact with technologically advanced societies is still with us.

One group of tribalists represent the serious side of this coin. They call themselves The Voice of the Earth and claim to represent 250 million indigenous tribal peoples. They are concerned with territorial rights, environmental protection, and retention of the right to continue a traditional life of hunting and gathering. Working under an umbrella group known as the Inter-tribal Committee, a Brazilian group that has led the fight to preserve the Amazonian rain forests, they secured wide support to hold a pre-environmental summit meeting called the Earth Parliament.

Common decency should encourage the international bureaucrats who manage the back rooms of international meetings to pay some attention to these people. There is no power in the constituent parts of this body — but there are 250 million human beings involved. They are not walking around with big money. They picked up $88,000 from the Body Shop International to pay for a U.K. office in London.

These traditional indigenous communities are small, seldom even noted on any map made in the industrialized world. No one can disagree that mining expropriation and commercial exploitation for lumber in tribal lands is common practice. Toxification by the chemicals employed in forestry and mining poison rivers and kill fish and other wildlife.

Displacement of entire communities for the "greater good" is a normal activity of governments to whom the welfare of indigenous peoples has been consigned, usually by the international community. (The ideology of the nation involved doesn't seem to matter.) Aboriginal people's already shortened life spans are made shorter by policies of governments entrusted with protecting them. No one argues about these facts. Any country with a respectable judicial system could bring second-degree murder charges against most of the senior officials of the aboriginal affairs departments and ministries in these governments. In fact, anyone thinking of taking a job with one of these agencies would be well advised to read over the Nuremburg court's findings about what constitutes genocide.

No wonder tribalism has allies among the small (and not so small) businesses that occupy product, geographic, or specialty marketing niches which can be cast in an "environmental," or *Whole Earth Catalog* genre. After all, tribalists are also a reiteration of the "small is beautiful" movement of the 1960s, which also contributed the mind-set which had as its credo "let's go to the country, get a farm, smoke a lot of dope, groove on nature, and not deal with the hassles of the city."

In the spring of 1992 a 10-part series called *Millennium* ran on North American television. It was billed as an exploration of the wisdom of tribal societies around the world. Promotion for the program included brown paper bags used to package items purchased from The Body Shop. On the bags were a series of statements:

"Every time a shaman dies it's as if a LIBRARY burned down.

"The wisdom of the world's indigenous peoples is the accumulation of centuries of living not just on the land, but with it.

"What can we learn from these cultures? We'll never know unless we act now to ensure their survival.

"History teaches us many unfortunate lessons about the ways in which contact with Western-styled "progress" has changed or destroyed indigenous cultures. Now it's time for us to learn and to ask:

"HOW WILL CONTACT WITH THEM CHANGE US?"

Primitive tribal societies worldwide continue to practice infanticide — usually female. When the baby killed is male, it is because the infant has a

---

The Body Shop's founder, Anita Roddick, plays the game honestly. Her company has supported activities like The Voice of the Earth since day one. It pays full commercial prices directly to Third World communities for the often unique natural ingredients used to manufacture the company's products. (The Body Shop sells only environmentally friendly bath oils, body oils, soaps, shampoos, cosmetics, et cetera.)

Roddick has a nice multi-branch, multinational business. But it is unlikely that she falls into the category of executives who can phone 10 Downing Street, or that she has the kind of influence we normally associate with the supporters of the New World Order. If it comes to push and shove, she hasn't got a chance.

congenital defect which would make him a poor warrior, hunter, fisherman or other culturally defined role. (Infanticide is seldom used in tribal societies as birth control. Tribal societies usually have such high infant mortality rates that the idea of birth control is pretty alien to them)

Shamans are not notably successful in clinical medical matters after we adjust for placebo effects. Tribal societies are typically animistic and shamans direct their skills to discovering which animal spirits are particularly malevolent toward people or are willing to act as familiars to do the bidding of those who would cast spells on others.

For the record, the way Westerners operating with resources of nation states since the 15th century have enslaved and exploited indigenous peoples is disgusting and generally obscene. We have behaved like the Golden Horde, or the KGB accountant who made the Gulags "pay."

But while it is noble to protect indigenous peoples from the negative effects of contact with more technologically advanced societies, the world deals unkindly with those who do not keep informed about the way the world changes. What good is a brown paper bag ("made from recycled paper") that attempts to impose a romantic, idealized view of peoples who have fallen between the cracks of the global mainstream? This seems to be just another kind of exploitation.

PREACHERS AND TEACHERS

In an era transition, as we have defined it, religion undergoes a pronounced resurgence. The simultaneous rise of fundamentalism and entirely new religions is not as contradictory as it might appear — both are reactions to the same collapse of historical authority. When a quantum jump in the level of abstraction suddenly provides explanations for realms that were previously dealt with by myth and faith, fresh religions provide a means to deal with those unexplored frontiers for which the new sciences have no answers.

Neil Postman, author of *Technopoly*, among other books, offers an anti-scientific rant which brings aid and comfort to the technophobes. He argues that the Western World has accepted and exploited scientific advances uncritically. His view is that contemporary science (Technopoly) is a "totalitarian technocracy." He writes that it is "without a moral centre. It puts in its place efficiency, interest and economic advance. It promises heaven on earth through the conveniences of technological progress."

Postman is a typical spokesman of the anti-science humanities communities. What few of these people realize is that they are the obverse side of the same coin with many senior executives in the corporate world, even in high technology industries. Neither the executives nor the romantic humanists seem to be able to separate *technology* from *science*.

There are other humanist voices with a different agenda. Paul Ehrlich, who hangs his ecological hat at Stanford University, has said, "I am convinced that a quasi-religious movement, one concerned with the need to change the values that now govern much of human activity, is essential to the persistence of our civilization." Another ecologist of some repute, Howard Odum, echoes Ehrlich's sentiments when he asserts that "The key program of a surviving pattern of nature and man is a subsystem or religious teaching which follows the laws of the energy ethic." He adds: "We can teach the energy truths through general science in the schools and teach the love of the system and its requirements of us in the *changing churches*" (emphasis added).

Are scientists trying to teach theologians to create new dogma and proof of the existence of God? Is somebody running the damn movie backwards?

This is not a time in history when you can create great stabilities. It is not a time when you write constitutions (unless your country has completely collapsed). It is a time when you learn to rethink your values, when you get as well-rounded an education as possible. It is not the time to memorize the world map. Realistically, we can assume that most of those things which we believed to be "writ in stone" will collapse under us.

The religious format that typically follows an era transition is puritanically fundamentalist and antagonistic to whatever old order existed. Its purpose is to address those issues which transcend the commonly accepted new level of abstraction, such as the nature of God, forms of worship, public morality, and social attitudes. The new puritans can be expected to attempt to impose their values on others in the body politic by offering a new social contract which is held out in lieu of the collapsed social contract of the previous era.

In our own time we see a New Age/Gaia movement that deals with unknowns, from death to the nature of God and the identity of self. The New Age anti-intellectual component is consistent with earlier religious resurgencies.

Contemporary fundamentalists, from the Shia Muslims to the "born again" Christians of the West, share this negation of intellectual activity with the New Age movement. The New Age runs counter to the fundamentalists in that it is very fuzzy on the edges.

"The Child Inside Me," rebirthing, past-life regression, alternative therapies, and the other unauthenticated alternative therapies (and 12-step programs) are all examples spun out from the pool we call New Age. They share an assumption of searching outside traditional value systems for relief from the impact and pace of change. These 'therapy' movements are focussed on finding a means of resisting or accommodating, within existing structures, the changes which are inherent in an era shift.

Realistically, we can expect a strong tide of religious experience to begin to become a common means for people to acquire a congruent personal epistemology — which will have little contact with reality and a lot in common with revealed dogma.

The above is not a prediction. It will not necessarily be the New Agers who will provide a basis of religiosity to help make this new era comprehensible. The religious closure usually tends to occur about halfway through the movie. The thing to watch for is fads with staying power.

CHAPTER TEN

Islam in Cyberspace: Loose nukes sink continents

In the scientific Renaissance (a.k.a. Renaissance 1.3), which happened during the 16th and 17th centuries, Europeans discovered how to couple creativity with freedom of inquiry. They developed conditions under which competing claims for "truth" or "fact" could be adjudicated without resort to doctrine, ideology, or people with big muscles, knives, swords, or guns.

In the Islamic world, as each new leader in whom our foreign offices have some, however misplaced, hope arrives on the scene, we hear pious pronouncements that the new leader is a true democrat and that he will finally fulfill his people's long-frustrated yearnings for a convincing Arab democracy.

The next time you hear of yet another home-grown Arab democrat, innocently ask whoever is selling this folktale believable only by small children how this latest paragon plans to eradicate the word *inshallah* from the vocabulary of every Muslim. *Inshallah*, which translates as "God willing," is a word you will hear a hundred times a day in an Islamic culture. It is the ultimate statement of Arab fatalism and the greatest hurdle the West and the Islamic world must overcome before they can have any kind of agreement about anything.

Earlier we saw how the discoveries of the Renaissance allowed the West to amend previously held ideas when new evidence makes such amendments compelling. We have institutionalized dissent and, with great difficulty, created formal social protocols to allow our scientific and political systems, and even scholarship in the humanities, where there are few trustworthy empirical tools, to accept challenges to authority without resorting to charges of heretical high crimes worthy of inquisitional investigation.

In the Muslim world, the pervasive use of the word *inshallah* changes every aspect of how the future is seen. In Islam, the single controlling feature of all projections is the surrender to divine intervention. According to this fatalism, man is a puppet to be manipulated by good or malign outside forces. These forces, whether they are the Red Crescent Society acting courageously in a civil war, or the CIA acting as tools of Satan, or an earthquake smashing hundreds of villages, are all working to carry out a divine plan — local effects of the action are essentially irrelevant to that plan.

The Islamic world is not one where we can expect to see Planck's quantum universe, Einstein's relativism, Heisenberg's uncertainty, or contemporary chaos models. The Islamic world accepts only a universe of straightforward cause and effect. God causes and the effects are God's gift to man. That is how the universe operates.

Islam will accept the flashy toys produced by the West, but there is no way Muslims can accept the underlying rules of that universe. That's the good news. The bad news is that Muslim scholars believe they have a choice.

Islamic fundamentalists have no conception of evolution as a random process in which genetic mutations are constantly tested in their environments. Creation, in the Koranic world, is the Adam and Eve myth (the *Koran* diverges from *The Bible* with its treatment of the patriarch Abraham and the appropriation of 'the word' of Moses). If they can't grasp this idea, then they must treat *all* events, whether chaotic, accidental, or the result of incompetence, as part of God's higher plan, which — *inshallah* — must be accepted.

A few years ago *Al Ahram* (the most prestigious daily paper in Egypt, if not the entire Middle East) printed a pre-Ramadan editorial that suggested the suffering of Muslims in Bosnia, Armenia, and the Philippines had been prolonged because "constructive efforts to alleviate the oppression of Muslim co-religionists by utilizing the mechanisms of international organizations or human rights organizations to help was never considered."

Muslims, *Al Ahram* continued, have no access to these kind of forward-planning strategies — which are, by definition, attempts to thwart God's will. Therefore, Muslims are left with a sense of fatalistic impotence, which leaves the ordinary person open to Imam-sponsored fulminating against the perpetrators. *Al Ahram* neglected to point out that one result of this fatalism is a ready climate for acts of terrorism which have their genesis in the frustrations brought on by assuming that, in all matters, anything the individual might do is of no consequence because events will only turn out the way God wills.

It is we in the West who must figure out how to transfer the method of inquiry to an Islamic world that is still locked into the residue of the Ottoman Empire. Whether it is possible to force-feed freedom of inquiry is something we shall see played out over the next few years as Islam tries to obtain our war toys without taking the query software. Muslim culture may not be able to absorb the level of abstraction necessary, which would cut it off from the next stage of human exploration. We've seen that option before in Russia and China, both of which missed out on the Renaissance.

ISLAM'S FATE MEETS HEISENBERG'S UNCERTAINTY

The break from the feudal, scholastic world into the Renaissance was started by a series of events which resulted in a quantum jump in the level of abstraction. When the level of abstraction is raised, a wide variety of events become more easily handled by a single explanatory rubric. The lawfulness of the universe becomes more pronounced, accessible, and provable. Superstition and flawed world-views become less viable and more easily dismissed.

We know that this jump in the abstraction level has a social price. The established orders are profoundly upset. Following the invention of the bill of exchange and implementation of the new mathematics in navigation, trade expanded and a new class of well-to-do merchants, whose wealth was renewable and who were very tough people, arose to challenge the established leadership cliques. In the Renaissance, that establishment's economic stability and power rested on the assumption that land, as well as the universe, was finite. With the discovery of the "New World," the finite geopolitics of the Medieval world became unstable.

The fate of the relatively inflexible Roman Catholic Church serves as a warning that religions, especially those with a significant temporal power base, are at risk during an era transition. From a purely secular viewpoint, religion serves to provide comfort and answers when we find ourselves enmeshed in events which transcend the known but not necessarily knowable. The commonality in the way most religious bodies direct us to deal with daily ethical issues are usually seen as a useful adjunct to the social control strictures available to the civil authorities and custom. Religions, in general, also hold out a view that humanity can transcend the world as we know it and further promulgate the local creation myth which customarily serves as a metaphor for community bonding.

When a new level of abstraction is consensually accepted, the mandate of religion to deal with a historical unknowable is taken over, amended, and incorporated into the new, widely accepted epistemology. Then religion must move on to a new level of unknowability.

If you were visited by angels in biblical times, you became a member of the cast of *The Bible*. If the visitation happened in the Middle Ages, the social response was problematical. If you went around urging political positions at odds with those held by the establishment, you were usually burned for heresy. If you merely reported that the angels had urged piety, without suggesting political change, you would end up in a monastery or nunnery as a highly respected potential saint. If you tried the angel visitation idea in 17th or 18th century Europe or America, you needed some pretty unambiguous miracles handy to avoid the local pest house. In our own time, if you're not really pietistic, be quick to find some unflinching true-believer followers and be cautious about who you talk to, otherwise it's the chlorpromazine route for you (or, in some medievally revisionist hospitals, electro-convulsive shock "therapy"). We humans have learned to be fastidious about who upsets what apple-carts, since we have a pretty clear idea how fragile our civilizations are at the best of times, let alone in their formative years.

New eras tend to develop congruent religious institutions that speak to the significant unknowables and usually find ways to oppress the followers of heresies. The present decline in mainstream church affiliation and increasing indifference to parental political and religious affiliation among newlyweds is all part of the breakdown of the previous age's historical authority. Meanwhile, fundamentalist churches continue to expand their membership rolls worldwide, which suggests that mainstream churches have become institutionally secularized, losing their capacities to address mysterious, mystical, and spiritual events. We can probably anticipate another global religious revival within a decade or two.

Much of the Renaissance world-view was unacceptable to the Roman Catholic Church and the temporal rulers of the time. But freedom of speech and thought were essential for the growth of the new science, and it is during the Renaissance that we see the beginnings of free speech and inquiry. The faltering beginnings of these freedoms are not easily recognized by present-day standards — certainly the European Protestants would burn you just as fast as the Roman Catholics would for deviation from orthodoxy.

The central thesis of this book is that those periods during which major changes occur in the world-view of developed countries and which we call era transitions have a common theme — that the genesis of the new world-view is a significant jump in the level of abstraction which is consensually accepted.

Further, there is good reason to believe that this type of change results in an evolutionary shift. It should be remembered that most of nature's evolutionary experiments are failures and that the outcome of failure is extinction. Under these circumstances, we should exercise caution about whom we chose to lead us into this next test of survival.

CENTRAL ASIA GOES BOOM IN THE NIGHT

While the governments of Egypt, Jordan, and Algeria face active fundamentalist opposition, the next spot with a high probability of mullah power is the C.I.S. nation of Kazakhstan — which has, among its many charms, the Tyuratam Missile Launch Site, the Baikonaur Cosmodome (the civilian space centre), and the nuclear weapons storage site at Ust-Kamenogorsk, which is close to the Chinese border.

As an editorial in the January 6, 1992, issue of the authoritative Aviation Week points out, as economic conditions worsen in the C.I.S nations, former Soviet nuclear experts could well be forced to sell their services to the highest bidder.

It is unlikely that the editors of the normally well-informed Aviation Week can really comprehend that in the former U.S.S.R. there exist six states in which the assumptions underlying modern industrial societies are over-ruled by the combined world-view of the Golden Horde and a stable majority of devout Muslim communicants. All of these states are in Central Asia.

These six states start with Azerbaijan, which has around 86,600 square unpleasant kilometres and a population of 7 million. Kazakhstan is geopolitically the most significant, with an area of 2.71 million square equally disgusting kilometres. Kirgizstan is about 198,500 square kilometres, with a population of 4.3 million. Tajikistan, with 143,100 square kilometres, has 5.2 million people. Turkmenstan clocks in with 488,100 square kilometres (if you can find a clock) and the smallest population, only 3.6 million. Uzbekistan has only 447,400 square kilometres, a population of 20 million and direct access to some of the world's most spectacular hashish.

Their southern borders abut Iran, Afghanistan, and the People's Republic of China, with whose populations there is, and has historically been, a significant degree of localized trade and intermarriage. This went on in spite of repressions by the Russian and Chinese communist regimes that included forced labour in mines and factories. At times these repressions bordered on the genocidal.

Kazakhs have, over centuries, had to bear more then their share of the burdens that life seems to impose on out-of-sight, out-of-mind places. Prior to the Communist revolution in 1918, local politics were notoriously unstable and bloody. Both the Tsarist and Soviet governments used the area as a buffer against potential Chinese incursion. When Stalin enforced collectivization in the 1930s, about 4 million Kazakhs were killed.

On January 13, 1992, U.N. inspectors in Iraq managed to get Iraqi nuclear scientists to admit to having the wherewithal to build a bomb which had not been turned over to the U.N. for destruction. The U.N. bomb cops had been tipped off to the production plant's existence by the Germans who had sold the plant to the Iraqis.

A couple of days previously there had been reports that former KGB commercial travellers were offering all the help necessary for the Iraqis to make their own real live bombs. Apparently, arrangements had been made to deliver these goods through Algeria, which had just elected a Muslim Islamic fundamentalist government intent on establishing a Koranic theocracy.

The new Islamic state of Algeria was immediately overthrown by the army. Since then, Algeria has been in a state of bloody insurrection.

Stalin exterminated the Muslim intelligentsia in Central Asia and moved huge numbers of people around while creating totally illogical "autonomous" states. Good old Uncle Joe, as President Roosevelt called him, realized that Kazakhstan was a place of immense potential. He also knew in his heart of hearts that the U.S.S.R. was filled with people who hated the Russian hegemony that was the underlying domestic principle of the Soviet government. And while Kazakhstan was not exactly a spot likely to be mistaken for paradise, it had little in the way of an infrastructure that would allow residents to leave or encourage nosy visitors.

Before the Soviet regime put up the two main space centres, Kazakhstan was a great place to drop off malcontents who weren't enough of a drag to shoot or put in a camp but who were going to sit around whining or getting ideas about the way things should be. For example, there are more than 80,000 Chechens (survivors and descendants of the original resettlers under Stalin's benign leadership) who sent money, volunteers and weapons to bedevil Mr. Yeltsin's SPEZNATS forces of moderation. Chechnya was never far from these Kazakh minds when they watched TV news of the glorious and heroic Russian armies taking down Grozny, the capital of Chechnya, brick by brick.

If you were an official in Almaty, the old capital of Kazakhstan, you would have these 80,000 Chechens on your case to let them get involved in the old homeland in ways like leaving to join the Chechen army, sending "humanitarian aid" which your experience told you would be a cover for weapons, or smuggling drugs to finance the "cause." Since you still wouldn't have anything recognizable as an infrastructure, you would be dependent on the Russians for survival supplies.

To add to that dilemma, Stalin frequently got rid of his problems by dumping them on Kazakhstan, so you have similar numbers of Volga Germans, Inguish Muslim neighbours of the Chechens, and Koreans whom Kim Il Sung had wanted to dump somewhere. By now these groups have developed general intuition that your government is not one the neighbours seem to trust.

All of this makes providing government in Kazakhstan an exciting business.

Its first act as an independent state was to replace the cyrillic alphabet of Russia with Arabic script. This nation is a curious mixture of modern cities and primitive, restless nomadic communities that hold to a classical social value system derived from 8th century Islam (in spite of the convincing arguments posed by the old KGB and its predecessor counselling services).

The inhabitants of the Central Asian republics did not abandon their faith and customs. They did, sort of, collectivize their herding activities, sometimes — and the Soviets finally settled for that. Racially, the people draw their roots and culture from the Muslim Caucasus, Tartars and Turks. The birth rate is one of the highest in the world.

To their east is China, where about 10 to 20 million Uighurs — a Turkic group related to Kazakhs — live in Xinjiang, where the Chinese test missiles and nuclear weaponry. Xinjiang is also on top of enormous oil and gas reserves. The Uighurs' notions of independence have recently won them the dangerous (for them) definition of a "separatist ethnic minority" by the Chinese Bureau of Social Affairs.

The few Western experts on the region are generally of the opinion that these technically sovereign states are among the most backward spots in the world. Some Slavic immigrants were dispatched by Moscow when some genius central planner irrigated a big chunk of Uzbekistan from the Aral Sea to grow cotton crops for which there were no cotton mills or clothing factories remotely nearby.

All the republics are exploring economic models which might allow them to have the basics. There is hope that the infrastructure of railways and pipelines tying them to Russia will remain intact.

Conservative Russian sources (which usually means the FSB, formerly the KGB) with experience in the region say that after the ordinary man in

---

What makes Tajikistan such a compelling tourist attraction? The capital, Dushanhe, has nothing to offer during the daylight hours and at night everyone, including the soldiers, are terrified to go outside.

In February 1997 a local band of night shooters kidnapped a party of U.N. aid workers who were there to help resettle "refugees." The usual targets of such troublemakers are the Russian army's "peaceful transition" support troops. Since leaving its old Red Army label, the Russian army has developed a strong dislike for casualties. But with the kidnapping of the U.N. do-gooders, the Russians had an excuse to respond with some real firepower and casualties from both sides began to clutter up the streets.

But who were the kidnappers? It turns out that they were Afghanis on the run from the Taliban forces who have taken control of Afghanistan. The Afghanis have decided that Tajikistan makes a good place to regroup and figure out how to run the politically correct Taliban forces out of the homeland from which they had so recently driven the Russians. The kidnapped U.N. aid workers wanted to resettle the Afghani northern army, which had been accused of having impure thoughts and being insufficiently Islamic for Taliban-run Afghanistan.

If you can follow this example of 'who's on first', check in with the human resources branch of the Russian army or the otherwise oxymoronic U.N.

the area has his yurt collapsed and packed on his ponies, he and his extended family are ready to disappear.

Pessimistically, these sources further believe that no one can have any realistic hope of organizing any of these six states. Their leaders are rather typical, ethnically indigenous Soviet bureaucrats who must keep the infrastructure-maintaining Russian technologists happy. The Russian technical experts are still aliens and a job in one of the six (when they were Soviet) states was never considered a great post. They do, however, eat well (if you like sheep, goat, steppe pony, and fermented mare's milk). And, unlike much of Russia, there is housing. Even though the locals prefer their domed, mobile yurts, the central planning clowns in Moscow allotted them the per capita amount of housing everyone else got.

The six Central Asian republics would probably support Russia in the case of another conservative coup attempt. The Central Asians have no reason to believe that the remaining Communist Party faithful have anything to offer them. An attempt by the Chinese to take them over as protectorates would result in stiff resistance. That is probably not an idea the Chinese would see as a winner. They already have about 20 million Central Asians and neither national group thrills the other.

Kazakhstan is still a primitive state with a very thin veneer of civilization that is losing what little ability it had to deliver benefits to a society already returning to its tribal way of seeing the world.

When the best a state travel agency can do to attract foreign tourists is a glossy leaflet describing the colourful yurt dwellers and families on ponies which are direct offspring of the horses of Great Khan (as did the pre-collapse Kazakhstan), you have a problem. You might have thought that the Russians of the U.S.S.R. would have realized that it is a good rule of thumb to keep things that go whoosh and boom out of the hands of people who write that kind of brochure.

Kazakhstan has been of concern for the past decade to Russian intelligence services who saw evidence of infiltration by various Muslim fundamentalist missionaries. If the FSB views these folks with alarm, think about how the world's dope dealers might view them. There is little in the way of the usual diplomatic pressures that will get their attention and they are right next door to Samarkand, the oldest dope trail in the world. The puritanical Soviets were rigid about dope dealing. Does the new government have the same priorities? (How about opening a bank in Kazakhstan?)

After the collapse of the U.S.S.R., Kazakhstan President Nursultan Nazarbaev found himself in possession of 1,690 nuclear weapons, most of them attached to short-range missiles. Any government in a nation of yurts has little interest in playing the international affairs game. The country's problems are much too basic, like avoiding reversion to a collection of nomads enjoying a high-protein diet.

The West was well aware that Kazakhstan had become, overnight, the newest member of the nuclear weapons club. It is also the most likely spot for leakages of weapons systems to other Muslim states. The Kazakh government could act as protectors of the former Soviet weapons scientists and their services could be sold until someone decided to take them out.

Kazakhstan's Turkic populations are historically Sunni Muslims and the republic's west borders on the Caspian Sea, which it shares with the fundamentalist Muslim government of Iran. The idea of Kazakhstan joining in some greater Prophet-based Club of Kabul with Pakistan, Iran, Afghanistan and the other Muslim states of the late U.S.S.R. is not just a paranoid fantasy.

In many ways, the post Cold War scenarios are more chilling than those of the most hyper anti-Reds of a few years ago. The FSB's argument is that Nazarbaev must deal with the survival problem — that of his people and ultimately himself. The present government has little in the way of industry to induce some level of civility in a culture where post-Renaissance assumptions are not a tradition. (Look at the problems the U.N. inspection teams have had in Iraq.)

The resources of Kazakhstan are principally oil, gold, natural gas, and a wide range of metals. This type of mining and petroleum exploitation requires engineering technology that can only be found in the West. To set up in the minerals business involves a long wait for a return on investment, but it's very unlikely that Nazarbaev feels that he or his government have the luxury of time. As if to emphasize the point, on the eve of one of Boris Yeltsin's official visits to London and Washington, Kazakhstan's sister nuclear power, Ukraine, announced a sale of machinery and weapons to Iran — and the Ukrainians aren't even Muslims!

That the West's attention was captured by the nuclear power status of Kazakhstan was obvious. In 1993 a Western delegation lead by Sir Douglas Hurd, the British foreign secretary, began holding talks with Kazakh officials. The seriousness with which the West viewed Kazakhstan's potential for going bump in the night could be seen from the rest of the party's makeup. Along with technical experts from NATO there was the French foreign minister, Roland Dumas, and Reginald Bartholomew, an American under-secretary of state. No one was underestimating the potential for problems here.

One thing you can rest assured about is that the states of Central Asia are one world. The core group are the Kazakhs, who, incidentally, contributed more officers to the Red Army than any other regional state excepting Russia and Ukraine. The linguistic borders of the Turkic populace stretch from China to the Balkans and Turkey. They are well aware that the Great Wall of China was built to keep them out. The Russians, from the time of Ivan the Terrible to that of Stalin, knew that they too needed a wall of some sort. This was why Stalin imposed the Cyrillic alphabet on them. It was an attempt to isolate Central Asians in the U.S.S.R. from each other and cut them off from their ethnic cousins.

From the Central Asian perspective, a new orientalizing and subjugation of Russia is long overdue. To look at the map of the world from a Central Asian aspect, you can see that the Mediterranean Sea and the Balkan mountain ranges are the only land barriers preventing the Kazakhs from solving their separation from their ethnic cousins by traditional means.

ISLAM'S INTERIOR GAZE

The Muslim world holds to an inward-looking focus. Without a trade or commercial force, it holds itself aloof from the "non-believer" community. It is this indifference to non-believers that makes the Muslim world a dangerous force.

Worldwide, Muslims are raised in a tribal community based on an extended family. The social safety-net services provided by governments in industrial states are the preserve of the extended family in Islamic countries. The rules of a theocratic state provide the faithful with a tribal identity. The individual is protected from Western materialism, which is not required for salvation. Fundamentalist religious leaders see materialist values as weakening the resolve of the faithful. Self-indulgence is similarly seen as an assault on faith.

A relativistic universe, with its emphasis on functional relations that are not necessarily causal, but are related, is not a world that Muslims would see as meeting the test of not being from Satan.

Muslims have potentially contentious relations with Europe and America. A minor one is the state of Israel. A major one is the relativistic universe of functional relationships. There is nothing relativistic about there being "one God but Allah" and as the relativistic world-view expands, we should be aware of the potential for it to be a flash point between the West and Islam.

Although Arab-owned banks are numerous, they are barred from usury. Their principal revenue comes from interbank loans to European (non-Muslim) banks, although they do charge fees to their customers. They will also guarantee a customer's loan from a non-Muslim bank. They even have banks exclusively for women. These Islamic banks are virtually all stand-alone units and there is none of the communications network necessary to a modern commercial banking system.

The harried technical managers and techie staffs of telephone systems in Central Asia and the Middle East are hardly thrilled with the idea of a few hundred thousand daily transactions of cash-dispensing banking machines. The infrastructure to support a global, time-sensitive, commercial trading economy is not available in the region.

When the abstraction level rises, the levels of unknowns also rise. Historically this has meant an upswing in religion as an explanatory fiction. Muslim countries with strong secular bases are at risk from their more conservative co-religionists.

In the 18th century, a religious revival movement began with an Arab leader, Mohammed ibn Abdul Wahhab. This movement was an attempt to break away from the brain-dead rigidities of the orthodox Islam of the Ottoman Empire.

It was Wahhabi fundamentalists who made life so lively for the Red Army in Afghanistan while the *mujahadin* competed with each other for religious worthiness as judged by the Wahhabi missionaries. By all accounts the Wahhabi are considered *very* aggressive in their sell-in approach. During the Gulf War, the Wahhabis supported Saddam Hussein even though the Saudis have been keeping them in petty cash since the mid-1940s.

In one of those diplomatic master strokes the Saudis are known for, they bit their tongues and managed to explain the deep needs of the former Soviet states in Central Asia for the Wahhabi message. So the Wahhabis are now wandering around Central Asia with a lot of cash and an unending supply of Korans.

The downside of this is that the Saudi handlers of the Wahhabis are being harangued at every meeting with a message that comes back as "they should be grateful but they say we should be grateful that they're willing to

---

In the Kingdom of Jordan, unauthorized ownership of a modem is illegal. This, of course, means that the people of Jordan are missing a chance to become acculturated to a significant part of education for the new era.

Already in a march toward fundamentalism and theocratic states, Muslims can be excused if they see themselves as the victims of a new series of crusades that will be fought over the invasion of Satanist literature littering the Infobahn. As long as Islam does not have a reformation, which should satisfy anyone's bloodlust, there is no way for Islam to adapt to the net's incapacity to suppress information. The idea of digitized made-for-TV movies travelling over the net must be the local imam's worst nightmare. If the ulema thought that Rushdie was a pain in the butt, wait until they get their telephone systems up to speed.

Another aspect of the Internet's challenge to Islam is that surfing the net is good (subliminal) training for the exploration of cyberspace. Subliminal, because the training is over before you realize that you've lost your faith.

take our money and I'm beginning to feel grateful." The Saudi intelligence service must be having a bad case of queasy stomachs as it sends off its best and brightest young men with more suitcases of cash and Korans, knowing full well that the Wahhabis will be shortly explaining to the young men that they (the young men) aren't good enough to be Muslims.

The nations of Islam are upset by the growth in support for fundamentalist imams. Political movements run by true believers with foot soldiers who have nothing to lose can get the attention of the established leadership, wherever they happen to live. With the examples of Iran, Algeria, and Egypt before it, the government of Saudi Arabia has recently had to set up a special accommodation to prove to its militant Muslim community that the Kingdom isn't being run by backsliders.

Saudi Arabia has retained the death penalty (as have all Islamic states) and has added the crime of drug smuggling to the usual list — adultery, murder, rape, treason, regicide or attempts thereto, second conviction for manufacturing booze, and blasphemy.

Ordinarily, execution is by beheading of the culprit in a public square. The means of beheading is usually an executioner and a really big sword. On occasion, however, the added theatrical elements deemed necessary to help onlookers achieve the proper level of edification has resulted in more advanced approaches. There was the case of an adulterous Saudi princess who was buried in sand; then a bulldozer blade was employed to remove the offending head. After an attempt to overthrow the government, the plotters and all their friends were shot from cannons — or rather cannons were fired with them tied to the muzzles.

In the past, executions have been held on Fridays after prayers. Recently there have been so many participants that the government has announced it will have to hold executions on other days.

Should the Muslim world be willing to turn its back on the West (unlikely), it will find in the east the Buddhist high-tech environmental movement. During the Gulf War, after Saddam Hussein dumped oil from the sea-loading pipeline and fired the oil wells of Kuwait, there was an intense Buddhist reaction. Arab diplomats have since expressed amazement at the amount of pressure Buddhist countries were prepared to exert. "Buddhists are supposed to be gentle, passive people," reported one, after Indonesian oil began to flow into traditional Arab markets. Arab embassies in Japan, India, Singapore, and Indonesia reported press attacks, solidly supported by local government officials, on all Arabs as environmental monsters.

Realizing that Islam is, perforce, in an extremely difficult position, it would be useful to understand the parameters involved in narrowing the gap between the West and the Muslim world. Islam's foundations are not built on assumptions familiar to someone used to the Christian tradition. It may be easier to think of Islam as one of the three global cultures with over 1.2 billion adherents.

To the Muslim, the great change wrought by our Renaissance and Reformation was that it released a great surge of individualism. Individualism provided the foundation for capitalism and democracy. The rights of man, so much a part of the American and French revolutions, are without a reference point to Islam. Islam remains locked into a world of the extended family and sees all of our social problems as evidence that, by supporting individualism over the interacting obligations of the extended family, each of us in the West is abandoned to a faithless universe which we face with fragile identities. In support of this thesis they cite American sociologists who have studied the fracturing of Western identity. In Islam the individual is the problem of the family and few Muslims think any institution can supplant the family.

Our world-view is struggling to accommodate the multi-dimensionality for which virtual reality is a metaphor. The world discovered by Planck, Einstein, Heisenberg, Schrödinger, and Dirac poses a great threat to the Ijma, the small, all male, largely self-selecting group of Islamic scholars that controls all — not merely religious — education in the Islamic community. The Ijma has four different schools of thought. Theological disputations between the four are the closest thing to what pre-Renaissance, pre-Reformation Scholasticism was all about.

Strict limitation on topics fit for disputation reminds us that this is a world which has never felt the need to leave the 7th century. A simple illustration is how the story of Adam and Eve is presented in Islam and in the West. In the West it is clear that the fruit of the tree of knowledge is the knowledge of good and evil, right from wrong. Original sin is the *disobedience* of God's will. The knowledge gained makes mankind responsible for all actions in the future. That is free will.

For the Muslim, man breaks God's law, God chastises man and the whole thing is done. No original sin and no capability to judge right from wrong. *The Koran* is completely determinist — God decides and man acquiesces. But the new era, as far as we can tell, has trashed determinism. Unless there is a way for the *Ijma* to fashion an accommodation, the Islamic world will be isolated, just as Westerners are by our abandonment of the extended family. There are no accommodations possible. We are the ones on the edge of the abstraction platform.

PART THREE

Life in Cyberspace

CHAPTER ELEVEN

Learning to Live in a Hyperspace World:
Does this mean our brains will change?

Adding a dimension to the knowable universe is not a new problem, as Renaissance art historian Erwin Panofsky reminds us. Panofsky points out that, prior to the development of perspective, the space in an image which would later be used to create perspective was set aside for God. Religious works produced in monasteries were set in a background of gold to remind the viewer that God need not be shown to be present. In the Eastern Church, we recall the vivid gold surrounding the figure in a Byzantine icon.

The apparent contradictions that arose in the Renaissance placed the established order at risk. In art, the intuitive proponents of perspective broke with classical authority and were, in some cases, accused of heresy by usurping God's place in paintings.

The challenges we face today are no more extreme than those of the Renaissance. The contradictions they faced were as daunting, in their day, as those of the present.

Defining abstraction is a problem to which contemporary cognitive psychologists have devoted much research. They have shown that money is one of the most abstract concepts most of us ever address. As children and teenagers, we spend 12 to 15 years learning to address the abstraction of money.

The invention of the bill of exchange is significant because it occurred relatively early in the Renaissance, spurred on by a widespread shortage of gold. Historians today believe that the gold shortage was a result of two elements. One was the large bribes paid by European rulers to persuade Muslim leaders not to invade. The other was that much of Europe's gold was in the hands of Jews who, denied citizenship, were required to live in ghettos. This gold was loaned out, principally to royalty, aristocracy, and others of the elite classes. Hence the term sovereign loans, whose surety was based on the ability to tax.

Under these conditions Europe's economy deteriorated. There was no money to finance trade. Rulers and clergy hoarded whatever coins came their way. In parts of Europe, no indigenous gold coinage was minted between the 9th and 13th centuries. The economy of Medieval Europe was for the most part a 'natural' and patronage economy. That is, it was highly localized and dependent on barter. Taxes on local and supralocal lords were paid in crop percentages. For example, a manor lord might provide a knight food, shelter and a few bolts of cloth, plus feed and stabling for the knight's horse, in return for the knight's pledge of service.

To move from a natural economy to a money economy requires at least some degree of specialization in labour and production. Of course, given the degree of unrest which plagued Europe during the Dark Ages, the natural economy appealed to everyone. (When we see a news item about the barter economy that holds the cities and towns of the C.I.S. together while the value of the ruble hovers at a fraction of a cent, we should remember that barter is how the entire Medieval world functioned.)

Life in the Middle Ages was one long fiscal crisis. The Church had banned usury, holding it to be a sin. Denied citizenship and the right to own land, Europe's Jewish businessmen channeled ghetto funds into loans. Since Jews were not Christians, and thus, in the Church's view, had no souls to risk through the sin of usury, they served as the money lenders of Europe. This comfortable fiction created money for loan (technically usury) while not officially approving of it. The shortage of actual gold made the loan business very profitable. (One of the main purposes behind the periodic Jewish expulsions and pogroms was to steal money and goods from Jews, or as a way for local rulers to avoid payment of debts. As modern bankers have learned, the sovereign loan business hasn't changed much.)

But if you run a bank without bills of exchange, you miss out on the multiplier effect that happens when you lend the same gold to more than one person simultaneously. By inventing the bill of exchange, the Lombard bankers also invented the 'float,' the multiplier effect on bank capitalization by which bank lending increases the amount of currency in circulation. The impact of bills of exchange on trade liberalization and expansion was massive.

LAWS OF GRAVITY

In a world driven by such a quantum jump in the level of abstraction as is ours, or as was the Renaissance, we are increasingly confronted with situations for which orthodox thought provides little in the way of solutions.

Era transitions only come in one size: huge! Smaller cycles of major change are termed here as "ages," which come with a major social or technological shift such as the invention of the steam engine, the automobile, or the passenger aircraft.

One way to get a rough estimate of the impact of a single new technology is to count the laws which are enacted to regulate it. For example, in the average North American state or province, approximately 25 percent of *all* laws regulate automobiles and highways.

One problem with which we are struggling today is the development of legal systems that meet the needs of the unfolding era. Legal systems are rooted in the need to provide rules that protect people from having their property taken from them arbitrarily, without just recompense.

It's easy to say "that's obvious." But that wasn't so obvious 500 or 600 years ago. Consider the idea of copyright and patenting an invention: it was primarily intended to encourage the orderly exchange of property. It was mostly a fabrication of the Renaissance.

Initially there were no patents or copyrights as we know them. Instead, a city would sell or grant a trade monopoly. For example, a city might grant a candle maker the exclusive right to manufacture or sell candles within the city boundaries. The enforcement of these patent laws was harsh. In Florence patent infringement was punishable by execution by garrotting. In Milan execution was by musket (the bore of the musket used differed according to whether the patent infringer was a Christian, Muslim or Jew). In Venice the malefactor was forced to drink poison.

These early patents were frequently used as political rewards or sold to raise revenues. They awarded to the patent holder the right to sell a product or service, often exclusively, and had nothing to do with primacy of intellectual property.

But as manufacturing inventions began to increase return on investments, the need to protect patent or copyright holders became pressing. Once again, the encouragement of the orderly transfer of property became a mark of a government's sovereignty and ability to support its citizens. By this point the benefits, in the form of increasing prosperity, had gone through a couple of iterations and were familiar to princes and governments.

The international patent process as we know it is relatively recent and was adapted from the monopolies when it became desirable to protect intellectual property. The need to provide such protections arose with the rise in global trade, which came about through improvements in travel safety, navigation and the invention of the bill of exchange. As commercial activity expanded, patenting conventions were adopted.

In the 16th century you didn't have to be a rocket scientist to figure out that if you could keep the means of manufacturing your invention secret, you could extend your patent coverage to other cities that wanted access to the benefits of your invention. So the patent process was shoe-horned into becoming a means by which the orderly transfer of property could be arranged and orderly commerce could be encouraged.

People of the Renaissance had more than enough experience with the disorderly transfer of property, which usually involved the sacking of a city or piracy at sea, both of which were dangerous to the possessor of the property.

COPYRIGHT BY THE BOOK

Era transitions occur when the level of abstraction is elevated, as is occurring in our lifetimes. When the abstraction level rises dramatically, there is a wide variety of forces for change.

For example, there is an expansion in vocabulary as the language adapts to the need for finer discriminations and an expanded environment. Media coverage grows as the perceived need for news and information is accommodated. News consumption rises as people attempt to remain abreast of events affecting their lives.

Most important, a perceptual shift occurs. The next thing that usually happens is that artists in the society begin to articulate their intuitive sense of this shift. The shift is typically seen as an altered epistemology and the society moves into discovering what is known and what is knowable at the newly accepted level of abstraction.

The Renaissance, for instance, had accounting techniques that served merchants well. When they adopted Arab numeracy, the number of people who learned or discovered advanced mathematics grew logarithmically. Merchants needed seamen who could navigate ships to the far corners of the earth. In much the same way, legal systems were developed which defined property.

A useful example of how copyright worked in the Renaissance can be seen by looking at how it affected Erasmus of Rotterdam (c. 1466-1536), one of the seminal thinkers in the history of mankind. He was a tutor to Henry VIII of England and a friend and contemporary of Martin Luther and Sir Thomas More. In our terms, Erasmus's books were consistently "best sellers."

Erasmus's books were published from Basel by a Swiss printer/publisher named Froben. The city of Basel gave Froben a form of copyright which worked fine — right up to the city limits. At one time there were 22 separate editions of Erasmus' work *In Praise of Folly* being printed and sold all over Europe, editions for which neither Erasmus nor Froben received any reimbursement.

This is what happened: a trader would come to Basel and buy books from Froben, then sell them to printers in other cities. These printers would, in turn, print their own editions and sell them without recompense to the original author or publisher. In fact, the local printer would arrange to be granted a local right to copy. (Don't let anyone tell you that "necessity is the mother of invention." If ever a time cried out for scanning hardware and software, it was the 16th and 17th centuries.)

From our rear-view mirror vantage point, we might assume that Froben was less than thrilled by this state of affairs. Realistically, there was little he could do. And after all, he did exactly the same thing with volumes secured from the self-same travelling merchants. Even though books were eagerly sought after, they were expensive, and the cost of shipping books would have been prohibitive. In every city in Europe there were printer/publishers anxious to get the latest book by Erasmus or any of the other star writers of the period.

Erasmus was a superstar, the leading spokesman of the new Humanism then sweeping Europe. A new volume by Erasmus would fetch a good profit for the traveller from printer/publishers in other cities, who would, correctly, expect to have a best seller on their hands. And what about Erasmus, best-selling author and big-time scholar? Typically, he and others like him met their financial needs by "dedicating" a book to a wealthy nobleman or prelate who paid for the privilege. No one expected the foreign publishers to give the author anything.

Incidentally, it is unlikely that *In Praise of Folly* would be published today. It is filled with a self-indulgent author's voice, which would be excised by a contemporary publisher's editors.

INTERESTING TIMES

The people of Renaissance Europe were presented with a new spatial plane that was empty and had to be filled. With the discovery of perspective came a perceptual mobility which actually altered the neurophysiology of human thought. Newly activated neurons fired the creativity and broad-ranging curiosity with which the Renaissance became synonymous, as people set out to create a happier, wealthier, and healthier world.

As the mercantile world faded into industrialism and a need for replicable inventions, there was an increasing need to regulate intellectual property transfers. As trade patterns became internationalized, it became necessary to make patents and copyrights enforceable internationally. Global patent recognition was not even discussed until the Industrial Age reached maturity — and has not been accomplished yet.

Toward the end of the Industrial Age it became possible for Third World countries to physically industrialize relatively inexpensively. Manufacturers, usually in collusion with the government, entered into "grey market" ventures that avoided patent and copyright acknowledgements. This became particularly true in products with high labour content. Low-cost labour could improve national living standards, which reflected disparities between those countries which underwent the Industrial Revolution earlier rather than later.

This is the world today. Once again we are involved in a paradigm shift, and there is no reason to believe that there is any benefit to be gained by avoiding it. We have the sad example of the former U.S.S.R., the People's Republic of China and various Third World countries.

We have the New World Order, proffered by George Bush, James Robinson III, et cetera, which claims to offer leadership for this new era. They would have us believe that the world will be more efficiently run if the rate of change is effectively controlled. They argue that transnational corporations are the most effective commercializers of the technological advances which seem to inundate us. They would argue, persuasively, that regional trading blocs will supplant many familiar functions of the nation state. Such a trading bloc is nearly complete in Europe and is becoming stabilized between the U.S., Canada, and more recently Mexico and Chile.

They would also have us believe that only large transnational corporations have the economic stability necessary to keep the economy expanding.

What fans of the New World Order forget is that the forte of this time in history is the transmission of ideas. We have social skills and technologies that bypass the social inertia that put the transmission of the forces of change on a relative "slow" in the past. They also conveniently forget that their allies, the transnational managers and senior government bureaucrats (who more and more frequently are the same people), regard innovation as the natural enemy of squeezing the longest possible product life-span out of a particular technology.

The new era is happening now because the assumptions behind the world-view of the industrial state no longer accommodate a world-view that incorporates the additional perceptual planes suggested by recent developments in physics and mathematics. The last time this happened was in the 15th century.

The new dimensions are temporal as well as spatial and require new skills in perceptual mobility. The new world-view must accommodate a universe which operates within a continuum of both space and time. No era has ever been confronted with the degree of change we face. It is not surprising that the wealthy and politically powerful would attempt to at least slow down this rate of change. It has been tried before with disastrous outcomes. The example which comes immediately to mind is Stalin's use of T. D. Lysenko to attack politically incorrect — but accurate — science. Then there was the political incorrectness of Galileo, whose papal ban has only recently been re-examined by the Church body that advises his Holiness about science. This agency has found that the Inquisition erred.

MULTIPLE DIMENSIONS AND STRANGE ATTRACTORS

The new world-view is based on an understanding that the universe is multi-dimensional. It is difficult for someone brought up in an essentially linear culture to understand N-space. Most of us don't even have the vocabulary, as yet, to talk about it, since descriptions of N-space are still couched in equations and proofs. Not many of us read theorems and equations for recreation, so the following analogy may suffice.

Imagine that you are a fish, a fish of a species that cannot see above the water line. Your hypothetical plane of perception encompasses a knowable world that provides food and oxygen, which you process through your gills. Then I put my hand into your pond, intending to tickle you under the gills with this hand. Initially, you will see only four fingers and a thumb. You cannot see the hand, nor can you extrapolate it, since it is above the water line, and hands don't exist in the watery plane of your perception.

Nothing indicates to our fish that there is a single controlling entity which, in our example, functions on another plane.

A few years ago, just after Pope John Paul II had been consecrated and installed, he issued a papal statement opposing birth control. That week the pope was on the covers of both Time and Newsweek. But someone whose curiosity about the world extended beyond Time and Newsweek might have gone home to find that his copy of Science did not have the pope on the cover. Instead, it had a picture of a three-coloured (or calico) mouse sitting on someone's hand, obviously alive and active.

That cover was, to anyone minimally literate in the biological sciences, utterly arresting. The gene that produces a calico mouse is fatal. (In cats the tricolour gene is only fatal to males, which is why all calico cats are females.) Yet here was a three-coloured mouse, obviously in fine fettle. It turned out that, in a feat of genetic engineering, biologists had excised the fatal gene from the embryo, then popped the altered mouse back in utero.

The calico mouse gave the new pope an entirely new credibility problem, which Time and Newsweek shared. The papacy objects to the birth control pill, which is, after all, a fairly low order of biological engineering. But the calico mouse is on a quantum higher order of bio-engineering control.

Institutions that continue to assess political or economic correctness from a linear perspective are doomed to triviality. Without perceptual mobility, the ability to even look for the right track is impossible. If we learn that events we don't anticipate are not really happening out of context, we can begin to learn to track the events which will impact on us.

Taking this analogy to a more empirical level, let us postulate a two-dimensional world. This world is a single flat plane. We could imagine some creatures existing on this two dimensional universe. If we use a piece of paper to demonstrate this, it helps. If we bend the paper from the upper right corner to the lower left corner we can see that what was, from the point of view of the creatures, the most distant point of the compass, is from our point of view the closest and most accessible.

But remember what we did. *We folded the paper.* That is, we took that flat plane and moved it through 3-space, a dimension which doesn't exist for those living in a two-dimensional world. (Kenneth Dewdney has written a book called *Planeverse*, which explains this idea much more thoroughly.)

Another part of the emerging world-view is a chaos theory formulation called the strange attractor theory, which holds that even the most minute actions may be related to other events in a way not anticipated by Newtonian physics.

Strange attractor theory deals with the changing relationships among three variables. In *Chaos: Making a New Science*, James Gleick describes the work of Edward Lorenz and others who work with order masquerading as randomness. "At any instant in time, the three variables fix the location of a point in three-dimensional space; as the system changes, the motion of the point represents the continuously changing variables."

Strange attractor theory allows us to discover the attractors between two data sets when there is another data set to suggest that an attraction exists.

When we establish relationships between two events that are "attracted" (i.e. have a functional relationship) to one another, we are using the terms used by cognitive psychologists to describe the way in which so-called "creative people" identify or solve problems that baffle everyone else.

In *Chaos*, Gleick describes how many of the most significant breakthroughs in chaos theory were not made by mathematicians, but rather by thinkers working in other areas with mathematics. For instance, Edward Lorenz is an atmospheric scientist who was interested in why clouds behave the way they do.

In this book we have been using the terms "tangential thinking" and "non-linear thinking" synonymously. Tangential thinking exploits some sort of inborn intuition which gives us the ability to reach out to the solution of a problem on the basis of apparently inadequate information and conventionally unobserved functional relationships.

The father of fractal mathematics, Benoit Mandelbrot, is not regarded as a mathematician at all. He is a computer scientist of great repute. It was he who laid the groundwork for virtual reality software. His work with fractal mathematics is derived from a point most of us would think to be only tenuously related.

The tangential thinker seems to be able to pick out connections that are apparently unrelated. Historically, this ability has been a relatively uncommon extravagance that went unrewarded and even punished in industrial and pre-industrial societies. The world of N-space rewards such non-linear thinkers. These are the people who, when they point something out, produce the response "why didn't I think of that?" Tangential thinkers are frequently at odds with those believed to be the holders of orthodox authority.

Throughout history, solutions to apparently impossible problems, which with the benefit of hindsight we think of as seminal thought, appear to have consistently involved tangential thinking. Arthur Koestler has studied this process and calls it "biosociation." He describes it this way: "biosociation means combining two hitherto unrelated cognitive matrices in such a way that a new level is added to the hierarchy, which contains the previously separate structures as its members."

History does not reward those who try to impede its orderly advances just because they occur without conventional, linear, cause-and-effect relationships. It would seem that there is a new world order; it is not the New World Order of George Bush. The real new world order agenda appears to be based in the perceptual alterations implied by Max Planck and in Einstein's relativity.

The concepts of cyberspace or N-space are difficult for most of us to grasp — but then few of us understand the internal combustion engine. What we need to understand is that the forces of N-space are likely to be

---

Tangentia

The idea of tangential thought has been kicking around for a long time. Remember the old children's rhyme:

> For want of a nail, the shoe was lost;
> For want of a shoe, the horse was lost;
> For want of a horse, the rider was lost;
> For want of a rider; the news was lost;
> For want of the news; a battle was lost;
> For want of a battle, a kingdom was lost.

We can imagine a long-dead tangential thinker teaching that rhyme to children so that the model would be chanted down through time until we needed it.

the engine of our lives for the future. It will be better if we don't ascribe magical properties to this engine, but recognize that there is a reason why the changes we see are happening, so we can make informed choices about the items on the smorgasbord of options being offered to us.

Stephen Hawking's book *A Brief History of Time* managed to stay on the *New York Times* best-seller list for over a year, to the astonishment of the North American publishing world. Similarly, that James Gleick's book *Chaos*, about the difficult concept of chaos theory, would also enjoy best-seller status makes it unlikely that the vision of the NWO and their World Corp. allies lie in the main track of history.

One of the major causes of the collapse of the feudal world was located in an unforeseen, unforeseeable event of the 15th century. As noted earlier, without the mathematics to support navigation, including Arab numeracy, it is very tough to sail out of sight of land.

For the better part of the 15th century, Europe was still feudal. Although the signs of ferment were obvious, the manorial economy still functioned on the basis that the available land was finite and what there was, was controlled through feudal obligations.

There is an interpretation of the consequences of the Columbus voyage which is not found in popular histories. This interpretation would say that the effect of Columbus' report of his trip was that land was not finite after all. This precipitated a confused land rush and the collapse of the feudal idea of "finite" land. Without finite land, the manorial economy, with its complex of interwoven obligations, received a fatal blow. (The Medieval idea that land was finite was well adapted to Church doctrine, which held that *The Bible* was indeed accurate and that God had created the world in seven days. The Church also held that God made the earth perfect.)

The Spanish royal house, which sponsored the Columbus venture, was thrilled when later expeditions reported the discovery of gold. The assumption of the Spanish court was that the New World could be seen in an extrapolative way and that management of the colonies' fortunes could be based on the feudal belief that land was finite. But while imperial Spain cautiously elected not to expand beyond its ability to control occupied lands, British and French settlers poured into North America.

In fact, fortunes were created in America which would challenge the existing order of Europe. The Spanish Main provided fortunes to finance the foundations of a new aristocracy in England. This new English aristocracy had its roots in trade rather than land (although they later acquired land from the luckless aristocrats who failed to survive the era transition of the Renaissance) and brought hereditary English wealth into the ventures of the East India Company, the East African Company, and the Hudson's Bay company. (Spain's attempts to resist the Renaissance would be paralleled in Czarist Russia's avoidance of industrialization.)

When Spain attempted to re-establish papal hegemony in Europe, it flexed its muscles to resist the ideas of Humanism. England's support of the Dutch against Spain is confused in most history texts today. To believe that the Spanish wars were about religion is to miss the impact of Renaissance thought on the technologies of trade.

By allowing the new technologies full and free exploitation, the Protestant north Germans, Dutch, and English were able to build unassailable mercantile empires. The religious aspects of this period are metaphors for the even more profound reality that the Renaissance had raised the level of abstraction, fostering a new perceptual mobility that threatened — and eventually overwhelmed — the existing order.

THINKING IN CYBERSPACE

A few years ago, if you were to ask a mathematician or physicist whether the fourth dimension existed, the answer would be simply "Yes." If you were then to ask the mathematician to show it to you, he would show you a set of equations. If you were to persist and ask to "see the fourth dimension" the mathematician would have been unable to show it to you in any other form. For one thing, there was no computer with sufficient power to display a graphic depiction of the fourth dimension.

Yet a working understanding of time and space is necessary for comprehension of the real new world order. Fortunately, the language to usefully describe these functions is evolving rapidly. Some useful graphical illustrations of the fourth dimension have already been dreamed up for films and television.

There are some excellent video games, written for personal computers, which require that the player assume a universe of four dimensions. There are some good books aimed at making this information available to wider audiences. Beside the Hawking and Gleick books, there is Gesa Szamosi's *The Twin Dimensions — Time and Space*, which while not way up there on the best-seller lists is about as good as it gets at explaining the roots of N-space. (Szamosi teaches math at the University of Windsor and his use of analogies makes sense of it all for someone who hasn't tried to understand the intuitions of mathematicians since undergraduate or high school days.)

But if a reader of this book were to ask for one volume to help familiarize them with the basic ground rules for a multiply-dimensioned universe, it would have to be Michio Kaku's 1994 book, *Hyperspace*. Kaku is simply a great writer and teacher. Without trying to take anything away from the others, Kaku's book is a pleasure to read and when you are finished you discover that you have, almost without noticing it, learned a great deal about a very complex topic.

The real survival problem each of us faces is to understand the intrinsic orderliness underlying the emergence of a world-view that incorporates N-space. This process is orderly, but the order is not that of the old linear and extrapolative framework.

What now appears to be randomly chaotic seems so because we view the universe with inadequate perceptual tools. There are new tools but, for most of us, they have been assigned a low order of priority.

Most business and government planners complain that they often miss windows of opportunity because the people they are advising take too long to get the point. Their real problem is that they themselves lack the tools, including consensual vocabularies, which will predict that a new window of opportunity is going to appear at point X. They need to develop tracking tools similar to those used by physicists.

Physicists have to deal with atomic particles in a universe in which motion and energy and position are mutually exclusive, depending on the observer. Prediction of future events (where these little electron and particle suckers will pop up next) is done using quantum waves as a probability generating tool, but you have to remember that by measuring any of the exclusive functions, you will influence the others. Physicists know that they cannot know the location, the energy or the charge of any molecule in a test chamber before they make a decision which constitutes an intervention on the part on the observer.

Any intrusion by an observer (i.e. a business or government planner) becomes incorporated into the structure being studied. By incorporating such notions, we can build strategies to inferentially plot where those windows of opportunity might pop out next.

The next problem for the hypothetical planner is that once we have improved the exposure time to the opportunity, we have to convince the boss that he has something. You'll recall us babbling on about how strange it must have been to be the first guy at your regional trade fair to try to use a bill of exchange. Our modern planner faces a similar problem — the audience is not particularly mathematically literate. What our planner must do is learn to be selective about which windows, in fact, offer useful opportunities and which windows are merely transient and end up far from the main evolutionary track. (Hey! Is it possible that we're saying that human beings may, *knowingly*, participate in their own evolutionary development?)

One thing our planner might do is learn to treat the abstruse metaphors of the more pristine disciplines (such as physics) with a bit more familiarity. There's no point in recalling high school days when this stuff terrified everyone.

When it's really new, teachers, textbook authors, and the scientists themselves don't really understand what they're doing. They usually lack a vocabulary to explain it to non-specialists. Breakthroughs have, in the past, required years to pass beyond audiences with highly specialized intuitive skills. By exploiting the graphics available in entertainment technologies, the new level of abstraction may be diffused throughout society at an unprecedented pace.

CHAPTER TWELVE

Culture in Hyperspace: This is not a computer game

Anthropologists have demonstrated the significance of the introduction of three dimensional art with research in which primitive people, whose own culture's art lacked perspective, had to *learn* to see it. To become aware of a new dimension, as happens when a person first sees pictures with a perspective component, the subjects must learn to see the three-dimensioned view. Later research used electroencephalographs to compare the responses of these objects with similarly stimulated EEGs from people acculturated to 3-D driven societies. The results showed different EEG patterns of glial cell activity sites when presented with the same perspective-based stimuli.

It took 300 years for people of the Renaissance to become comfortable with the ideas, art, and literature that accurately depicted the world-view which had at its heart a universe dominated by assumptions of three dimensions. The dramatic increment in the generalized level of abstraction, which became the norm, resulted in massive changes in the way people thought and the level of abstraction at which that thought began to be manifested in daily life. Critical to a widespread acceptance of the quantum jump in abstraction was the exploration of the limits by the vigorous arts communities, from the painters to the playwrights. Music became more mathematically based. New instruments were invented to more accurately reflect the ideas in composers' heads.

Initially, artists marked three-dimensioned pictorial statements explicitly by placing them in a separate part of a painting, such as a window. The paintings themselves were a device give to viewers a clue *how to see* the 3-D picture.

Unless you have been brought up in a culture using artistic or other graphic presentations of perspective, you have to learn to see pictures employing a third plane.

In the West, it is common to place a mobile over an infant's crib to stimulate neural processes. Studies of infants' abilities to distinguish events in the third dimension show that the child's 3-D viewing and discrimination skills are enhanced by use of a mobile.

The mobile was a natural outcome of the groundbreaking work exhibited by Marcel Duchamp and others at the 1913 Armory Show in New York, although Duchamp left it to Alexander Calder to make a career out of this 3-D art form.

We also know that in those whose society admits to the existence of a third dimension differ in abstraction-management skills from those whose society has not discovered perspective.

THE COMPUTER AS VIRTUAL LIFE

The cultural differences of national computer industry success occur on parameters closely related to problem solving strategies. There is now some research to suggest that cultures with exposure to N-space will experience radically altered glial cell activity and probably different access to abstraction.

In the Renaissance, the city-states of the Lombard League attempted to keep the way perspective was generated as a guild secret. That was a non-runner. The idea that a group of artists could maintain a secret was pretty strange.

Similarly, we may ask what nations produce world-class software. Certainly North Americans can claim to have cornered the world software market. There are a number of reasons that help account for this. For one, corporate America, unimpaired by World War II, was able to invest large sums in computerizing many applications while foreign countries were rebuilding.

When other countries' computer manufacturers tried to play catch-up from industrial strength bases they were less successful. Some used their manufacturing expertise in TV sets, printers, electric typewriters, or other electronic devices, but no one has produced anything they could parlay into building real computers that could be sold across borders. It wasn't long before everyone understood that no matter how good your chips were or how well-engineered your computers were, without great software no one would buy your computers.

One factor that appears to have been overlooked was that computers in North America took on a certain chic and young males took to "playing" with them. In this case the word "playing" means obsessively learning about computers and software in the company of peers. By the mid 1970s, the travelling social skills of the 1960s had become absorbed into the entire youth culture and kids started travelling to computer fairs. Hobby kits were available and the first Apples were being built. Universities were engaging in competition to produce the best computer science departments. By the mid-1980s it was not uncommon to overhear 14-year-olds in grade nine arguing about the relative merits of MIT, Cal. Tech., Carnegie-Mellon, Waterloo and Rochester and planning how to get into their school of choice. The real wealth of North America began to show.

The Apple IIe and the Commodore 64 came out and thousands of young males conned their parents into financing their new obsessive habit. Texas Instruments proved that the new industry would not tolerate industrial management. The growth in sales of personal computers amounted to a dedication of a significant part of a generation's self-selected learning, before the education system was ready to teach. That generation had a problem with being told "you can't do that." They proceeded to make computers do things which the few textbooks available said could not be done. Even more interesting was that a whole underground culture was growing up around computer stores and a lot of kids were able to get jobs right out of high school. If you could write 30 lines of error-free code a day, you could look forward to steady employment that provided the latest in hardware.

The disciplined academic systems of Europe and the Far East, with their elitist structures in Europe (90 percent of secondary school graduates go to apprenticeships or to on-the-job training) were unprepared for what they and their governments thought was a competition between the European and the North American post-secondary education systems.

That was not the field that the Americans had chosen. The competition existed at the student level! After the 1960s North Americans saw the social change rate as a human issue, not an academic issue. The North American hacker community was very real and the North American post-secondary system was prepared to deal with students who held no particular brief for a historical authority which had been demonstrating clear signs that it was in failure mode. This was just as well, because there was very little historical authority in the computer sciences.

In fact, most computer programs came from other established departments such as applied math, electrical engineering, and physics. The North American schools were not only able to cope with students who were fully aware that the schools had no legitimate authority, but the schools themselves had no investments in protecting a class system.

The American university system had renewed its physical plants to deal with post-war veterans from World War II and Korea and one way to deal with "mature" students is to give them lots of projects. After the war sapiential authority had achieved a strong value on North American campuses.

With little to teach and four years to teach it in, most computer science professors turned to their students' abiding interest level and put them to work on directed projects just as if they were "mature" students.

The students found themselves with unlimited time and the best equipment. Another thing happened that made life more bearable for the programming fraternity: in 1982 the cyberpunk writers started to publish. They were able to explain the new ether of cyberspace to the satisfaction of the programmers who were experiencing it daily. (One of the cyberpunkers even coined the term cyberspace.) Because a lot of programmers are pretty uncommunicative, the cyberpunk literature meant a lot to them.

That France, Germany, the U.K., Japan, India, the Netherlands, Russia, and Italy have all failed to be serious contenders in the global software field suggests that some heretofore unidentified factor is at work. It is not simply that the world's operating systems were developed in the U.S.

The British produced the BBC computer with distribution of courseware and instruction manuals through radio, TV, and partners in the educational world. Clive Sinclair, with significant City of London backing, produced an inexpensive computer, the Sinclair.

The French gave away keyboards and modems for the Antiope videotex systems. They also stopped supplying phone company customers with print-based telephone directories in major cities substituting free, continuously updated electronic directories.

The Italian industrial giant Olivetti tried to use its typewriter business base as a jumping off place, but never got to the point that anyone else was interested in its sales performance. Olivetti also made one of the great egregious errors, equalled only by the Texas Instruments personal computer disaster.

Olivetti tried to start using a unique formatting system for its PC machine. The rest of the industry was mystified as to why anyone would be this stupid when everyone else was thriving on a compatibility bandwagon that left Apple out there cultivating the artistes and package designers. Olivetti also attempted to end-run its own product with a single-application word processor electronic typewriter. Philips Electronics also tried to enter the game with a dedicated word processor.

A few years ago Japanese computer companies announced through MITI that the government and private sector would combine resources in a "national effort" to be the first to produce a "Fifth Generation" computer. (That is a computer that would make every other computer in the world obsolete.) After trying for a few years the Fifth Generation project fizzled like a firecracker that had been rained on and then dried.

France's Bull bought a minor American player, Honeywell, and tried to get market share with Bull's smart card. Honeywell should have told Bull, in whatever fractured French it could manage, that no one gets to be noticed with a minor product that requires a massive infrastructure.

Mitsubishi of Japan produce respected mainframe and supercomputers whose sales, while international, are spotty and don't impact on the ink supply of anyone else's sales charts, even though Japan remains such a major player in the DRAM and other chip games that the E.U. is trying to get restrictions on imports.

There has been an argument that the North American English grammatical structure is ideal transport into the cognitive syntax needed to "visualize" the computer environment. Whatever the truth is, we North Americans have a substantial running head start in developing the one essential tool for the Information Age.

There is, however, one single explanation for all the successes and failures that have occurred. What is interesting is that even the successful practitioners probably can't identify it. In all cases that have been commercial successes, the company has been driven by an awareness that the endeavour was fuelled by something larger then the sum of its parts.

Just as the universities had to run with a non-hierarchical model in those early years, so does the computer industry. Few marketing executives have any technical training, the financial people are pretty good with spreadsheets and can, over time, learn to use those swell options spreadsheet makers talk about as being so easy, the senior executives are mostly deal makers and the truth is that anything that matters happens on the programming floor. Successful CEOs lead their troops and understand them.

At a meeting in Toronto on February 2, 1994, *The Globe and Mail* quoted William Esry, chairman of Sprint Corp., saying skeptically about the consumer market hype surrounding the mass benefits to be awarded by getting the "information highway" up and running, "Aren't these the same people who have trouble programming their VCRs... Make sure every child can read before every child is hooked up to the information highway."

At the same meeting Nicholas Negroponte, director of MIT's Media Lab, assailed another speaker, Ted Rogers, a cable TV tycoon, saying "50 percent of what Ted Rogers said is wrong." He went on to add that his plans to invite Rogers to become a sponsor of the Media Lab "are probably best forgotten."

Rogers, who heretofore had been considered a well-informed deal maker, was carrying too much industrial baggage to understand what was going on. We should remember that for most computer or communications executives to be invited to be a sponsor of the Media Lab is a privilege for which they would cheerfully sell their first-born.

Another key ingredient to the North American success was that the IBM open architecture, Microsoft DOS-based computer was *allowed to invent itself.* It offered options like six or eight slots for boards which neither IBM, nor Microsoft had the slightest idea of what they would be used for. A modem manufacturer wants to put a modem on a board? You want to add memory? Whatever.

In the case of Texas Instruments and all the others who lost at an obvious business, at no time was the company out of control of its managers. No one knows how many clone manufacturers there are, and no evidence exists that anyone at IBM or Microsoft was ever in control of very much. The IBM open-architecture computer invited everyone in the world to build applications for it.

Others attempted to put out this product of the new era under rubrics suited to Industrial Age mind-sets. Most of the post-industrial world still hasn't learned this lesson. One of the rules of the game is to *stay as close as you can to the abstraction level that is driving the era.*

Invariably, these companies would bring their historic strengths to the table and lose out. No matter what they did, they blew it. What has making chips got to do with building computers? Nothing! What has making TV sets got to do with computers? Nothing! What has running a state post office got to do with running a computer system? Nothing! What is it that justifies someone in the electronics industry thinking they can run a computer company? Nothing! If you have a respectable market share in the typewriter business, can you use that as a springboard to get into the computer business? Nope!

They refused to recognize that the closer you get to the level of abstraction the less you have to say about what is going to happen.

HOW TO CHANGE YOUR MIND

While our understanding of neural activity is, at best, primitive, there are some things we do know. We know that certain parts of the brain are active today which were inactive in the past. We also know from physical anthropological research that members of isolated societies are often unable to comprehend an unfamiliar unit of information. We do not know what triggers a "ready" state for reception of a breakthrough in the level of abstraction.

If the West was still using Roman numerals, it would have been unlikely for the discovery of calculus to have occurred in the 17th century. To understand perspective, our brains have to be able to manipulate the world of the mind in three dimensions.

Another factor which affects a breakthrough in the abstraction level is the ability to abandon historical assumptions about the way the world is ordered. We, as individuals, may have all of the "facts" concerning a change in new symbolic processes and still be unable to incorporate them into a personal world-view because they conflict so harshly with our personal historical assumptions. Men who retire from active careers frequently have great difficulty abandoning the lifestyle patterns of 30 or 40 years.

We went on at great length about North American supremacy in developing the critical tool for the new era. What was important was that the culture respected the aspirations of the programmers. The young men had little to unlearn. The computer industry has an assumption that if a problem exists there is a solution. The problem is one of exploration and discovery. We do that well. We don't have a tradition-bound culture. We respect sapiential authority.

Our young people are encouraged to be idealistic. We can understand that for many people the computer industry, with its close connection to the abstraction level, can have a sense of vocation to it.

The present world-view shift may have been significantly speeded up by the introduction in the 1960s of perception-altering drugs. The endemic availability of LSD and the other perception modifiers provided a generational group with a learning tool, which was supported by strong peer approval, for wide-ranging perceptual mobility and experimentation. This generationally-based shared perceptual exploration was further supported with a popular culture expressed in art and music.

This is not to suggest that drug use is likely to enhance the ability to explore cyberspace today.

But at a critical time in the movement of the new era these drugs came to be widely available. It meant that the next generation had been shown that accessing perceptual mobility was possible. They were given crude tools of language, film, music, and graphics with which they could begin to engage in perceptual exploration. They also had another tool, the computer, which would allow them to explore a virus in three dimensions. They could model events in ways that either slowed or speeded up time. They could morph graphics. The computer could enhance pictures from space and allow our knowledge to crawl away from speculation that could never be proved or disproved. The physicists had told us that a universe of N-space existed. The computer proved and demonstrated that they were right. Nihilism and anarchism ceased to be attractive to our youth. The computer gave them back a vision.

READING THE RUNES

At the various times in history when major leaps in the level of generally agreed abstraction have occurred, the process of moving the new level of abstraction into general availability has usually meant pretty severe dislocations because no one understands what has really happened. The further from congruence with the actual new level of abstraction you try to implement something, the more likely it is to be wrong or a transient fad.

The world-view undergoes a profound shift as the society scrambles to accommodate new information being transmitted in unexpected contexts. Once the society adjusts to the new world-view, there is a period of implementation, a period when commercialization and invention are based on the new level of abstraction. The inventions and commercializations are, in fact, very primitive because the new world-view is not widely accepted yet.

For example, given the state of public health in the Renaissance, with Plague and sexually transmitted diseases, and the relatively early invention of the telescope (final quarter of the 16th century), we might have expected the microscope to have been invented right away. But it was nearly 200 years after the telescope before the microscope became available.

The fact is that people of the Renaissance had no realistic expectation that Plague and syphilis could be cured. By and large, the populace assumed that it was God's Punishment, and looking around at the behaviour of their friends and neighbours, most residents of the Renaissance would be hard put to name a more worthy crew for God's attention when He was going into punishment mode.

Naturally some existing cultures are more adaptive to the emergent level of abstraction than others. This is also the time when the expansion of the more successful states begins in earnest.

The combination of entertainment and information delivered together makes control of the media relatively easy, as was seen in the Gulf War. But what happens when we are presented with information which we don't understand or where we see the content as trivial? What happens when information is encoded in terms which are averse to our values yet do not offend our legal prohibitions, for example, against obscenity?

The contemporary literary underground follows what has been a common strategy for avoiding being seen as subversive. It writes in ways which are either not understood or dismissed as trivial.

Cyberpunk literary forms are found in almost all media. Stylistically, cyberpunk is dense with information and reads as though the writer had an over-release of endorphins that were enhanced with a stimulant. One consistent theme, regardless of the medium or genre, is the hero as an outlaw.

While most cyberpunk draws on a speculative fiction base for its settings, it is not essential for a writer to use science fiction to be a cyberpunk author. It is probably necessary for the writer to be, at least, aware of the technological assumables to carry off an authentic cyberpunk voice. (There are no techno assumables, for example in *Dr. Who*, the BBC sci-fi program so beloved by your neighbourhood post-adolescent aesthete, except the ability to suspend disbelief that interdimensional and cross-temporal travel is possible.) Cyberpunk writers use irony, which is essentially logical, to highlight the bizarre under a microscope of logical analysis. In the course of an era transition, many of the events are not only estranged from our sense of historical authority, but are beyond any of the usual extrapolative models' capacities to be predictive. In the end you can only look at a writer and see if the author's work cuts down on the frequency or level of surprise you experience.

Cyberpunk can qualify as a post-modern style because it doesn't discriminate between pop cultural sources and "serious" resource materials. This bias was first understood by Marshall McLuhan and accounted for much of the misunderstandings he encountered from conventional academics.

The greatest risk, from the point of view of the NWO leaders, is the same one the Aztecs faced. The Aztecs had a closed-loop society of abundance in which an oligarchy held all of the power. When the oligarchy began to make serious mistakes there was no "loyal opposition" to perk up the government with a fresh team. Spanish classes anyone?

The rock and roll music of the 1960s thought, self-indulgently, that it was politically radical. Large record companies, themselves usually flaccid arms of conglomerates, with their burnt-out flower children executives, no longer unwittingly publish what is unacceptable ideation. Try finding a copy of the Leslie Spit TreeO's "North American." That certainly set off the alarms at Capitol Records.

The stuff that challenges mainstream values, we are told, is left to non-mainstream black performers, although the customer demographics for such records, tapes, and CDs have highly white representations and get heavy play from DJs at "raves" and dance party events.

Emanating from both Europe (principally Britain) and the U.S., black musicians have learned that when electronic sampling of musical phrases was overdubbed with repetitive electronic drums, they could create two new art forms, hip hop and rap music. The entertainment industry has, since the days of Shakespeare's *Othello*, imposed on blacks a metaphorical quality of sexuality and music. Both the rap form and hip hop dance music draw on the oral traditions which remain close to the surface of black culture. It is not surprising that the black performing artists would take to electronic art forms so readily and successfully. There is a strong affinity to the expression of material transported by the rules of oral traditions, since post-literate electronic forms seem to obey many of the same rules.

Rap musicians appear to attract more attention from censors then do any other group of new artists because they can be understood by a wider audience. The subject of their material tends to combine explicitly sexual and political content. Groups such as Public Enemy have been targeted for legal action responding to calls for censorship.

Watching the underground cultural literature is a useful way to get a feel for understanding the post-industrial world as seen by the most influential "underground" media.

Practitioners of cyberpunk are considered the most creative and incisive in the overall "underground" media. Cyberpunk is one of the more aversive forms of the political, post-industrial "underground." The aesthetics of cyberpunk become significant when it is realized that cyberpunk is the cultural definer of the contemporary creators of this time in history. The intuitions of the cyberpunk writer, painter, or filmmaker may jar the sensibilities, but they provide a guide to the esthetic maps of the designers of everything chip-based.

The smothering pall of orthodoxy is where the NWO is most intuitively comfortable. This affection for orthodoxy was also true of the British industrialists of the 1850s. Other groups, such as the North American political left and the trade unions, seem to harmoniously share this orthodoxy with the admirers of the NWO.

The place where underground cultural media made an identifiable, significant difference in the 1980s was the Soviet Union. In 1922, Lenin promulgated a law banning private ownership of the means of print reproduction. Lenin, of all people, understood that no good could come from letting malcontents get their nasty hands on the means to print leaflets and flyers. After all, turning the crank on a mimeograph machine was an old 1930s Left icon.

By 1970, young people in the U.S.S.R. had appropriated Western rock 'n' roll as their own. Country and western music tapes surpassed blue jeans for desirability on the black market. It is now indisputable that rock 'n' roll had, by 1980, become the vehicle enunciating the need for freedom of expression that was the precursor to the collapse of the U.S.S.R.

The freedom expressed by leading rockers, coupled with the intonation of singers such as Jim Morrison, needed no translation. As Marshall McLuhan had warned us earlier, "the medium is the message." Young Soviet musicians started playing smuggled electronic instruments or building their own. Their words began to match the messages of the freewheeling rock music of Britain and America. In one of those ironies that occur in history, Soviet officialdom had approved blank tape as a consumer item that did not impact on the Soviet defence requirements so cassettes were allowed to be made in the Soviet Union. With a ghetto blaster, you were your own music publisher. Russian rockers saw that the system was not omnipotent. They could be their own publishers and never had to get jobs through the Brezhnev years. Their names never showed up in those cross-referenced records in all the ways that industrial states have developed to keep track of citizens.

They could sell their tapes at informal concerts and introduce freedom of expression in a medium which neither Lenin nor anyone else had thought to regulate in 1922.

Today in the West there is an interesting argument which may spell the end of the recording industry as we know it. A lot of musicians, young bands, and "indie" record companies (independents not affiliated with the large entertainment conglomerates) are distributing their music on the Internet. This, of course, cuts out the distributor, record pressing, tape duping, poster making, advertising, and packaging. About all that is left for record companies is to promote music to radio and TV stations.

While the Russian rockers sold tapes and ideas to their peers, Western journalists had to deal with special import rules for photocopiers. One aspect of Soviet life that struck right into the heart of the Western mind-set was the KGB's view of photocopiers. When you consider the frivolous way we treat photocopiers, it's not surprising that few Moscow bureau chiefs of Western news agencies could, in their Western naiveté, resist writing a piece about Red paranoia around photocopiers. The bureau head had to prove to a clerk in the special section of the KGB that dealt with foreign journalists that the office photocopier could not be surreptitiously used by some unauthorized person. The KGB's reasoning went something like: God only knows what those perverts who peck out typewritten samizdats, would do with a colour copier with a collator and binder.

Samizdats were unauthorized books reproduced with a typewriter and as many as seven carbon copies. They were the product of the country's artistic elite and were critical of the government. Possession of, writing, or typing a *samizdat* could and occasionally did result in arrest and the perpetrator being sentenced to a gulag. This was mostly an illusion. The writers and distributors of *samizdats* were seldom at risk after the death of Stalin. They lived better than anyone else in the Soviet Union and the idea that they were risking their lives or freedom was a romantic myth.

For example, there is an apocryphal story told of one major Russian poet who was in a gulag camp and who shouted to his barracks mates one day after a particularly vile meal, "Courage comrades, only in Russia do we care enough about our poets to imprison them. American writers live like dogs. No one cares enough about them to imprison them. That is why their poems have no sense of passion." That story was published in a Russian book, authorized by the Writer's Union and the KGB.

There is a term from entropic physics which helps to explain why extrapolation is such little help in understanding why the world is acting the way it is. This term is "the real stuff" and is used to describe what happens in a closed system when you attempt to change the system and the changes become part of the system. With the cultural events described above, the events themselves destroyed the predictive strategies which depended on linear models.

When a whole generation became familiar with an unlicensed and unregulated chemical called LSD, it made perceptual mobility skills easily accessible.

The skills involved in perceptual mobility *without drugs* became readily available to the rest of the society. To have predicted in 1963 that endemic availability of LSD would result in a wide curiosity about perceptual mobility could not have been possible because the established order could not imagine its tactics of social control breaking down so completely *among the middle class.*

In 1967, no one could have foreseen benign consequences to this principally youthful experimentation. To have done so would have required someone to say "it requires a special learning to apprehend the time-space continuum Einstein describes."

It might be better to start the learning at a perceptual level and make it easier to conceptualize a fourth (or higher) dimension. Today a number of literary formats glibly discuss a post-Newtonian universe and there is wide comprehension of what is at issue. Think about the coffee-table characteristic ascribed to Stephen Hawking's best-seller, *A Brief History of Time.* Now Errol Morris, Hawking's film translator, can have his work described by film critic Michael Corvino in *Film Quarterly* as: "It's as if Norman Rockwell, whistling on his way to work, bicycled with easel and palette into *The Twilight Zone*" and have these mixed metaphors understood by literate English speakers. Even more amazing, Morris was able to get a bank loan on the basis of the book's success.

A final comment on the cultural component to this era. Remember Rubik's Cube, the toy that took Hungary off the international bankers' credit-watch list? Those kids on TV shows, whizzing through to the solution, were doing manipulations in N-space in their minds!

CHAPTER THIRTEEN

Government in Hyperspace: The twilight of the nation state

In the Western world, there are three major legal systems. The British Common Law system is the most stable. The French Civil Code influenced most of Europe's juridical attempts to manage the industrialization of the 19th century. The American system was structurally based on the inherited Common Law and has an impressive capacity to creatively respond to changed conditions, whether economic or social.

The greatest weakness facing all three systems is that too many disparate issues are reaching the courts while legal reforms fall drastically behind the rate of technical and social change.

The court systems are losing contact with a useful base of precedents. At the same time, there are significant pressures on legislative bodies to enact laws to regulate emerging areas of innovation, invention, manufacturing, and marketing. The policy analysts, who fear that new laws will inhibit development in post-transitional industries, try to slow down simplistic legal responses. It is difficult to rescind dysfunctional laws, so legislators are being advised to hold off on regulation until the new industries become more mature and the real issues are clarified. The result is that the legal systems that regulate society are becoming less relevant and less able to arbitrate disagreements.

Social pluralism is another major problem affecting the delivery of government. When you can't develop some kind of consensus it becomes very difficult to arbitrate divisive issues the way governments are supposed to do. The collapse of the linear, Industrial Age Left-Right political stabilities is being accompanied by expanding social pluralism. Think Trekkies or other regions of fandom and think of the merchandise industries associated with fan behaviour. The product and ideational loyalties of these kinds of perceptual peer groups are beginning to provide services similar to the alliances and identities that have, for the past 500 years, been offered by nation states.

Another predicament of government is money. The Industrial Age tax base is being eroded — but states, faced with increasingly pluralized electorates, try to win approval from each pluralistic sector by supporting and paying for everyone's limited, competing, single-issue agenda.

But perhaps the most obvious breakdown of our governments' ability to deliver government is in the area of immigration.

Refugees are a fact of life all around the globe. They come in all sorts: refugees from war, refugees from terrorism, refugees from police-run death squads, refugees from armies that murder street children, refugees from religious oppression, and refugees from countries where political dissent of the mildest variety puts you into the refugee business. Then there are the economic refugees — people looking for a better life than overcrowded housing and intensely competitive employment conditions. They are pursuing a dream — to become middle class.

Finally, there are those refugees from places where tribal leaders have begun the "final" settlement of centuries-old feuds. These refugees could be thought of as tribally challenged. Western governments are terrified that these escapees will bring their old habits of fratricidal warfare with them.

Of course, mass migrations are not unique in human history. Indeed, they are one way to rejuvenate a society. But mid-June of 1993 may have proved the great disaster period for those who wish for more compassionate treatment of refugees. That was when the FBI busted a crew of fundamentalist Muslims who were in due course convicted of planning to blow up one of the tunnels into New York City, the U.N. headquarters, the Secretary-General of the U.N., the FBI's New York headquarters and Senator Al D'Amato of New York.

The same day a Kurdish group ran a terrorist operation against 16 Turkish diplomatic and commercial interests. The sites were all across Europe but focussed on Germany and involved the usual hostages and property trashing.

Naturally, the media benefits to Islam's fundamentalist warriors and the Kurdish independence movement were high, as they got editorial attention globally. Equally naturally, immigration agencies began to see every refugee as someone plotting to build a support base for freedom fighters.

The American Immigration and Naturalization Service (INS), tired of waves of illegal immigrants from Haiti and elsewhere in the Caribbean, has opened a camp at the U.S. naval base at Cuba's Guantanimo Bay and secured the assistance of the U.S. Navy and Coast Guard in intercepting ships carrying illegals. These illegals are then returned to Haiti. To accomplish this, the INS had to seek the U.S. Supreme Court's assurance that they were not infringing on the rights of the immigrants.

The U.S. has also been embarrassed by refugees from its allies in Latin America, along with its perennial problem of Mexican illegals who disappear into the barrios which now reach as far north as Chicago and New York.

During the bad old Cold War days, officials from the People's Republic of China held two aces up their sleeves in discussions with the British about the fate of Hong Kong. One was that Hong Kong's water supply is in China. The other was that China could stop impeding the "blue ant invasion" of hundreds of thousands of would-be Hong Kong immigrants. There is no way Hong Kong alone could keep such a stream of refugees out.

Recently, prior to its turnover to the P.R.C. authorities, Hong Kong forcefully repatriated thousands of illegal immigrants from Vietnam after negotiating with the Vietnamese government to accept an international observer agreement to assure the safety of the deportees.

Under Hong Kong rules, anyone classified as an economic migrant is deemed illegal. In the first two months of 1992, the number of illegals from China rose by 50 percent. At the same time China's southern industrial provinces drew a massive number of incoming rural labourers, all fully qualified illegals. In Hong Kong's labour-short economy, a farmer from China can make more money in a day than he can make in a month on a mainland rice paddy. The current cost to be smuggled into Hong Kong via boat is the equivalent of $450 (U.S.). The penalty for getting caught is an automatic 15 months in jail.

Things aren't much easier in China proper. A report from that upriver idyllic spot Guangzhou (formerly Canton) said the cops had rounded up 250,000 unemployed rural farm-hands whose internal passports weren't good for big city life and shipped them back to their collective farms. Then there is Beijing, where the internal passport factor is particularly dicey after the events in Tiananmen Square. There, the authorities sweat out an estimated 15,000 rural residents who each day still manage to find their way into the capital.

China's "blue ants" are on the march — in search of food, housing and jobs.

DESTINATION EUROPE

To paraphrase Winston Churchill's 1946 speech, from Stettin in the Baltic to Trieste in the Adriatic, economic and environmental refugees (plus assorted political losers) are breaking through that rusty old iron curtain.

In the mid-1980s the 12 nations of the emerging European Union set up a European travel zone to make borders less inhibiting to movement within the community. The E.U. also established common rules defining who was an economic refugee and who was a political refugee. These plans have been trampled by the exodus from the former East Bloc.

Italy and France are under pressure from legal and illegal immigrants from their former African colonies. In France, a right-wing presidential aspirant, Jean Marie Le Pen, has triggered some of the nastiest anti-immigrant backlash effects going these days. Le Pen wants to abolish France's traditional position as a sanctuary for political refugees. He also urges a ban on tourist visas for all Africans and Arabs. (He would like all other visitors to put up a deposit of the equivalent of about $20,000 prior to entry into France.) A recent poll showed that 40 percent of French citizens generally agree with Le Pen's ideas about refugees.

Italy was equally unprepared when boatloads of Albanian economic refugees started arriving (18,000 on one day alone). Italian authorities believe they are facing a refugee flood from the port city of Trieste, which seems to be becoming the Ellis Island of Europe. Trieste, a city with a strong multicultural heritage, is easily accessible by road for most East Europeans. Its port provides employment at jobs Italians don't wish to do any more and it has, over the centuries, developed lots of experience with migrating populations. Trieste has learned that migrants will move on if you help them catch their breath and don't let them get too comfortable. Since Trieste is currently part of Italy, the Italian government fears that the rest of Italy will become their ultimate destination. They contend that most, if not all, of the refugees today fall into the E.U.'s category of "economic refugees" and should be returned to their last point of departure post haste.

It's easy to adopt a liberal view that any attempt to keep out "refugees" of whatever variety is xenophobic. To recall the failure of Western countries

---

On the Italian political right, the Lombard League has scored domestic points with the electorate by demanding the government impose the "necessary" draconian measures to stop the flood of foreigners.

The original Lombard League was formed in the middle of the 12th century to resist attempts by European princes conspiring to occupy and unite the city states of the Italian peninsula. The contemporary Lombard League calls for a strong anti-corruption stand and more efficient government. Its local branches call for a return to the city state on the grounds that the city states of Renaissance Italy were prosperous and delivered effective government. The League is strong in Northern Italy, where it concentrates on municipal politics in Milan, Florence, Brescia and the like. Recently in Brescia 25 percent of the electorate voted to separate and become a city state again.

Since the Lombard League's electoral pluralities have increased, it has changed its name to the Northern League. Its literature makes it clear that it holds firmly to the convictions so beloved of the forward-lookers of the Renaissance.

to provide asylum to Jews trying to escape from Hitler's Germany is the rallying cry from the humanist centre/left.

But the industrial states of Europe and North America are going through political upheavals of their own. The peoples of both the E.U. and North America are on the edge of changes in their mores and cultural identities. Many among the middle class and working class, on both sides of the Atlantic, are fearful. The rate of change these ordinary citizens face is unlikely to make it politically profitable for politicians to offer much in the way of overt assistance to the latest wave of global immigration.

Both Germany and Austria have been inundated with refugees from former East Bloc countries and anticipate many more. Germany, which has 60 percent of the E.U.'s asylum applications, also has deserters from Red Army units still stationed in the former East Germany.

Arrivals from the east used to be called defectors and "freedom choosers." Now refugees from the former Yugoslavia, East Germany and other Warsaw Pact countries, plus the thousands of "guest workers" from Turkey, have worn down what little goodwill is left for refugees in Germany. The German government has amended the constitutionally-based aid for refugees (the most generous in Europe), making it highly restrictive. This action occurred after an anti-foreigner movement was given muscle by street based neo-Nazis.

Switzerland, as usual in the vanguard of anything relating to money, has made permanent entry difficult for many years. The Swiss, already with four languages, are only concerned with maintenance of their existing standards of living and avoiding the instabilities they see around them.

As we saw earlier, the impact of catastrophic environmental changes could set millions on the move in the next few decades. If that happens, the Swiss may need more than mountains to keep the world out.

CAN GOVERNMENTS STILL GOVERN?

To think that the New World Order, or any government, can still write the rules is to make assumptions that are not necessarily valid. For example, since the Great Depression of the 1930s, we have assumed that the central bank of the state would act as the guarantor of the nation's currency.

Today currency control requires an ability to regulate a computer network — the financial clearances network. The high end is the Bank for International Settlements, located in Switzerland. The problem lies in the question of how you regulate what may, in fact, reside in another jurisdiction.

Earlier in this decade a database called Covia, which supplies airline seat availabilities to travel agents all over North America, decided, unilaterally and without notice, to exclude information on flights to Cuba — *wherever the flights originated*, be it Mexico, Canada, or the Caribbean. Travel agents in

Canada, where Cuba is a popular, inexpensive winter vacation destination, just about went ballistic. Covia's explanation for excluding this service was that its attorneys had advised that supplying this data placed Covia at risk from U.S. government regulations barring trade with Cuba.

The Covia action is the kind of thing that can sink NAFTA or any other trading bloc. The Canadian media reported the story loudly, calling it an imposition of American policies on Canadian sovereignty. With a Canadian election looming, the Canadian nationalists and other foes of the free trade deal greeted the news with outrage. More to the point, most Canadian media looked to opponents of NAFTA as legitimate commentators to explain the action of Covia. No wonder the Conservative government and its new leader found themselves declining in the polls, with free trade as the major cause of dissatisfaction. Suddenly, a great many voters started to grasp the abstraction that information can be impeded as a tool of domestic politics or a weapon of economic warfare.

For example, a significant part of northern North America's weather originates in Siberia. Imagine what would happen if someone were to exclude that weather information from the U.S. If you don't know, ask a commodities broker whether a Russian leader who talks about a breakdown in the former U.S.S.R. has a bargaining chip with which to negotiate for aid.

As we noted earlier, satellites are not distance sensitive. That means you can maintain a bank account in a jurisdiction that maintains your privacy without significantly adding to your bank charges. It also means that many of your records are in another, sovereign jurisdiction. If you work for a transnational corporation, you need not pay taxes. Wherever you live is just that, a residence. There is no record of your having an income. There is a cost to set up this situation, but that cost is not onerous if you happen to be in the upper hump of the increasingly bimodal income distribution curve.

Bimodality of income distribution occurs when the centre (the middle class) is eroded. Since 1971, the Canadian and U.S. governments have watched, with varying degrees of dismay, as the familiar bell-shaped curve that portrays a typical democratic, industrial society began to crumple in the centre. Data from the two countries showed the U.S. middle class to be collapsing at a somewhat slower rate than in Canada, but in most cases the trends since 1979 have been consistently toward fully bimodal distribution.

Some of the middle class move into the upper part of the bimodal curve and others fall into the lower hump of the distribution. (Policy analysts usually define middle class income as lying between 75 percent and 150 percent of the average.) Those falling into the lower hump become marginalized and begin struggling with compromises that confuse life for those who become detached from familiar values.

It used to be that to set up a tax avoidance scheme like the one mentioned above, you had to be in the upper 0.5 percent of the population of a developed industrial state. Now, thanks to satellites, the game is more wide open. It also means that if a state wishes to have a non-convertible currency, as did the former U.S.S.R. and as does China, its citizens can acquire convertible funds, usually through a black market, and vote with their money by moving it around without trace.

On a smaller scale, the *Scientific American* of November, 1991, carried a full-page ad for the South German State Lottery which made all the usual claims for a lottery and invited the reader to participate with a thinly disguised offer to help place winnings beyond the reach of any taxman. Throughout the advertisement, reference is made to "investments." One might expect that the readers of *Scientific American* would have a higher than average level of numeracy, and at least a modicum of comprehension about probability theory, but that is between the South German State Lottery and its media buyer. Much more interesting is the overt offer to help winners hide the money from their governments.

For some years now there has been an increase in the number of people who work as consultants, doing specialized jobs for specified times. For employers, the incentive is that the consultant is paid a flat fee or other remuneration that ends when the project finishes. The employer is not obliged to provide the benefits the core work force expects, which must be capitalized. As one successful consultant phrased it, "Consultants don't get invited to the office Christmas party. Instead, we take our families to Vale or the Riviera."

The term consultant used to denote special expertise. Today consultants are often contractors employed on a "just in time" basis for a time-defined project. If you ask consultants who are successful and not merely "between jobs" to define the benefits of a consulting career over a conventional job, they will give you an answer that is worth thinking about.

They will tell you that the corporate worker, the government worker, the institutional employee — even the employee of organized crime — must adhere to alien, principally administrative agendas that detract from any benefits which may be inherent in the job. The consultant takes pride in being a hired gun who can enjoy a job and can afford to do it well without accommodating the inferior quality agendas of the workplace.

The temporary employee market, whether for typists or for project managers on multi-million-dollar developments, places an increasingly large number of people outside the administrative thrall of the conventional workforce.

GOVERNMENT FADES AWAY

The constitutions of most nations require that an accused be granted a "speedy" trial. This is, by and large, done. When it is not done, appeals courts usually slap the wrist of the trial court.

Civil litigation is another matter. There are no constitutional guarantees of a speedy civil trial. In a number of jurisdictions, when the criminal courts are clogged, administrators find new facilities to clear the criminal log-jam by further delaying civil cases. So there is a strong trend toward privatization in civil litigation.

By allowing this, the state is abandoning part of its most jealously guarded right — the exclusive right to deliver justice. In terms of national sovereignty, the dichotomy between civil and criminal courts is an administrative fiction. By abandoning the protections of the sovereign's law, the state is proclaiming its inability to govern.

NWO adherents are strongly committed to the idea that less government is good and that the trend to privatization of the courts puts government costs under free market discipline. The idea that there is a loss of sovereignty implied would not be seen, necessarily, as a problem.

They would say that those using the courts should, ideally, pay a user fee for this service. They would reject the idea that the "king's justice," freely accessible, is needed to assure equity in the system. It is unlikely that they, with their strong ties to the mythologies of the American southwest, where there remains a "bounty hunter" tradition, would see that a logical extension of privatizing the courts would be to privatize the means of enforcing the court's decision.

Their simplistic view of other events in the world would indicate that they might be unaware of the historical abuses of natural justice that occur when the justice system is withdrawn from the responsibilities of the sovereign power. It is highly unlikely that any arbitrator has addressed the issue of a settlement which might intrude on "public policy."

As the rate of change becomes faster, governments — federal, state or provincial, and municipal — seem to become more dysfunctional. In 1972, a policy document called the *Pluralistic Society Papers* was commissioned by the government of Canada. It pointed out that the major problem governments would face by the 1980s would be, simply, the delivery of government. The document said that, as society became more pluralistic, governments would have difficulty finding a consensus to provide a basis for action.

When a government department fails to deliver the services it is legislatively obligated to deliver, it places the whole of government in disrepute. The failure to deliver government services is proving to be the dominant political issue for this decade.

Jeremy Bentham, one of the founders of the University of London, made his living writing constitutions for newly founded industrial states in the 19th century. Anyone considering career options today should look at the constitution-writing field. There will be lots of work, most of which will happen during recessions (just look at eastern Europe).

Constitutions are the rules under which a body of people agree to live together as a nation state. Most modern constitutions — say, those constructed after 1750 — are facing imminent collapse.

Constitutions are seldom recognized for what they really are. They are a plan for managing a country for the *foreseeable* future. Countries with constitutional problems today should realize that it is very tough to write a constitution at the beginning of a new era in history. Anyone attempting to write a constitution today would have to plan for the effects of the greatest era transformation in the history of the human race. A new world-view, with new assumptions about what constitutes reality, will change the face of the planet far more than the events of the Renaissance. If you were going to attempt something similar in 1492, you would have needed to foresee that the Mercantile Age, the Reformation, the Counter-Reformation and

---

Bureaucracies, over time, become structurally ineffective. Political operatives learn early that when you want to do something that is really worth doing, the last place to go is to the government department with the mandate for the area in which you're going to act.

Let us say that you plan to take all the trainable mentally handicapped people in government institutions and put them to work in a controlled environment at jobs they can do. The end result is a bit more dignity for the currently institutionalized, while their productivity will pay for more attractive housing. The argument for doing this is two-fold:

• It will ease the burden on the public purse.

• It is genuinely more humane then present strategies (which are effectively warehousing).

The arguments for not doing it are essentially bureaucratic.

If you were to try to sell this idea to the department of mental health you would soon discover that many individuals who represented vested interests in the department would resist what you are doing. To use current jargon, there's nothing in empowerment of patient populations for the bureaucrats. If the program works, they could lose their jobs, or, even worse, have to manage a program that was designed to encourage innovation.

The thing to do, as any successful government manager will tell you, is to give your program to a department without a vested interest. It will immediately see it for what it is, a chance to earn a reputation for managing innovative programs, and the promise of a promotion.

the Industrial Age would all be direct consequences of the Renaissance.

The countries whose constitutions have best stood the test of time are either out of the way (Iceland) or have extremely limited mandates (Switzerland). England has survived without a "written" constitution since Oliver Cromwell's Commonwealth experiment left the English with the clear idea that they were better to draw on flexible "custom" than attempt to agree on any formal charter, which would create monstrous amendment problems.

Of course, in 1867 Walter Bagehot published his book *The English Constitution*, which codified British constitutional assumptions and which has currency as an "informal" constitutional document. By writing this book Bagehot effectively rigidified the British constitutional process and began the now widely acknowledged British constitutional decline.

Constitutions in the West have become the victims of too many second rate minds becoming social scientists whose commitment to the latest fads have resulted in a plethora of "rights," which politicians exploit to bribe people with their own money. Nations that do not make superior products cannot expect to be able to add to the guarantees of their constitutions.

No nation state today can be regarded as stable. As the new level of abstraction emerges, stabilities that have achieved the status of national identity myths can be expected to crumble. Nation states will lose the props that hold them up.

That happened to the U.S.S.R. in 1975. By then, the KGB had clearly identified that the U.S.S.R. was in imminent danger of collapse, and its plan to salvage the Rodina took on the Byzantine moves which are the hall-mark of any government of the Euro-Asian land mass. They decided to arrange to have a top Soviet bureaucrat appointed to head the service.

This pleasantly surprised the Kremlin's Party hierarchy, who believed that by placing one of their "own" in charge they could count on KGB assistance in the damage control operations that followed the widespread corruption of the Brezhnev regime. (Secretary Brezhnev was the worst nightmare of a dedicated socialist. He and the clique around him were massively corrupt. Authoritarian socialist states have no means to deal with corruption.) Reformers saw the move as a means of cleaning house of the "bad apples" while the carry-overs from the Brezhnev regime saw the move as a tightening of the authoritarian regime, which would give them a few more years until graceful retirement.

The KGB thesis was that by getting an honourable, competent chief they could tell him the truth — all of it — and get a sympathetic hearing.

When the new head of the KGB was announced as Yuri Andropov, Western intelligence agencies unleashed a campaign of vilification against him, which blessed the KGB plan's authors. Andropov, as a senior Kremlin official, was well-versed in the KGB's client response capabilities. When he checked in for work at Dzherzhinsky Square, the senior executives presented him with a briefing.

This was the crucial point. The briefing was voluminously supported and documented. It said that the Cold War was lost and worse, the Soviet economy was in chaos. It recommended that Andropov himself become the next General-Secretary of the Party and effective head of the Politbureau and the Presidium. It further recommended that planning commence forthwith for an orderly succession. The KGB's analysis was correct. Andropov bought the scheme and a doorstop leader, the geriatric Chernenko, succeeded Brezhnev.

There was not much that could be done with the domestic economy. Andropov's major thrusts were international. He had to negotiate with the West to ease the heat and allow the Soviet Union's collapse to occur gently. Given the medical information on Andropov — available, of course, to the KGB — steps were taken immediately to groom a successor.

Mikhail Gorbachev was virtually unknown. He was bright and had been doing yeoman service in the agriculture ministry. He was a lawyer and a number of KGB senior officers saw him and his wife socially. His wife, Raisa, could be unleashed on the West. She had a sense of style. For the first time since the revolutionary cabal had fought their way to power in 1917, a man's wife was significant in his selection for leadership support. One other factor delighted the puritanical KGB heads. The Gorbachev children, a boy and a girl, weren't bums. That fact alone made Gorbachev stand out among his peers.

During the Andropov period, 7th Avenue in New York decided that the "Soviet Look" was in and a little girl from New England became Andropov's guest. No one watching could fail to be impressed. The KGB had launched a PR campaign far beyond any level of sophistication seen before from the U.S.S.R. Obviously, the American Communist Party was not involved, nor even probably told. With an eye clearly on the West, Gorbachev announced his intention to show the "human face of Communism."

The sands of time, however, were flowing too fast. History would not forgive the Russians for arriving at industrialization so late.

SOCIAL STUDIES

Meanwhile, in the West, and particularly in the United States, the bimodality of income distribution was becoming more evident. While commercial television sold a consumption-based, materialist good life, too many Americans were slipping through the cracks.

In the past few years the term "underclass" has crept into the North American language. Initially this term was used in a denigrating way to identify a group in society who were perennial users of welfare and who did not contribute to the communal well-being, except as consumers.

Canadian opponents of free trade with the U.S. have frequently cited cases where the absence of a social safety net of guaranteed medical insurance resulted in some particularly heartbreaking story of what happens to a non-insured, low income person in the U.S. who needs expensive health care services. Canada's universal health insurance system works. Americans who fall into the lower end of the bimodal income distribution die when they are seriously ill.

The Rodney King assault case in Ventura County, California, is another example of systemic stress on the institutions of society. The civil stresses became manifestly apparent in the riots that followed the Ventura County jury's findings in the trial of the four police officers who were charged with assaulting King. When you institutionalize a wide section of a society into holding no stake in that society, you can usually guarantee unpleasant results.

The jury's findings were perfectly predictable. Most common law jurisdictions have property qualifications for prospective jurors, the assumption being that jurors should have a significant stake in the community. This is usually addressed by requiring that jury lists be drawn up from the assessment rolls — that is, people who own or rent property of a certain value.

People who move frequently are under-represented on juries, as are those to whom jury service would constitute a serious economic hardship. (Salaried individuals usually have their pay continued by their employer, while hourly employees may suffer significant loss if a trial is prolonged.) Legal scholars have called for higher pay for juries, but it will remain difficult to avoid selecting juries that under-represent low-income citizens. Aboriginals from treaty reserves do not appear on assessment rolls. Married women who are not employed are frequent choices for jury duty, which further skews the source of female jurors.

For a lawyer defending a police officer charged with improper use of force, denial of civil rights, abuse of authority, or denial of due process, the usual strategy is to find some rationale for the actions for which the officer is being charged. But the main thrust is to get across to the jury that, as a society, we ask police officers to take high personal risks and make split-second decisions. The defence further adds that it is not unrealistic to expect officers to make, from time to time, human errors.

Finally, the defence will point out, probably accurately, that if an officer is to be punished for one of these "human errors," the likelihood of fellow officers being willing to continue to take these risks in the defence of "our lives and property" will be placed in jeopardy. The implication, of course, is that hordes of looting, murdering thieves and rapists are only held at bay by police officers who sacrifice themselves so that we (the defence lawyer and the jury) will remain safe.

In other words, no matter what the officer has done *in the line of duty or in pursuit of a fleeing felon*, if there is no evidence of personal malice, the realistic defence is that it is forgivable human error.

If you are offended by the outcome of the trial of the officers in the Rodney King case, be aware of what factors prevailed and what you would be willing to change. The jury certainly understood and were not prepared to change anything. Given their socio-economic background, which would put most of them in either the high end of the lower hump of the income graph or, at best, in the low end of the higher-income hump, they certainly wouldn't want to put their own somewhat tenuous socio-economic status at risk.

CHAPTER FOURTEEN

Challenges to the New World Order: Watch out for falling dinosaurs

An era transition is not a happy time for most people. In its early phases, the nascent era must compete for a place in the sun with the established, if somewhat creaky, old order.

Hollywood screenwriters and other revisionist historians have created a selectively romantic view of the Renaissance, which they accompany with the mythic values of the idealized Renaissance person. Actually, the turbulence of economic and social violence, plus a religious reorientation, left no one untouched.

We have also seen that a new era tends to be resisted by leaders of the establishment. It would be foolish to think that people relinquish power, privilege and status voluntarily. In the Renaissance those who represented the papacy, the feudal nobility, and, to a large extent, ordinary people fearing change certainly did not look with favour on the disruption of their lives.

On the other hand, the burgeoning middle class was trying to survive in a society that was geared to a manorial economy. The leadership of that pre-Renaissance society saw the newly rich merchants, traders, small manufacturers, and explorers as uncouth tradesmen whose principal good point was their contribution to the territorial state's revenues. Yet there was no infrastructure to tax the new middle class — and they were not particularly eager to volunteer money to church or state.

In our own time we see the same conditions. We see an elite managerial class trying to patch up the latter-day Industrial Age — engaging in an activity psychologists call denial.

In the face of global system collapse we see political and other sectoral leaders attempting to establish regional trading blocs, using the thesis that the only way for transnational corporations to expand is through globalized trade. The capital-intensiveness of trading zones favours the transnationals, for whom the benefits of rationalizing markets outweighs the direct capital costs. Another benefit which cannot have missed the eagle eyes of transnational corporate thinkers is the negative effect on their local or national competitors, who, without an international strategic baseline, become even more combatively marginalized and financially stressed.

Of course, this model of global economic management omits the fact that the corporate elite have a pretty poor track record of competence in managing the shift to an Information Age economy. Their basic management personnel strategy — exclusionary focussing without long-term strategy — is a death-wish. You can't run a privately held empire when the change rate on which your core business is to be built cannot be predicted a year in advance.

When our leadership establishment is criticized in a way that seizes its fleeting attention, the response is usually a demand that the critic offer some alternatives. Since criticisms are usually specific to a minuscule part of the systemic breakdown and deny the complex relationships which exist in global economies, these criticisms are much better seen as metaphors for the situation.

SPLITS IN SOCIETY

There is a disturbing trend that, if their public actions and statements are to be believed, meets with the approval of the New World Order's enthusiasts. This trend is the departure from a statistically normal distribution of income, where the stability of the middle class is the high middle of a bell-shaped curve. Instead, we can see a trend toward a bimodal distribution of income between two ranges. For example, CEOs in American industry often are paid 100 times the salary of an average worker. A Japanese CEO will find that he has topped out at 17 times the line-worker average.

In December 1991, when General Motors announced that it planned to lay off more than 70,000 blue and white-collar workers and close 21 plants, it set off a chain of events, not all of which were entirely happy for "the General." Critics were quick to point out that no cuts in executive jobs or salaries were included in the announcement. It was also observed that, since Japanese auto companies were doing well using American workers, GM's problems must lie with the executives.

Starting at the top, Roger Smith, subject of the movie *Roger and Me*, held the position of chairman and CEO through the '80s while GM's American operations managed to lose market share not just to the Japanese automakers — as American car industry spokespeople want us to believe —

"They [corporations] cannot commit treason, nor be outlawed nor excommunicate, for they have no souls."
— Sir Edward Coke, Lord Chief Justice of England, Case of Sutton's Hospital, 1628

but Ford and Chrysler as well. With some perverse logic of its own, GM's board then voted to raise Smith's pension from $700,000 to $1.2 million a year. At this time GM was losing $500 million a month. Someone with a calculator pointed out that Roger Smith, as a retiree, every 16 days makes (not 'earns') what an average line-worker makes in a year, assuming the line-worker is not one of the 70,000. But maybe we are comparing apples and prune juice. Chairman Roger's salary, during his 10-year tenure, was four times that of the heads of Nissan and Toyota.

On January 3, 1992, the Dow Jones news service reported that the value of bonds and other commercial paper issued by GM and its financing unit, General Motors Acceptance Corporation, was falling off due to fears of a downgrading by bond-rating agencies. Even before the bond-raters spoke, GM's notes were being quoted at a spread of 1.8 points above U.S. treasury bills, compared with the month-earlier spread of 1.3 points. The debt markets were losing faith in GM's ability to pay them back.

And what did GM officials have to say? They joined in the chorus of complaints about Japan.

One step that established orders usually take to defend themselves from a new order is to demonize the forces that threaten to supplant them. Demonizing is what the power elite of the Renaissance did when they set up the Inquisition. Demonizing allows the establishment to secure consensus in a society which has become highly pluralistic. Since the friends of demons are not a particularly popular or well-connected constituency (usually a few psychotics whose fragmentary delusional system is notably loathsome), the institutional masters may use arbitrary powers of state terrorism to harass those who are, in the earliest days, espousing the emerging era in paranoid ways. Thus the established order can claim to be protecting us from evil.

In an emerging era the distinction between good and evil may become blurred. In the Renaissance, the line dividing pirates and traders operating under letters of marque was indeed thin. In the past decade the unstable markets of the information industries have seen piracy of both software and hardware. Some knowledgeable people argue that to assign ownership to information implies an exclusivity that is difficult to enforce and that, at this immature stage of the Information Age, it is not necessarily a good thing to enforce copyright. This argument is based on the public policy idea that it is essential to enable the largest possible portion of the population to become computer-literate.

The opposing argument says that unless a society can assure software and system developers of a return on their investment by creating an orderly market for computer-related development, the potential benefits will be lost.

With the Cold War over, the War on Drugs enables North American governments to engage in arbitrary search and seizure to harass various grey markets. When these steps are being taken, you can be sure that the established order fears that its days are numbered.

IS INTELLECTUAL PROPERTY THEFT?

Have you wondered why there is such a hue and cry about protecting intellectual property on an international level? We are being forced to address the absence of international agreements defining intellectual property. At present no legal system has managed to begin to rationalize digital materials. Lawyers advise anyone who troubles to ask them to keep property off the Internet.

The world's trading patterns are such that it is impossible to police borders for knock-off imports. Digital technology allows someone to copy or alter everything from text to games to art, music, and databases. The Internet is so porous and without legal controls that it is an appropriator's paradise.

Copyrights, patents, trademarks, et cetera, offer holders the right to control reproduction and distribution. The catch is that holders of copyrights, et cetera, are required to actively police their intellectual property. Policing your property means sending ominous legal letters to anyone you discover using your property without your permission. Failure to police means you lose the rights to your franchise (see the case of Bayer and its lost Aspirin in any high school business law textbook).

Knock-offs can only be controlled at the country of origin, which means that country must have the bureaucratic legal infrastructure to support the policing of intellectual property. In the western post-industrial world that infrastructure is in place. Less developed parts of the globe have never needed such complex governmental resources.

In the November 11-17, 1995, issue of The Economist, well after the headline stories, was an article whose implications were so far out, they were in. The story (on page 85) was titled "Hunting the Big Mac in Africa." Datelined Johannesburg, South Africa, it concerned the decision by the golden archers to open up in South Africa following, rather late, the lifting of American sanctions on trade with that country.

McDonald's had, as politically correct globalizers, trained two local franchisees (one black, one white) and was just about to open two succulent dining emporiums when horror struck. A South African company, Dax, was operating under the trade name MacDonald's.

"Displeased," shouted Big Mac's local law wranglers. "That extra 'A' in the name is covered in our trademark and we're in the cultural icon industry."

Changes brought by GATT and the evolution of the World Trade Organization's dispute settlement rules mean that every signatory nation is supposed to have the capacity to respond to a complaint about intellectual property abuse from a co-signatory country in a timely and effective manner that meets international standards.

International standards are being negotiated in a U.N. council called the World Intellectual Property Organization, which grew out of the old Berne Convention. At present, the WTO requires every government to rationalize its laws respecting intellectual property so that the individual signatories' regulations are compatible.

There are two rubs that will make this possibly the most acrimonious international issue of the next decade or two. First, even countries that had some semblance of intellectual property laws have, in the past, been open to domestic political pressures. For example, Bulgaria is not one of the big international trading nations, yet it is second only to the People's Republic of China as the source of bootleg music and recordings.

The other is that the digital revolution is creating new definitions of intellectual property. No one can agree whether information stored in a computer's RAM is transient or stable. No one can even begin to consider if a morphed picture is the property of the original owner or a separate work.

Politically, things aren't much better. Setting up the government infrastructure to enforce WTO regulations is not a priority that is voluntarily high on the list of "low labour cost" countries faced with 50 percent unemployment and social services being delivered by some religious sect promoting a theocratic state.

The truth is, all of the international instruments that allow the orderly transfer (no killing) of what we think of as copyrights, trademarks, and patents have to be rethought to accommodate the new era's discoveries.

The court replied "how awful for you, but here in sunny South Africa the rules of peaceful conduct say if you don't exploit your intellectual property within five years you are deemed to have abandoned your stuff." (Just like in a rooming house: you split and, after a locally defined time, the landlady can sell your stuff.)

The court added that the Golden Arches and all the other trademarked goods involved may indeed be icons to South Africa's elites, but there is no evidence that the average majority black South African has any idea of what they mean. Following an appeal, McDonald's regained many of its trademarks, but Dax continued operating its MacDonald's restaurants.

The problem for would-be global corporatists is, how do you protect intellectual property in places that are playing catch-up?

Can a state ban the international electronic transfer of its currency? Currency controls were the key to the economic management of World War II by both the Axis and Allied nations. When the G7 put out the idea of taxing international fund transfers, there was considerable doubt such taxation could be done, especially in light of the Maastricht treaty establishing a common E.U. currency.

Copyright, trademarks, and patents are tools that severed intellectual property from the territorial state. These legal tools were invented as a defence against search and seizure without due process. As we enter a new millennium, we need to make our legal systems, drawn from thousands of cultures, sufficiently congruent to be useful on a global basis.

The United States can bring pressures diplomatically. GATT, the WTO, and regional trade zones such as ASEAN, the E.U., and NAFTA can use the dispute settlements available. But if a nation wants to refuse the findings of the dispute settlement process it can probably get away with it, as we have already seen in other attempts by the United States to isolate Cuba, Libya, and Iraq. What will happen when one of these disagreements is used against the U.S. or another first-world power caught in the bind between domestic political pressures and its international obligations?

A year or so after its South African debacle, McDonald's found itself suing some guy named MacDonald in Scotland who was dealing in burgers 'n' fries. The corporate counsel thought they were in a Common Law court and instructed the local solicitors to rip out the guy's throat. Wrong! They were in a Scottish court, just as ancient a tradition and with many common charters, but some real differences, too.

Not least of the differences was that the chief of the clan MacDonald was brought in as an expert witness for the defence. He testified that MacDonald had more rights to the name than the boys from the Arches. End of the case. Scottish judges understand the Scottish National Party's aspirations to independence. If they had allowed the case to continue they might have found themselves ruling on the political legitimacy of the Clan MacDonald versus an American hamburger company.

There is a reason why Scots all over the world run banks, armies, hospitals, great universities, and can listen to bagpipes for hours on end. They've been running an underground clan culture since 1749, usually under unpleasant persecution. Stupid is not one of the characteristics you easily find among them.

NWO FINDS BYPASS SURGERY IS PAINFUL

The forces we think of as the New World Order are not likely to succeed at very much in the way of their self-designated goals. Their problem lies with the vehicle they have decided to ride along the road to oligarchic power. The idea held by the North American division of the NWO, that a transnational trading base can be used to ensure dominance of market share in the Americas and resist further market penetrations by Japan Inc. and the E.U. while dominating home governments, is not high on the probability scale.

The idea that North American society can exacerbate its drive to economic bimodality without serious fissuring, up to and including a constitutional crisis in the U.S., is not likely.

The NWO is unlikely to reach its goals — that is, maintenance and enhancement of a status quo which is endangered by forces neither understood, nor even publicly recognized, and an orderly continuation of economic "progress." This progress, of course, necessitates imposing bimodal economies on the Western world at the expense of the middle class. At the present time NWO adherents employ a lot of people under relatively stable and humane conditions, as long as we're not talking about jobs in the Third World. But for all the nice things you can say about them, they can be dangerous to all of us.

Eventually those in favour of the NWO model will realize that, ironically, not only is history not on the side of the Marxists, history is not on their side, either. In fact, history is bypassing them completely. When they arrive at this juncture, they might begin to randomly kick some butt, as the sordid side of their personalities comes to the fore.

The obsession with a success definition based on power, the commitment to large — very large — corporate structures, coupled with total amorality within a pseudo competition ethic, heralds some real disasters. On consideration, this amorality may be the most significant factor to consider. Most of the players are pleasant enough people, with strong personal ethical standards. However, along with their collective amorality, they are absolutely ruthless. As has been said before, "they make the trains run on time."

The strength of the industrial world is waning as unanticipated changes come on-stream. For example, it is highly probable that primitive fission power will be displaced by quantumly more effective and safer fusion reactors. This will alter global energy resource requirements.

Governments worldwide are concerned about the capacity of the former U.S.S.R. member states or successor states to guarantee the security of their nuclear weapons stockpiles. The truth is that facilities for the destruction of nuclear weapons are booked up for the next three years and unless someone sells some nukes to another state with a "what have we got to lose?" philosophy, the surplus nuclear weaponry will be cleaned up in about eight years.

As the less stable middle European states (which were essentially creatures of the Industrial Revolution) become more unstable, we can anticipate that this problem, or its analogues, will become more pressing.

For example, it has been popular since the Industrial Age stabilized to criticize national boundaries established by colonial powers. The past 30 years of wars in Africa and the Indian subcontinent show what happens when natural and historic boundaries are interdicted, yet there is no longer a colonial power to maintain order. The NWO would say that resolution of these issues must be the concern of the regional trading blocks.

Those who express horror at the killing fields of the Caucasus, the Balkans, Africa, and some spots in the Far East should remember that tribal wars by their very nature take place for the purpose of genocide and/or converting the losers into slaves. Anyone who supposes a global transnational might be willing to stop one of these regional bloodbaths had better have an answer for the question, "What's in it for us?"

The idea that someone could stop international arms dealers trading in chaos-creating commodities forgets the role of transnational oil companies (working through international weapons merchants) in the Nigeria/Biafra war.

In December 1992, a short item was reported on the BBC World Service. The Russian civilian intelligence service had intercepted a number of Russian nuclear weapons scientists at Moscow's airport, where they were about to leave for Iran on a plane belonging to the Iranian national airline. This item was not picked up by any of the major wire services or North American TV news networks.

The question is not whether the NWO should be challenged. In fact, every time a development occurs outside the NWO paradigm, the NWO is tested. It was on that basis that the NWO was announced in the course of a war about oil by an American president whose personal wealth was based in the petroleum industry.

The transnational oil industry is a primitively managed business engaged in exploiting a diminishing resource. In a world of N-space these folks have real problems because fusion energy has been developed in the United Kingdom at a research centre which is jointly controlled by the technologically advanced partners of the E.U., and ultimately controlled by the North American NWO's largest competitor.

Certainly, one thing the past few years have taught us is that corporate employers cannot be trusted to show any sort of loyalty. Even the feudal lord had a sense of loyalty to those above and below him. In the Renaissance leaders led from the front, not while enshrouded in a golden parachute.

History is not on the side of those with the most divisions. History is on the side of those who can most quickly adapt to a world-view that incorporates N-space. The divisions will gather around them, as the leaders of Commonwealth of Independent States are finding out the hard way. This is the truly profound situation in which the peoples of the world find themselves.

But it is unlikely that those who lead the NWO are overly endowed with an understanding of this level of abstraction. It is even more unlikely that they have the skills necessary to manage a world in which information is accessible and storable in N-space. If this is true, then we should anticipate a sharp upswing in errors of judgment, like the ones managed by those big spenders at General Motors.

We have seen from cyberpunk literature how certain information can be aimed at an audience with less baggage to jettison, an audience that is not confused by tangential or lateral thinking. But the paucity of imagination, the absence of any higher aspirations demonstrated by the NWO's leadership, suggests that they are avid fans of a relatively infantile view of power. This view says that the only real purpose of power is to perpetuate itself. In other words, power serves neurotic, infantile needs. (If Freud were intellectually respectable, we could say that the neurosis which NWO adherents and leaders share is carved in anal fixation — hence the popularity and almost respectability of the term 'asshole.' Our psychoanalytic comment could add that this neurosis is so strongly ordered that, just as we observe in drug addicts, all efforts are directed to the service of this ego.)

We see no indication that those in charge of the NWO have any urge to accomplish great goals, to govern wisely, or to serve mankind in such a way that the human condition will rise above the fragile veneer of civilization that it presently grasps.

CRITICAL THINKING

Probably the most dangerous belief among NWO adherents is that it is unnecessary, and probably undesirable, to encourage the ability to exercise critical thought and functions. If your responsibilities do not call for operational or strategic decisions, why would you need a wide range of explanatory referents and the skills to acquire such information?

Critical analytic skills are survival tools for every one of us today. If the children of North America don't learn these skills, they will end up on the left-hand side of the NWO's bimodal income distribution curve.

Proponents of the NWO seem to suggest that they have a capacity to define a new rate of entropy — which, if true, would require them to have discovered a new kind of physics not subject to the established laws of the universe. In other words, in the long run, the NWO as we've defined it here will lose, no matter what happens. Given the change rate, even the long run will be short. The truth is that just as this is the worst possible time to attempt to write a constitution, it is also the wrong time to establish a secular mercantile empire.

The computer industry has demonstrated that this is not a time when you can find stability with mature product lines. As fast as you churn out what, in an industrial society, would be a mature product, someone turns out something based on a newly-revealed level of cybermath and their new product is not just competitive, it is a completely new iteration of a world-view that is incomprehensible to your industrial mind-set. In the computer industry this reality is summed up in the well-known saying, "IBM cannot compete with four guys in a garage."

If that is even remotely true, the best strategy is probably to remove yourself from the orbit of the NWO and support the evolutionary process at the level where it makes no territorial claims. The worst option is to try to hide within its orbit, to be a change agent from within (a.k.a. getting the security, the salary, and the pension plan, then claiming you're trying to reform the less pleasant aspects). Anyone who opts for that line, you can be sure, will go down with the ship because they voted against buying life-jackets at the behest of management. These are the ones who, as the ship is sinking and the management is getting away in a luxury motor launch, will cheer that the boss is going to get help.

One thing you find in NWO supporters is a decided anti-intellectual bent. A new scientific finding must have a readily identifiable application, something which can be commercialized, before the finding is seen to have value or pose a threat to the existing order. For example, when mathematicians recently discovered a new prime number ($2^{756,839}$ -1) the discovery's announcement was given a relatively high profile in the city where the author lives. The day after the announcement the author found himself at an upscale luncheon club where, in addition to the bad food, he was assaulted on all sides by executives wanting to know what the new prime was "good for." The author explained it had no use that he knew of, and

---

The mass-marketed, self-improvement 12-step industry is predicated on the idea that we are all victims. The range of this victimology, in which all suffering is relative, is evidence of a wealthy, discomfited society in which every middle-class person is sufficiently well-off to self-indulgently wallow at the trough of dysfunctionality.

It also suggests why none of our governments are able to deliver the services they promise — along with becoming an incredibly wealthy society, we have become pluralistic to an extraordinary extent. The degree of consensus required for the exercise of political will is simply lacking.

that new primes usually came out of testing new supercomputers and that this prime was a little big for code generation. The questioners were genuinely confused as to why the media had put it at the top of the TV news line-up and on front pages the day before.

In such company, it's always wise to avoid telling one's luncheon companions that the people who design supercomputers usually have an unnatural fetish for either prime numbers or extractions of even more integers to the right of the decimal in π. There seems to be a lack of understanding that basic research occurs at a significantly higher level of abstraction than the usual research and development, which is the topic of budget meetings in corporate North America. The idea that basic research is essential for application research seems to have escaped their comprehension.

Currently the corporate world is attempting to influence the direction of university-based research without understanding that basic research cannot be vectored to their view of the universe. This results in a large percentage of our corporate leaders attempting to deal with changes in scientific direction, despite having little in the way of the necessary support for understanding the implications.

It isn't that we should expect corporate decision makers to be rocket scientists. But we should be able to expect some basic scientific literacy. It also means that our education systems should think about how to sustain and enhance basic science and humanities throughout life. Some psychologists have given a lot of thought to self-reinforcement of learning — this might be important to our survival.

If we are all immigrants to a new era of history, it should not be too much too expect that the leadership try to learn enough to read a subway map. They should develop some literacy, if for no other reason than their own survival.

The solutions to present-day problems are not political; nor are they economic. Not until a wide base of individuals achieve a degree of fluency in the language of cyberspace will the solutions be spoken of in political or economic metaphors.

HEROES AND HISTORY

The mergers and acquisitions activists have been, perhaps, unrecognized for their contributions to the environmental movement. In the rush to dump on the junk bond dealers of the '80s, it should be understood that their real function was to act as corporate garbage collectors and to hold corporate garage sales.

They randomly enforced recycling of senior executives, whose contributions could be put up to multiple random scrutinies. The issue was, after all, management. When a business becomes mature, there is little in the way of innovation, either in products or administrative strategies, possible. And as the NWO's birth rate declines we should assume that growth would only come from entrepreneurial action. Nowhere is it written that there is a role for management of the nonexistent. Managers only manage what exists. Mature industries are run on management formulas.

The junk bond excesses of the 1980s paralleled the excesses of the labour movement. Management's professional organizations are no different than a mob-run union whose method of enriching the union leaders was to featherbed the work force, thus increasing the flow of dues.

History, as we have seen, has been filled with quaint tales of economic heroism which, in two or three generations, are seen for what they really were — romantic conceit! When was the last time you heard anyone speak well of the following?

- The French nobility and men-at-arms at the battle of Agincourt.

- Owners of clipper ships after the 1840s.

- Lord Cardigan, Lord Lucan and General Raglan. Two are remembered for their fashion statement. We may celebrate the courage of the 600 (actually a little over 700) men of the Light Brigade, but their commanders were not fit for what we tell children.

- Religious authorities who opposed anaesthetics for women during childbirth.

- The elitist Allied cavalry generals of World War I. They justified trench warfare as the only base which would allow an artillery-supported, sustainable infantry breakthrough, which the cavalry could then exploit like Confederate raiders in 1862, destroying the enemy's rear support and thus winning the war.

- The American admirals of the 1930s who refused to believe that capital ships were at risk from carrier-based planes.

- The Polish cavalry. In 1939, the Polish cavalry was the finest in Europe. In 1940 there was no Poland. It is instructive to read the memoirs of German General Heinz Guderian. His anger at successive Polish governments and the Polish general staff for promulgating among young Polish men the romantic conceits around the calvary to which the young are susceptible is coupled with his disgust at having to play the butcher's role.

- The Legion d'Etranger at Dien Bien Phu, where the French general staff rejected intelligence estimates of General Giap's logistical management capabilities and opted for yet another dreary replay of the theme song from the Maginot Line soap opera.

• The American and European automobile manufacturers who only saw growth in the "back in" and replacement parts side of their industry. They could not believe that anyone in the world would want a Japanese car over one of theirs. So they adjusted their quality control and innovated the idea of built-in obsolescence.

• The Province of Quebec's proponents of extending the massive James Bay power generation complex when their principal customers, the State of New York and the New England states, were passing or had passed legislation requiring that utilities purchase only from suppliers who could pass their (American) environmental regulations.

• The world's nuclear, hydro, coal, and petroleum generation industries, wiped out by clean, safe, fusion-derived energy. (Oh, sorry, that doesn't happen until 2009.)

It is really curious. Humanity is quite ambivalent about these romantic vanities. On one hand we applaud them so that selling self-sacrifice will be easier. On the other hand, to hold these and qualitatively similar romantic narcissisms is contraindicated for a good life. Besides, in the West it is a matter of public policy not to reward suicidal behaviour.

JOINT VENTURES AND WORLD WAR

Following the Renaissance, the Industrial Age assumed an orderly and systematic universe which, until about 1900, remained relatively stable. The Victorian and Edwardian years took from the sciences what they could readily understand.

The 19th century was a time of inventors. In Germany, chemists, tool and die makers, and metallurgists contributed another phase of industrialization. In England and America, Fessenden's (not Marconi's) long distance wireless led to the multifaceted versions of radio with which we are familiar. George Stephenson's steam engines brought about railroads, which widened the market range for the new factories and allowed the efficient, albeit somewhat disorderly, opening of the North American West.

In the U.S., a uniquely American world-view of the new industrialism came about with Samuel Morse, whose telegraph lines paralleled the railroads, along with the one-time Morse code telegrapher Thomas Edison, George Westinghouse, and Henry Ford.

In the 19th century few British inventors were being pushed by the sciences. Most British inventors of any stature were inveterate tinkerers, and usually trained as artisans. But the Germans and French maintained a scientific base. German chemistry, engineering, and metallurgy led the world. French chemistry began to offer discoveries upon which the French chemical and pharmaceutical industries would be based. In Britain, a global patent-medicine industry arose based on coloured water and alcohol coupled with highly skilled marketing.

Superficially the world-view was orderly. But assumptions of incremental trade growth coupled with an extended life span assured that World War I would break out as the industrialized nations of Europe competed for markets. The reason that this war became the first world war was that no part of the world had been left untouched by industrialization.

That war was imminent was widely understood and accepted for a number of years prior to its actual outbreak. Even the word "outbreak" is significant. It suggests the war had been ongoing, but constrained, and the constraints had broken. World War I was a war about colonies with raw material resources and markets.

It is quite possible that some form of trade war will emerge as Europe and Japan flex their muscles. With the threat from the Soviet Union gone (and, indeed, the U.S.S.R. itself), the Eurocrazies and the Mishima-lovers at Japan Inc. are feeling that the time has come to put the U.S.A. in its rightful uncultured place.

CHAPTER FIFTEEN

The Superpower Trap: America's dangerous gamble

There is more to the world around us than we can conventionally see. Marcel Duchamp suggested that the 'normal' world, as we see it, is some kind of a shadow existence, like a projection on a flat surface of solid things in the real world. By amending the flawed epistemology that we inherited from the late Renaissance of the 18th century (the Age of Reason), which assumed a deterministic and rational universe, we can perceive this real world. With the insights provided by Planck, Einstein, Heisenberg, Schrödinger and Dirac, we are able to construct an epistemology which permits us to know that new ideas of space and time are legitimate aspects of the world we can see.

It is pretty much agreed that the change rate which we are experiencing is greater than any humanity has weathered before. There is also wide-spread agreement that the problems which result from that change rate, plus the problems brought on by the accumulated detritus we didn't pick up over the past couple of hundred years or so, is competing for our attention with the pollution of the planet.

The second greatest nation state of the past age has collapsed and its people face at least a decade of near, if not actual, starvation. Commenting on this Cold War collapse, the President of the United States, George Bush, said in his State of the Union address on January 28, 1992, that the world has been left with "one sole and pre-eminent power — the United States of America." Oh well, January 1992, was the beginning of the primary campaigns for a presidential election year and Mr. Bush could be excused for a small exercise in hyperbole.

It is unlikely that France and Germany plan to allow the U.S. to become the world's only superpower without a struggle. It is equally unlikely that Japan Inc., which is inextricably linked to the 'spirit' of Japan, will find the idea of one pre-eminent power something that fits with ASEAN (a.k.a. the Greater East Asia Co-Prosperity Sphere). In all, there are probably four groups who aspire to compete with the U.S. by becoming power states of the commercial/mercantile period we are entering. These are Japan, France/Germany, and Britain, with its corporate financial services industry in alliance with some members of the Islamic Conference. (The latter don't see themselves as commercial competitors but as the sustainers of timeless moral and spiritual Koranic values.) Finally, there is a highly unpredictable actor: China.

GERMANY AWAKES

Historically Germany has dominated commercial and financial activities throughout mittel Europe, including European Russia and Ukraine. From about 1860 until World War II, German companies were the principal managers of the bread basket of Europe in Ukraine.

Germans have long been world leaders in machinery, from machine tools to Mercedes-Benz cars, and in sciences such as chemistry and physics. Reunited, the Germans are now looking to their historical markets in the East. The German commitment to taking a leadership role in the European Union has been a less than happy surprise to the French.

Germans are celebrating their newly recovered power. They aren't exactly flaunting it — they are letting this new power speak for itself. Today Germany is the No. 1 economic power and the most populous country in Europe. Diplomatically, Germany's leadership is less resentful than disdainful of the United States and more comfortable with the U.S. than are France's leaders. In recent years Germany has shown that the country's diplomatic service is unwilling to play the silly games which exemplify the Quai d'Orsay, home of the French diplomatic service.

On December 23, 1991, Hans-Deitrich Genscher, then the German foreign minister, personally announced that Germany had recognized the independence of the breakaway Yugoslav republics of Croatia and Slovenia — and that the European Union would follow suit. Opposing this move, France had argued that the Serbians would be insulted and the U.N. secretary-general's peace plans would be thwarted. Cynics, however, viewed the French and German posturing as all too similar to events leading up to World War I. That the secretary general's peace plans were well and truly thwarted is attributed by world opinion to Serbian bloody-mindedness and the events which followed have made loving the Serbs an impossible task for any PR firm, no matter how well the French funded them.

Genscher's dramatic announcement was particularly noteworthy because it was the first unilateral diplomatic move by Germany since the end of World War II. This coup was quickly followed by another intuitive step by Genscher, who suggested that NATO forces might be used as an in-place U.N. peacekeeping force. New life for NATO!

France and England were further irritated when a German delegate to the E.U. suggested that, instead of each of the 12 member countries appointing individual ambassadors to the ex-Soviet republics of the Commonwealth of Independent States, the E.U. should appoint one ambassador to each C.I.S. nation, using the Maastricht treaty as the legal rationale. The French were outraged, since they had already established embassies and missions in the new republics, with the plan of winning preferential trade agreements for France. The British, whose concern was simple nationalism, saw one of their most unlovely nightmares becoming real — the idea that the Foreign Office could end up going the way of the pound sterling was not one a British civil servant would wish to take back to Whitehall.

Finally, Germany's mission at the E.U. in Brussels suggested that German become the third official E.U. language, holding equal status with French and English. For this piece of entertainment the Germans brought in their superstar performer, Chancellor Helmut Kohl, who politely pointed out that German was the "most widely spoken language" in Europe (it is spoken in Germany, Austria, the greater part of Switzerland and Holland). Not a bad few weeks work for a diplomatic service that until then had been so discrete as to be invisible.

It was apparent that Chancellor Kohl had decided the day of apologizing for being German was over. Germany was also through tugging its collective forelock and duly walking three paces behind its betters. When Kohl was asked at a press conference if he didn't expect some difficulties overcoming harsh memories among Russians who remember the war, his reply was, perhaps, the most illuminating event of all. He said: "When you always want to be loved, then you will not shape or move anything." That statement alone meant Europe was entering a period of radical change.

FRANCE THE SPOILER

France feels that it has been French genius which made the E.U. viable. France also feels that the United States has dismissed her as a second-rate power. Few French products are popularly accepted in America (always excepting Perrier water, Evian water, and wine).

France is driven by a myth of France's historical greatness. French foreign policy since 1945 has been to ensure that the glories of France are treated with respect by all who deal with her. This has not been easy and successive French governments have repeatedly sacrificed significant power chips in pursuit of their goal. Excepting the E.U., France's post-World War II foreign and domestic adventures have been mostly disastrous.

The French myth of superiority was personified from 1940 until 1945 by the autocratic General Charles de Gaulle. De Gaulle's establishment of a government in exile following the French defeat by Germany in 1940 helped create the myth that the battle in France ended in defeat because British allies abandoned the French northern line and failed to provide air cover.

After the war came the loss of the French colony of Vietnam, ending with the debacle at Dien Bien Phu. This, says the revised myth, was the result of the abandonment of a war-weakened France by the U.S., which wished to take France's place of influence in the Far East. The loss of France's oil-rich Middle Eastern virtual colonial interests is also attributed to a U.S. plot to give American oil companies control of the Middle East at the expense of France and Britain.

Then there was the 1956 joint venture with Anthony Eden's Britain at Suez in which, again, the U.S. abandoned its two wartime allies. Then there was the war in Algeria, which became France's political equivalent of America's Vietnam War. Out of that one came the greatest threat to post-war France, the abortive putsch plot of the officer corps, headed by the so-called colon generals of the Army in Algeria, who argued that they had been betrayed, yet again, by the politicians at home.

The reason the war in Algeria was such a mess is that France claimed Algeria was an overseas department of Metropolitan France like Tahiti, or

---

A common failing of people the world over is to perceive foreign leaders in terms of their impact on international affairs. Political leaders, who also tend to see the international stage as the "big board," play on it to the detriment of their commitments to the job for which they were elected.

Imagine you are head of the government of an industrial state, a middle power like Sweden, the Netherlands, or Canada. Most of your day is spent meeting with your senior civil service advisers or your political advisers. Your day is about 12 hours long and is filled with problems which bedeviled your predecessors and to which it is unlikely your government or your successors will find any answers which are more than Band-Aids.

The only people you ever see are so thoroughly screened that the meetings are completely predictable and your completely scripted responses, thoughtfully provided by advisers (see above), are mainly an exercise in not saying anything. It is heady stuff indeed to be sitting in one's office under these circumstances, fielding calls from leaders of Great Powers who are asking favours.

Naturally enough, you begin to discover it is more pleasurable to deal on the "big board." For one thing, when you travel abroad, the media are nice to you. Even your own country's journalists, travelling with you, take on an aura of fellow conspirators:

"Look guys, I'm sure they told you in the briefing before we left home what we're really after with these [insert name of natives of host country here]. Today's

St. Pierre and Miquelon, or Corsica. The official view was that the war in Algeria was technically a revolution and not a "war of national liberation." When a cabal of officers who had served in Algeria began openly plotting and issuing calls to overthrow the government, General de Gaulle was recalled as head of state, electrifying the nation with his call of "*Je suis France.*" The plot collapsed while de Gaulle presented himself as a head of state above party politics.

De Gaulle's support came from a sector of the French body politic referred to as *le droite classique* (the classical right), whose view of de Gaulle was, romantically, that he had restored French honour on an almost chivalric battlefield during the war. Not only did the plot to overthrow the French government collapse, but the French economy, which had been impoverished by the Algerian war, recovered in the buoyant days of the 1960s. But French diplomatic policy became fixated upon recovering French pre-war prestige — and in its pursuit of that prestige France's foreign policy was often seen by its European neighbours as playing the spoiler when it could not secure movement toward that prestige.

In 1967, de Gaulle came to Canada as part of the celebration of Canada's centennial and greeted a crowd in Montreal with the cry "*Vive le*

---

meeting was really tough. They're not much interested in budging. Now, if you could get out there tonight and tell the local press that unless their government is more reasonable these meetings are going right down the toilet...? Tell them if that happens, the only thing I'll be able to do is cave in to the opposition and [name horrible consequences here]."

The press, who at home hate your guts, scurry out to do your bidding and the other nation's leaders get asked rude questions and get beat up by their national media for being intransigent.

On the big board, even the food is better. International fare for foreign leaders tends to be well-prepared and not too weird, although George Bush might take issue with this.

Naturally enough, people at home see most of your foreign travel for the boondoggle it is. The same press who were your pals and accomplices when you were all chowing down on other people's expense accounts now assail you for your lavish lifestyle, the number of aides you took and your accomplishments. Your immediate constituency asks why you were unable to get your whole shopping list and no one at home is impressed with the foreign editorials praising you.

When you lose the next election, the foreigners are amazed that your country has turfed you out and call you a force for international justice, truth, beauty and peace who will be sorely missed in international affairs.

Quebec! Vive le Quebec Libre!" Canadian Prime Minister Lester B. Pearson reacted immediately and angrily. He advised the French president that Canadians had, after all, played a significant part in the liberation of France when France was unable to do so herself. The Canadian ambassador in Paris was called home and did not return until after Pearson left office.

At this point the French foreign service pulled off a minor coup with the organization of the *Francophonie*, an association of former French colonies and independent states where French speakers formed a significant portion of the population. It has been a useful forum for the members (largely indigent African states) and France is secure as the titular leader of this organization, through which France funnels most of its foreign aid and provides funds for a permanent secretariat.

The most successful of France's post-war ventures by far has been to provide the impetus for, first the European Common Market, the wider-ranging European Community, and finally the European Union. The E.U.'s top civil servant in its formative years was a French bureaucrat, Jacques Delors (now retired). French citizens are the largest national group within the E.U.'s bureaucracy.

However, even with the successes of the Francophonie and the E.U., the maintenance and, if possible, enhancement of the French myth remains France's principle international goal. And so France could not let the '80s pass without another disaster.

In 1986 the internationally respected environmentalists-with-attitude group, Greenpeace, was getting set, along with others, to harass the testing of another French nuclear explosive device in the South Pacific. While a Greenpeace ship was refitting in New Zealand, France's military spy outfit was ordered to give them some trouble.

Like any other spy shop in the 1980s, the French intelligence planners jumped at the chance to do a real operation. According to information leaked by the Australian security service, a team of seven agents was dispatched to New Zealand, where they proceeded to blow up the ship — and drown a freelance photographer on board. *Mistake.*

This was murder, not silly spy games. It was no longer in the hands of New Zealand's limited counter-intelligence force, which might have responded with some form of quid pro quo. So the real cops came in — and then the disaster happened. The real cops caught two of the French thugs and dropped a murder charge on them.

A few years before, when France had announced an earlier series of nuclear tests, the government of New Zealand had decided to send a naval ship to break through the safety blockade of international waters established by the French navy. This move was greeted with consternation in France and widespread public support in New Zealand. Then New

Zealand had a cabinet crisis: the government had decided that two cabinet members would go with the navy ship, just in case the French actually blew them out of the water. But the entire cabinet wanted to go!

When French spies actually killed someone, the New Zealand government was not about to negotiate anything unless every TV camera in the country was watching. For France this was not a happy event. France was not merely embarrassed; the glory that once was France had been humiliated. And worse was yet to come, as the spies talked to anyone who would listen. In France, opposition deputies whined about dishonour and shame.

The whole world was laughing at France. What kind of an intelligence service gets caught by the New Zealanders? A little pastoral country of 3.5 million souls? It was really so unfair. The *Quai d'Orsay* had never trained French diplomats to compete with a nation of farmers who might act out of principle.

JAPAN'S DAY IN THE SUN

Japan, the scapegoat of the future, was barred by a U.S.-supplied constitution from participating in the Cold War. Japan's business community thought this was just swell, as its electronics industry became eminently well-prepared to supply components for U.S. weapons and military computer systems.

Now Japan has begun to feel that any hint of subservience to the U.S. is an insult to its cultural superiority and racial purity. As Japan-bashing in the U.S. increases, the Japanese are clearly unwilling to see their culture denigrated.

Japan is currently undergoing a bit of constitutional and financial services industry reassessment. Akio Morita, the recently deceased founder of Japan's mega gadget company, Sony Corp., co-wrote (with Ishihara Shintaro) a book whose title is usually translated as *The Japan That Can Say No*, which enjoyed momentary notoriety for its criticism of Japan's close relationship with the U.S. The authors argued that Japan must once again become a free-standing nation with an independent military option.

Originally the book was not intended for translation into English. The Japanese publisher issued a Japanese-language edition and sales were limited to the Home Islands. But sales figures and public outcry were sufficient to encourage the publisher to authorize a U.S. publication. Mr. Akio insisted that the parts written by him be excised from the American edition. In the original text, however, the authors contend that America has been corrupting the spiritual values of Japan. Little notice was paid at the time of publication to another argument the authors made, which called for Japanese companies to change their priorities from a headlong battle for market share to one placing more emphasis on increasing dividends and enhancing employee benefits.

When Japan's economic prosperity began making a global impact, Japan's elite started to get restive. Its first diplomatic initiatives were to commence delivering — without much fanfare — aid to less developed countries. In short order, Japan became one of the major aid suppliers to the Third World. Japan's strategy differed from that of other traditional donor nations. There was no effort to secure an immediate return in market share. There were no mega projects in Japan's agenda, and as Japan-bashing rises to new crescendos in Europe and America, the Third World sees Japan as a responsible global partner. In South America particularly, Japanese influence is strong.

In January 1992, the distinguished economics journalist David Crane wrote a column in *The Toronto Star* comparing North American management with Japan's corporate managers. He cited his own research and an MIT study (*The Machine that Changed*), along with a book by a reputable U.S. auto industry analyst, Maryann Keller (*Rude Awakening*), plus the widely recognized U.S. management authority Peter Drucker.

Crane vividly described U.S. business leadership as "inferior management," pointing out that Japan practices a different form of capitalism than that which evolved in North America. In Japan goals are achieved by working through consensus to attain progress for the entire group, which is profoundly different from North America, where the focus is on the individual.

Crane's research is solid and legitimately disturbing to any North American, whether a worker, an executive or a government official. However, Crane's analysis is incomplete and his criticism, lacking a fuller commentary, is defective. (This may simply be the function of the word-count limitations on a daily newspaper columnist.) The Crane column, headlined "Japan beats U.S. car firms on superior management," failed to acknowledge the profound cultural limitations of using such simplistic comparisons.

North Americans live by a cultural myth that places extravagant value on an assumed right to personal space and the lack of group accountabilities over our lifetimes. The ordinary North American lifestyle is almost unimaginable to the Japanese psyche. In a nation where there are 130 million people packed into the Home Islands (about the size of one of the Great Lakes), you make sure you have a degree of social consensus before you do anything. You also develop some interesting ways to develop consensus, ways that are usually inaccessible to the Western psyche. When you live in houses with paper walls, you learn, very early, not to express your emotions.

Every Japanese knows that this is a land that was made for feudalism. Japan needs a stable government. Since there isn't much chance of that, they have successfully opted for stable corporations and looked for a stable royal family. Given what they had to start with, the royal family has historically been held as tools of shogunate court factions. The last shogun sold out to U.S. Admiral Perry in 1865 and, with Emperor Hirohito's denial of his divinity in 1945, Japanese identity became unstable.

David Crane's column ended with a quote from Ross Perot, a man who proved that it was still possible to give American career politicians, regardless of party affiliation, a nervous twitch. A few years ago Perot sold General Motors his highly successful computer service company, EDS, and joined the GM board. Perot later fell out with the chairman, Roger Smith, over management practices and made public statements casting aspersions on Smith's ability to administer a one-car funeral. Perot also managed to pull off a jailbreak in Teheran when the Ayatollah refused to pay Perot's bill and tossed two of Perot's staff in the slammer.

Perot, among others, was less than amused with President Bush's pre-election trip to Japan, where the president, accompanied by U.S. auto industry leaders, converted a wave of nausea into a photo opportunity where the only winners were the dry cleaners who held the contract for the Japanese prime minister's suit. Perot said: "A great tax base only comes from a country which makes great products and that can compete and win. This trip was just a joke."

Crane's summary comes close to the real problem. He wrote: "Until there are fundamental changes in the quality and attitudes of top executives in the United States and Canada, as well as new relationships between business,

---

The Japanese word wah translates roughly as inner tranquility, being spiritually at peace with one's self. For example:

Trading Company Executive (calling company chairman at home): "I hope I am not disturbing your wah, Lord. I have a fax from our American subsidiary saying the American Congress wants to ban our consumer products from the U.S. market for six months because in 1982 our disgusting Korean subsidiary sold the same computer chips to the excremental Russians that we had sold to the U.S. military."

Company Chairman (wah obviously beat on): "Apology not accepted. My grandfather, hero of the Battle of Port Arthur, where he led Japan's torpedo boats against the incomplete abortions of the Tsar's fleet in 1904, would have told you to slit your belly. Instead go to France and sell the snail-sucking French the warehouse full of obsolete computer chips. And apologize to the fools in the American Congress."

A culture in which the language has a commonly used word that is as heavily loaded as the term wah will take ideas of civility and politeness very seriously — which is so alien to us that we treat it with parody.

labour, and government, Japan will continue to hold all the aces in the deck."

What is really happening to American-Japanese relations is actually two separate problems which are occurring at the same time.

Japan's achievements in quality and productivity result in a massive trade imbalance between the two countries. This trade imbalance exists between Japan and just about everywhere people can afford to buy a TV set. The imbalance with the U.S., however, is particularly embarrassing and the size, when compounded with all those T-bills Japanese banks buy, raises the problem of what the U.S. would do if Japan were to withdraw from U.S. investment markets. Recent Japan-bashers seldom mention the degree of participation by Japanese investment dealers in the weekly American T-Bill auctions and the ability of the Japanese investment community to absorb a disproportionate amount of corporate America's debt and equity.

No objective commentator would disagree that Japan has practised protectionism which the international trading community believes to be unfair. However, it does seem to be a dubious argument to say that, because American managers perform badly, Japan should compensate them by offering access to its home markets.

If, on the American front, the variable is simply that American leadership — political, corporate, institutional, and trade union — is inefficient, incompetent, slothful, and possibly corrupt, that is one problem. But what if the American problem runs deeper than that? What if it is not the Japanese leadership that is more productive and efficient? What if it is Japanese *culture* that is outperforming American *culture*?

North American culture happens to operate in a bountifully endowed part of the world. Put someone from any other part of the world in a North American supermarket and show them the aisle dedicated to pet foods: their disbelief that an economy of such wealth could exist is a reaction for which most North Americans have no answer.

Cultural amendment is not something which people lightly or gladly embrace, except under severe stress of a type North Americans have never experienced. If the bad news is that our problem is cultural, the good news is that the era transition we're facing is going to demand cultural adaptations anyway. So we get another chance. But only if we successfully read a new set of entrails.

JAPAN AND AMERICA: A MONSTER OF A PROBLEM

The Japanese problem of political legitimacy swoops in on us in some weird ways. Usually we don't even notice.

In 1954, America awoke to a new bit of cultural incongruity when a Japanese film studio, The Toho Company, released a film into the American market which was to set a new benchmark in weirdness. This flick, called *Godzilla*, was the story of an evil monster that rose out of Tokyo Bay and began to stomp on Tokyo. This was obviously a job for the Japan Home Defence Force! And they responded magnificently. Jeeps freshly refurbished at the Toyota plant careened down mountain roads with JHDF troops as the extras. The (real) JHDF fired U.S. 155mm howitzers, locally retrofitted after use in the Korean War, at the monster. Not to be outdone, the air arm of the JHDF bravely fired rockets at this paleolithic creature from Korean War-vintage surplus Saber jets, while the sea arm of the JHDF sped around Tokyo Bay in its coastal patrol vessels, making hooting sounds.

When *Godzilla* debuted in 1954, the author was living in Tokyo after personally "stemming the tide of Communist aggression in the war-ravaged peninsula of Korea." It was a strange experience to go to this monster/morality movie with a group of Japanese friends who were officers in the newly minted Toda, who were all totally enthralled by this allegorical treatment of U.S.-Japanese relations, with its theme that Japan was redeemed but not yet renewed. The rapt attention shown by the all-adult audience rattled me at the time. After all, this was a kid's movie. Right?

For many of us who saw that first Godzilla movie, some of the dialogue is unforgettable. In a scene near the end, after a *kamikaze* attack by one of the Rising Sun-adorned Saber Jets had proven futile, a JHDF officer says to his assembled staff and his American scientist consultant, "Our computers are not strong enough. We must have the best and fastest computers in the world." He then says to the round-eyed American scientist, "Can you get Washington to send us such a computer? *Only America can save Japan now!*" (Emphasis added — I think.)

Here is some comparative data on the problems facing folks who don't live in the wealthy nations.

A few years ago, a pal of mine was writing speeches for a senior official of the U.N.'s World Health Organization. I once went with him to see his boss provide after-lunch entertainment to the kind of folks who get that kind of luncheon speaker. In the course of his speech the official noted that "there are 10 cities in the world where the public health services are imminently expected to break down."

Afterward, I asked, "what is the operational definition of public heath service breakdown?"

My friend replied in the matter-of-fact tones used by those whose daily lives are made up of administering reactions to the disasters of an imperfect world.

"Oh," he said, "that's where they don't pick up the bodies of the dead from the streets within 24 hours."

No one laughed. America sent the world's most powerful computer and Tokyo was saved. Fast forward to 1992. Over the years, in North America, Godzilla movies have achieved cult status and produced lots of foreign revenue for Japan. Toho has become a world recognized film production studio. As for Godzilla himself (Godzilla has always been male), the after-market merchandise has been a real windfall. Toho's scriptwriters have portrayed the monster with an ambivalent moral swing most of his fans find to be refreshing. Sometimes he is a good creature seeking redemption, sometimes he is his own evil twin. At times he has battled other monsters from the depths of wherever. Whatever else may be said about Godzilla movies, the writers have never bored us with consistency. Of course, that is to assume that Toho bothers to hire scriptwriters. Actually, the dialogue is mostly there to link one special effect to the next.

A few years ago, while living in a city with a large number of Japan Inc. subsidiaries and personnel, I took my then 10-year-old son to a movie house where the latest episode of the Godzilla saga was to play for a week. On Saturday we arrived at the theatre for the first show. It was packed with 10-year-old Japanese kids and their dads, who all seemed typical Japan Inc. representatives — well-dressed sararimen. Many knew each other and there was lots of ceremonial bowing. Interestingly, the fathers all smiled at me, not in a friendly way, but approvingly. I was doing the right thing, taking my kid to see Godzilla.

When the movie started, the same rapt attention I had noted in Tokyo in 1954 took over the audience, only this time there were muted comments pronounced by sucking in breath. Occasionally there was gesticulation, as a father pointed out the significance of something on the screen. After one such exchange between the father and son sitting beside us, the kid, who had been sharing his refreshments with my son, said that his dad had just pointed out the house in which his aunt lived. It was apparently identifiable in the model.

Early in January of 1992, the Associated Press reported that Toho was about to release a Godzilla movie with a story-line that was sure to surprise some of the mutant creature's round-eyed fans. This time, Godzilla would be squashing Americans. Whoever passes for a story editor at Toho had decided that people from the 23rd century, many of whom bear a startling resemblance to Americans, return to our present in a time machine. Their dark purpose is to alter the past and prevent Japan from becoming a ruthless superpower in the 21st and 22nd centuries. The weapon of choice for this dark deed was to be the flying, three-headed dragon-like Ghidrah, who the bad guys from century 23 turn loose on the long-suffering Japanese. The Japanese turn to Godzilla (who else?) to save them from the twin horrors of Ghidrah and the blue-eyed devils from the 23rd century.

Toho spokesmen denied that the film was anti-American. Instead, they said, the movie focusses on the soul-searching that currently engages Japan about its economic prowess and its global role. Anyone in North America or Europe hearing that, without the benefit of having seen a Godzilla movie in a theatre where the preponderance of the audience is Japanese, could be forgiven for believing that the producers of Godzilla movies are being pretentious and self-indulgent.

Formulating policies that respond to Japanese domestic political events is difficult enough, but for North Americans the gaps are cavernous. The differences begin every morning. The constant psychic goal for the Japanese is to find their own national centre. The Home Islands are small and based on (by geological standards) recently active volcanoes. The country is also earthquake prone to a degree that makes California a sea of geological tranquility by comparison. In this kind of environment, it's tough to find your own centre, let alone a national one.

NORTH AMERICA'S GREAT FRONTIER

The Cold War period left the nations of the world hooked on fortress men-talities and simplistic pseudo-solutions which benefited only the major weapons-system manufacturers and the military bureaucracies of nations that had been converted into weapons-system states. Now these nation-weapons systems have no targets. Perfection of control of when or if new technologies come to market is the goal of the bureaucrats who adminis-tered the capital concentrations of the industries and governments which became weapon-system states.

During the Cold War, one of the salient features of both West and East was that national identity was abandoned or subsumed to the foreign policy diktats of ideological positions which had little to do with the daily lives of anyone. Military redundancies were like national debts: they were so great that they had lost any meaning.

As we have seen with 4th century Rome and the feudal world, the uni-verse has way of dealing with such systemic collapses. It changes the rules! When the rules change, we call that an era transition.

North Americans are particularly fortunate in that the new rules have been largely local products, founded by Germans and other Europeans who were part of the greatest intellectual migration ever known. The problem for North Americans is that the leadership has the wrong goals.

Essentially, the New World Order of the corporate West is attempting to shoe-horn the management precepts of the high Industrial Age into the post-industrial period of a new era. The result of this attempt to perpetuate industrial management processes will require repressive forces beyond the capabilities of the transnational corporation. In other words, it won't work. The Great Corporation mentality is not up to the task.

North America is the logical home of the automobile. To get a driver's licence is both a perceived "right" and a "rite of passage" toward adulthood. In Europe the automobile is a luxury. It is extremely difficult for Europeans to comprehend the distances which North Americans assume. Compare European highway traffic law in Europe and North America. In Europe highway traffic legislation is a small part of the legal system. According to research by the Canadian Law Reform Commission, highway traffic law in North America constitutes around 25 percent of the body of law affecting the ordinary person.

Recent Japanese acquisitions of wilderness vacation properties in British Columbia and the way Japanese tourists use these environments suggests that, coming fresh from Japan's high density prefectures, the tourists treat the open space and unexploited mountains as a fantasy. The tourist has great difficulty in suspending the disbelief that such space may be used. The North American wilderness is profoundly different from the amount of space their daily lives teach them is a fair and equitable allocation.

Every North American should be profoundly troubled that the domestic automobile and light truck market has been taken away from the domestic auto industry. How dare the custodians of GM, Ford, and Chrysler get beaten by the Japanese? This was not a market share defeat. It was someone else making our icons better than we did. Inadvertently, the Japanese became cultural imperialists. That wasn't their goal. They just wanted to employ their people and make the best of a lack of natural resources by maximizing a disciplined labour force.

The car enabled us to explore our lands. North Americans revere the forefathers who pushed the boundaries of civilization across the continent. The car enables us to experience the geographic diversities from the semi-tropics of Florida to the Arctic of the Peace River to the tundra of Alaska to the deserts of the south-west. From the Atlantic fisheries through the granaries of the mid-west and on to the Pacific, the automobile reminds us of our pioneering heritage. It is this cultural commitment to being in the forefront of discovery which has been placed at risk.

For both Americans and Canadians the automobile retains its iconographic value, denoting a central core myth about the mastery of the immense distances and hostile weather that faced North America's cultural founders.

Americans identify with the "wagons West" myth, of the settler beginning at Virginia and moving across the continent, opening up the prairie, Lewis and Clarke reaching out for a route to the Pacific.

Canadians share this mystique, which allows us a feel for the land expanses which neither the Europeans nor the Japanese can ever know in their innermost being, although, the metaphors for Canadians are different.

For Canadians there are the *coureurs de bois* of New France, the Hudson's Bay Company factors and traders, the settlement of Ontario and the Maritimes by United Empire Loyalists, the great march west of the North West Mounted Police, the building of the CPR with a search for a pass through the Rockies by Col. Rogers, which assured that the country would be joined and the settlement of the west by immigrants from Central and Eastern Europe.

All of these myths are celebrated by North Americans as part of a heritage which has a great part of its identity in the challenges of survival-class frontiers.

This core North American myth, with its focus on frontiers, is crucial to the culture. Among North Americans, frontiers are arbitrary and seen as barriers to progress.

This is why the idea of free trade seemed so logical to the North American business community. The reason there is so much acrimony in the dispute settlement process is that the negotiators failed to recognize the profundity of the differences between the American and the Canadian identity myths.

But since the negotiators were civil servants being urged on by political masters of the respective governing parties and the corporate elites of both countries, there was little likelihood that there would be anything approximating consideration of issues that would poison the treaty relationship of the two countries and their real (informal) relationships with one another.

CHINA: LOOK FOLKS, CLEAN HANDS

After Premier Leader Deng's funerary extravaganza, replete with the official and representative mourners being urged to weep "hot tears," the political deals, which are always the high point of obsequies for any powerful politician, were buzzing with speculation as to the identity of the new leader.

The operative word is Power. Deng, to the very end, maintained a death grip on the levers of power within the CCP. Finally, Party spokescreatures trotted out to report that the 12th party honcho was to be the former mayor of Shanghai, Jiang Zemin. Jiang was a middle-of-the-road choice.

The Chinese party has never been one to let a leader ease into the job gently and Jiang's entry was no exception. His CV emphasizes his career as a party bureaucrat in bold type. Each new job, as he climbed up the ladder, had been marked with increasing complexity.

For example, his efforts in picking up litter after the Red Guard rampages marked him as a comer. When it was judged that Mao's wife and the other errant members of the Gang of Four needed a trial, Jiang was there to see that there was always a courtroom available and the PLA guards had clean white gloves. When Deng decided to reactivate Shanghai as the mainland's answer to Hong Kong attitude, Jiang was there. In Shanghai, Jiang was an outstanding administrator; his successor Zhu Rongji was shortly to follow him to Beijing.

Mr. Zhu is extraordinarily tough while exuding considerable charm, a vital survival trait in post-Deng China. His CV is a good example of how China has substituted optional creds for the participation in the 1934-1935 Long March.

Until now the first step to politburo appointment required Long March veteran status and conduct during as the first element of the CV check. Currently a political comer will find his records being scrutinized for how he behaved during the Cultural Revolution, when bureaucrats and intellectuals were being detained prior to being rehabilitated by peasants and workers and the gauche and even thoughtless children of the Red Guard. In Zhu's case, the Red Guard sent him to work on a rural swine production facility.

Rural pig works do not lend themselves to specialization. Everyone gets a chance to micro-manage the distribution of swill for the pigs' lunches, herding the porcine friends from one stop to another in the pork production line. China's communes use techniques perfected 4,000 years ago. The slaughtering methods are noted for recycling efficiencies that leave the ground fertilized with an abundance of decomposing pig feces and urine. This is why typical pictures of pig works show the staff are not wearing shoes.

The social life of the workers at a pig producing collective is assumed, by most China watchers, to be less sophisticated than say, the fleshpots of Beijing, Shanghai, or Hong Kong, even though pig workers usually have two set of clothes. Anyone would be rehabilitated after the four-and-a-half years of often thoughtlessly insolent treatment by his Red Guard case managers that Zhu would have endured. The Red Guard did, however, return Zhu as a promotable executive.

When Jiang became China's new leader, Zhu's successes in reestablishing Shanghai as China's financial capital were rewarded with the number two job behind Jiang as prime minister.

The new regime spotlight was shining on Jiang, where the new boy was a big hit visiting Russia. Boris Yeltsin hugged him and his spinners happily reminisced about the power-shift exemplified by the good old days in 1956 when Jiang was what was euphemistically called "a young fraternal brother" at the ZIL limo factory in Moscow, where he was learning to build cars. Unfortunately, the Chinese delegation was unable to extend its schedule to permit a visit to the ZIL plant, perhaps because the ZIL plant was closed and in the last stages of bankruptcy.

In his North America excursion, Jiang dealt effectively with Chinese-Canadian and Chinese-American dissidents holding up rude signs in English by expressing his disinterest in "the incident" or "the events" in Tiananmen Square. The "incident", et cetera, is the way this untidy happening is referred to by Chinese officials when they are pointing out that those bits of street theatre are of "little interest" to the average citizen of the People's Republic of China or to even the lowest clerk in China's officialdom. Jiang entranced Western politicians and bureaucrats with *après café* talk about what he had to buy over the next 20 years and how much he wanted to do his shopping in NAFTA land and how difficult this shopping would be if people kept obstructing his attention from his shopping by interfering with sovereign China.

This was a big improvement on former president Li Peng who allowed himself to be humiliated on a visit to Moscow in October when he handled Chinese dissident complainers in an undiplomatic and testy fashion. Jiang's demonstration of cool under similar harassment made Li look stupider than usual.

With Jiang on his world tour, Zhu had a chance to do the necessary due diligences back home. Addressing the economic impact of the Asian financial crisis, Zhu ordered China's central bank to close its provincial offices and open regional offices where Beijing could maintain more rigorous scrutiny. Zhu also off-loaded zillions of stiff loans on the three remaining domestic banks. That made the flaky loans rimbi-denominated and left both the central bank and the powerhouse Bank of China, the facilitator of China's "no sweat" international trade dragon, unencumbered.

When Jiang returned from his friendly and enlightened talks with the foreigners Zhu was able to announce (are we surprised?) that the economy was a little bit shaky and it would be necessary to close down about 3 million state-owned businesses that owed hundreds of millions of uncollectable yuan and rimbi to China's hapless domestic state-run banks.

The chairman of the central bank was on hand to announce that there was no chance that either of the currencies would be devalued and China would be making a contribution to the aid package being cobbled together by the IMF. It would appear that Mr. Zhu had learned all about tough decisions, even if he was too young for the Long March, during his tour at the pig works.

The yuan may be internationally traded or used for repatriation by external investors. The Rimbi is restricted to domestic usage and may not be externally held. The bad loans have disappeared as far as the external world is concerned by being dropped on the People's Bank Of China and the other domestic banks.

The idea of having two currencies is a trifle baffling for most of us, who were taught that simple is good and there are less cracks in the floor to lose the change. China's bulging foreign exchange reserves have been buttressed by this creative monetary policy and the two currencies have managed to create a new category of "not Mexico, not drug money being laundered, not in bed with the Yakusa and not Indonesia."

On the evening of September 12, 1997, just before the Party congress (held once every five years), Jiang demonstrated his Party credentials when he described China as still being in the "primary stage" of socialism. Marx must have been doing pirouettes in his grave at that, but it was, in fact, a very good party line. In Marxist-speak, this is the way to describe a state whose socialism is not so strong or deep that it can't be reversed or remoulded. The delegates to the party congress were duly impressed and Jiang was acclaimed the leader.

Jiang was available to talk to the West about market economies and other events of mutual interest. He wasn't even in Beijing or Shanghai for that matter when "the incident" was happening but "the events" did occur in a number of other urban centres where CNN had no cameras recording anything out of the ordinary.

A CNN bean counter was once asked how much it would cost to give China full coverage. His reply was instructive: "China cannot be reported on. You can't get reporting teams permission to go in where some interesting things are happening, even when they're positive. The only reason that Tiananmen Square got the coverage it did was that it happened in Beijing."

Among the factors that favoured Jiang's selection were that he was not carrying any baggage from the Long March. He was a true Child of the Revolution and could be expected to survive for 10 or 20 years.

Jiang's stoicism was tested when the North Korean intelligence head defected to the South Korean Embassy in Beijing. It was Jiang who worked out a face-saver from the mortification that goes with a high-profile defector announcing his new affiliation. Jiang managed not to be publicly tied to the defector's subsequent arrival in Seoul where the line-crosser chattered on about invasions and Silkworm missiles landing in Seoul, Tokyo and Yokohama.

It would probably be wise if graduates (survivors) of a multiyear stretch in the Red Guard's version of boot camps are not seen as primitive ex-commies by the people we tend to send on missions to China. North American and European bankers, CEOs, union leaders, and bureaucrats have no idea how tough you have to be to survive the pigs and pig by-products, or the production team leaders and the Little Red Book catechism, self-criticism, and the rest of the local Red Guard's ideas of how to deal with someone who had lost their sense of political correctness.

The people we usually send on missions to China are incapable of understanding the disciplined fortitude needed to just survive one's sentence during the Cultural Revolution. Currently China is desperate for two-way trade deals. In about 20 years it will be less anxious but it will remember any government who tried to bully or otherwise diss China.

PART FOUR

How to survive in a multi-dimensional world

CHAPTER SIXTEEN

Life in the Cyberspace Era:
How to survive and even enjoy an era transition

It may seem obvious but, when you build a house, you build it to provide security from the elements. For example, an adobe house in the arid southwestern U.S. can be quite pleasant. It is cool without needing artificial air-conditioning. But no matter how much you might like the style and form of an adobe house, you don't build one in England, no matter how homesick you are for Arizona. Building world-views is very similar.

This chapter is about how to survive and even enjoy an era transition. The problem with era transitions is that a lot of people you like are not going to make the transition. If you've made it this far, you probably are fully aware that the road ahead is rocky and not well-built. In fact, you should have realized by this point that any road building that gets done will have to be your own work. It is unlikely that our leaders — business, institutional, or political — will admit to us that they have no idea where this bumpy track is going. It's not unrealistic to expect that they will impede our way. They, after all, have a lot to lose, and are not noted for their altruism.

The scouts who went ahead — Planck, Einstein, Heisenberg, Schrödinger, and Dirac — were not exactly the most concise and explicit map-makers for the coming era. Their idea of the good life might not match yours. So this chapter is not a road map. It is about some things to watch for on the way: some things to avoid, some to simply appreciate, some to grab hold of, and some daisies that grow along the way that are worth taking a break to sniff at.

Historically, governments have tended to be minimally useful in this kind of situation. One difficulty with era transitions is that you can seldom legislate them. When there occurs a quantum jump beyond the previously accepted level of abstraction, events tend to start seeming random. That's because the rate at which people understand the new abstractions is randomly distributed, as is social approval of that understanding.

Implementation of these separate understandings is also random in its distribution over the population. Each time the new abstraction level is implemented it becomes part of the conventional wisdom and the overall population becomes a little more aware. Adherents to the previous level of abstraction try to hang on like grim death (and it is a grim death for them).

Suppose you work in a junior personnel capacity for a pharmaceutical company, responsible for recruitment of scientific staff. The company is probably a transnational corporation with a broadly based product list and a multi-disciplinary research program. You would have a firm grasp of industrial safety law, employment law, employment and pay equity as it applies to the jurisdiction in which your office is located, recruitment strategies, an understanding of dealing with personnel consultants, and screening applicants. You should also have an idea about the instructional skills reputations of various graduate schools from which you recruit.

You would be able to supervise personnel clerks and be sensitive to the dynamics and working conditions of the company's current working groups, which employ scientific staff in the areas for which you are responsible. You will also be familiar with industrial espionage and screening techniques to identify persons who are likely to be a security risk.

One day you are requested to recruit a technical writer for the microbiology group, which is working on anti-viral compounds. This writer should be familiar with writing technical documents for professional specialty and general journals (medical and microbiology), consumer publications, educational journals (for doctors, nurses, and lab technicians), as well as possessing general journalistic skills and familiarity with writing submissions to regulatory agencies.

It is critical that this person be able to meet with members of the microbiology team (which includes two Nobel laureates) and be able to accurately write authoritative reports of their work.

One of the things you must screen candidates for is a solid understanding of contemporary mathematics. Further, the writer must have some clues about contemporary computer technology and be able to knowledgeably discuss the stages of molecular modelling which the research group's work has gone and will go through. The manager of the publications office and the director of the microbiology research group will not be amused if they must screen out mathematical illiterates and the seriously computer challenged. Besides not knowing how to do it without getting slapped with some kind of nasty lawsuit, they assume such screening is your job.

If you had taken such a job 10 or 12 years ago they would have hired you if you had a B.A. or an M.A. in personnel psychology, or even a degree in one of the social sciences, such as sociology or anthropology. A writer applying for this job, 10 or 12 years ago, might have been, with a bit of luck, a science journalist on a daily paper or trade publication, or a person with some technical writing skills and an undergraduate life science degree.

In the last five paragraphs we have seen how an average junior personnel administrator begins to achieve functional literacy in the applications of the new era. Through a combination of daily exposure and personal research (accompanied by a healthy dose of enlightened self-interest), a junior personnel manager has acquired the necessary superficial information about the abstraction level which is running the world these days. If this knowledge seems illusory, very few of us could describe how an internal combustion engine works, yet most of us use one daily.

SURVIVAL OF THE FITTEST

With the discovery of perspective, the invention of the bill of exchange, and the adoption of Arab numeracy in the Renaissance, a new world-view came into being. The feudalism and Scholasticism of the Middle Ages impeded any attempts to raise the level of abstraction.

In the face of the new mathematics the force for administering the orderly social cohesion, the Pax Romana (the Peace of Rome), began to come apart at the seams. The Church and its offshoot, Scholasticism, came under increasing criticism from the Humanist intellectual movement. The new mathematics delivered the means by which trade and commerce expanded exponentially. This resulted in a new middle class, the bourgeoisie, whose wealth was based not in land, but in the trading of goods.

This new class, whose wealth was independent of the existing order, supported a world-view that was congruent with its interests. This new world-view exploited the new learning, which was based on a new level of science. This new science was noteworthy in that it was highly applications-driven: Pacioli's accounting techniques and his assistance to both painters and architects resulted in an outpouring of applications in Northern Italy. It also resulted in the boys' school attached to his Franciscan order house becoming the school of choice for the sons of the regional nobility.

The Renaissance brought forth the Reformation of the church. Conventionally, our school system speaks of the Reformation as if it were only about religion, but it was also about a level of abstraction that was too limited to address the new discoveries and new institutional structures based on a vastly expanded world of ideas.

This world was profoundly altered and needed a new epistemology to explain the expanded mental universe. It needed new theories of economics and new systems of accounting to reconcile the new wealth. It even developed new ideas about ethics, severing the ethical from the religious.

The difference between the two became obvious by the time the English Reformation was underway, when England's writers were in the fore. Probably the most significant figure for our purposes was Christopher Marlowe.

Marlowe, who was killed in an argument over a bar tab, started off the right way. The poor son of a tailor, he managed to get a full tuition, room and board scholarship to Cambridge. At the time, two of the Cambridge colleges were regular hotbeds of papist intrigue and Sir Francis Walsingham arranged a scholarship for Kit much as we arrange scholarships for football players. Marlowe didn't have to run fast with a weird ball, all he had to do was catch papist plotters. Which he did with great frequency.

Kim Philby and Anthony Blunt, the British intelligence officers who turned out to be Soviet spies, would have been as much at home in Cambridge of the early 17th century as they were in the 1930s. Secretary of State Sir Francis Walsingham knew a winner when he saw one. After he had sent Marlowe to France to check out the papists' spy school at Rheims, Cambridge was loath to award him his M.A. degree. The Privy Council office sent the Cambridge dons a rocket which would appear to have got their attention.

The letter basically said that Marlowe was a good kid and to get off his case because when he was not at school he was saving the realm from the forces of evil. The letter added that Her Majesty, Queen Elizabeth, would really hate it if one of her staunchest defenders was turfed for defending said realm. The guardians of Cambridge weren't slow about this sort of thing and presto! Marlowe got his M.A.

Marlowe went on to become the finest poet in English history and would have probably surpassed Shakespeare as a playwright if he had lived. Certainly Shakespeare thought so, since he frequently "borrowed" Marlowe's plots and even lines.

It is worth a glance at Marlowe's *Faustus* because in it we can see the seminal idea behind the Puritan movement. *Faustus* is about a man who sells his soul to the devil — a popular theme ever since. Here we see Lucifer and Faustus. Faustus thinks there is something to negotiate.

Faustus: O might I see Hell and Return safe, how happy were I then.
Lucifer: Faustus thou shalt at midnight, I will send for thee.
Then we see that Marlowe understood the new Protestant worldview and how it dealt with repentance — the sinner who truly repents will be forgiven. God has granted Man free will. Marlowe confronts his audience with an allegorical challenge as Faustus' guardians wrestle for his soul.
Good Angel: Faustus repent: yet God will pity thee!
Bad Angel: Thou art a spirit: God cannot pity thee.
Faustus: Who buzzeth in my ears I am a spirit? Be I a devil, yet God may pity me — Yea God will pity me if I repent.

But stupid Faustus cannot repent. His sin, after all, is not the absurd sale of his soul. His sin is the sin of hubris. He believed he could avoid eternity in Hell by outsmarting God and Lucifer. He thought he could get away with visiting Hell and "return safe."

Faustus does not, in truth, repent his state of hubris. In fact, at no time does Faustus even acknowledge the sin was hubris. To the end he keeps whining about his less-than-believable soul. This is the world-view by which the Renaissance rejected the legalisms of the Medieval scholastic world. In the end Faustus finds that he has bequeathed his soul to Lucifer irrevocably and this is just. After all, Lucifer himself was also thrown down to hell for, of course, the sin of pride. The Protestant world-view held that no one is saved by good works, but only by Grace.

Marlowe's *Faustus* is not a Medieval mystery morality play. Marlowe does not ask his audience to affirm the basic goodness and justice of the socio-religious system. Rather, Marlowe is railing at the religious order as offered by the "one true faith." *Faustus* portrays the new Renaissance man. The old order limited the aspirations of man.

The Renaissance said by your own efforts you can aspire to goals which you can even invent. Only in the matter of salvation was man fettered and the Grace of God was all that stood between man and the fiery pit of eternity.

In everything else man could try to reach beyond his dreams. Individuals could abandon their feudal obligations and strike out on their own. More important was that this awful choice to abandon the sureties of the Medieval world was made by each individual.

SURVIVAL IN A POST-INDUSTRIAL ECONOMY

One thing that happens in the course of an era transition is that the language grows in size to accommodate the new level of abstraction which has to be communicated. This language growth and change must describe the new inventions, the retrofitting of social changes, and the new world-view.

Our word "virtue," for example, is rooted in Latin. As a way-station on its trip to us it passed through the Italian Renaissance where we find the word *virtu*. But virtu was used to describe the principle of man's force to achieve in and for himself alone. Such an idea spelled the death-knell for the collectivism and the feudal obligation which had been the basis of the social order since the classical Roman time.

You should be considering how to earn a living if your current job collapses. Remember, there are few "safe" jobs any more. Lots of IBM and GM long-term employees thought they weren't vulnerable.

One thing to pay attention to is the language changes that reflect changing social realities. As the economy becomes increasingly bimodal, watch for terms like "urban armour," "disenfranchised," "propertyless," and "computer illiterate" to become part of a growing list of terms, along with "marginal," to describe those who do not possess the social and economic skills to be part of the emergent era's mainstream.

"Marginal" is increasingly used to describe people who fall into the back hump of a bimodal income distribution. Marginal people are not central to the main society's requirements. They are outside the mainstream of society. They do not work for large organizations, so they have minimal health insurance. Their access to information is relegated to the public media, not the new electronic databases which are coming on-stream and are still capital and social skill intensive.

Why have we seen a massive rise in the market value of entertainment and multimedia companies? Why did Seagram buy out MCA and, later, PolyGram? How come Disney acquired its very own TV network and why did Time Warner borrow even more to bounce into Ted Turner's increasingly amusing arcade?

During the high point of the recessionary cycle, one of the safe places to nest cash was in the video rental industry. Blockbuster, the retail video rental chain, enjoyed such apparently unrestrainable revenues that the conventional investment analysis tools could not explain the market performance and market-share growth.

The reason was quite simple. People who were laid off, fired, placed on shortened hours, or otherwise made economically unproductive watched a lot of TV. If they were over 45 it was unlikely that they would ever return to stable employment.

As a growing part of society caught on to the new level of abstraction, it was increasingly apparent that many school drop-outs and over-40 products of the out-placement experts would never hold "productive" jobs again in their lives (which would be extended by each new "advance" in health care).

In real estate, the old saw about assessing value says the only three factors are location, location, and location. If you want to open a video store the best location is an area of government-assisted housing. Video store owners in these areas are never heard to complain about "welfare bums."

If the only real job growth is in the knowledge industry and the low end of the service sector, it's a good bet that society is in one of the transition stages from the Industrial to the Information Age.

The chronically underemployed and unemployed who live in the "projects" have few skills that cannot be readily obtained for a lower wage offshore. The likelihood that these chronically unemployed can be retrained, in the event they were ever trained, for jobs in the knowledge industries is highly improbable. The service industries (burger flippers and retail clerks) tend to hire the young and attractive (post-pimples to 25).

The knowledge industries require at least a modicum of motivation among employees to raise their level of access to a higher level of abstraction. Someone who dropped out of school in grades nine or 10, because they were overwhelmed with those abstraction requirements in literature, science, and math, required by a latter-day Industrial Age high school, is unlikely to have experienced an abstraction epiphany since their grim high school days.

This phenomenon is not just North American. It pervades the whole Western world. Third World people, however, see the process in different terms. For them the view is opportunistic.

They see the jobs, for which they can underbid our marginals and under-classes, as a way station on the road to middle class for themselves or maybe just their children. The inhabitants of the Third World find these transitions quite hellish but at least their mobility is upward.

The Third World sees a lot of Hollywood-made movies. They see our middle-class life-styles as heaven on earth and are often willing to sell their children into all kinds of nasty slaveries to achieve that middle-class life.

The reality facing everyone is that the linear projections with which most of us are familiar, and by which we plan our lives, are becoming incrementally fallible and those grade nine and 10 drop-outs who lack the skills to easily manipulate linear projections will be totally lost in a world where access to a cyberspace outlook offers the only chance at mobility.

Most of the world is going to be busy just initializing the new era. Providing jobs for those who the era shift has dropped into marginality or the underclass will not be a priority for the next 50 years.

And that's why Seagram, Disney, and Time Warner are borrowing all those inflated dollars. The way they see it, it's like having the only stone quarry in town when some Roman emperor needed to build a new circus to cool out the restless plebs who might otherwise turn cranky.

BRAZILIFICATION AND OTHER HORRORS

While language shifts are certainly not trivial, they pale beside the effects of a different world-view of time coming down the pike.

Communal societies have a massively different view of time than do industrial people. We children of industrial societies acknowledge these differing temporal perceptions in many ways. We speak disparagingly of "Indian time" or about any group which does not treat time as a compulsive ordering agent.

How long will it be until "marginal" becomes a pejorative term? At the present time, the term still offers a range of connotations. It may used by those in this category to simply describe their vulnerabilities.

Douglas Coupland, author of the gentle and wry novel *Generation X*, has a term for this economic bimodalization of the global and social economy which seems to fit. Coupland's term is "Brazilification." It certainly looked like a snug fit of particular suitability for anyone who watched the U.N.'s Environmental Summit held in Rio de Janeiro, Brazil, in mid-1992.

The Brazilian government felt it should first resolve the problem of potential demonstrations by the city's urban slum dwellers. (Among connoisseurs of slums Rio, and Sao Paolo are neck and neck for the worst in the world, and this world has some really tacky places.) The authorities simply blocked off the slums from the rest of the city. In effect, they turned the slums into an urban concentration camp. This is a place where the "death squads," who are really off-duty cops in the pay of local business people, hunt down and kill abandoned children who have survived long enough to become street kids.

In Coupland's novel, he chronicles the lives of college educated, under-employed offspring of the middle class who have fallen off the mainstream somehow and have no expectations of recapturing the lifestyle their parents brought them up to. The author is too gentle to forthrightly ask whether his characters' children will be fodder for some North American urban death squads recruited from the police.

People who have unstable occupations, regardless of income level, are marginal. As we saw earlier, the phenomenon of just-in-time supplies for a production line is also applicable to personnel. Whether someone is a temporary secretary or a temporary middle manager, they are hired for a the term of a project and when the project is finished, their employment is over. The company supplies no safety net and neither has any obligations to the other. Some consultants are very well-paid but, as noted earlier, they don't get invited to the company Christmas party. In large organizations the trend is to build a core group of permanent employees at all levels while the rest are temporary and employed by "virtual companies."

Governments have understood this one for years. Contract employees are paid from slippage in a large budget. The funds never appear as a significant above-the-line budget item. And the employer avoids obligations for pensions, health insurance, holiday pay, dental plan, disability insurance, and perks. The contract employee can be discharged with a limited impact from wrongful dismissal charges.

The employer has another benefit. Without long-term obligations, trade secrets and other sensitive matters are restricted to permanent employees. The temporary employee is not expected to build a set of obligations which result in institutional loyalties. As more people become marginalized, the carrot of permanent, stable employment becomes a recruitment edge.

If you derive your identity from where you work and your security from "belonging" to a large organization, being marginal is a bad thing to be. If you doubt that large organizations are likely to be any more secure than you can be yourself, it's okay to be a successful, statistically marginal person.

Being statistically marginal is having a skill-set which gives you mobilities to move out of conventional job boxes when those job boxes are outpaced by technological or social change. When you lose your job and/or go down in income or social status and remain there, you are effectively marginalized. It is possible to keep your job and lose social status!

Lawyers are in a field which has historically been marginal. Lawyers are vulnerable to being personally responsible for client loss. In a firm with 300 lawyers you can stand out and be a full partner really quickly if you have a corporate client with big billings. If your biggest client is a company that is taken over in a merger you'll probably discover that the individual who was really your client was just a salaried employee. When the company gets bought, you were just a hired gun.

Think about the hero's comic-relief pal in a Western movie who the hero keeps around out of some sort of neurotic charity. The departed CEO has a great golden parachute but your partners will only have words for you. You're just a hired hand. There won't be a golden parachute for you. From a straight financial point of view, better you should have become a criminal lawyer with a good sense of how to get a positive high media profile. Crooks are very marginal people, but they like to associate with prominent people, even if they're just pleading guilty.

If you are a temporary secretary and your temp agency has lots of stable, steady customers, you're less vulnerable than the permanent secretary at the law firm described above. Your temp status makes you more marginal. At the law firm, a big client goes and five floors of offices gets downsized to three. A secretary of the partner who is "no longer with the organization" has longer tenure than you, so you get bumped.

I'M OK, YOU'RE MARGINAL

Architects are marginal.

Artists are marginal.

Actors are marginal.

Film directors are marginal.

Spies are marginal (agents of influence especially).

Being an ideological terrorist is marginal. Your paymasters might lose and have to turn you over. Just ask Carlos "The Jackal" Sanchez.

American and British defectors in Russia are marginal. Not only can't they go home, but the only other countries they can go to are worse than Russia. That is *very* marginal.

Anyone with AIDS is marginal.

Being a token anything is marginal. (The group you are a token of may cease being seen to be threatening.)

Being a street drug dealer is marginal.

Being a manufacturer, designer, or seller of T-shirts is marginal in a world of ozone depletion.

Being a construction labourer is marginal.

Being a long distance contract driver-owner of a tractor-trailer for a just-in-time supplier is marginal.

Being a serving-person in a bar where you have to wear a minimalist costume is marginal.

A journalist who writes a contemporary commentary column for a free entertainment directory/weekly newspaper is marginal.

Being a writer is marginal.

Being a fundamentalist pastor with a sexual control problem is marginal.

Social workers are marginal. (The group you are supposed to be helping might be seen as one that could be cut adrift, without loss to the wider society, during a budget downsizing.)

Being a product manager of a national brand is marginal. (The company may sell your brand to a competitor to get closer to our core business.)

Being an honourable politician of any stripe is marginal.

Being in the military is marginal.

Flipping burgers at McDonald's is marginal. (In his novel *Generation X*, Douglas Coupland's term for a marginal job is "McJob.")

On the other hand, being an international internal auditor for a transnational corporation is not marginal.

Being an external auditor for a revenue agency of any government is not marginal (even Chad).

Being in the R&D group of a transnational corporation's core business area is *not* marginal.

Being a Jolt Cola bottler in Silicon Valley is *not* marginal.

Being a cartographer is *not* marginal.

Being a good follower is *not* marginal.

Being a good salesperson is not marginal.

Being a good teacher outside the public education system is not marginal.

Being an HIV or other virus researcher is not marginal.

Being a salesperson for a cosmetic which is an effective UV-B blocking agent is not marginal.

There are, however, worse things than being marginal. You could end up being "underclass." Underclass makes "marginal" seem like fat city.

Being a bagperson is underclass.

Having government revenue agencies autoerase your name from the tax rolls as "unproductive to process" is underclass.

Being chronically schizophrenic, but not crazy enough for the state psychiatric hospital to let you in, is underclass.

Being in need of the services of a social rehabilitation agency after a spell in a government institution is underclass.

Requiring special facilities for work because of a physical or mental disability is underclass.

Being an informant for anti-terrorist squads is underclass.

Being turned down for a $5,000 insurance policy, as unlikely to be able to meet the premiums, is underclass.

Underclass is being permanently set into the far end of the back hump of that bimodal distribution of income. Moreover, the word underclass comes from the German Nazi period legal term *Untermenschen*. It applied to Jews, Gypsies, Slavs, homosexuals, those with congenital disabilities, the retarded, and the mentally ill.

CHAPTER SEVENTEEN
Women in Cyberspace

The women's movement has been highly successful in North America since its first steps in the 1960s. (In other parts of the world the gains have been more problematic.) Now its greatest weakness is the rush to institutionalize its values. The enormity of the era shift is so profound that to institutionalize anything as it now exists has the highest probability of failure.

Earlier we spoke of the difficulty of writing a national constitution at this stage in a new era. Every day we hear calls to write new laws to regulate and control phenomena and events as the new era settles in. Think about the demands for censorship of the Internet, surely the most obvious example. (Jordan, for instance, outlaws private ownership of modems, which should do some really bad things to Jordanians' chances of contributing to discussions of the era and its issues.)

The problem that the women's movement faces in attempting to institutionalize its gains is that anything that can be regulated in your favour can also be regulated against you, or worse, used to justify excluding you in changed conditions. Today, any smart government will be careful about what it bans or promotes. Sooner or later, after enough politicians and civil servants have been burned, we're going to see some very permissive governments. As that pendulum swings, we'll find that they are just as bad as the aggressively regulatory governments of the past.

In the 1960s, the parental generation lost much of its traditional authority. Recreational drug use, which was conceptually unavailable to the parental culture, became a metaphor for an explosive change rate. In the Western world, mood and perception-modifying drugs were available to most young people.

Those who initially experimented with drugs, such as marijuana, LSD, and the rest of the alphabet soup of psychedelia, tended to come from upper-middle-class and middle-class homes and had higher than average educational backgrounds. Recreational drug use became the icon of a massive rupture between generations.

The lack of social engineering around the introduction of another drug has profoundly altered the social realities of the industrialized West. This drug, of course, was the oral contraceptive, which confronted legal systems with having to totally reorganize the legal basis of marriage, support of children, property, and divorce.

As social pluralism increased, the pressures on legal systems to legitimize various pluralistic sectors rose in ways that were totally unanticipated. For example, a homosexual couple who have gone through a form of marriage wish to have the courts order one partner's employer's health plan insurer to allow spousal benefits to the other partner. "Not on your life," says the insurer. "Such unions are not factored into our actuarial risk analysis for this employer's group. Besides, the plaintiff's life-style places him at higher risk of sexually transmitted diseases (STDs) than the sample normative population. The cost of such additional coverage will raise the premiums to be paid by the employer."

The employer, who has dodged involvement in this litigation up to this point, echoes: "Not on your life. We negotiated this health plan with our employees' certified bargaining agent in good faith. This benefits package represents a significant portion of our overall compensation package." The union says, "The contract was democratically approved by a majority of the members of the bargaining unit." The trial judge mutters to himself, "No matter what I do here, we're talking appeals for the next ten years" and ruminates about early retirement.

No parent in the 1960s had ever lived in or been socialized to a world in which control of conception was possible. We need only consider the weight of the social and sexual taboos that humans lived under and how sexual mores evolved. The evidence that conventional historical authority had broken down was clear by the early 1980s with public campaigns designed to slow the spread of AIDS. Explicit television spots and other commercial marketing techniques were brought to bear on the social acceptability of condoms, and most parents stood passively by while public school boards debated placing condom dispensers in schools. Public health agencies began to exchange clean needles for dirty ones with street junkies, who are vulnerable to the spread of AIDS through shared needles.

At the same time, the technologies of the new era started to come online. Members of the parental culture, who had spent innumerable Saturday afternoons watching space serials that featured the fictional characters of Buck Rogers and Flash Gordon, suddenly discovered that space exploration had become real. Astronauts and cosmonauts, who were people just like us, were out there on yet another new frontier, inexorably opening its doors.

The computer lost its superficial mystique as millions gained access to PCs and mainframes via networks. Certainly, most computer use was pedestrian and limited to unsophisticated databases, word-processors and spreadsheets, but the world began to abandon its consignment of computers to some fuzzy future. Stephen Jobs, Jack Tramiel, Steve Wozniak and Bill Gates were likened to Henry Ford, and achieved folk hero status. The adoption of computers was occurring at about 10 times the pace that our grandparents had been socialized to the automobile. From watches at 10 percent of the price of less accurate timepieces to computer-managed elevators and microwave ovens in our homes, the computer on a chip began to order our lives.

The American civil rights movement was another hallmark of the 1960s. Racism was seen as evil and ugly, especially once the increasing social pluralism allowed more people to minimally experience the brutality that was the lot of minorities. Children of the middle class found themselves marginalized for guessing wrong about the directionality of the changes. Television news coverage of the civil rights marches put into question the parental culture's acceptance of institutionalized racism.

The effects of the bombing of Hiroshima and Nagasaki had made everyone aware that another war would be a disaster which all of humanity might not survive, producing an anti-war movement that was truly global in character. In England the Aldermason marches led by philosopher Bertrand Russell developed a counter-institutional character.

Youth movements reflected a generation that had not experienced World War II. The participants were the children of the middle class. Their parents began to feel that their lives, spent surviving the Great Depression and the war, were being seen by their children as valueless. The parents had never experienced a time when there was the assumption of general economic growth, nor had they experienced youth when control of conception was readily available and the raging hormones of adolescence and early adulthood could be satiated without fear of pregnancy. Parents lost their authority.

The 1960s did not address the issue that women were largely excluded from roles which would allow them to participate in a society in ways which would give them some say about matters that affected them. The 1960s did however, provide women with a right to participate in "movement" causes and, from these roots, the women's movement rose to become one of the most significant events of the 1970s and on to the present.

UP FROM CHATTEL

In post-Battle of Waterloo, England, in the early 19th century, a series of legislative maneuvers known as the Reform Acts included among their provisions regulations for hours and conditions of work. These laws also excluded women and children from onerous and dangerous workplaces. The Reform Acts established a new idea, that the state had a right to intervene in employment issues around health and safety. Further, the state should protect women and children who were employed in mines, where both were used to draw ore through spaces too small for a man to pass.

The early years of the Industrial Age were not a happy time for anyone. The social dislocation coupled with new machinery made working-class people particularly vulnerable to dangerous working conditions.

In the mid-19th century, the Utilitarianism of Jeremy Bentham was providing the intellectual underpinnings for Western liberal thought as the Whigs evolved to become the British Liberal Party. Bentham's theories were expounded on by John Stuart Mill, who wrote his essay "On Liberty" in 1859. In 1869 Mill published his essay "On the Subjection Of Women." It was written as a Utilitarian attack on the contract of marriage as it was known in the early- to mid-19th century. Mill wrote that marriage, as it was legally implemented in Europe and North America, was a means by which society oppressed women unjustly. Mill was outraged at a society in which a woman who married gave up all rights, economic, social, and personal, to her husband. Her husband was also given all of her property or other assets.

The use of the word "Subjection" in Mill's title is no fluke. The American Civil War had ended only four years earlier. The British Anti-Slavery Society was exposing the African, European-colonial and Arab nations for their maintenance of slavery and Mill, good Benthamite that he was, pointed out that women were held in a legal servitude right there in England. His readers were told that the legal subjugation of women was one of the conditions for a woman to become married. In other words, to be married, a woman must agree to voluntarily enter a state of servitude.

Throughout the decade from 1859 to 1869, we find Mill supporting the institutional suffragette cause but, more importantly, he found it intolerable that women's minds were being wasted because of the social inhibitions and restrictions on intellectual mobility solely by reason of their gender. It would become clear that Mill and the rest of the British liberal establishment, not merely the "radicals," should support, in a heartfelt way, feminist principles.

"A woman is not a person in matters of rights and privileges, but she is a person in matters of pains and penalties." — The common law of England.

"No woman, idiot or criminal shall vote." — The Election Act of The Dominion of Canada (copied from the British legislation in 1867).

To read Mill's work over the decade separating the two essays is to recognize that he was familiar with the persons and work of women who were not only breaking down gender barriers, but being exceptions to these exclusionary fences. It was not just the suffragettes on whose behalf Mill spoke out. He wrote on behalf of a wide range of women scientists, scholars, and institutional innovators, like Florence Nightingale.

Mill argued from a purely Utilitarian (greatest good for the greatest number) position that women's capabilities were being wasted by the intellectual and occupational restrictions placed upon them. He also argued that society was being unjustly deprived of the fruits of their labour.

Many of the original publications of Mill's essays were in a liberal, general circulation magazine called *Fraser's Magazine*. *Fraser's* encouraged a spirited Letters to the Editor section, and if we check the issues following Mill's publication of "On the Subjection of Women," we do not find any great outpouring of criticism of Mill's views on the desirability of removing the inhibitions on women economically, socially, biologically, or in terms of intellectual or work-related activity. Criticisms of Mill by *Fraser's* readers are limited to attacks on his political applications of Bentham's Utility.

Mill's arguments for extending the voting franchise, expanding associational freedoms and institutionalizing support for science were apparently a more useful target in the eyes of Mill's fellow Utilitarians than his support for expanding the role of women. (Mill had been arrested as a young man for distributing pamphlets on contraception. The charges would have been related to the obscenity laws.)

In other words, feminism has been an accepted part of the mainstream of Western intellectual thought for the past 15 decades! And yet the lame rhetoric of opposition continues.

Supporters of this gender disenfranchisement went back to classical Rome and Pauline Christianity for their authority. Regrettably, they did not go back to the Christianity of Byzantium where, even more classically, they would have discovered women were fully economically and socially emancipated and that, while the clergy were all male, the church of Constantine allowed its priests to marry (as it does today).

Mid-19th century Britain was a place where the idea that women should be treated with respect and encouraged to be part of mainstream scientific, cultural, and intellectual activity was commonly held, particularly in more liberal circles. It was a time when "enlightened" men would admit that women were intelligent, but would argue that their sensitive feminine natures would be irreparably damaged by being exposed to places of work. Academia was struggling to expand its freedom of inquiry but barred women from medical schools because of the coarse language "they might overhear" and the disgusting sights they would be forced to witness. It was a society where community social services were largely limited to those provided by the churches.

This was a time when admitting a woman to a hospital for delivery of a baby was tantamount to a death sentence for the mother, due to the lack of sterile procedures in filthy hospitals. In Vienna in the 1840s, the work of Ignaz Semmelweis proved that the probability of death from post-partum infection increased massively when you placed the woman in a hospital and had the delivery done by male physicians, who did not wash their hands before touching patients, rather than a midwife.

Throughout the 19th and 20th centuries, women's rights to employment, property ownership, and participation in public affairs expanded continuously. In the 1960s, a new trend became apparent: middle-class young women began to spurn traditional female employment ghettos.

The idea behind the female employment ghettos was that most women would be in the work force for only a short time. It was assumed they would, after a brief period of employment, get married, have children, become homemakers, and be lost to the labour force. Social policy of the time held that women should be protected from physically strenuous work and the crudities of many workplaces. This was a very middle-class viewpoint and was shared by both the artisan and white-collar communities.

In the conventional wisdom of the middle classes and the skilled-labour classes, it was assumed that families would be supported by a single income. If a wife worked, particularly after the birth of the first child, her husband was deemed to be a failure in handling his responsibilities.

There were jobs a respectable woman could take that were structured to support her right not to be exposed to "unladylike" conditions, and which made allowances for what was seen to be her "physical and emotional limitations as a female." These occupations were expected to allow her to be feminine and nurturing, in keeping with what were seen as "natural female characteristics." For the middle-class woman, secretarial jobs; school teaching (primary grades were generally reserved for women teachers since the nurturing function was seen as solely owned by females and pedophiles, and the latter were generally believed to be exclusively men); switchboard operation (because women have superior motor skills — it's similar to darning socks and knitting — and besides it's tedious work and women will be happy not having to think); and nursing. Whoever assumed that nursing would protect women from the crudities of life had little experience with the way people behave in real pain, or how the human body functions when organ systems collapse or are traumatized by external forces. The few males who entered such "pink collar ghettos" did so at the risk that they would experience whispering campaigns that placed their masculinity in doubt.

In contemporary North America double-income families are now the norm. Less than 5 percent of urban married adults are from single-income households. The growth of the double-income family had repercussions far beyond anything anyone really anticipated. As the economy expanded in the post-war period, inexpensive automation replaced the mechanization that marked the Industrial Age. As more employment opportunities became available, women started to achieve unprecedented fiscal independence. They actually had their own money. (Blue collar families had always assumed that the wife would work unless encumbered by infant children, but if the husband achieved artisan status, the wife would remain at home as a matter of propriety.)

Most jurisdictions established spousal-type protections for both parties after a period (usually two years) of cohabitation. Courts also acted to provide precedents for the protection of each party in common law marriages and "palimony" equity became widespread.

Some jurisdictions had repressive laws on the books. In Arizona, even into the 1960s, the law stated that a woman's husband could come to her workplace on payday and claim her pay as his property. Her employer was legally required to turn it over to the husband on demand.

More recently, lenders such as banks, savings and loan institutions, trust companies, and finance companies refused loans to a woman unless her husband or some male relative co-signed for it. But as the credit card became common, banks discovered they were losing money by not applying the same lending standards to women as they did to men. The financial services industry began to lobby governments to change laws that required them to loan to women only when a responsible male was present in the transaction.

By and large, the differential pay scales for equal or similar work began to be seen as irrational and unfair. Large organizations that were noted for the efficiency with which they managed work forces — such as IBM — had long held that equitable employment standards were the rule. Underneath this was the view of top management that "special treatment" was an administrative impossibility — and expensive. The first all-male bastions to fall were in marketing. It was impossible to have pay differentials for men and women when all pay was based on productivity, as in the case of sales managers.

The most significant gains of the women's movement for the 20 years following 1970 were in the realm of equal employment opportunity and movement into the high status professions: medicine, law, accounting, and other employment sectors requiring post-secondary and post-graduate education. Some simple data about women in the law in California will put these professional groups in perspective, since they can be generalized to other graduate degree-requiring jobs.

Other data report that women lawyers are almost twice as likely as men to be unmarried. This can probably be accounted for in four ways. First, the tradition of men in North America is to marry women less educated and less socially mobile than themselves. We must also factor in the non-traditional marriage option of a "relationship" without legal bindings or obligations. A third factor might be that a number of middle-class women began to delay marriage as an expression of fiscal independence. Finally, there is evidence that women in law tend to be more conventional and would be expected to be more traditional.

Data on earnings are also instructive. Among white male lawyers in practice for 10-19 years who worked at least 35 or more hours per week, only 8 percent earned less than $50,000, and 20 percent earned over $200,000. Among comparable women, 14 percent were reported earning less than $50,000, with 9 percent earning more than $200,000. One of the reasons for these disparities is probably that women tend to be under-represented in the best-paying specialties in law, such as corporate, intellectual property, and investment law, and legislative and bureaucratic lobbying. Women are over-represented in the less remunerative fields like family law, community affairs, juvenile, constitutional "rights" areas, divorce, and as individual practitioners. The areas of property rights law and employment and pay equity law are also disproportionately female.

Each economic sector had its own barriers to participation by women. And while some of the barriers are still in place, the roadblocks that remain are largely informal and related to specific working groups. Most administrators, those with their wits intact, understand that discrimination on the grounds of gender is illegal and an expensive luxury no self-respecting nickel-cruncher would tolerate.

The cutting edge for women remains economic. Superficially, men will tell you that the cutting edge is sexual harassment. Sexual harassment is simply gender discrimination on another level. Sexual exploitation and various forms of extortion are increasingly seen by men as placing the entire

Gender and ethnicity of California lawyers (percentages)
Years In Practice

	Less than 5	5 -9	10-19	20 or more
White male	49	56	71	93
White female	39	34	22	4
Asian	4	4	2	1
Black	3	2	2	1
Hispanic	5	4	3	1

business at risk. Every community has had a few high-profile cases and, when it happens today, the administrative executive is perceived as having allowed the entire business to be put at risk and is thus de facto incompetent.

When a woman has to resort to a formal human rights complaint or file a criminal complaint, morale in the entire workplace disintegrates. The common law system is ill-suited to such matters. When a case of sexual harassment occurs, other women working in the same place are put under pressure to quit by their fathers, husbands, and boyfriends, which tends to support the action of the complainant. Senior management sees line managers as unable to manage, and the male accused is seen as placing the other males at risk. The other males, in turn, get pressure from their wives and girlfriends. Investors write blunt letters to senior management and to their brokers. Customers stop calling. Everyone in the workplace experiences becoming, to one degree or another, a pariah. Under these conditions, few women will press such complaints lightly, and administrators take their responsibilities seriously. It has, in a relatively short time, become bad business to allow gender discrimination.

The other goals of the women's movement are about to change, along with all of us, as issues of the era transition become more intense. The feminist movement in North America has largely been directed by and for middle-class, well-educated women who live in the wealthiest society ever known. Now, the other shoe is about to drop.

The men in their lives have become irresponsible. As the independence of women has been impressed on them, men have come to see no benefits in any of the various permutations of historic responsibilities between men and women. Women are increasingly seen as competitors, but lacking the socialization that allows men to treat work as a game. Women have become prominent in the media and in jobs requiring strong interpersonal skills. As the "relationship without marriage" is accepted in the wider society, men appear to be less prepared to accept obligations that inhibit their socially-approved (by other men) irresponsibilities.

As the era transition becomes more pronounced, women will, if they wish to maintain separate gender roles, have to stake out "territories" within which their contribution is seen as valid.

In the 14th century, Saint Benedict said in his rules for the orderly function of Benedictine order houses, "After the last prayers of the day a monk may read as long as he does not disturb the other monks." The reason for this rule was that in the Medieval world when someone read, they did so aloud. The commonly accepted level of abstraction did not permit silent reading, and the reader was anxious to concretize the transfer of information from page to brain. This rule was, over time, adopted by most other monastic orders. The rule is seldom found in Medieval orders of nuns.

This monastic support for reading resulted in scholarship becoming gender-biased for men.

Early in the Renaissance, there was little in the way of generalized social pressure to provide women with education. While few women were educated in the sense of being learned or practicing the arts, neither was it rare or exotic for women of the nobility or from successful merchants' families to receive a well-rounded education.

Upper-class Renaissance women had little in the way of illusions as to their real worth. Marriage arrived early; many girls were married as young as 12, although 13 to 14 was more usual. When the girl reached 15, her parents were starting to become anxious, and if she remained unmarried when she was 16 or (gulp) 17, it was a full-scale disaster, and the family would be opening negotiations with a nunnery.

But the sex-bias of education changed. Girls from noble or merchant families were educated by tutors. The 15th century Renaissance man Cardinal Bembo once wrote: "A little girl ought to learn Latin. It puts a finishing touch on her charms." We have many examples of 10-year-old girls writing Latin letters and memorizing pages of poetry written in Latin. Girls were tutored in most of the same subjects that boys studied — obvious exceptions were that boys received long training and acculturation in the martial arts and girls were taught embroidery and dance. As well, 10- or 11-year-old girls started to learn the rudiments of supervising servants, although most of their domestic management training was deferred until after marriage, when their mothers would have dispatched a couple of servants along with the newlyweds.

In the Northern Renaissance, the daughter of a merchant was expected to assist in her husband's business and take his place, supervising the clerks and apprentices, when the husband was away. Earlier we noted the evolution of the salon, which was "business entertaining" without the tax break.

Marriage was seen by upper-level families as an extension of court political life or mercantile venturing. The alliances of the court's political intrigues and the alliances to trade, or fight in some foreign land, were cemented by arranged marriages. Paternal authority was supreme in the Renaissance household. As grim as it sounds to us, that life was marvellous compared to that of the lower classes.

When a woman of the commercial class was married, she would have an extensive wardrobe. Household management was not a big problem since servants and slaves were readily available. The wife would have time to develop a salon and be expected to entertain. If her husband was usually indifferent to her life, he was probably a generation older than she. He was also engaged in different day-to-day activities. Women tended to die from the effects of frequent child-bearing. Their husbands were killed by wars, shipwrecks, and injuries resulting from disputes and brawls. Both men and women were often victims of plagues and common illnesses we now treat preventively with sanitation management.

By the early 16th century, a new woman had emerged among the middle class who was literate and socially apt. This new woman was placed on a pedestal. She was romantically idealized by poets and painters and her youthful education became more trivialized, as did she. (Botticelli was all about trivializing women through romanticism and placing them on pedestals — a really uncomfortable place to be, especially if you're not allowed to move.)

CAN WOMEN HAVE A SAY?

Today women face an era transition from a different position in society than that of their Renaissance ancestors.

We will see productivity as the *openly agreed upon measure* of employment and power. Addressing historical injustices will become recognized as an unproductive exercise, while those who persist in practicing it will lose out in the market place.

What will happen is that the economic world will shortly be divided into two camps: explorers and stay-at-homes, risk-takers and risk-aversive consolidators. Both will be legitimate. There will be those who have moved into a relativistic world-view. Within that world-view, there is great risk and, if you're successful, great rewards. (We're talking about the kind of rewards that set up your family for generations, even if your progeny generate normal statistical ratios of fools, criminals or other ne'er-do-wells.)

The other camp — the majority — will opt for conventional stabilities and a general circle-the-wagons attitude.

Unless women are seen in leadership roles, able as individuals to move mountains, then in 75 years or so, women will be right back to having junior manager jobs, at best. It will be a guy's club again.

When men go to work for one of those on-the-edge leaders, they know what they're in for in mythic terms. They have been gravitating toward the computer industry for the past 20 years. The space program is another spot for them. Genetic engineering is another. In other words, the high-tech industries that are the exploration bases of this era are being occupied by men.

The women's movement is about to be tested in an era transition. In a lot of ways this is unfair, but fair/unfair doesn't mean anything. No one has any "rights" in the way an era transition works. Women may try to go for establishing their own ground and style rules. If they do that — and win — then its women's rules for the next era. Era transitions are truly non-sexist. The only thing that matters is how the whole society comes out.

We should return to the greater simplicity of the Renaissance. Imagine how different our world would have been, just in terms of the social and political legitimation of women, had there been a Lady Francine Drake who trashed the Spanish Armada and explored some very wealth-producing countries. Or a Countess Lorraine Sforza who set European banking on a road to control the economy of the world. Or a Mistress Alberta Dürer, whose art brought perspective to Germany; a Mistress Ida Newton, whose renown was such that she was the only logical candidate to head the Royal Society; a Mother Superior Lucinda Pacioli, who supplied the mathematics used to explore a new planar dimension; or even a brilliant poetess Beatrice Portinari, who pined for a wastrel youth, Dante Alighieri, who was probably unworthy of her, and whom she only saw once in her life, from a distance. If it were she who had left us such extraordinary poetry that it is still read today, and if she were the author of the poetic allegorical journey to hell and then to heaven, would we still have had male writers in the majority since the 15th century? What was the chance that a Wilma Shakespeare would have been a writer of plays in 17th century England? Would young Mistress Shakespeare have even managed to get out of Stratford-On-Avon?

But that was not the Renaissance, at least not on this time-track. On this time-track, Venice had the most and the busiest hookers, (sorry, courtesans) in Europe, in spite of professional hazards that included flogging for trafficking with Jews or Turks and the high risk of getting the terrible "French disease" (syphilis), which hazarded their careers as well as their lives. Venice was home to 12,000 harlots, who were required to celebrate religious holidays even though the republic lost tax revenues when the city's cut of their take dropped because of the enforced holiday. At the time when there were 12,000 prostitutes, the city had a total population of 300,000. That ratio gives us a clearer picture of the benefits of marriage to an artisan.

To someone who says it's not fair, that women have not had time to develop the population base of participants in the power structure from which leadership emerges, the reply must be that it doesn't matter. Era transitions have always been a period when new leadership replaces the faltering old era's leaders. Era transitions have always thrown up new classes, and there are women who deserve to be at the forefront of this era transition. One such is Fiorella Terenzi.

Dr. Terenzi has a doctorate in mathematics, while her area of specialty is astrophysics and astronomy. She also studies music composition and performance. Her first album, *Music from the Galaxies*, was created by taking input from a radio telescope, digitizing the waveform and turning it into music. If you want to talk about unfairness, here is a final bit of information: Terenzi has that kind of beauty which Botticelli taught us is timeless. She will be beautiful when she's 90. The Lombards strike again!

Mainstream media seems intimidated by women like Terenzi. "She's too unfocussed," says one editor whose magazine shovels out pop iconry. "If she wasn't so damn multi-talented. No one can identify with her. She's too beautiful and brainy, so the feminists can't stand her. An interview with her leaves you with quotes about her ideas, and those ideas threaten everyone with the way she applies science to art and art to science. Scientists see her as being trivial, and artists attack her for actually understanding the technology and science which is the medium for her art."

In the spring of 1995, *Time* put out a special issue on cyberspace. The issue included an outrageous full-page picture of Jaron Lanier, the guy who laid down the basic laws of virtual reality, juxtaposed with a two-inch photo of a youthful Bob Dylan and a CD-ROM interactive version of his 1960s album *Highway 61 Revisited*. Flip the page and there Terenzi is, still only 30, and now bearing the imprimatur of *Time*. But *Time* still managed to trivialize her by quoting a description of her as "a cross between Madonna and Carl Sagan." This is the kind of really bad journalism that shows the mainstream media is not the place to look for information.

Another extraordinary woman is Melissa Franklin, a tenured professor of physics at Harvard, co-discoverer of the top quark, and an outstanding jazz saxophonist. When Franklin earned full professorship at Harvard, only 10 percent of physics graduate students were female; within a few years they made up 30 percent.

In an environment as overloaded as our information systems are, it will take more Terenzis and Franklins to provide women with the role models necessary to effect leadership in this era shift.

There is another factor, to which our historical model is sensitive. We are going to need military captains again, at least for this cycle. (Look at all of those places where minorities aspire to "national independence" — Serbia, Croatia, Bosnia, and Cyprus) and the places where there are old enmities to be broken open again. There is little in the mythologies of the women's movement to inspire the formation of great captains.

This is not necessarily a fatal flaw. Military leadership is likely to be peripheral to the main event as we play out this era transition. But unless women begin to become leaders in the applications of the source of the new level of abstraction, one might suspect the applications will continue to express a new dominant male culture.

CHAPTER EIGHTEEN

This is the Information Age? Loaded canons and crossed wires

Entering this new era we find ourselves in its first 'age.' We call it the Information Age. History will probably call it something else. Most of our descendants will think of us, when they are forced to at school, as pretty underwhelming and primitive. We think of ourselves as rather overwhelmed by the job of reordering the basic survival information we inherited from a latter-day Industrial Age.

All humans enter the world with the same basic strengths and weaknesses. Our gestation period is governed by the size of our brain cavities — if our birth occurred at a more mature stage, our heads would be too large for the trip down the birth canal. From the moment of birth, we can suck and we can make a fist (which enables us to grasp our mothers more easily while they deal with predators). These are the sole intellectual accomplishments with which we enter life.

Because of our early birth, we are born with fewer abilities than other placental mammals. We are born highly vulnerable to the environment. Somebody has to take care of us for longer than any other creature.

Unlike other placental mammals, and most other living things that get most of their information downloads via DNA, much of our survival information is transmitted to us by our parents and the community, using reason and instruction as the principal vehicles. This non-innate learning strategy stipulates that learning to reason is the most valuable resource we acquire. It is the root of all of those other uniquely human abilities that apparently don't download very well to other placental mammals with longer gestation cycles.

We acquire reason and initial use of abstraction from parents and the community. The other intellectual activity is learning the language; at the end of the initial language-exploration cycle we begin to use these original verbal skills to discover and explore the abstract world.

At around four to five years old, a child's brain begins firing the neurons that allows it to start exploring the abstractions behind its concrete world. Metaphors and similes are linguistic tools that extend abstract concepts beyond the simpler, more limited, concrete verbalizations the child started with. Wise parents will not rush a child into this period. The opportunity for exposing household embarrassments is high until the kid learns a little discretion.

From five until 14, we learn the survival skills that enable us to pull through the traps set for the young by the world and its predators. With a lot of stops, starts, and way stations, children slowly begin to act as responsible citizens. That is, we hope they will begin enhancing the values and shared benefits of the wider community.

The mean age for a child to be judged fit for adulthood (fit to become a parent) has been, until very recently, about 14. We also start on the road to skepticism around then, since we are encouraged to test information by seeing if it will stand up to the consensual validation of our inputs from peers and family.

AUTHORITY BREAKDOWN

The time from birth to four or five years old is spent getting two basic learning skills to the point that they begin to work as if they were products of our autonomic nervous systems. One is exploring the environment under the supervision of parents, grandparents, siblings, and assorted "babysitters."

Watch these exploration tutors to see which behaviours they reinforce — what the child gets smiled at and cuddled for — and which they do not. (Frowns are interpreted early, and are very similar worldwide.) It is only when the environment is fragile or predatory that these first lessons become specialized. While we are checking out the environment, we begin to get a look at the way the adults make a living and frequently play at "working" with other children or alone. If we live in a matrilineal society, among the Trobriand Islanders for instance, and if we happen to be male, our mother's brother will begin to take us fishing with him when we are about three. If we are very good, and manage keep from getting under foot, he will let us help him unroll and roll his fishing net. Later we will take the fish from the net, and still later we will learn to throw the net and catch fish like every other adult Trobriand male.

But what happens when the historical authorities bequeathed to us by our parents, the community, and even the environment lose their power to guide? What do we do when we, ourselves, are without the skills of parenting for a heightened level of abstraction? Our parents couldn't teach *us* to parent in this kind of enhanced speculative environment.

So we fall back on basic reason. Over the years we have learned that there are other sources of information. We've also learned that you must treat that kind of unauthenticated information with more skepticism than your grandparents did when the traditional historical authorities were relatively intact.

As for living in an era transition, you know that this has happened before, because you have been given access to history, and in the case of the Renaissance, the documentation is pretty good. It appears that a new era only emerges under extreme pressure, when the previous world-view has collapsed completely. Then there is a quantum jump in the level of abstraction, which provides a way out of the prior era's inability to cope with the information generated by enhanced understanding of the laws governing the universe. When you try to make sense out of the bewilderments of our time, you know that the events of the mid-15th century were qualitatively as difficult as the problems you face.

One thing critics and editors of historical novels watch closely is the author's accuracy. Film critics are less inclined to demand accountability of films, except for documentaries.

In the *QUATTROCENTO*, they lacked a Renaissance to look back on. What documentation they had exceeds our spectacle movies for crappiness, and few of us take Hollywood spectacles seriously. Imagine if all the information we had about the Renaissance was a Hollywood mega-movie, set in Florence but actually shot in Spain because Madrid was "close enough" to what Florence looked like — and who could tell the difference, anyway?— and the scriptwriter was more concerned with strengthening the dramatic elements of the story than the facts.

Editors for science fiction publishers are really cautious about a writer's scientific fidelity. In that editing trade, you make one obscure boo-boo and the collection of Nobel laureates' autographs accompanying vituperative mail grows exponentially. (One such editor has over 50 "autographs" that he shows, in painstaking detail, to any new author with a propensity for sloppy research.)

"Popular" science writers such as James Gleick, the biographer of Richard Feynman and ideas such as chaos theory, have established a standard to make the discoveries and critical thought of our times accessible without being simplistic or patronizing. Another example is Richard Dawkins, who has explained the current classical Darwinian view of evolution in his *River out of Eden*, which is one of Basic Books' The Science Masters series.

Like most pioneers, the residents of the Renaissance were so preoccupied with surviving that they were less than concerned with future generations. They had little time to consider how to best exploit their situation. Windows close really quickly when your important information comes by sailing ship.

We have analytic tools; theirs were censored by church and state. We have tools of reason that they honed for us. We do not have their superstitions, which made them believe that the plagues were the result of God's judgment on sinful mankind. Then again, many of our contemporaries get their news of the era from tabloids sold at supermarket check-outs.

We know how a pretty effective health system works. The directionality of our shift appears to be providing some benign health spin-offs. In fact, we may be faced with the largest life-span expansion ever to hit any species. But would you rather have to face a plague with only soiled alchemists to turn to, or face up to the fact that there is no country in the world with an actuarially solvent old age pension plan?

This chapter is about managing the information resources available to you. It offers some suggestions on how to use them and how to rate them. It is also the most tangential in structure.

INFORMATION INFLATION

One of the survival strategies everyone should adopt is to develop a strong sense of caution about the information services one subscribes to. None of us can be too careful about who we allow to sell, trade, or give us information.

Before we get into talking about sources of information, it might be a good idea to understand why the first stage of this new era is being called the Information Age and why our information gathering strategies should be so different from what was deemed adequate by the schools we went to.

In the past few years, every minor-league cow college professor it was our misfortune to run into seemed to be whining about "information overload." The truth is that there is no information overload. What we have is an overload of trivial drivel masquerading as information and a lot of twits treating this drivel as though it were significant. We have *information inflation* because we don't know how to access a lot of the information we actually need.

In a new era, a lot of the old rules are changed. The new era requires a greatly heightened level of abstraction to understand the events triggering it. A specialized Information Age in which we can refine the transfer of knowledge makes a lot of sense when the era is addressing such a jump in abstraction.

We find that media requiring a lot of concreteness are less useful to articulating the variegated emerging parts of the new era than those more adapted to abstraction. The era's grammar rule seems to be: the more concrete the message, the less accurate the content will be.

Before we start looking at information resources, we should examine what it is that we expect from the information reservoir we have inherited and are creating.

To appreciate the impact of the printing press on the collective psyche of 16th-century Europe, consider the case of one London bookseller, Andrew Maunsell. Remember, this is just one guy with a store, trying to make a living less than 100 years after the Renaissance got started. His catalogue listed over 6,000 volumes, divided into three sections. First came "Divinitie," next was "Science," followed by "Humanities." The latter consisted of Gramer, Rethoricke, Lawe, Historie, Policie, et cetera, "which," this worthy book merchant reported, "contain matters of delight and pleasure."

Maunsell's Science catalogue lists works "mathematicall as Arithetick, Geometrie, Asronomy, Astrologie, Musick, the Arte of Warre and Navigation and also... Physick and Surgerie" (sic). There is a further note that Maunsell also carried a wide range of books on architecture and cooking.

As John Hale tells us in *The Civilization of Europe in the Renaissance*, what all of this pot pourri had to do with each other was that the topics represent applications of knowledge useful to *every* reader in leading his daily life in those years. A Renaissance person had many widely ranging interests because new ideas were cropping up in every direction. He needed to understand the context of these breaks with the past's conventional assumptions, or else develop ways to obliterate learning curves. He had to

---

Graffiti may be the last bastion of free speech. The dissident wall posters in Tiananmen Square were a precursor of the Democracy Movement sit-in. One of the reasons for the student sit-in was to protect the wall posters, and other graffiti, from destruction by the army or the secret police.

Graffiti has seldom been a respecter of property and is usually pretty rude. Some students of contemporary media have speculated that one use of a computer virus could be as an electronic graffito. It's an interesting experience to see the effect on an audience of computer industry executives and academic computer scientists when someone proposes the idea that a virus could be used as an electronic graffito. They go absolutely, totally ballistic. Yet it's being done regularly. One of the effects of Java, the Internet-specific language, is to make it really easy to write viruses, even inadvertently.

When Arab programmers wrote a virus that was triggered on the anniversary of the Intifadah (Arabic for the "uprising," specifically of Palestinian teenagers who threw stones at the Israeli army), the message that appeared on computer screens said: "Your computer has been stoned," followed by a reminder of the anniversary. The virus was quickly dubbed the "stoned virus" and after a short time, the news media began to tell us that "stoned" referred to drug use. A number of computer industry stalwarts and publishers were outraged and appalled that political activists could use viruses as a sort of infoterrorism.

understand, quickly, the manner in which the breaks arose, and how he might profitably exploit them.

Earlier in this book we had some suggestions for a civil servant who learns that he or she will be the senior official in the department whom the intelligence services brief, and included some strategies for evaluating their offerings. With some minor editing, the same guidelines will help you evaluate your everyday information services.

Keep track of specific news items your information services have provided. Once you have about three months' worth of data on hand, you can start to codify the data. First note the source and the date. (It isn't Apples and PCs. It's information and information.)

The source said X event had happened. Did it really happen?

The sources said X would happen in such and such a time frame. Did it?

The source predicted that if X happened, Y would be the consequence. Was it?

The source said because X event had happened, Y and Z would follow as secondary consequences. Did these secondary predictions turn out to be right?

The number of such items you want to track depends on your information needs and on how many separate items and subsidiary consequences you can manage without becoming confused. Here are some more questions:

How often did your source provide you with information that was 'spun' in a way that enhanced another agenda of the source's?

Does your source help you find other sources that expand on the information it provides?

Does the source give you a new point of view for an ongoing problem? In other words, does the source enhance your understanding of the problem?

Do its editors have a grasp on how to tangentially relate items to each other?

Is it independent from advertiser pressure, social pressures, secret police pressure, terrorist pressures, the publisher's personal political agenda — or is the independence openly qualified?

Can you trust it to keep you informed on topics that affect your welfare?

Will the source follow up on its own early analysis?

Does the source give you consistently useful information? (No matter how unhappy you are with the way your daily TV news fails to cover your special interests. You have to remember that all information is connected. That is, it's all tangential.)

Does the source address complexity well? (It is important to find sources that address complex problems in a way you can understand, and deliver the information in a usable format.)

For the Humanist Renaissance man, the classical scholastic education that had been the core of schooling in his father's time was insufficiently broad to include the ideas that were becoming commonplace. His tangentially based education, incorporating perspective, would have been structurally too abstract for his grandfather to understand.

Tangential thought processes are employed today as a means to express complexities that have not found a vernacular expression, as our new era frequently lacks the vocabulary to specify events that have become commonplace. These events can only be properly defined by the use of technological or specialized jargon terms. Such rapid transitions from the language of the specialist to the vernacular occur because of an expanded world-view.

We see similarly rapid adaptations in pronunciation. For example, Halley's Comet is pronounced "Hawley" by astronomers, who learn the pronunciation in a lecture hall. Similarly, psychologists first learn of the "Hawthorne Effect" in the classroom, where the professor pronounces it "Haythorne." The general public first ran across "Hawley's" Comet in the press when the comet was leaving its every-75-years tail in our sky. The mispronunciation became accepted as the norm when the broadcast journalists got it wrong. Business students learned about Hawthorne's industrial psychology experiments in environmental manipulation at Westinghouse from instructors who also learned of Hawthorne in print — as a result, Hawthorne heard the common pronunciation of his name changed in his own lifetime.

Psychologists have found tangential thought to be highly correlated with creative thinking. Anyone uncomfortable with that can take solace in the fact that a number of psychiatric texts of 20 years ago argued that tangential thought or speech was indicative of a serious disorder. It isn't surprising that in an era transition we find an increment in tangentially ordered ideas, both in the written and spoken word. The conventional world appears chaotic, and conventional associations no longer fit or indicate the associations they once did. At the same time people are searching to relate new concepts to familiar ones for which the language may simply lack synonymous terms.

It is easier to talk about "virtual reality" in "cyberspace" than it is to assure yourself that the person you are speaking with understands Planck and Einstein. This is useful, especially when all you want to talk about is how the time element of the time-space continuum was bent to produce the graphics of your favourite video game.

Our society and parents were ill-prepared to transmit relevant information about functioning in the Information Age. They were even less prepared for the explosion of dimensions we call cyberspace, which is inaccessible to our conventional senses.

Most successful industrial states think that a good time for society to intervene in educating the young is when they are five years old. Since World War I, really prosperous industrial state governments have offered pre-school programs because they want to assure themselves that the next generation is prepared for the rigours of primary school. Pre-school is particularly important if the industrial society has a serious apprenticeship program, starting usually after graduation from primary school. In the North American scenario, we have gone the high school/junior college route and looked to immigrants for the kind of skills that go with five- to seven-year apprenticeship programs. Had the Industrial Age continued, it is likely that this strategy would have continued.

Our education system was geared to extending middle-class values and social skills. However, the Industrial Age has been transferred to the Third World and, as the level of abstraction increases in the former industrial world, the ability of the family and state to implement a congruent epistemology is lacking.

The reason most of us have never, or at least seldom, heard the word epistemology is because once the era becomes stable, its epistemology is pretty well unquestioned by everyone, except the mentally unbalanced and politically deviant. Everyone knows what its content is and conforms, more or less. Until the new epistemology evolves and is articulated, the education system

---

Incidentally, contrary to what you may have learned in art history class, and what you may have thought this book was saying, the people of the Renaissance did not invent perspective. They discovered it, centuries after it was used in ancient Egypt. One example was found recently at the KV5 Site in the Valley of the Kings, in the tomb of Rameses (1279-1213 B.C.). It has been alleged, on some of archaeology's flimsiest evidence, that Rameses was the Pharaoh who had the labour dispute with Moses.

In Rameses' tomb is a painting of his Queen, Nefertari. The painting is claimed by art historians to be the first rendering of the human face in three dimensions using a technique called chiaroscuro. Chiaroscuro lacked the mathematical framework that would have supported its knowledge transfer, but it did produce a 3-D image. This is the kind of discovery that an artist makes intuitively, lacking the intellectual context to understand what he has tripped over. The item gets seen, the artist gets hot, he sells a few pieces at dramatically inflated prices. If our intuitive artist is lucky or, more to the point, if we're really lucky, he finds an apprentice or maybe a son with talent, to whom he transfers the skill. He has managed to do a technology transfer to the next generation through one person, and all that one person gets is the "secret". So he also sells a few pieces at inflated prices, and the discovery goes nowhere without the knowledge-transfer tools. One break in the

is bound to be pretty chaotic, and some of the information that is just floating around out there is often seen as an attack on "family values." Meanwhile, our college and university systems try to maintain their infrastructures while they await the new epistemology, which will come to them in a memo from the head of the state or province's education department.

The rest of us can, however briefly, look at the way we get information and start to understand how we will learn about this expanded world-view we find ourselves in. At least it is now clear that we are on a learning curve that will last all of our lives. If we handle it well, we might be able to stay in place. Most of us will never see the curve's asymptote.

THE IDIOT BOX

Admirers of television never tire of telling us that most of us get most of our news from the tube. Television news is well-suited to brief bursts of unrelated news items, since well-chosen video persuades the brain to process both pictures and sound as combined content.

Television news items are selected by editors whose standards for choosing an item are whether the video footage accompanying the item is sufficiently gripping to stop us from changing channels, and whether the item is offensive to the channel's owners. As a medium, television does not require the viewer to exercise much in the way of attention-span management.

---

chain — a son who wants to go into embalming, an apprentice who doesn't get it, a daughter who marries a guy with a talent for herding goats — and the whole intuitive hit is down the tubes.

The Egyptians did nothing important with chiaroscuro, unless you have a fetish for classy funerary objects; chiaroscuro objects have only been found in tombs. Remember the Egyptian priest Ahmes, who actually discovered π around 1650 B.C.? He did nothing with it except to meditate on the mystic metaphysics of π.

There is a benefit to Newton's scientific method, which requires the timely publication of findings. With requisite publication, you can literally mobilize your entire discipline, plus a bunch of onlookers from other disciplines. In a show of their indifference to justice, the Lords of the Universe may allow someone from the onlooker crowd to use your discovery for some scheme of their own that makes a better explanatory model of your discovery and takes the chance for a Nobel away from you and your discipline.

That kind of media prospecting requires time to put your information source aside for a moment and think about the implications and consequences of what you've just learned. What do you do when that takes longer than the 15 to 30 seconds that television allows?

Television's current archival strategies are ill-suited to retrieving the context of film or tape. Indexing systems for both are shoddy and anachronistic. There are some interesting algorithms that could be amended to enormously improve the retrieval of film and tape footage. But, on the surface, that looks like a very expensive job. The people who make those decisions are money administrators or CEOs, and because they have no clue about computer algorithms and no access to people who do, it doesn't get done.

This is what we call baggage. As the baggage increases, you have to lay off such executives before they sink the ship. The Renaissance solution was to pay navigators twice as much as ship's captains.

The biggest problem with TV is that over the years, various hacks at the networks — while carrying out executive "revenue sensitive directives" — have implemented "industry standards" which, over time, have neurally conditioned the viewer's private time management to favour the agenda of a nascent oligarchy.

If you have any worry that the book is at risk, you may rest easily. The book is a piece of very user-friendly, interactive technology. The book is efficiently delivered: it can go to any level of abstraction you require and, with a simple change of delivery package, can address entertainment interests of the reader, all without taking control of the reader's private time management. But the multimedia global corporation has a vested interest in maximizing audiences, and thereby its return on investment.

A&E channel, which is owned by a consortium of ABC, NBC and Hearst, is touted as the private sector's answer to the quality of programming that is ascribed to public broadcasters. A&E is sold to advertisers who wish to reach a demographic consisting of upper-middle-class executive males, 40-65. That is why its contemporary history programs, ingenuously cobbled together from old film footage, define accuracy as what the conventional wisdom of that demographic deems to be true. To get there, you selectively edit out facts which conflict with that conventional wisdom.

In January 1996, A&E ran a series of features on the Gulf War. As usual, the editing was impressive. It proved that President Reagan was right all along. Video games do a really good job of simulation and training for politically acceptable, visually sanitary, odorously non-offensive, and auditorily modern warfare. No matter where you looked, there were no body bags, and no bodies. It was just video game footage, and the video cameras that accompany the weapons delivery systems delivered not bad — if not quite studio quality — programming material.

The only criticism voiced was that the shots of the "Highway to Hell" sequence — which includes the instant incineration of fleeing humans and was criticised at the time of the original fighting for being in doubtful taste — were dumped on for being repugnant.

TV news writing is universally bad, since the style manual assumes that the viewer has, at most, a 30-second attention span. For the news source, there is a benefit. Before the viewer has had a chance to ruminate on an item, let alone question the incompleteness of the coverage in terms of addressing even the most obvious consequences, the power of the images supporting the next item have driven the viewers' questions from their minds. Over time, the medium's style manual has extinguished any chance that TV viewers will develop or, even less likely, heighten any sense of critical thought about the world.

PRESS BARONS AND MEDIA MOGULS

If the style manual of TV is intentionally structured to ensure that critical thinking by viewers is discouraged, we can expect that critical thought and critical discussion will be deliberately excluded as TV content. We know how the Industrial Age sense of time was shaped to serve the requirements of the new industrial workplace. We can see that any significant shift from the massification of media would threaten the maximizing of the revenue sources available to the new media's ownership. Would this level of information control not be the basic requirement to shape the political bias of the new era's epistemology to favour an oligarchy?

The issue of mass media ownership then becomes more relevant when that ownership is global. Suppose, for the sake of argument, the world's media are ultimately controlled by 20 or 30 people who sincerely believe that media ownership is not just another business but one that allows them to control, at a macro-level, how an audience with few critical skills and limited information comes to support the agenda of such an oligarchy. Suppose they also believe that journalism has no vocational character, whether one is a publisher, an editor, or a journalist. These owners, in all sincerity, believe that "content" carries no moral caveats or imperatives.

The late Roy Thomson, founder of the Thomson mass media empire, strongly believed "news was what you used to separate the ads." Thomson started out with nothing, except a strong commitment to stop being poor, and managed to turn a few papers in Northern Ontario into a chain that grew into a global force. He solved the poor Scots immigrant heritage by picking up the *Times* of London, which led to a peerage.

His son Kenneth expanded upon the mandate of never being poor again, since he never had been poor. Thomson's assets now include broadcasting properties, electronic publishing interests and newspapers in Canada, the U.S., and the U.K.

Conrad Black, who is chairman of the Hollinger group of newspapers, is charming, bright, and a witty, provocative, romantic writer in his own right. He has authored a decently written and well-argued 700-odd page paper on a period of Quebec history, which would be accepted by professional historians as adequately thorough. He has vigorously opposed the idea that putting out a newspaper is a calling or vocation. He should know — he owns a lot of them. He believes that no chain owner should ever hire a publisher or an editor who will disagree with corporate policy, because a publisher or editor is there to implement the corporate policy.

When one of his associates was asked to explain why two Hollinger papers in different countries espoused different political views, he replied that each of the papers held a different community "franchise", and that the performance judgment by head office was on revenue and net profit, not content that is of no interest beyond the communities involved.

These are only two of the small group of media barons who decide the ground-rules by which many of us get the information we need to understand the forces at work today. Since their interests are in a more developed status quo, they would appear to have little interest in supporting critical analysis of this new era, except as it affects the revenue streams and share prices of their properties. They have usually found that the powerful interests of the world make the best allies, since regulators frequently disallow desirable purchases on the grounds that media should be competitive, or at least not monopolistic.

Whenever the industrial West has exposed itself to the luxury of commissions of inquiry into the media, most of the discussion of media ownership has focussed on the subjects of censorship and monopolistic practices. There have been few inquiries focused on *global centralization* of ownership.

MAGAZINES

Magazines have been undergoing a massive shift in style, design and content. Before looking at a selective list of them, it's probably useful to ruminate, in a McLuhanesque way, about magazines. Generally, magazines are published weekly or monthly. There are pressures on the editor of a weekly magazine to be more topical, while a monthly can take a more reasoned view.

One reporter, happily employed at *Newsweek*, compared working at a news magazine to having been at a party and recalling, the next morning, all the clever ripostes that you could have made if you could have thought of them at the time. If you work at a news magazine, you're able to show how clever you are, because the weekly news magazine has a seven-day approach-path to deadline.

In theory, journalists at news magazines enjoy a more leisurely approach to writing than is possible for their broadcast and daily newspaper peers. In actual fact, because of the group effort that goes into developing the editorial content, news magazines are more frantic than the newsrooms that produce multiple editions on a daily or hourly basis.

Time, the crown jewel of Time Warner, hoplessly compromised itself and clearly demonstrated that its vaunted editorial control system was dysfunctional when it produced its horribly innacurate July 3, 1995, cover story about pornography on the Internet. That cover proved *Time*'s editors could not be trusted. (If *Time*'s readers are looking only for entertainment, then the failure of editorial control is not germane.)

The more perilous result of the feature was that serious commentators raised the question of the potential for conflict of interest when an information provider is burdened with a high debt-load. A million dollars a day in interest charges assures that that the steps taken to conserve revenue will inevitably corrupt the product by the intrusion of financial jugglers into the editorial control process.

In other words, information providers are in the business of providing timely, useful, accurate information filtered through a predictable editorial process. It doesn't matter if there is bias in the process. The user can take that into account. But when the editorial judgement is impaired by cost-cutting, you can be assured that the people who ultimately control the information provider have not got the slightest idea of the place that integrity plays in the value of the product. This is why *Time* doesn't even rate consideration on our short-list of magazines.

Monthly magazines, at the cost of timeliness, can use longer deadlines to deliver more depth in covering emergent and past events. The following list does not constitute a canon by any means, but is reasonably useful in helping the reader pick up on events that matter and, because of their disparity, will help to develop tangential skills, since the overall content usually has some surprising connections. None are specialist publications, and all are readily available.

Scientific American attracts good contributors and has editors whose concept of accessibility assumes the reader has a mind that is prepared to work if the evidence warrants it. The editors are also good at avoiding the false dichotomy between "pure" and "applied" science (a dichotomy that occurs at the level of abstraction). At the same time, these editors are not going to confuse you with non-science stories. They have a clear picture of their readers; the informed layman and the specialist who is trying to avoid the exclusion that often accompanies intense focus on career research.

If you feel you must read a news magazine, the London-based weekly *The Economist* has a less bent editorial policy than any North American publication. The circulation department does not push a regression-to-the-mean readership recruiting strategy. Best of all, the editors have a wider aperture than North Americans are usually exposed to.

The Times Literary Supplement is the best literary review for a North American reader. It will give you a clear picture of what matters in the world where the written word is still taken seriously. Its reviewers not only have specialized expertise, but they take their critical function seriously while producing entertaining reading in their own right.

As a final recommendation among traditional magazines, *The New Yorker* is still capable of consistently producing some of the best journalism in North America.

Mondo 2000 is the place to go if you really want to see the edge pressures of the imminent future. *Mondo 2000* is published quarterly (sometimes). It is committed to challenging the norms of publishing, on the assumption that when a new era is crashing in, that is the best time to try anything that looks difficult. Of course, there are some problems with that kind of a publishing policy; sometimes it works and sometimes it works on something you couldn't care less about. Then there are those times when it doesn't work and you feel the frustration of a bright person who fails to understand something and assumes they aren't getting it when, in fact, it simply doesn't work.

Mondo 2000's readership is highly discriminating. The editor (R.U. Sirius) wants his readership to have fun with the ongoing revolution. He and the other editors have two missions. The first is to see what they can do with state of the art of computer graphics and publishing technologies. They are also concerned with writing styles that work in the here and now, when there is no evidence of an epistemology that offers a reliable guide. With those two statements, plus its erratic alleged publication schedule, *Mondo* has cut itself adrift from any possibility of attracting a mass readership. As for attracting advertisers, it does well, all things considered.

If you go into a hip advertising agency, a top-of-the-line design shop, or a bar where regularly employed film and TV art directors congregate, you will find that the personal reading art directors will prioritize, over almost everything else, is on those wonderful days when R.U. Sirius has managed to ship another issue.

Mondo's readers are typically more experienced in managing high degrees of information density than is expected of readers of mass-market magazines. The readership has an affinity for exploiting the latest technologies to the fullest. The readers are further along on the abstraction learning-curve than subscribers to mass media. (Those of us who might find *Mondo 2000* somewhat intimidating should realize that so did the first LSD experimenters.) With that kind of readership, there is strong support for putting *Mondo* on the buy list of any client who will stand still for an off-the-wall campaign.

Another magazine that is noted for special, one-off advertisements placed by big-money technology companies is *Wired*. *Mondo 2000* and *Wired* also share certain design philosophies. Both attract a similar advertising mix of computer hardware and software and computer-assisted production hardware for multimedia workers. The advertisements are worth looking at because neither magazine accepts ads that exhibit discontinuity with the magazine's style. (The ad featuring two male babies peeing, which solved Logitech's identity problems, was first seen in *Wired* after being turned down by other, more conventional advertising venues.) Both magazines feel that advertising should be seamless with the overall design and editorial values. *Wired* even hires *Mondo 2000* writers on occasion, including R.U. Sirius.

Revenue management problems aside, *Wired* has been the magazine success story of the last half of the decade. When the premier issue was released in January 1993, it sold out, literally overnight, in all major markets.

There are times when it pays to have friends in high places. One such friend was at the World Economic Forum in Davos, Switzerland (where all those heads of central banks, treasury officials, ministers of finance and their corporate equivalents meet annually to lie to each other), when *Wired* hit the stands.

Wired's editors and owners were less surprised when their constituency turned political than Rolling Stone's hippie capitalists had been 25 years earlier.

Rolling Stone's conversion of drug use into a metaphor for political oppression had been tough a sell and had needed the civil rights and anti-war movements to gather those who recognized that the decline of the nation state was apparently going hand-in-hand with the increasing dysfunctionality of conventional Industrial Age political values.

A generation later, the nascent thought that a new era might require new politics became obvious to a population that was vulnerable to randomly distributed radiation. This was how Rolling Stone became a political rag of outrage over the Johnson and Nixon White Houses.

Wired's constituency has more of an engineering world-view than the humanistic orientation of Rolling Stone. At the newsstand where Wired's customers hang out, there is a distrust of the Renaissance's simplistic Humanism and the ease with which it could be subverted.

The hacker ethos intuitively understood the nature of the revolution hackers were undertaking and that the implements they were producing would terrify the established order. Today the Internet, a vehicle highly touted by Wired, is under massive attack by legislative forces and police agencies using the same constitutionally convoluted tactics that were directed against marijuana users.

He had just started to read the inaugural issue when he saw something of interest to the CEO of some Euroscam multicom. The mogul, who was sitting next to him, glanced at it, went ballistic and ripped off the magazine. Back to the hotel newsstand, which had 50 copies when the original purchase had been made an hour before; there were two left, one of which was air-mailed to the author.

Anyone claiming media literacy when they saw that first issue had to realize that *Wired* was aimed at a market poorly served by *Mondo 2000*, whose editors, at the time, seemed to be fetishizing smart drugs. Further, its production values were so flawless that it could get away with engaging in the wildest experimentation in style, print, and graphics. Produced on a top-of-the-line Macintosh desktop publishing system, that debut issue of *Wired* also said to the world's magazine industry and production unions that desktop publishing was not only here, but it could meet and exceed all magazine industry production standards.

BOOKS TO LIVE BY

The infrastructure for books is pretty inexpensive, except for one part — readers. Reading has become a really expensive outdoor/indoor sport. The time required to read a challenging, engrossing book is under serious competition from entertainment, lean-mean workplace demands, quality time with the children, and using up frequent flyer points.

The list of competitors for book-reading time is endless. However, you will only find the information that will allow you to select your best survival options in books. Books have an integrated reflective quality that is hard to learn to use these days.

The infrastructure for books also requires publishers. Publishers of mass market books are in the entertainment business. They are, more and more frequently, owned by entertainment conglomerates. A real publisher is someone who sees the job as permitting the luxury of an occupation that is also a vocation. With the vocational territory goes accountability, the understanding that the definition of a publisher is someone who makes an author's work public.

You can learn a lot about the 19th century's move into a full-blown Industrial Age from reading Charles Dickens. Dickens will also tell you a lot about why Social Darwinism was such an easy sell to the British and American business communities after about 1875. It's a good idea to understand Social Darwinism, which has the virtue of being unparalleled in the world of bad ideas. It has *no redeeming qualities* and assured that the fruits of the British Industrial Revolution would be quickly lost to countries with a less egregious coloration to their national disposition.

Books as sources of information offer the reader an aesthetic option. Aside from being the vehicle of choice for the initial dissemination and archiving of important ideas, books are a part of the entertainment industry. As to books being superficial, pop entertainment, we should also take Andy Warhol's "15 minutes of fame" quote and recognize that a lot of books are not just entertainment, they're someone's 15 minutes of being trapped in the the pseudo-spotlight of celebrity and exposed as being without distinction (although Warhol neglected to point out that risk).

While there is nothing wrong with getting entertaiment from a book, the pseudo-spotlight is no beacon and offers no informed guidance for those of us whom history has given the opportunity of living in the first years of a new era.

Most popular books are entertainment, and it is unlikely that anyone is writing anything that is more than transiently helpful. Here are some starting points that can be useful as signposts.

HAROLD BLOOM LOADS HIS CANON

What with electronic publishing, computer-based texts and a lack of time to read in the face of a steady diet of electronically enhanced entertainment spectacles, it isn't surprising that we are losing the ability to read efficiently. Things have gotten to the point where Japan Inc. effectively trains its middle managers with comic books and treats its workaholic workforce to badly animated pornography.

Harold Bloom, who professes English Literature at Yale University, apparently dissented from that option. His 1994 book, *The Western Canon*, was a whacking great success at book store cash registers. That must have been as much of a surprise to Bloom as it would have been to his agents, his editors, the publisher and the publisher's author tour manager.

During the Renaissance, books, in spite of the relatively high cost of paper, had much wider right-hand margins than do books published today. That was because the reader was expected to write points of agreement or disagreement with the author in the margins. Dr. John Dee is famous for his adversarials, as these marginalia were known. Dee, the most widely respected alchemist (and much else) in Elizabethan England, possessed the best and largest (7,000 volumes, manuscripts, et cetera) private library in England.

The interactivity touted by the computer elite is not any more "interactive", and possibly much less interactive, than Dee's adversarials. His books and papers are very expensive now, yet are snapped up by great universities with large library endowments. His library remains a treasure trove to historians because of the detailed lore in his adversarials.

What did Bloom say that justified the accolades? *The Western Canon* is a trenchant critique of those players in the 20th century whose work he charges with being not just uncanonical, but without intellectual standards. His sense of political directionality is pretty open. On the right, there are those who attempt to subsume the Canon under a wholly fictional moral agenda, which validates works that advance the neo-con academic right-wing agenda. Then there are those who are usually thought of as being on the left; Bloom identifies them as the "school of resentment" or "the whiners", and charges them with wanting to destroy the Canon to speed their agenda of social change.

Bloom, like a Gilbert and Sullivan character with a library card, has a little list of those who never will be missed. The list is sufficiently generic that it reads like the membership roster of the Association of Academic Victims Unjustly and Suddenly Deprived of Their Only Epistemology. On the list we find all of those who have dedicated themselves to reminding the rest of us of our failure to advance our understanding of the latest shifts in thought among the politically correct. Like a tribal shaman on a bad day, Bloom points the finger of fatality at the Marxists, the Freudians, the Feminists, the Afro-Americans, various academic multiculturists, Jacques Lacan and his happy little band of Franco-Hungarian psycholinguists, and Michel Foucault (who has uncritically inspired some strange, almost occult historicists). The semioticians, like the mysterious deconstructionists, are included among those Bloom committed to the trash-heap of history, not because he finds them politically offensive — just aesthetically.

Bloom targets them because they offer nothing to posterity. His argument is that for a writer to achieve canonical authority, the writer must have been influential for at least two generations and be acknowledged to possess a high degree of aesthetic power. One of the standards Bloom insists on for inclusion under the appellation "canonical" is that each work must make a unique and critical contribution in terms of literary value as well as addressing the critical ideas of the time in which it was written.

Bloom's taste for what has been clasically canonical is impeccable. His starting point is to argue that the biblical prophets are addressing a world of Chaos, and he assigns them the task of breaking through the Chaos. His formal Canon then begins with Chaucer, Dante and Boccaccio. He negotiates an argument that then moves the focus on to Shakespeare. His central thesis is that all else that follows, all that is canonical, is related to and defined by the influence of Shakespeare.

Part of Bloom's defence for this thesis is that all literary history can be separated into four distinct periods. Bloom properly attributes this literary periodic table to Giambattista Vico (1668-1744), who produced the somewhat seminal *Scienza Nuova* (New Science), a pre-Diderot attempt to systematize the ideas of the Renaissance in the manner of the Scholastics and their classics.

Vico's systemic view begins in Chaos and cycles through three stages before returning to Chaos. As humanity distinguishes the crisis of meaning and identity, the place of self in the cosmos comes to centre stage and the paramount concern of society is to differentiate itself from this a chaotic universe. Enter the prophets.

In Vico's system, Chaos is followed by a Theocratic literary period in which authors make these yearnings public ("Thank God, other people feel crowded in by this Chaos, the way I do") and propose solutions. Once the fundamentals of the theocratic oeuvre — addressing the nature of the god(s) — is achieved, the human relationship with the god(s) is exposed.

Once the approriate condition of man *vis à vis* the god(s) is resolved, it is time to address relationships with authority. This next stage is the Aristocratic phase, in which the voice of the canonical author zeroes in on the question of who is legitimately superior to whom. The subject of Aristocratic canonical literature is how the leaders and followers should carry out their obligations and how to tell the differences between those who have legitimacy as leaders and those who are ordained to follow. This is a problem that recurs hourly, if not oftener, for anyone in the Renaissance. Unsurprisingly, Bloom places Shakespeare in the Aristocratic phase.

This is also where Bloom gets into trouble. For instance, he does not tell us how to judge Shakespeare's willingness to become a huckster for those wretched Tudors. Certainly the Lord Chancellor would have liked the most recent film production of *Richard III* as well as he liked the original, because he liked anything that justified the usurpation of the throne from the House Plantaganet.

Are we to forgive Shakespeare's bending to the Lord Chancellor's rewrite directions? Bloom says yes, because the aesthetic power of Shakespeare, coupled with the aesthetic influence that power wields up to the present, obviates any other flaw.

The next stage Vico and Bloom identify is the Democratic phase, when the muse moves authors to introduce the universals of feeling and experience. The human condition is now extended throughout the society. In the term we have been using, the Democratic stage is the point where a new, ready-to-go-to-work epistemology is primed to be disseminated. The final phase in Bloom's Canon is Chaos, which encompasses mostly works of the 20th century.

Bloom's Canon is an elegiacal means of looking at Western letters and identifying the chroniclers of the great ideas of the West, from the Middle Ages up to Samuel Beckett. Reason, enhanced by the view from the tower

Bloom occupies at Yale, should tell him that the period addressed by *The Western Canon* is over, yet he is admittedly unenthusiastic about suggestions that his work is an elegy.

But the great flaw in Bloom's argument is one that his catalogue of "whiners" and "school of resentment" no doubt share with him. What Bloom has missed completely is a gaping deficiency of such magnitude that it could make a decent national park.

THE NEW CANON

If Harold Bloom wants to go on about aesthetics, he would be well advised to read *Hyperspace: A Scientific Odyssey Through Parallel Universes, Time Warps, and the 10th Dimension* by the theoretical physicist Michio Kaku, whose aesthetic standards are more clearly enunciated than anything Bloom, or anyone in his Canon, has trundled out. *Hyperspace* is so simply and gently written that you'll be revelling in the author's writing before you realize that he has taken you to the edges of today's theoretical physics — and there isn't a single welt on your body.

Kaku's work is also the best source this author has found for the life of the man considered by many to be the greatest mind of the century: Ramanujan Srinivasa. He was born in 1887 in a place called Erode, which is near Madras, India. This was not a good place to be if you planned to be a world-class mathematician. His family was of the highest caste, Brahmins, but his father was a clerk in a clothing store.

By the time Ramanujan was 10, the whole village realized that he was some sort of human calculating wizard, and he was given a scholarship to high school. (The British Raj of the day was always on the watch for really bright kids who could be turned into low-level clerks.) At high school, he managed to flunk his exams (shades of Einstein). Playing with esoteric equations of high order number theory doesn't help you to prepare for the exams developed for very dull English boys at the end of the Empire.

His family used up whatever connections they could muster and got him a low-paying job as a clerk for the Port of Madras Trust. That solved the problem of starving to death and even gave him some free time to get on with the math. (Remember Einstein, clerking away in the Swiss patent office.)

Ramanujan had read a completely uncelebrated book on mathematics by George Carr before he was trapped by the downscale effects of his school. This was his sole contact with Western mathematics. In 1912, he wrote letters to three of England's leading mathematicians, hoping to introduce himself to minds that shared his sense of vocation. Godfrey Hardy of Cambridge found his letter strange.

It began: "I beg to introduce myself to you as an accounts clerk of the Port Trust office of Madras on a salary of only 20 pounds per annum...." He went on to lay out 120 theorems with original proofs neither Hardy nor anyone else had ever seen before. What Ramanujan had managed to do was to re-derive the previous 100 years of European mathematical history. Hardy knew he was in contact with a mathematician of "the first order."

Hardy once rated the abilities of leading mathematicians. He gave David Hilbert an 80 and himself a 25. Ramanujan he graded as 100. Hardy and John Littlewood, another Cambridge math don with whom Hardy had shared the letter, went through whatever hoops people like that have to when they want to drag someone out of a Madras office and in 1914 Ramanujan showed up on their Cambridge doorstep. He stayed for three years.

England in 1914 was a bad place for Ramanujan, with a solid base of nasty bacterial infections, wartime food, and British weather. In 1919, Ramanujan managed to return to India where he died, probably of tuberculosis. During the three years he was in England, he was in and out of sanatoriums. In those three years, however, he produced an amazing stream of theorems.

Ramanujan's work was in the area of modular functions, which describe and discover how to protect the mathematical identities whose symmetry would, if left alone, be destroyed by quantum theory. In his time in England, Ramanujan produced three notebooks filled with 4,000 formulae on 400 pages. This mass of work consisted of theorems that were extraordinary in their power but maddeningly without any notes or comments. These notebooks have led mathematicians on a search for what seems to be the greatest mathematical breakthrough in 2,000 years.

In 1976, another cache, now known as Ramanujan's lost notebooks, turned up at Trinity, one of the Cambridge colleges. It was in the form of 130 pages of scrap paper. This work was done in one year while he was dying and the output of this one year has been described as "the lifetime work of a very great mathematician."

All of this has to do with a branch of mathematics called superstring theory, which, as Kaku explains, lead us to a 10-dimensional universe. Historically it has been argued that "the laws of nature simplify when

---

Nature's Numbers by Ian Stewart is part of Basic Book's Science Masters series. Again, written so well and with explanations so clear and accessible you'll wonder why they made math so difficult to understand in school.

Chaos: Making a New Science by James Gleick is an outstanding introduction to chaos theory. Gleick records how a cast of non-mathematicians happened on the mathematical principles behind strange attractors, the "Butterfly Effect," and other concepts that are right out on the leading edge of research tools.

expressed in higher dimensions." But when we have a clear understanding of quantum theory we have to say that "the laws of nature simplify when *self-consistently* expressed in higher dimensions." It is at this point of self-consistency that Ramanujan's modular functions kick in and push the level of abstraction at which exploration is being undertaken to the 10th dimension.

If the contents of Ramanujan's final notebook prove to be as useful as it is presently assumed, the coming jump in the level of abstraction will be exponentially greater than anything we have experienced so far. It is a troubling idea that a sick guy, working in Cambridge in 1919, could produce solutions to a problem that wouldn't be around until the 1980s.

Can we forgive Bloom's inability to include mathematics and physics in his Canon? True, most math and physics authors are not big on plot development or Aristotle's Poetics. But Kaku considers it part of his discipline to explore aesthetics and describe them, not merely describe the experience of them. This is the fatal flaw that the literary person finds waiting for them after 40 years in Yale's libraries, even with a faculty stack permit.

At this stage of a new era, we have no Canon. Bloom is important to our canonless time because his Canon is the distilled essence of the epistemology the Renaissance has remaindered to us. If, as is argued here, we have to build a new epistemology, it helps to have access to the old one. It is only available in books. There is no guarantee it can be repackaged as infotainment and no assurance it will entertain.

NOT A CANON, BUT WORTH READING ANYWAY

The rest of our Canon falls under the genre of "cyberpunk." The cyberpunks are usually classified as science fiction, but they are a class by themselves because they perform a journalistic service. (The degree to which they anticipated the hard edge that emerged in the '90s is impressive.) Cyberpunk writers are the guides to this era transformation, just as Erasmus and the other Humanists ushered in the Renaissance. Their writing is popular among computer programmers and others whose work has taken them to the edges of the topographical universe, where we find the engines driving this era shift.

Don't whine about the literary value. The cyberpunks are first and foremost describing a period of history while it is just being invented.

Rudy Rucker started the genre in 1982 with two books: *Software* and *Wetware*. Even the most avid readers of science fiction are less than amused when they open these books. The first few chapters seem to be the worst space-opera, schlock science fiction ever concocted by an author needing the publisher's advance to buy a drink that morning.

If the reader perseveres, however, he will discover that Rucker has ensured that readers committed to banal and culture-free pornography will drop the book. This device of deliberately confusing anyone looking for ersatz literary value allowed Rucker to collect a dedicated and broadly literate readership who were hungry for information and psychic support. Rucker's books are definitely noncanonical by Bloom's standards but contain information that was priceless when it was published.

Rucker is the great, great, great grandson of G.W.F. Hegel and teaches mathematics and computer science at California's San Jose State University. The tangential lateralism Rucker exploits in his writing is the very quality that creative mathematicians assume to be a perfectly ordinary way of thinking. If you think Rucker is a crazed freak and you can't handle his serio-comic literary equations, then read his *Infinity and the Mind*, which was published by the Boston publisher Birkhaüser, also in 1982. It is popular among mathematicians, mathematically inclined philosophers, and physicists.

In his books, Rucker brings his mathematical intuition to bear on the problem of what Turing defined as artificial intelligence. He asks, "How can we bring into existence robots which we don't know how to design?" His revelation is to *let the robots evolve*. Rucker understands contemporary psychology and neurophysiology much better than most of the computer scientists who are active in the AI field. He realizes that the problems of AI are at the level of density — data indexing, data packing, and the power of information processing. (As opposed to the more mundane *data* processing approach.)

Readers who are offended by cyberpunk and think of its writers as having lively thought disorders have to be prepared for Rucker inserting phrases and asides in machine language. These aren't essential to the plot or information characteristics of the book. He does this in the way a more conventional author might incorporate an obscure foreign language as a piece of literary humour or pretension, assured some of his audience will figure it out.

William Gibson's trilogy, *Neuromancer*, *Count Zero* and *Mona Lisa Overdrive*, encapsulated the world-view of young programmers at a critical point in history. When *Neuromancer* (the book in which Gibson coined the term cyberspace) was published in 1984, the young programmers were beginning to realize that they were the intellectual cannon fodder in a revolution of far greater potency than their employers and managers were capable of understanding.

In the unheated valley garages and on the corporate programming floors of North America, the programming fraternity were much like an army in wartime. They were mostly young males. They worked the outrageous hours that only the young can sustain. That they had jobs was a blessing for their mothers, who could finally clean their rooms. Most of them "had no life" aside from writing code. Their work spaces had microwaves to heat food and large refrigerators to stock high-caffeine soft drinks.

The programmers were inspired by the idealism the young find so easy to live within. The managerial elite were calling the period the Information Age (or, using the U.N.'s pop term, first expounded by Robert Theobald, the Communications Age). They used industrial similes to explain to themselves what they were doing. But the programmers knew the new period was bigger than the Industrial Age. It was they who faced the enemy daily and in so doing got fleeting glances of the dimension-hopping foe.

These programmers were the first to discover Gibson, and BBSs usually devoted to arcane technical issues sang his praise. After publishing a few article in *Omni*, Gibson (working on a typewriter) was already articulating the dreams, hopes, and terrors of the hot-shot hackers who had the best sense of the new era. He did it entirely from his intuitive sharing of the lore of the dragons these youthful knights were meeting and slaying daily.

To the young code writers, Gibson had performed a rite of magic which has always been used by shamans. Gibson named the beast and assured those idealists on the front lines that they were not alone.

A few years ago a computer industry trade magazine asked its readers who in the industry should the U.S. Post Office put on a stamp. There were a few votes for Charles Babbage, a few for Jobs and Wozniak, even a few for Ada, Countess of Lovelace. About 75 percent voted for William Gibson.

Reading Gibson's trilogy is almost essential to gaining an understanding of our new era. (Reading Gibson's more recent books isn't a bad idea either.) Not reading Gibson is like time-travelling to Shakespeare's England and not going to see *Richard III* version 1.0 because the Lord Chancellor thought it was subversive.

With the hyperbole about the Internet that besieges us, it is also vital to read Bruce Sterling. If the new era goes through a period of Inquisitions and censorship "for our own good" or "to protect our children," the first cyberpunk work that the NWO should put on the Index is *Islands in the Net*, which satirized the "Information Highway" to gridlock back in 1988. Sterling is a Texan whose literary style owes much to journalism, which makes access easy for the reader. In *Islands in the Net*, Sterling offers a painful look at those who substitute loyalty to a corporation for the loyalties usually given one's self, family, and nation by using a computer network as a metaphor for the relationships between employees and executives in a transnational corporation.

Neil Stephenson leapt into the front rank of cyberpunk writers with his third novel, *Snow Crash*. Our knowledge of our own time is too sketchy for anyone but a novelist to speculate profitably on our immediate future — and with *Snow Crash* and his latest, *The Diamond Age*, Stephenson has shown he is one of the few who understands the new era. In *Snow Crash* he writes: "The human mind can absorb and process an incredible amount of information — if it comes in the right format. The right interface." Then he adds a truly McLuhanesque touch: "If you put the right face on it."

Alexander Besher is a sometime consultant for the Global Business Network, specializing in the Pacific Rim. In 1994, Besher published *Rim: A Novel of Virtual Reality* and anyone with assumptions about N-space being a comfort station was straightened right out. This book is probably the best cyberpunk novel so far, excepting Gibson's *Neuromancer*.

Mary Gentle, author of *Grunts*, is the last novelist who is absolutely essential. If you believe that the next generation does not see itself as living in an increasingly hostile world, Gentle will disabuse you of that notion.

Grunts exposes the romanticism of the fantasy genre, typified by *Lord of the Rings*, by being a fantasy book that adheres to the rules of the genre — except with attitude. In effect she says, "look at the people you've marginalized and defined as 'underclass.' Look at the effect that has on the society we're inheriting. Kill Bilbo, that fucking wimp of a Hobbit. He's of no use to the oligarchy or in fighting the oligarchy and doesn't deserve to survive!" The parental culture has done a good job of teaching the constituency Gentle addresses about values. Gentle teaches them about a world that has none.

MIND'S EYES

In the Renaissance, as we saw earlier, it was necessary to go through some neural conditioning in order to *see* the new perspective-based art. Those glial cells had to be coerced into firing in some way. This was accomplished by way of the sheer abundance of the art that anticipated and reflected Vico's *New Science*.

In our own Renaissance, the initial artistic interpreters of our era have been writers. Where we do find graphic artists who are able to bring an intuitive sensibility to the new world-view? The answer is the film and TV industries and the video game world. Unfortunately, the creative uses of cyberspace must support the dramatic requirement of the story-line. We are supposed to focus on the actors, so the deliberate intention of the director is to use the strongest possible virtual realities to enhance the dramatic element of the film. Most of us lack the neural processing time to deal with both points of view simultaneously. As a result, we are largely unaware of the contribution made to a theatrical film by our "new sciences."

When TV commercials use these technologies, it should be acknowledged that the advertiser wants nothing that will interfere with the "message." The cyberspace effects are designed not to upstage the product's stardom. Still, because the effects are seamless or even subliminal, their role in helping us to understand and begin to neurally exploit cyberspace probably results in a high ratio of people gaining on the learning curve, steep as it is, toward integrating higher dimensions into their thinking.

Dealing successfully with our new era means understanding that information is being processed with increasing density and acceleration. One film that deals with this is *Blade Runner*.

Blade Runner intellectually excites only a very small part of its audience. It enjoys cult status for a wide range of viewers and is used in film studies courses for a variety of reasons. And then it is rented by people simply looking for entertainment.

Ridley Scott, *Blade Runner's* director, drew casually on the classic sci-fi story *Do Androids Dream of Electric Sheep?* by Philip K. Dick. Over the years the film has become a metaphor for the way the world seems to be unfolding. Those who saw the future with unbridled and uncritical optimism found the film depressing. The term "Blade Runneresque" has infiltrated the language as a substitute for "post-modern" where a hard, high-tech cut is being taken.

The film's real star is the set. It was designed by Syd Mead and inspired by a comic book story, *The Long Tomorrow* by the French artist Moebius. William Gibson realized that a great deal of the power of this film came from the fact "that Ridley Scott understood the importance of information density to the point of perceptual overload."

Scott brought this densification to the screen and, as such, *Blade Runner* was a precursor for understanding that the density and velocity with which computers transfer information would make an impact on the literature of the future. Interestingly, this approach to density and speed is seldom discussed by people in the film industry, who should know better.

VOICES FROM UNDERGROUND

Over the past 30 years, we have all been forced to become more media literate. This is particularly true of youth. None are more aware of this than the people who run our education systems. In North America, almost universally, educators have implemented "media literacy" courses, usually at the high school level, and in spite of budget cuts these courses have been widely accepted and seen as progressive steps to help the young cope with the modern world.

But what happens when kids open up their own information pathways, unsanctioned by the parental generation? What happens when information is encoded into terms which are aversive to the authority culture's values and norms, yet do not offend against legal prohibitions — for example, against obscenity? The result is "underground" media, which mainstream society finds aversive either because of the intellectual content or because of the esthetic.

The "underground" media of the 1990s follow a common strategy for avoiding the risks of being seen as subversive. The strategy is quite simple. Authors write in ways which are either not understood or dismissed as trivial in the greater society. Rudy Rucker created the genre of cyberpunk but cast the first two books of the genre in ways that would repel many readers. Remember what we noted about the functional relationship of rock 'n' roll music, which the KGB could not analyze and the *kultura* elite could not hear, and the overthrow of the U.S.S.R.

Since the 1960s the comic book has enjoyed increasing appreciation as a legitimate art form. Desktop publishing, supplied by the personal computer industry, speeded the process, as anyone with access to a photocopier could publish their own 'zine. The comic book has almost replaced the novel as the form of expression for an entire generation, and standards have risen so much in recent years that it is no longer sufficient to be able to spell "fuck." Yet comic books, despite their highly political nature, are still seen as trivial by the parental culture.

Alexander Shulgin, alleged inventor of the hallucinogen STP and general all-round technology guru, once said this of institutional secrecy: There are three levels of socially mandated secrecy. The first is industrial and it is so porous you'd think they were trying to give it away. The second is the military — it is slightly more difficult to crack. Finally, there are the private secrecy systems. These are almost impossible to break.

This description certainly fits the comic. It is distributed as mass culture and is treated as trivial by those against whom it addresses its japes. Since pornography is counter-intuitive to the values it espouses, it satirizes porn. It assumes drugs to be endemically available and unnecessary to promote. Its principal artistic devices are irony and satire and graphics that look like mediocre soft-porn. That makes the comic book about as safe from current censorship strategies as it is possible to be.

In the comic book *Give Me Liberty*, published by Dark Horse Comics, authors Frank Miller and Dave Gibbons made assumptions about the bimodalities of the world which were sufficiently aversive to parental values to cause mainstream Americans to dismiss or otherwise trivialize the content. Yet their kids, the same generation the educators wish to reach with their media literacy programs, found the series more accurately reflected daily events than did TV, newsmagazines, or daily papers. The point of view of Give Me Liberty is that the only escape from an oligarchical world, which exploits everyone who is not part of the elite, is to learn to identify an oligarchy and make your choice now about what side you're on. The authors are on the side of fighting it.

Dark Horse is also quite capable of putting out some pretty wholesomely tame satire for an ordinary 12-year-old mind-set. If you find a kid reading *Flaming Carrot Comics*, they are getting some satirical, instructional commentary on American teen-age mores. This tells a 12-year-old not to take it too seriously when the big 13 rolls around. It also puts that media literacy course under enough of a microscope to pump up the kid's residual skepticism.

Tank Girl is a whole other thing. *Tank Girl* is from the same British school of comic books that gave us *Judge Dredd*, *2000 AD*, *Robo Catcher* and other mythic-quality comics that combine getting in your face with a well-developed sense of puritanical zeal.

Tank Girl comes from a not-too-distant future in which the promised environmental crisis has come about. Her mission is to coyly admit that women, for better or worse, are independent and will accept no pushing around from anyone. Her level of coyness is best understood when you realize that the tank of her name comes from the military tank that is her personal transportation. Her best friend, another young woman, is a techie with a Harrier Jump Jet as a personal vehicle. She, of course, is called Jet Girl.

Tank Girl manages to set the preceding generation of baby boomers' teeth on edge, regardless of sex, but especially those following conventional employment routes. One jarring factor in Tank Girl's life is that her love interest is an escaped product of military bio-genetic research to produce a mix of the gene efficiencies found in kangaroos and humans.

For anyone born before 1960, *Tank Girl's* satire is stronger stuff than we remember in comics. But if you were to spend time with Western European and North American young men and women between 25 and 35, who are beginning to be identified as that birth-decade's style setters — the bond traders, the successful non-traditional business owners, and the film industry's technical and business people — it is hard to find anyone who doesn't know and approve of *Tank Girl*.

Within that age range, disapproval of *Tank Girl* comes from women who are committed hard-line feminists, men who see women as toys, and men who consider themselves to be feminists. The gender skewing toward women indicates that this is not a generation of women who will wimp out under the stresses that go with being on the ground floor of a new era. As one young woman said of Wonder Woman, whom a lot of the parental culture equate with Tank Girl, "she's a token superhero, but still a slut."

The movie *Tank Girl* enjoys less approval from its key demographic. It is seen as having made too many compromises with Hollywood. One suggestion: if you are in a position where you are expected to be on the cutting edge of censorship, don't try to censor *Tank Girl*. Review the comic, see the movie. Do you really want the kind of people who see *Tank Girl* as offering accurate social and political commentary to be pissed off at you personally? "I was just following orders" might get them into even more of a rage. A lot of them are actually conventionally literate.

CHAPTER NINETEEN

First We Kill All the Censors: Why censorship is suicide

With the quantum jump in the level of abstraction, we can expect the rise of new and, as yet, undefined social management problems. We see from the past few years in business that conventional systems of management are unlikely to suffice. IBM and Xerox have failed to implement first-rate developments from their own labs; the American automobile industry has managed to lose its own home market; in Europe and America, the domestic home electronics business has been lost to Japan, which has also taken a large part of the chip business. Reading over the above reminds us that Einstein wrote: "Perfection of means and confusion of goals seems — in my opinion — to characterize our age."

We know that the "New World Order" seeks perfection of control, which really means not letting things get out of control. Elites have a bad habit of dealing with control by looking at their world through filtered, blinkered vision systems. The NWO is looking for a society in which the highest accolades and rewards are reserved for those who manage global corporations and advise and subsidize governments and political parties. This would reduce the impact of individual members of society and create an oligarchy of the corporate elite.

If you want to create a political oligarchy, the first thing you do is get out the tools of censorship. That's because, if you want to secure the powers inherent in an oligarchic government, you have to make some political changes.

First you push the many virtues of your target population's national, racial, or religious characteristics. Then you exterminate any expression of different family values. You destroy the middle class and replace them with a marginalized class who will never have security of home or health and who live in fear of joining the underclass. That means you have to create an underclass to make that idea really concrete. (Nothing abstract for the marginalized!) Then you decide how few people you need to run your oligarchy and you become the supplier of the stuff that keeps them onside — health care and secure housing, for example.

During an era shift you can do all this if you restrict access to the operative level of abstraction — and that's not too hard, given that most people don't want to know.

Now you understand those huge white-collar lay-offs at IBM and AT&T. Why do the faceless pension plan managers who forced those lay-offs keep tightening their grip? Because this is the time to go for power, even if your understanding of events is only visceral. Of course, oligarchs tend to die in really ugly ways.

CENSORSHIP: IT'S THE ECONOMY, STUPID

As the ferment of the Renaissance and its subsidiary event, the Reformation, rolled on, all parties agreed that censorship was absolutely essential to maintaining public decency, stamping out witches, and making the world safe for supporters of law and order. The part that they could not agree on was what should be censored.

The Inquisitions and the Star Court Chambers of the world got most of their cachet from their ability to provide a legal framework to legally stamp out crimes like blasphemy, obscenity, selling occult products (eye of newt, bat's whiskers, et cetera), teaching erroneous beliefs, and advancing unacceptable political ideas.

Some of these charges were easier to prove than others. The bottom line was that proof was obtained by torture, or from witnesses who had been tortured, or whose testimony indicated that they were less than disinterested parties. (Giordano Bruno was nailed for speculations he had published.)

Supporters of censorship are usually promoters of some single-issue cause. But the problem with censorship is that you can't abolish only something that is offensive to you and your friends. Civil servants who write laws know that after some experience with a new law, someone will always want to amend it. So if you want a censorship law what you get, as part of the original law, is a law investing the state with a statutory right to censor, period. Then they put in, as a regulation, whatever disgusting conduct you and your friends wanted quashed.

Next, someone else will use your law to extend the act's provisions to cover some deeply held conviction of their own, as regulation number two. Once you consent to censorship, by creating the law which allows the suppression of information, anyone with minimal lobbying skills can censor literally anything.

In the early 14th century, most of Europe's political leaders were not very numerate. The monasteries trained clerks who could do simple sums, but as long as they continued to use Roman numerals, the most simple arithmetic was really pushing the envelope.

By the time Fra Luca Pacioli had triggered the Renaissance and perspective was discovered, most of Europe's educated laity had learned of the new Arabic numeral system through painters and architects illustrating and illuminating the rules of perspective. Alchemists, both lay and clerical, found that a numerical system which included zero could accommodate infinity and give them the underpinnings for the beginnings of science as it has evolved down to us.

Scholasticism began encountering questions, and the questions became really boorish when its historical antecedents began to provide less and less authority, and the number of answers that were obviously in error started to pile up. The Church saw the challenges to Scholasticism as challenges to its own authority and brought in the Inquisition to stamp out what was perceived as heretical activity.

At the beginning of this book we talked about the heat that came down on fra Angelico and other perspective painter clergy for using "God's space" as the space for perspective. (This was the space catechists used to prove it was possible for God to exist even though God was unseen.) Luther and Machiavelli were both banned. In the case of Luther, the Inquisition went to the length of banning not just specific works, but *everything* he had ever written and everything he might ever write. Apparently the inquisitors believed the likelihood that he might see the error of his ways and return seeking penance and forgiveness was too imperceptible for them to grab on to.

If the goal was to progress in farther reaches of the knowable universe using the new learning, what was needed was a way to challenge the historical authority of the feudal world-view that did not result in one or the other disputant ending up as the centre of attraction in a huge bonfire. The new Humanists had to find a way to allow for a wider contention than the Medieval world permitted

Just in case you thought that the idea of free speech came along as part of the package with printing, you can forget that right now. Institutionalized legal censorship was initiated in Cologne, the same colourful Rhine town where Johannes Gensfleisch Gutenberg set up the first printing press. In 1475 the powers of the day at the University of Cologne invented censorship to deal with a moral problem of some magnitude.

The university petitioned the pope to allow the school's governing council to licence the publication of books, and asked for the authority to punish those who published, printed or read unlicenced books. The law didn't mention the need to control the specific conduct of the usual dweebs who were on the pope's and the university's list of trouble-making perverts. It merely authorized the punishment of those who broke a licencing law.

What had happened was that people who disagreed with the conventional wisdom, who could already be refused permission to teach or preach, were using the new printing technology to get around the preach-and-teach ban by publishing tracts to distribute their bad ideas. The university's officials didn't like that.

Eventually, it became obvious to the Humanists who took over the universities that they needed a way to challenge authority so that scholarship, especially in the sciences, which were fueling the Mercantile Age, could expand and grow.

When that context was made clear to the civil authorities licencing the universities, they realized this was more than harmless philosophic squabbling between obviously unemployable academics. The Protestant princes put their minds to the problem and came up with the obvious solution — don't change the laws, change the regulations.

By the late 17th century, the sciences had already demonstrated the capacity to incorporate new, empirically demonstrated findings that were at variance with classical and conventional wisdom. It took a long time before it was recognized that the secular benefits of the right to publish — that is to make public — this information resulted in economic benefits to the entire society and not just to the author and publisher. But over a period of about 500 years it became clear that ideological and religious censorship was a luxury which no new world order could afford if it wanted to take advantage of its discoveries.

In other words, the real argument for free speech, a free press, and free inquiry are found in improvements to the economic life and general betterment of the community. If you want to get into the censorship game, it

---

In 1922, Eamon De Valera, born in Brooklyn, U.S.A., of Spanish and Irish parents, found himself president of something they were calling The Irish Free State. For De Valera and his Irish nationalist friends it was the first step in a progression they hoped would bring total independence from Britain. But to move forward De Valera needed some force that would bring Ireland together.

Post-Renaissance figures like Cromwell and William of Orange used the country as a shooting gallery with a brutality that has marked the people of Ireland into our own time. The thugs of the I.R.A. and the equally thuggish Protestant Black and Tans from Ulster were delicately balanced in their ugliness at running a war.

De Valera's problem was that he and his political supporters wanted a unified Ireland, including Ulster. That meant an Ireland totally free of English control. He had to get the Irish Catholic population to provide support in this venture, which allowed everyone to share in the horror.

But De Valera realized that to push for full independence he needed some institutional support. Word of his plight found open ears among Ireland's Catholic clergy. The bishops of Ireland agreed to provide the help De Valera needed — in return

is important to know that suppressing speech-related freedoms has a high probability of creating an economic disaster.

Censorship is not just an exercise in the fuzzy abstractions of civil libertarians. After Gutenberg, the benefits that came with being able to read the output of the printing presses and printers that began popping up all over Europe have been clearly economic.

Censorship is a crime against the economy; all censorship is ultimately economic. In our own time, when various attempts to censor the Internet are finding increasing favour with political, economic, and historical underachievers, it is probably wise to remember how high the price of free thought and speech has been.

FREE SPEECH IN THE WIRED WORLD

In the late 19th century, France's secret police services complained to the government about the introduction of telegraph on the grounds that they could no longer surreptitiously steam open envelopes of letters. (This is what you get when you seek policy advice from cops.)

The Internet as we know it will disappear, except as a switching system, because too many Industrial Age politicians worldwide will try to police, censor, and control it. The telephone companies may adopt switching as their new revenue point, which will also make the present Internet unfeasible from a consumer's viewpoint. The free Internet will be replaced by commercial system operators, who will be essentially local. There will still be a global e-mail system, but the nation state will make a last stand around

---

for the most rigorous censorship and repressive life-style laws in force in Europe at the time. Indeed, the bishops of Spain were so deeply impressed with De Valera's vision that when General Franco was looking for assistance in 1937, the Spanish bishops were able to point out the Irish precedent.

Ireland had missed out entirely on the Renaissance and the Reformation. Irish Catholic clergy were uninvolved in the counter-Reformation. Indeed, the number of the domestic clergy who had ever heard of these developments can charitably be described as nonabundant. So Ireland retained the characteristics of a Scholastically-based early Medieval community.

The Church preached support for De Valera's political agenda and the Irish Free State became the Republic of Ireland. And three generations of Irish writers left Ireland and relocated in England, France, Austria, Italy, and Switzerland. The waves of emigration toward Liverpool spoke as loudly as the virtual expulsion of writers and other artists. It takes a special kind of political talent to effectively outlaw, in his native land, James Joyce.

"national, cultural, and linguistic values" against the Internet as it is now.

At the 1996 G-7 meeting, the president of France gave a major speech in which he said the use of English as the principal language of the Internet was something the French government would not tolerate. The Russian Republic has had it with American fundamentalist "missionaries" who use a lot of net time to keep in contact with each other. The People's Republic of China has announced its intention to run a Chinese net — China's leaders already have their own problems with the electronic graffiti coming out of Hong Kong and Taiwan.

Chinese National People's Congress Deputy Chairman and 19th Vice-President Li Peiyao was sent on a one-way trip to meet his ancestors in

---

As we move into a fully formed Information Age, the first age of the cyberspace era, it is important to realize that the net is really a giant educational system that teaches users how to manage life in a data-flow culture.

To oversee dynamically shifting data requires a different kind of literacy from the Industrial Age's static, print-based environment. Earlier we considered the implications of the Industrial Age's need for a literate working class. Cheap paper, John Wesley's bible, penny-farthing newspapers, and three-penny novels provided that time with the facilities to spread reading and writing.

In light of the non-negotiable requirement for literacy in an Industrial Age economy, commercial Internet service providers should not be surprised that U.S. Vice President Gore has consistently assured anyone who listens that access to the "information highway" should be universal.

From the earliest ARPANET days, when working defense scientists had exclusive access to what is now known as the Internet, it was obvious that even the best and the brightest could be rendered perceptually dysfunctional by virtue of computer phobia. Frequently ARPANET was the major source of information about colleagues' progress in one's field. Alternatively, one could wait for a journal article 18 or so months later. This proved a strong incentive to get rid of computer phobia.

Now the net is a virtual schoolroom, comfortably located somewhere in hyperspace. This school includes a rich social life and even games designed to enhance the student's skills at dealing with the learning curve.

And just as with our own reading primers, the content is often unsophisticated compared to what we shall soon see. Criticizing the Internet's content is easy — if you know nothing about learning theory. That huge database is ideally suited to addressing the state of the individual user's learning curve. Almost certainly, history will see today's net as the point in time where we modified our data and information management skills to accommodate a quantum jump in information diversity.

early February 1995, by a burglar he surprised in his Beijing home. Who needs the net under those conditions? Better a Chinese net managed by the Bureau of Social Affairs, so that there is no confusion about who is reading your mail. Not on your life will China stand still for Phil Zimmerman's PGP encryption software being available to any jerk who wants to turn every monitor in China into a Tiananmen Square wall poster.

As for the Islamic world, many of its leaders enjoyed the spectacle of how quickly the Internet access provider CompuServe tugged its forelock for the Bavarian state prosecutor in the City of Munich, who ordered it to shut down access to parts of the net. (Then again, Islamic states don't seem to give a damn about what happened to the Spanish economy when Spain decided it was going to pass on the Renaissance because Philip II didn't think he should buy into anything that had the Reformation as part of the package.)

The Bavarian prosecutor's success came in the first week of 1996, when they convinced CompuServe to ban Internet access to pornography deemed offensive to German sensibilities. The Bavarians thereby usurped the attempts of United States Senator Exon to be the first on his block to ban Internet porn.

It's easy to understand why CompuServe would cave in at the first hint of pressure. And it's not much of a surprise that it was a Bavarian state prosecutor in Munich who said providing global access to what appeared to be 200 sex activity-related newsgroups was a violation of German law, particularly laws to protect minors. Munich was, after all, the place where Hitler got the Nazi party off to a such a swell start in a beer cellar. Munich was also where the Nazis held their first book-burnings. Bavaria is the German state whose most noteworthy past ruler was Mad King Ludwig, who built all of those fairy-land castles that inspired Michael Jackson's adventures in architecture as an attraction for children. He also bankrupted Bavaria, an event focal to the establishment of Germany as a nation state that used a Prussian model to establish a new national identity.

Let's think about this. The current Bavarian state prosecutor's predecessors couldn't figure out what to do when the head of state was suffering from a severe mental illness and the state was slithering into insolvency. A later state prosecutor's office cooperated in implementing Nazi legislation affecting Jews, gays, retarded people, gypsies, and Lutheran ministers named Dietricht Bonhoeffer (who was executed by hanging in Flossenbuerg, a concentration camp conveniently just south of Munich, in Bavaria), besides employing pyromania as a tool of literary criticism. This track record entitles them to chose what the rest of the world can see and read?

(Or maybe someone at the U.S. Department of Justice just wanted to see who would yell about censoring something without a statutory authority.

Why not try getting the State Department to lean on our gallant and thinkalike good friends and allies in the Bavarian state prosecutor's office? But this kind of paranoia ill befits the intellectual and sensitive nature of readers of this book.)

One wonders what steps CompuServe will take when some really pissed-off Islamic Imam who reads the legal news realizes that here's a precedent he can use because he wants CompuServe to delete any pictures of women who aren't wearing chadors. Or when said Imam's competitor from the minaret down the street says he wants all information from the Scottish single-malt whiskey web site expunged so as not to contaminate the eyeballs of the faithful, or he'll lay a *fatwah* on the CEO.

Let's assume we should ban access to pornography on computer-based information services. But given the amount of data that exists on the Internet there is no way for an Internet provider to check what is out there manually, although another large commercial Internet service provider, America Online, has been trying.

The system operator will have to check electronically. That means using a search algorithm that finds offensive words. These exist. One could even write another algorithm that would spot pictures of genitals. (No more pictures of the Logitech twins peeing?) To do it effectively, you would have to be running that software all of the time on everything.

Consider the effect of this on a medical service that uses the Internet to offer physicians in communities without a top-flight oncologist access to timely expert opinions on cervical and breast cancer. All its data transfers will be ripped open by the censors. Given the history of censorship world-wide, there will be leaks of these legitimate medical images. Wouldn't some of the tabloids pay well for those pictures of a celebrity? It shouldn't take long for the image processor to decide to stop the electronic transfer of data.

This has already happened in one case. It's not that they were doing anything illegal, it's the explaining they have to do when all the would-be censors get checking up on them. The same holds true for a medical publisher's e-mail. Don't forget, every cop agency from local sheriffs to the Feds sees the Internet kiddie-porn industry as a source of relief from the budget slashers.

The Inquisition and its Protestant equivalents agreed that it was that it was better to "let 100 innocents be burned lest one heretic escape and go free." Hitler, who thought the Inquisition were sissies, failed to understand the economic implications of censorship, which can bankrupt a country and lose a war. South Africa learned that being isolated had a downside. That's why South Africa is one of the more open countries now.

CompuServe and America Online managers are right in line to join the "good Germans" who were "only obeying orders." Do you really trust that prosecutor in Munich not to let 100 women with cancer die from neglect rather then chance one porn-pusher going free?

THE DICTATOR'S FRIEND

If there was ever any doubt that censorship is counter-productive, the development of science in the Renaissance showed those involved in intellectual activities that it was not a luxury any country with aspirations to survival could afford.

Nevertheless, as various countries experimented with authoritarianism in the early years of the 20th century, the idea that censorship is not regressive was played out again and again. In the Stalinist Soviet Union, the attempt to promote the wretched Lysenko's theories about evolution showed that Russia, having missed the Reformation, was clinging to a world in which Byzantium had never fallen as a refuge for political legitimacy. It was this failure to absorb the lessons of the Renaissance which doomed the Russian Revolution of 1917 to repeat the absolutism of the Tsar and ensured that neither the government nor the country at large would have any way to absorb and distribute amendments to conventional wisdoms and assumptions about the nature of of the world.

Similarly, when Germany chose to deal with its post-World War I economic debacle by electing a government that was so anti-intellectual that its racist policies had the effect of driving its scientific community away, it had failed to learn the lesson of the Renaissance: that authoritarian governments are economic disasters.

Both Hitler's Germany and the U.S.S.R. bequeathed by Lenin to Stalin depended on a wide-ranging policy of censorship to hide the weakness of the state and to demonize the state's foes, whether real or appointed. The Marxists and the Nazis both made the mistake of insisting on an agenda that used economic theories to address problems that had more to do with the world-view of their respective societies being out of sync with the discoveries of the world's scientific communities in the first 20 years of the century.

It is ironic that Hitler's one-issue politics of anti-Semitism caused him react against the "Jewish ideas" of Einstein and insist that Germany's science be "cleansed of Jewish pollution." German science had been the cutting edge of a new era in history, but Hitler's referents were all Medieval. His anti-intellectualism, his brutality, and his dependence on charismatic leadership were all traits we would expect from an Otto I, a Charlemagne, a Rudolf of Switzerland — or Frederick II, sitting out the onset of the Renaissance in Sicily without a care in the world.

THE CORPORATE INQUISITION

In 1962, *The New Yorker* magazine published a book called *Silent Spring*. The book anticipated Love Canal and other eco-disasters that have since come to fruition. The issue sold a lot of magazines, and *The New Yorker* almost went bankrupt because corporate America's ad agencies responded with an advertising boycott. As we know, *The New Yorker* survived. But it was a close thing.

In 1995, Bruce Necht, a *Wall Street Journal* reporter, heard stories that Chrysler Corporation wanted magazines to provide advance warning of editorial content that might be offensive or provocative. (*The Wall Street Journal* used to be a dowdy little rag until it was purchased by Dow Jones, an outfit with years of experience in writing reports that were the epitome

---

When the People's Republic of China discovered the BBC World Service was saying rude things about the late Chairman Mao's less than conventional sexual proclivities, they quickly cleared up the Australian-born media mogul Rupert Murdoch's failure to understand George Orwell's place in the new level of abstraction.

Murdoch got into the mess first because he made a speech to some advertisers on September 1, 1993, in which he said Orwell had gotten it all wrong. Orwell thought high-tech communications would help authoritarian governments crush the masses even more than usual. In his little pep talk, Rupert pushed the idea that fax machines made it possible for latter-day samizdat dissidents to out-publish the dreary propaganda of government-controlled print media, while direct-dial telephones made it really inconvenient for the security forces to maintain proper one-on-one surveillance. The final zinger was his assertion that satellite TV beats cable hands down because you could thumb your nose at those control freaks who run government-controlled TV stations.

Murdoch's Star TV service covers Asia by satellite, just as his Sky 1 and Sky 2 services blanket Europe. What he was suggesting to advertisers was that you could sell anything without interference from authoritarian governments. Rupert would probably accept booze ads for broadcast in Iran.

This was where the prime minister of China. said "watch how fast I can make it a jailing offence to own a satellite receiving dish." It was about this time that Rupert learned he could become a New-Age sensitive guy because he felt the prime minister's pain so much that he turfed the BBC off Star TV.

Since Murdoch's partner in Star TV is the Hong Kong multi-zillionaire Li Ka-shing, who is well-regarded in the corridors of Chinese power, Murdoch may have thought Mr. Li could get the prime minister off his back. The Chinese bureaucrats are still on Murdoch's back and while Murdoch and Li will probably swing it in the end, it won't be without more pain than Murdoch likes to put up with.

of offensive and provocative, if terms like "fly-by-night" and "world-class expertise in Chapter 11" qualify. A lot of leaders of corporate America have read a Dow Jones report and saved themselves from looking stupid.)

According to people who know Mr. Necht, he has an inquiring mind, and his curiosity got the better of him. Necht became curious about what constituted "provocative or offensive" editorial content in the minds of guys who had a string of used car lots in their corporate quiver. What he found was that Chrysler's ad agency had written a letter on January 30, 1996, that said "In an effort to avoid potential conflicts it is required that Chrysler Corporation be alerted in advance of all editorial content that encompasses sexual, political, social issues or any editorial that might be construed as provocative or offensive." Further research revealed that Chrysler spends about $U.S. 270 million a year to flog its cars and trucks.

Necht discovered that many similar letters had been sent to the leading U.S. magazines by the ad agencies of America's corporate elite. He discovered, for example, that Ford's executives were pretty challenged by *The New Yorker* when a full page advertisement for the Lincoln Mercury division ran adjacent to a "Talk of the Town" piece that quoted explicitly and caustically sexual lines from the lyrics of the musical ensemble Nine Inch Nails.

Necht's list grew and grew. The tobacco industry and the booze barons want warnings about abusers of their products being profiled and showed particular sensitivity to Jerry Garcia's high-profile death. Baby telcos like Bell South and Ameritech turned up on the list, along with Foot Joy Worldwide and the makers of Titleist golf balls. Necht found that Robert Mancini at J. Walter Thomson was willing to mouth off, for the record, about Ford's squeamish attitude toward Nine Inch Nails. (Are the tires on Lincolns and Mercurys particularly vulnerable to that length of nail?)

The list of advertisers and agencies who wished to be given advance warning was getting pretty long and it was spring in New York, so the *Wall Street Journal* went with what it had. And so should we, but before leaving the estimable Bruce Necht, et al., we should remind them that the next time they feel inclined to extend their philological vision, they might look up the words "Faustian" and "hubris."

CHAPTER TWENTY

A New Kind of World: a new kind of literacy

Future historians will probably describe the half-century since 1945 as the Golden Age of an era which began with the Renaissance and its Mercantile Age, played intellectual catch-up with the Age of Reason, and encompassed the Industrial Age.

This Golden Age was the highest point to which the human race could climb with an amended world-view based on the one that accommodated the discovery of perspective, a numeracy "borrowed" from the Arabs (who had "borrowed" it from India and China), and new mathematics that bred sophisticated navigation and accounting tools. These made global trade commonplace, financed through an incredibly abstract invention: the bill of exchange.

The quantum jump in the level of abstraction, which included perspective and the bill of exchange, was principally implemented in the Mercantile Age. An amended world-view was installed as the profits from the Mercantile Age were used to capitalize the beginnings of Industrial Age, arguably beginning in 1750.

The Renaissance world-view was amended — and it was only an amendment — to accommodate the emerging Industrial Age. The new world-view was, at best, a patchwork piece of business. The political disasters of authoritarianism during a period of increasing individualization became the great contradiction of the first half of the 20th century. Those who allowed their countries to adopt an authoritarian form of government paid a brutal price for getting the trains to run on time.

As the 20th century unfolded, it became increasingly clear that the patchwork world-view of the industrialized West was becoming increasingly dysfunctional because it took Laplace's embellishment of Newton and attempted to account for all events by simplistic, linear cause and effect. In 1900, a new world-view came under construction with Hilbert's 23 problems and Planck's quantum theory. This world-view received another major component in 1915 with Einstein's theory of relativity, and was nearly completed in 1926 with Heisenberg's uncertainty principle and, finally, the discovery by Heisenberg, Schrödinger and Dirac of quantum mechanics.

Golden ages tend to be relatively short-lived. The Golden Age of Greece is identified with a short period of the life of one man — Pericles. Typically golden ages tend to live off the products of their forbears. Ours is now over.

Now, those of us whose culture is based in the traditions of Western European values get another kick at the can. This is the value-add we get for grabbing the brass ring of the Industrial Age. We in North America are immensely better off than any part of Europe was during the Renaissance. We have a great strength in the biodiversity of our gene pool. Diets in industrialized countries are relatively healthy. Even more significant, for the short-run, is the cultural diversities of populations that have a widely accessible public and post-secondary education systems.

But this does not mean we automatically get to initiate the high point of the cyberspace era. On the contrary, because we are carrying so much baggage (and our leaders carry even more), the probability that we can maintain the pace into next breakthrough diminishes significantly.

Even if we do bring on the next level of the new era, the probabilities of it being we who will make the major implementations are slim. England,

---

There are a number of steps we go through before an abstraction becomes concrete. The first step is to "name" something that is only an idea.

For example, think of our word "blue." For us, the colour blue comes in many shades and hues. (colour theorists regard cobalt blue as the "most blue" of all because there are fewer reds in its spectrum, but computers can generate thousands of different blues.) We know what another English-speaking person means when they say "my new shirt is blue" and even what they mean when they say "I'm feeling blue." Imagine trying to describe "blue" to someone who has been blind since birth.

The early Greeks were the first Europeans to "name" blue, a pigment that was, for them, hard to come by. Their source of blue pigmenting material was lapis lazuli, a light blue gem and pigment the Greeks got from Egypt. They originally referred to this scarce material by a word which has come down to us as ultramarine, meaning "on the other side of the sea," because they got it from the other side of the Mediterranean. So where did our word "blue" come from?

The word "blue" in its various forms is common to all the European languages — except that in its root it means yellow. "Blue" in its basic root refers to something bright and light, as in a light sky. Over the years, since blue is a light colour, it came to mean blue as we know it.

the country where the Industrial Age began, was on the outer reaches of the Renaissance.

In the 1550s, two decades after Henry VIII's dissolution of the monasteries, one-fifth of the nation's land was up for sale, and England's merchants and lawyers were eager buyers. If one of the new wealthy class aspired to politics, he would read "the murderous Machiavelli." For those after the social cachet of being gentlemen, there was a delicate volume known as *The Courtier* which bred over a dozen imitative discourses, many in the form of letters from a fond father to a son. (How-to books aren't exactly new.)

England's poets and playwrights borrowed shamelessly from Italian writers, while scholars mined the rich ore of the European Humanists. The English language changed, as borrowed words from those countries in the forefront of invention and ideas were tacked onto English. There was little in the way of original thought, but if King Henry VIII could be educated by Erasmus of Rotterdam, then Shakespeare, Marlowe, Decker, and Middleton could borrow a plot or two.

This nation of secondary sourcers was not a country that would have been expected to move into the number one spot. But from the days when Henry VII had the bright idea to subsidize the English merchant navy with money budgeted for the navy, the English had their eyes firmly on the ball labeled "trade and commerce."

INQUIRING MINDS SURVIVE

Inquiring minds survive era transitions. Have you learned to enjoy understanding the implementations of the new era? When someone at your place of work wants to resist implementation of a new technology, do you join in the resistance, or do you recognize an opportunity to learn? Do you recognize an inappropriate technology when you see one? Does the tax structure of your country encourage invention and new enterprises?

If you work for a branch of a multinational company, does it have a product development mandate and a manufacturing mandate? Does your employer encourage employees to acquire new skills? (It is more efficient to promote internally than to recruit from outside the organization, but not if the promoted employee carries a load of baggage that makes her/him the corporate antiquarian.)

Do *not* associate with losers. If the company you work for is not actively ready to change, what are you doing working there? No one escapes the impact of an era transition.

How good are you at understanding what is going on in the world? Did you really believe that the collapse of the Soviet Union would produce a "peace dividend?" In the absence of a peace dividend, do you feel your leaders have betrayed you? Do you believe that your country will not lose much sovereignty, especially losses unanticipated by your government's negotiators, if your nation joins a new trading bloc? Do you believe that it is possible to return to a more stable world based on familiar truths? Do you believe that it is important to right old wrongs, such as fighting your tribe's ancient enemies?

If you believe or believed any of the above, your personal epistemology is seriously flawed.

The message of this book is that an era transition is not something you can manage or guide. The most you can do is discover its properties and try to understand its various implementations. Keep your eyes open for the ways those properties can make the world a little better for all of us. If you can make a bit of money implementing the new level of abstraction, so much the better. Having money will help you cope with those parts of the shift which may be unpleasant.

Each era transition carries the seeds of its own destruction. It is only at the beginning of an era shift that any integrity (as in classical Greek philosophical use of the word "quality") can be established. As soon as the era gets openly under way, the compromises begin. If the quality of the era can be enhanced at the beginning, our great (plus) grandchildren might get another couple of hundred years out of this era we're installing now. So you can actually do something, at this time in history. You're not just putting in time.

An era transition is a time of discovery. If you do not participate in that discovery process you are just a waste of carbon at a time when the human race is changing its assumptions about the nature of our place in the universe. It is the time when we humans push back the walls holding off chaos a bit more and flex our non-deterministic minds once again.

It's also more fun to be part of the change process than to trying to play at being the little Dutch boy with a finger in the dike — especially when the whole sea-wall has collapsed.

An era transition occurs because of a quantum jump in the level of abstraction, which happens because the previous level of abstraction can no longer account for the facts of the known world. (The level of abstraction can also be expressed as the world-view or the conventional wisdom.) This results in a complete shift in the course of human events. When this shift has happened we are in, to quote the Renaissance cartographers, *terra incognita*. We can no longer treat the future as an orderly extrapolation of the present.

This era transition began in 1900 and was fully in place by 1929. We are now participants in the era of cyberspace, hyperspace, N-space, or the Relativistic Era, or whatever name historians of the future assign to it.

Our leaders fumble in this unfamiliar territory, while seemingly contradictory information make us think that our world and our lives have turned to chaos. Demagogues will try to seduce us with short-term solutions that feed their own fragile egos.

The equations that would allow reasonably effective modelling of the problems we face are of such complexity that they remind us we are unprepared to face such a time. Experience is a harsh, imprecise, and brutal teacher. Yet this is the time when we must select which lessons we can pass on to future generations — who, if we are even marginally successful, will live in a gentler time than ours.

This is the only time in which we can build quality into the new era. Only in the fresh foundations of the new period is it possible to establish values, so we should ensure they are positive values. That is why it is important to resist the stifling despotisms which are offered at this stage of a historical epoch. It is also important to learn how to be strong, so we are not a burden on those who love us. There are no surpluses during an era transition.

There are many pitfalls in any new era. A familiarity with history teaches us to accept nothing without question. Humans don't succeed when they try to build utopias or dystopias. Humans succeed when they create something *better* than that constructed by previous generations.

HOW THINGS FALL APART

In our time, while our traditional institutions are battered by economic, political and social instabilities, their flaws are becoming increasingly obvious. For those who insist on benchmarks, let's look at the collapse of the Medieval world in the middle of the 14th century.

These years saw the revolts of the Ciompi in Italy, the Peasant's Revolt of Wat Tyler in England, and the weavers and cobblers of Ghent in Flanders. The Church was confronted with the Lollard movement, John Wyclif, Jan Hus, and a lot of other like-thinkers who introduced the novel idea that the Church needed reforming.

The European territorial state, which had supplanted the city state, had demonstrated its ability to deliver an effective centralized political, military, judicial, and administrative government. Now this territorial state was, in turn, being superseded by the the nation state.

The first European territorial state, founded by Alexander the Great, was based economically on conquest, not productivity. At the beginning of the Renaissance, the leading class was a warrior cult typified by mercenaries like the White Company, who propped up a chivalrous knighthood inherited from the Middle Ages. As the Renaissance's world-view came into being, these knights tried to retain their myths, but they were soon overturned by new classes.

The journeymen were products of guild-administered apprentice systems and, unlike the ordinary Medieval person, they enjoyed mobility and political influence through the guild chapter house to which they were attached. Merchants, lawyers, and other members of the emerging middle class were similarly able to influence the aristocratic political leaders because of the increasing tax base they controlled. The nobility held land of diminishing worth and increasing overhead, which was particularly at risk from periodic labour shortages due to Plague and illnesses caused by poor sanitation and non-existent personal hygiene — diseases whose causes were completely beyond the "medicine" of the time.

In spite of laws against leaving work on the land to move to the cities, the migration to urban employment was steady. (One other factor, which would be politically unpopular to study today, is that we can assume that this rural-to-urban migration had a detrimental effect on the rural gene pool — which has been borne out by modern genetics research. It was the more venturesome and brighter people who were motivated to escape hard and monotonous work on the land.)

The growing cities, with their demands and opportunities to take advantage of the enhanced level of abstraction, drew the more innately intelligent rural population, who would be happily challenged by the enriched urban environment. Once a bonded person escaped from the manor's control, he was pretty safe from recapture unless he ran afoul of the law. Even then, municipalities would usually turn a blind eye, since their need for labour far exceeded any sense that they should return an eloped villein to some noble 20 or 30 miles away.

The warrior class — the knights — were corrupted and decimated by ruinously extravagant wars. By the end of the 1300s, not only were most of Europe's knighthood unfit to fight, but even their horses were fat and overfed. The knights had become softened by the good life as part of the minor aristocracy in a closed-loop society. Meanwhile their rulers, in their perpetual quest for cash, were knighting merchants and even, heaven help us, government administrators.

The adoption by the European knights of the new heavy plate armor has been too frequently discounted by commentators. The fact is that plate armor was a technology that didn't work — if a knight were to be unseated while wearing it, it was difficult to rise without assistance. Pages attended their lords on the battlefield to support them, and there are countless cases of knights dying from heart attacks brought on by the heat from the sun in the new armor. Dysfunction from exhaustion was the rule rather than the exception. One of the things we should all remember — which is essential to surviving an era transition — is that new technologies may not only fail to work, but some applications may even be a retrograde step.

The economic base of the territorial state was in land, which lacked the potential for revenues that lay in middle class ventures such as banking and activities related to trade and technical productivity. In the face of diminished revenues the custodians of the knighthood myth were unable to sustain it.

The lack of substance to the knighthood myth became obvious at the battles of Crecy, Poitiers, and the Crusade of 1396 against the Turks at Nicopolis. At Agincourt in 1415, the defeat of the numerically superior French nobility by Henry V's English yeomen confirmed that European knighthood had lost its ability to protect manorial property. The English mounted nobility did not play a significant role at Agincourt, as the flower of European nobility was annihilated by Henry's commoners.

Each new revolt, whether politically or religiously based, further demonstrated the inability of the warrior class to maintain public order and to play a meaningful role the delivery of effective government. With the increased urbanization of the state, other forces emerged that were better able to manage the new political climate.

Together with the merchants of the expanding cities, masters and artisans had gained physical mobility and lost their connection to the waning feudal social structure and the manorial economy. The bourgeoisie, the newly strengthened and stabilized middle class, were the only ones with money to pay the expenses of government. They were less and less amused to watch the wealth they created go to support an increasingly parasitic class that wasted funds that could be better employed elsewhere.

Every popular revolt of the time was a consequence of a breach of the social contract by the Church and nobility. None succeeded — not Wat Tyler, not the Lollards, not the Jacques in France nor the *popolo minuto* of Florence. But the Protestant movement of Wyclif and Hus laid foundations for others to question a Church whose affiliations with the manorial economy blinded it to the powerful new world-view that was shifting power from the nobility to the middle class.

Throughout this book, the New World Order of George Bush has been, admittedly, used as a "straw man" to portray a political and economic constituency who represent, in historical terms, the same constituency as the Medieval Scholastics, Roman Catholic Church and Holy Roman Empire — basically, the feudal power elite who lived in manors with the comfort levels of a drafty barn.

In other words, the NWO has been a metaphor for a part of society that believes it represents the forces of order, decency, fiscal probity, rectitude, and administrative competence, and whose right to govern is, by an obscure natural law, claimed as their reward for having defeated the Evil Empire of International Communism.

Gutenberg's movable type spread the new world-view at a speed unimagined by the Medieval minds of the establishment. The nobility and clerical orders had little conceptual access to the marketing systems which arose from the new printing technologies. It is a big leap for a Medieval mind, accustomed to acquiring a "fair copy" of a book, laboriously hand-copied by a monk, to imagine 500 copies of a book turned out on a press and made inexpensively available through public markets and fairs. Feudal-minded leaders could not comprehend the speed with which information started to move through Europe.

With the collapse of its world-view, the Medieval universe went into self-destruct mode. By the year 1500, the Renaissance was in full flower.

DANGEROUS TIMES

While having the Renaissance backdrop to our own time is useful, we are still faced with paradoxical events — things that happen when our predictive tools fail. For example, when the drug Thalidomide was given to gravid women, there was a high probability of fetal damage — children were born with deformities of the limbs. When someone is taking some anti-depressant medications and eats cheese or barbecued meat or drinks wine, there is a possibility of elevation of blood pressure to the point of death.

These pharmacological problems display the kind of obscure interactions with which we have no historical experience. But addressing problems like these will become easier as the intensification of computing speed and density delivers new power that will change the ways we use computers.

Computer literacy is part of survival in the new era. The uses of virtual reality data management systems will be focal to understanding the complexities of the new era. It is these complexities which will result in the collapse of the more familiar political systems. Most of our contemporary political models simply won't respond to the multiple diversities that will change the priorities of our lives. This means that our school systems will have to deliver some kind of appreciation of mathematics beyond algebra and calculus. High schools in North America will have to find their way into chaos theory, if we want to start using strange attractor algorithms in data management software.

The potential for disaster — the ordinary kind of disaster — is increasing in our time because of the increase in the amount of materials or information being controlled. Accidents on the order of a train crash spilling a load of volatile chemicals, a transient bug in a computer program that is managing a nuclear reactor, a faulty computer chip in a weapons system, the crash of an aircraft flying over a crowded city, or the inadvertent release of toxic waste from an industrial factory in a densely populated area, are bound to increase.

Today, computer systems lead in the employment of cyberspace. But no matter how much redundancy is built into software solutions, the human factor is always present. One of the benefits of automating many routine jobs is that the processes can control far greater and more wide-ranging events than the antecedent mechanical procedures. When the automated procedures fail, for whatever reason, the result is usually more catastrophic than we, who were brought up in the late Industrial Age, have been socialized to accept.

Because industrial managers, regulatory officials, and politicians don't understand the vulnerabilities of such control systems, they are willing to cut corners they don't understand *are* corners because they didn't learn to appreciate the mathematics driving the world when they were in high school.

We can accept 200 dead and injured in a train wreck as part of the price of having a railroad system with passenger cars that carry more people than do stage coaches. Human error is comprehensible, but the horror-show that was triggered by a Union Carbide employee turning the wrong valve and releasing clouds of chlorine gas on the factory's neighbourhood slums in Bhopal, India, is more than we thought we had bargained for.

The achievements of science and technology do not suggest any kind of infallibility among scientists and technologists. Since the beginning of nuclear energy, engineers have always duly noted whenever some electrical utility wished to build a new nuclear-powered generating station, that nuclear plants have a productive life cycle of 40 years. After that, the place will be "too hot" to use. If pressed, the engineers would admit that there is no technology which would enable them to dismantle the radioactive site. Privately, they admit that there is no hope of such a technology on the horizon. Publicly they claim that, before the proposed plant has reached its

---

The insurance industry is aware of new forms of risk, and tries to avoid the level of liability they pose. Space missions, often loaded with satellites, have found it increasingly difficult to obtain insurance. The cost of the launch vehicle, plus the cost of the payload, along with the infrequency of launches, defies the mystical forecasts of the actuary. Making such insurance actuarially sound is impossible because there are too few events to provide a valid sample of the risk level.

In August 1993, a Titan launch missile blew up two minutes into its journey with a payload of three satellites. The satellites were the last of a series used by the American CIA to watch the Soviet fleet. A number of U.S. congressmen were less than amused when the bill of $2 billion (roughly a billion for the launch vehicle and a billion for the satellites) was reported. One congressman was quoted thus: "We know where the Russian fleet is. It's rusting in its harbours."

40-year benchmark, fusion will be commercially feasible — so the dismantling question is academic.

Around the world there is an increasing glut of mothballed nuclear facilities, each awaiting the arrival of the technology to dismantle it; a technology which is as distant as ever. Think about all those rusting Soviet nuclear subs, beached, with their nuclear reactor cores intact (maybe).

What this means as we enter a new era is that the optimum sizes for political or institutional structures will become much smaller than we might have expected. The appropriate size of an organization will be defined by its *manageability*.

TRADE — THE ONCE AND FUTURE FLASHPOINT

Trade is a fundamental part of human existence. Simply put, trade is what we do when we take a product, raw material, or service which, hopefully, is surplus to our needs and sell it to someone else.

When trade gets more complicated, as in multinational trade pacts, we try to establish rules of foreign trade. Because of differences in culture, law, language, financial systems, and social values, there are inevitably disputes about trading rules. Sometimes these trade disputes are insoluble, and nations become very angry with one another.

A few years ago, the government of France was trying very hard to protect its family farms by paying high subsidies to support the food produced on these farms. The U.S., Canada, Australia, and other countries argued in the negotiations of the General Agreement on Tariffs and Trade that their food trade was being unfairly discriminated against. The French looked to their European Union partners to help defend the position, which has been a contentious point since the first days of the European Common Market, the predecessor to the E.U. France also became the E.U. point for protection from the American film and TV industries.

Obviously, if the globe is to be divided into regional trading zones, the stakes become much higher. The final GATT meetings in Geneva did produce an agreement on food. Belgian farmers rioted, Canadian farmers' pleasure at being able to export into the E.U. was muted at the prospect of a wind-up of the country's marketing boards and an onslaught of U.S. farm products, and French police agencies prepared for more riots from French family farmers. A change in the global rice marketing agreement strategy sent Japanese and Korean officials off to consult their riot police.

In most countries media coverage of the GATT was sparse. The agreement is so complex that print media have a difficult time getting it in one-syllable words, while the TV folks' traditional 30-second sound-bites lose their flavour unless they have pictures of farmers dumping manure at the base of a national monument or burning excess crops. Fans of the economist Lester

Thurow would argue that it was all academic anyway (see chapter 21).

The final success of the GATT and its successor, the World Trade Organization, is not necessarily good. Medium-sized and small countries discovered that the E.U., NAFTA, and Japan Inc. now carry much more weight than they had imagined would come down, and that their concerns were not even getting a passing glance.

Whether this deal will work minimally, or at all, is still problematical. What happens when one of the three trading blocs gets into a confrontation with the others? Japan is very strong in aid and other foot-in-the-door ventures in South America, where the Monroe Doctrine does not address an Asian intruder.

At the present, these three trading blocs are well matched for resources of the type which count today. But the tools to stabilize them are not evident.

All three have serious vulnerabilities. One event that points up the short-fuse potential is that all three trading blocs have taken a leaf out of the Cold War book and begun entering into client-state relationships with smaller nations, e.g. the E.U. and Eastern Europe, or the NAFTA group and the Caribbean and South America, or Japan and the populous mini-states of southeast Asia, as well as South America.

Alternatively, the main event could happen while the world wrestles with the dual environmental crisis of the whole place heating up (not only metaphorically) and a lot of people being buried because they are tanning challenged. The worst possible case is not that North America loses, the worst possible case is that none of these global trading partnerships works.

It may well be rational to assume that the new currency of the E.U., the euro, will provide a stable and trustworthy financial system. But pollsters have reported that citizens of Britain and Germany do not believe the euro is, or ever will be, "real money."

If citizens don't trust the euro, it stands to reason that they will change their euros into something that they do trust. Will it be gold? Not likely. How about American Express cheques? Nope, Amex is not a nation state and would freak if the float became that big — it would lose effective control of its paper, and the investment community would dump its stock and bonds.

Then how about good old U.S. dollars? They're easily changeable for goods and services all over the world, more acceptable than Amex, and readily counterfeited.

And what would it be like to run the weekly T-bill auction when no one had the slightest idea what the American M1 money supply actually was? Has anyone at the U.S. Treasury thought about what could happen if the people of Europe resist the euro?

This is the most complex global economic environment the world has ever seen. In the history of armed conflict, things often seem to get out of hand as a result of apparently innocuous events that are the culmination of a long series of "irritants." For example, delegations to many non-governmental organizations usually vote as their governments direct them to. World fairs are much sought after by cities worldwide, and the organization responsible is the *Bureau International des Expositions*. If the E.U. members advanced a policy set down in Brussels, other states might claim the E.U. was over-represented with 10 (or more) votes when the Maastricht agreement, with its common foreign policy provisions, means the historic votes of individual member states are no longer valid.

The E.U. members would still have to deal with their own electorate and their hometown fans. This becomes an international Catch-22, because the complaining states would have hometown problems too. A succession of such problems could result in international disputes of significant dimensions. The scenarios are endless.

WHY WE NEED TO KNOW WHAT WE KNOW

At this time, the most important questions for humans appear to be *how do we know what we know?* and *is what we know truth?* Questions about the general acceptance of our tribe's creation myth and what happens to us after death do not compare with the issues posed by our theory of knowledge, although they're effectively the same problem.

A theory of knowledge allows you to test new information before you incorporate it into the conventional wisdom. While it may seem pretty esoteric, and has limited value for telling us how to cure cancer, or improve our living standard without adding to the national debt, this theory of knowledge guides all of our political and moral management. How we know something to be true or false determines how we incorporate new events into our lives.

For example, currently there is a strong interest in research on aging. The baby boomers now understand that too many pension plans are not actuarially sound. Most government pension plans are invested in low- or no-interest capital projects with the idea that the next generation will make the pay-outs for the previous generation. With declining birth or immigration rates, it is unlikely that our children will be thrilled with this idea. (Isn't it time that the life of Ponzi be made required reading for every civil servant or politician?)

Realistically, few of us can expect to experience the "retirement picture" painted by personnel managers explaining an employer's pension plan or the advertisements of insurance companies.

Research on arresting the aging process will bear fruit in the next five decades. Information being generated by research on AIDS, cancer, et cetera, is providing some solid direction to investigators in the field of aging. Of course, friends of the Third World will wind up the guilt machine, but for now, the research vectors are so basic that no one, not even the scientists, knows why they are getting all those swell grants.

People in the nanotechnology business understand this one. That's why they talk about gene repair machines as being imminent. If you think we have a crazy breakdown in the capability of individuals and institutions to respond to the early signs of the era shift, wait until some nanotechnologist announces that the average life span has just become 150 years.

Back to the theory of knowledge — epistemology. If we can increase life spans to 150 years, should we do it? If such a life span increment were possible, what do we *know* about the effects of such a change from the biblical three-score and 10? In the Industrial Age, our theory of knowledge didn't have to be strong enough to deal with scientific breakthroughs of that level.

The congruent epistemology of an industrial society uses extrapolative models quite effectively. But the potential for disaster in changing the mean age requires a stronger epistemology. Think of all the information that goes into a decision of this complexity. And think of the consequences if we make the wrong choice.

PANIC IN THE PREDICTION MARKET

Prediction, in the kind of an environment described in this book, is not an activity for the faint-hearted. Fortunately, neither Lord William Rees-Mogg, former editor of the *Times* of London, nor James Dale Davidson, founder of U.S. National Taxpayers' Union, who normally are the principal writers of the thriving *Investors' Monthly*, have the slightest hint of cardiac giddiness. In 1987 they published *Blood on the Streets: Investment Profit in a World Gone Mad* and managed to predict the collapse of the U.K., U.S., and Canadian real estate markets. They also forecast the U.S. savings and loan imbroglio.

In early 1992, their publisher released their latest screed, *The Great Reckoning: How the World Will Change in the Depression of the 1990s*. Given that Rees-Mogg's and Davidson's record of getting it right from time to time in both their earlier book and their monthly tip sheet, it was worth looking at the new set of predictions.

Besides, they also provide an uncensored glimpse of the assumptions under which the self-described right-wing elite of the Anglo-Saxon life-force conduct their lives.

Their predictions are pretty hard-line, based on what they call "non-linear" thinking. (That's the same as tangential thinking, I think.) They use a strategy that, they say, gives them access to a "three-dimensional land-scape," which is better than the viewpoints held by conventional gurus. (So far, so good)

They are convinced, with a lot of supporting data, that there are cycles which run about 500 years in length. (OK so far — there has been one cycle.) These cycles, they argue, begin with major paradigm shifts in productivity, after which the political process regurgitates a new political power-base. They say that the last such political flip was what they want to call the "Gunpowder Revolution", which resulted in the European worldview becoming the prevailing version of what was right and proper. (It sounds like they missed a step here.)

Then they say that following World War II, the United States replaced Britain as the king of the castle, but that didn't involve much change in policy. They argue that the next shift is due to the production achievements of Japan Inc. Hence, their conclusion that a new shift is on, from the U.S. to Japan.

They also want us to believe that the American economy, with its horrific debt-inflated condition, is headed for the big collapse. They expect that the big money-centre U.S. banks will go belly-up; that inner-city Hispanic and black youth gangs will get it on with vigilantes; and that the state and federal governments will get into mass layoffs and firings — which, no doubt, will gladden the hearts of all those card-carrying members of the National Taxpayers' Union.

The folks who still have some cash will abandon the great cities, elite cores, and suburbs to head for those idyllic rural towns that still have basic essential services. (Sounds like people in the late 1960s and early 1970s who believed the rural life was ideal for growing pot and selling it back to the cities that had hassled them into the rural life.) They believe that taxes will go wild, especially for the wealthy, and real estate prices will collapse. In this scenario the poor will have to work for subsistence welfare while fundamentalist religion becomes a growth industry.

The U.S. will be damaged worse than Britain in 1946 or Germany in the 1930s. Internationally, according to Davidson and Rees-Mogg, if Canada stays together, it will be marginally better off than the U.S. Most of C.I.S. states will become fascist. Islamic theocracies will pop up all over the Middle East and Israel will be in jeopardy.

The two authors claim to be optimists, but their thesis is severely flawed. If they want to go "non-linear" in their thinking and treat data as "three-dimensional," they need a bit more experience in cyberspace.

Nations engaged in realpolitik ask only one question of a nation with whom they would engage in some form of warfare. That question is: "What is it you have that we want?" In the unstable world of the 1990s we should wonder — how many nations are asking this of us?

They have not accounted for the roots of the era transition of the Renaissance, which happened 500 years ago. They also fail to acknowledge the increment in the level of abstraction.

They also have, apparently, little understanding of the internal cultural contradictions under which Japan functions. The March, 1992, decline of the Japanese securities market and its sluggish response to that decline suggest that to give the new crown to Japan is probably premature.

Japan's computer industry has not done very well. Its patent library is sparse (even its laptop computers are highly dependent on American patents). Japan has yet to produce any world-class software. The written Japanese language creates severe difficulties in computerizing administrative functions. Even the largest Japanese trading companies use fewer computers than you would find in a western company. This is important because it means that in Japan and other calligraphy-based nations, a significantly lower proportion of the population has daily hands-on experience with computers.

Japan is probably pushed to its productivity limits now, and the North American recession of 1990-94 caused a breakdown in the "engine" that has fuelled the Japanese economy. Japanese trade bureaucrats have encouraged direct investment in Asia, and it is probably not unreasonable to expect that Japan will concentrate on developing and managing its Asian-Pacific clients/partners.

Japanese banks are capitalized differently than are Western banks — most of the capital of the so-called super banks is in the form of equity in Japan's large trading companies. When Japanese industry has to drop its prices below the profit point simply to maintain market representation, life becomes complex. When the trading companies release their annual reports, the banks have to adjust their stock-based capitalization. This loss of capitalization could cause more than one of the largest banks to be found to be insolvent.

Davidson and Rees-Mogg failed to alert their readers to this potentially fatal flaw in the economic structure of Japan Inc. More important, they disregarded North America's culturally built-in capacity for renewal.

In writing off America, the authors neglected to account for the North American culture's enthusiasm for innovation. They failed to recognize that countries with the cultural mix of the U.S. and Canada have a head start in any innovation contest. This cultural and genetic mix will be one of the most powerful of North America's weapons in the competition over international trade.

Davidson and Rees-Mogg earnestly and touchingly believe that the American constitutional system will remain stable enough to avoid total disintegration. Instead, they forecast a "crash-landing." Because they follow the conventional wisdom of Social Darwinism, they expect us to accept a crash-landing and be pathetically grateful that we're only crippled.

They display a near-religious assumption that the American Constitution can cope with change-rate. But the Constitution has already been rendered arthritic by the contradictions in cyber patents and copyrights. It is simply not possible or desirable to write or even amend constitutions this early in a new era.

This is why it is so important for us to undertake the steps that will lead to a renewal of historic North American values. The corruption in business, government, and daily life is no longer tolerable. Maybe adding a "search for excellence" to the culture's assumptions would create enough craziness to make the society functional.

VALUES WITH VALUE

North America is probably unique in that it is possible for it to succeed itself. We are not conquered, and our productivity is high. We are, however, undemanding of ourselves. We are over-consumptive of the world's non-renewable resources and over-indulgent around our whims.

About 1 billion of the world's population will go to bed hungry tonight. Having been brought up amid apparently limitless natural resources, we have developed some bad habits and have become thoughtless about the

---

A more recent arrival on the big-picture scene is Paul Romer, an economist. Skimming Romer's affiliations reveals that he is one of the hottest new stars in the economics firmament. He received his BS in 1983 from the economics department of the University of Chicago. Currently, he is a Professor of Economics at Stanford University's Graduate School of Business and a Fellow at Stanford's Center for Economic Policy Research, the Hoover Institute and the Canadian Institute for Advanced Research.

Published in a time of serious recession, Romer's doctoral dissertation, Dynamic Competitive Equilibria with Externalities, Increasing Returns and Unbounded Growth, helped initiate a new study area in economics: growth. His growth models have collected a wide variety of academic and professional economists as apostles. The Economist calls Romer's work the "new orthodoxy." Speech writers and policy analysts for both Bill Clinton and George Bush are among Romer's avid fans.

Romer believes in something called an "ideas-based economy" which is driven by a new epistemology. Romer thinks that the U.S. and Canada should abandon the old industries which rely on unskilled or semi-skilled labour. If this is not done, North American workers will end up with their job rates converging with those of Mexico, Thailand, Malaysia, and, sooner or later, Africa.

management of the environment, both in conventional terms and in our assumptions about the limitless nature of resources.

On the positive side, North Americans are inherently nonconformists and, more important, we're really bad losers. This comes from being short on history and very close to our pioneering past. When pioneers lose, they don't pass loser genes along. They do pass along a lot of immediate references to what happens to losers.

But if we do not find a way to renew our global leadership, we will probably disappear from any significant role in world affairs in a few generations. We will go into history as the people who disintegrated even when they knew what to do.

Never before has a society, at a time of transition, known what to do. That's why the most important thing for us to do right now is to start building an epistemology — a way to define how we know what we know. The New-Agers would have us discover the "truth" of the events around us by "channelling." Those who have opted for an authoritarian political system would tell us that truth is whatever the beloved leader for life says it is. Those who have made a religious commitment to a fundamentalist creed will urge us to accept what is revealed as a sign of God's special favour, while the scientists will tell us that the scientific method assures us of their

---

Romer's theories still result in more questions than answers. When he blithely urges political leaders to stimulate the ideas economy, he wants them to prioritize education and training by addressing the question of drop-outs and tying apprenticeships to the education system, upgrading worker's skills, and raising the research capabilities of universities. But he assumes that an epistemology sufficiently congruent with the new era is within sight.

Romer's growth theory postulates that politicians are wrong to concentrate so exclusively on the business cycle. But then politicians have always concentrated on economics they didn't understand, such as Keynes's demand management after 1945, or Milton Friedman's monetarism of the 1970s. (Most arguments between economists are over such small distinctions that no one except other economists can comprehend the dispute. An apocryphal story is told of the economist who was asked to explain a technical dispute between John Kenneth Galbraith and Milton Friedman. He said the world thinks the difference between them is A to Z when in reality the difference is A to B.)

It is unlikely that Romer has even started on a new epistemology, but he recognizes the need for one. He might learn a little psychology and a little philosophy and a whole lot of interactive models of history. His work until now, while impressive to economists, is naive in these areas.

statements within a range of acceptable probabilities.

In other words, the methods for discerning truth or reality that were acceptable under the old epistemology do not work any more.

In approaching the new level of abstraction, we are continually pushing past where our conventional assumptions offer some guidance. Science is one of the few systematic purveyors of knowledge with a built-in capacity for correction, but it is still subject to culture-bound limitations, besides human error and corruption.

In a world of *virtual* realities, neural networks, nanotechnologies, genetic engineering, and an environmental crisis, all of which require long-range solutions, we must try to understand how to organize what we know. It took the Renaissance about 300 years to evolve an epistemology that could handle the information generated by a new era. We don't have 300 years.

It may well prove impossible to construct a workable epistemology immediately, but if we can't build one, we should recognize that we have no system of knowing what it is we know and we must assume that our knowledge may be flawed, just plain wrong, or, at best, suspect.

In the past, accurate information was so sparse that "learning" was held to be a major societal goal. Today we hear complaints of information overload. For the first time, we must add a coda to the specifications for a new epistemology. In addition to a theory of knowledge, we need a component part that enables us to choose what is worth knowing, or even knowing how or where to find knowledge which we *may* need in the future. Until we get this new epistemology together, any tinkering we might do with the education system will be just that — tinkering.

A number of years ago, I became interested in the shift from the Industrial Age to the Information Age. I decided that it might be easier to understand the economy if I could think of it in terms of "Industrial Age dollars" — those earned in Industrial Age pursuits — and "Information Age dollars" —those which had their genesis in Information Age systems.

First, I tried to identify capital pools or family fortunes which had crossed from the Mercantile Age to the Industrial Age. Very few made the transition. Those that had typically lost about 90 percent of the invested value by the time industrialization was stabilized. But the remaining investment had risen by 300 percent in real value.

It seemed to me that any rational financial manager would be moving a percentage of funds under management into Information Age investments.

What I found was eye-opening. Yes, the managers of large industrial-based cash pools were buying into Information Age companies, and they were doing badly. They were losing their shirts when they bought into a company as passive investors. When they brought active management to the table along with their money, they also lost their pants.

Next time a politician urges you to support him or her so that he or she can upgrade the education system, remember one thing: we don't know what to do. Surely we have figured out that simply throwing money at boards of education is not going to get conscientious and competent teachers pounding on the school doors, looking for jobs. Remember, a major component of a public education system is to prepare people for being productive members of society 15 or 20 years in the future.

As we saw earlier, a number theorist may tell us he can compute π to two-plus-billion decimal places. Do we need to know this? What does it imply? We are told that in a bit over a decade we will have a petaflop computer chip and that today's supercomputers will exist on a single chip. Will this unimaginable computing power change the way we deal with the questions we choose to ask, or change how we manage society in the first decade of the 21st century? Or will it only make us aware of new problems of even greater insolubility?

Will a new puritanism hold us accountable for what we know or what we *should* know? Is this to be the new political correctness? This is why we need a new theory of knowledge to accommodate not just how we know what we know, but whether we need to know it and what the implications are for knowing something. We can now see a language form evolving from tangential thought processes. Perhaps it is here we shall discover the roots of a new epistemology.

Medieval science/alchemy in the 14th century attributed the Black Death (1347-1349) to astral influences and emphasized an airborne mode of transmission. Their clinical observations of the Plague are surprisingly

---

The worst scenarios came when the investor thought there was a natural mix, e.g. Remington Rand, General Electric, or Westinghouse in the computer business, or Texas Instruments and its personal computer enterprise. Or when some genius at Exxon decided to go into the information systems business because Exxon was such a big user of information technology. They all learned an expensive lesson about mixing mature and immature corporate cultures.

It is now obvious that the same pattern holds true for transferring capital across eras as it did for transfers from the Mercantile to the Industrial Age. It is hard to invest in a field in which there is a strong cultural discontinuity between the investor's corporate or social cultural background. (Exporters learn this lesson early.)

There are ways for a corporation with a mature product mix to invest in the new, post-Einstein industries, but they don't involve being confused about power. The most naked form of power today is the knowledge held by one person — which another person has no way to acquire because of the intellectual baggage they are carrying.

good when you consider the confusion around two carriers (the flea and the host rat). They even noted the connection with the sea, but could not have imagined the bacillus *pasteurella pestis*, for which there was no technology to permit discovery. As a result, the mystery surrounding contagion resulted in a wide variety of attributed causes, with most falling into the category of "God is angered with mankind's sinfulness and is allowing the Evil One to punish humanity."

The second great plague, in the 17th century, found human knowledge in this area not significantly improved. The abstraction level had not reached a point where it could cope with the idea of a bacillus. The epidemiology of various viruses that trouble us in our time is little understood. But as we bring new strategies to bear on these diseases, and new technologies to hasten our understanding of them, we can anticipate clinical tools which will allow us to control them. For one, we can expect to see virus-based illnesses like AIDS largely eradicated. The research tools coming on-line are designed to give fresh insights into protein infrastructures at levels heretofore unapproachable. The birth control pill was certainly one of the most wide-ranging causes of social change, but as a piece of pharmaceutical engineering, it is elegant rather than exotic. Beyond it lies the technologies of molecular modelling, biotechnology, and genetic engineering.

The magnitude of the era transition we face is unprecedented. Above all, do not listen to Jeremiahs who would tell you that all the instances of change are omens of an impending end of the world. This too has been said before, and the prophets have seldom been right. In fact, there has been no occasion in history when they were right.

On the other hand, most of us will have to go through some big adaptations, probably a whole lot more then we ever expected. Kicking away a lot of historical assumptions, which are of less and less value, should take up a large part of our time on the activity wheel of life for the next few decades.

In the sexual politics of the 1980s and early 1990s, the women's movement started to speak about "sensitivity" as a desirable quality in men. It is unlikely that "sensitivity" will offer much in the way of a survival charac-

---

To understand how limited our epistemology is, try to define a simple term as if it were just coined and not enjoying wide usage. Take, for instance, the word "knot." Ian McDonald, a British novelist interested in perceptual shifting as a literary form, tried with this word: his definition was that a knot is a self-binding topological structure in a one-dimensional system. Planck, Einstein, Heisenberg, et al. would be comfortable with that one.

teristic. As the new era unfolds, we can expect to see things become a lot tougher than anything humanity has experienced for a long time.

CHAPTER TWENTY ONE

All Aboard for a New Era: leave your baggage at home

*We have sought for firm ground and found none. The deeper we penetrate, the
more restless becomes the universe; all is rushing
about and vibrating in a wild dance.*
— Max Born

That a cyberspace world is beyond the ken of our leaders is by now
painfully obvious. This is why we see such widespread rejection of our
politicians and political systems. Each of us feels we are venturing into this
new era alone and that we are unique in experiencing the alienating challenges such an era shift presents.

The challenges come from an (as yet) unexplored cyberspace. We lack
even the words to describe this new world, in which the level of abstraction
has shifted so dramatically.

One place where we differ from our forebears of the Renaissance is that
we have the *concept* of an era transition. In the Middle Ages and the early
Renaissance, people were misled by the magnitude of their change rate and
felt the changes offered a chance to gain access to a more spiritual plane of
existence.

Niccolo Machiavelli, though he lived in the midst of the high
Renaissance, had little idea of the nature of the change-rate. In *The
Discourses*, Book 3 Chapter IX, entitled "Whoever Desires Constant Success
Must Change His Conduct With The Times," he saw change rates in
centuries, but most of his allusions are classical, frequently drawn from Livy.

Machiavelli is an example of a good analytical mind swept up in the
times and failing to comprehend the juggernaut qualities of the period. He
was unable to deal with the level of abstraction his era had risen to. Rather
than understanding what was really happening under his nose, his best
advice was drawn from the liberal rhetoric of his day and used classical allusions to avoid any sense of the intuitive.

Lorenzo de'Medici, the actual prince to whom Machiavelli's better known work *The Prince* is dedicated, understood the needs of the times for military captains and wisely rejected Machiavelli's proffered services.

The alchemists argued that a shifted level of understanding of the nature of the universe would allow for a transmutation of the soul, rendering it purer and thus closer to God. The alchemists' talk of the transmutation of common lead to gold was a metaphor for moving to this higher level of consciousness.

The reason that the central bankers and leading economists confess to being baffled by the loss of their ability to predict outcomes of the economy is that, like Machiavelli, who was, after all, the quintessential liberal-minded civil servant, they are unable to understand that new forces — some plainly obvious, and others more subtle — have changed the fundamental nature of economies worldwide.

Few can comprehend the degree to which superconductor-based computers will radically alter the economic universe. Central bankers need more of the intuitiveness of Lorenzo and less of the tortuously constructed explanatory fictions that so appealed to the liberal mind of an earlier era.

Most central bankers are, by definition, lacking in any of the perceptual skills essential to understanding this time. To become a central banker who also has such skills would mean that somewhere along the road you would have had to deviate from orthodoxy sufficiently to have been found by your peers and elders to be "unsound." You would have had to have survived your early spells of prescience and learned to deal with the consequences of being right when your peers and elders were wrong and calling you rude names like "erratic" and "flaky."

And so we find ourselves rendered leaderless, waiting for new guides to emerge. The era won't wait for us. Its time has come.

THEORIES OF THE FUTURE

Lester Thurow, former dean of the Sloan School of Management at MIT, has written that three models of capitalism are the principal competitors on the world trade scene. These models are: the individualistic one of the Anglo-Americans; the corporatist image offered by Europe; and the conglomerate structure employed by Japan Inc., with its strong participation by the Japanese government through MITI. (This is a rebuttal of the arguments of economists such as Robert Reich, who believes that national origins are of little significance in the decisions made by transnational corporations.)

Thurow believes that global competition is principally between two of these philosophies of business, the Anglo-American "individualistic" style and a "communitarian" world-view, which has a European iteration and an Asian expression of amended feudalism centred in Japan. It is Thurow's belief that the Anglo-American "individualistic" thrust is in decline and will only succeed with a strong improvement in the human resources of North Americans. He doesn't seem to think that this outcome is likely. His scenario predicts the Europeans will regain full ascendancy in the 21st century.

According to Thurow, current world trade agreements will be largely supplanted by the decisions made in what he calls the "triad of capitals" — Washington, Bonn/Berlin, and the home base of Asian commerce, Tokyo. Thurow argues that these three will devote the balance of the 20th century to going "head to head" in "quasi regional trading zones," which will hardly come as news to any literate person.

Thurow argues that what we have termed here bimodal income distribution has resulted in two-thirds of working Americans experiencing a drop in real income (after inflation) of almost 20 percent since 1973. Thurow's data are from official U.S. government sources and Canadian data are similar, so the phenomenon is at least North American. These data also show that in 1980, 28 percent of male workers in full-time jobs couldn't earn enough to match the government's own definition of the poverty level. By 1990, that number had risen to 40 percent. The fate of young women is even worse.

What the Thurows and the Reichs of this world miss, while playing with statistical permutations of dubious raw data, is cultural assumptions about how people communicate and deal with one another. That will have more to do with where economic supremacy falls than any other factor.

One thing is clear. Those countries of the Third World, or those tribal/ethnic/religious enclaves emerging technically as nations, will not have much to say about anything unless they do it with bloody, attention-getting wars. If the North American business community maintains its usual anti-intellectual stance, then it loses. But the European and Japanese models have serious problems, too.

The Germans are the engine of Europe. The cost of absorbing the unification of Germany will limit any German government's options for the next decade at least. The inter-European competition between Germany and France over becoming godfather to the C.I.S. has been capital intensive, and the pay-off, if there is one, is proving to be a long way downstream.

The idea that one (or two) of the arms of Thurow's triad might collapse (or lose) is a concept that might excite the romantic boy scouts of the New World Order. It is not a winner for anyone with a semblance of reality

---

A terrorist is merely someone who has been stupid enough to sign on with an army that has no air force — and feels the call of duty whenever someone suggests delivering a bomb by messenger.

working for them. Compared to the collapse of the U.S.S.R. into a starving, politically dishevelled Russia and a motley collection of independent yet non-autonomous states of no economic rationale (though some possess nuclear weaponry), the collapse of one of the global trading blocs will provide entirely new definitions of "disaster area."

As we saw in chapter 15, President Mitterand of France, like most European leaders, managed to restrain his enthusiasm when George Bush announced in 1992 that the world would be a better place if there was only one superpower, namely the United States. That President Clinton will reject the aspiration to single-superpower status flies in the face of political reality.

If our Renaissance benchmark works, we can expect that all significant changes and real growth activities, such as scientific advances and implementations of those advances in ways which improve general well-being, will have their genesis in post-Newtonian physics.

We should also ask whether the Industrial Age mind-set which is the world-view of the American corporate elite has a lock on understanding the "perspective" of our time, or whether their understanding is uniquely centred on the U.S. We have argued that an understanding of the functional level of abstraction will determine whether the U.S. — or anyone for that matter — is to be the single superpower.

The quantity of information available to North Americans is the best in the world. The quality is a more open question. Institutionally, we discourage information hoarding or censorship. But most of the sources of our information exist in formats aversive to the average person, which says more about our educational system than anything else.

THE INFORMATION REVOLUTION

It would be interesting to know whether the entertainment moguls who control Time Warner's destiny are aware of the potential for problems posed by the Internet. *Time* (as a metaphor for the print publishing industry at large) will be seen by our children as a sarcophagus that, since Gutenberg, has frozen information and data alike into rigidly isolated units of either information or data.

The algorithms beneath the interfaces of the Internet mean the net disregards, as a matter of course, spatial caveats against exploring functional relationships and obscure interactions between information sets — interactions that have been inaccessible until recently. The subtleties implied in these kinds of information and data interactions will give us access to a much greater understanding of our universe than anything ever imagined.

This beginning of a recognition of the true dimensions of so-called "information overload" will shortly result in our perceiving a *shortage* of information. The net we have today is the Model T Ford of the infobahn. The information management tools now in the workstations of software designers will shortly open whole new dimensions of perspective.

In other words, we only see information overload as a problem because our existing information management tools and skills are not much different from those of the Renaissance, 500 years ago. The dynamic interplay between different information sets has been effectively screened from us by our own information management tools. Without applications that exploit higher dimensions, we are doomed to continue using data environments ill-suited to the complexity that the knowable world has foisted upon us.

This is why tangential thinking is so important at the time of an era transition.

As the new era unfolds, not only will the information overload we all commonly experience disappear, but a new epistemology will begin to emerge. One part of the urgently needed new epistemology which seems to be gaining some credence is that the entropic process with which we are familiar appears to shift with a jump in the level of abstraction. Entropy probably slows down as a function of the heightened level of abstraction.

For those who have enjoyed the dinosaur craze of the last decade of the 20th century, remember it all began in *Jurassic Park* with the idea of a mosquito biting a dinosaur, becoming entombed in a crypt of amber and (only in the movie) later being recovered, still containing enough blood to make a clone from the DNA. If you thought all that required a "suspension of disbelief," as the theatre folks say, wait until you see what the microbiologists et al. are up to. This is probably the big one for life as we know it. The offshoots of microbiology will require suspensions of disbelief that no Hollywood director would dare ask of an audience.

No matter how you look at it, the Human Genome Project can spell nothing but disaster for a politician. Remember what was said earlier about the Islamic world's pre-10th century mind-set? How do they deal with this kind of thing? The Imams at Al Azhar might get really upset about this one. And they were careworn about the U.N.'s report endorsing reproductive choice. Remember the tricolour mouse on the cover of *Science*? Then there's the *fatwahs* on Mr. Rushdie and Egyptian writer Naguib Mahfouz. Realistically, it looks like time for another alliance with the Vatican.

This means that it has become justifiable to expect researchers to identify the fragment of DNA carrying defective genes, such as Tay-Sachs, Huntington's Chorea or sickle-cell anemia, to prevent their continued distribution through inheritance, and eventually to treat present sufferers. To understand the magnitude of this project, imagine a map of the United States that shows every house. Assume that there is a blown light bulb in one of these houses. The Human Genome Project is designed to enable a physician to detect the blown bulb *and change it*. This is the order of magnitude of the problem which scientists worldwide are addressing. Their work will do more to affect human health and welfare than anything in the past 500 years.

The term Renaissance is actually a misnomer popularized by those who were attempting to revert to the finite world of classical, pre-Medieval Europe. The period we call the Renaissance was not a time of renewal, but a time of discovering new cultural and economic forms, the beginnings of comprehension of time and space, and a time when the classical era and its Aristotelian-Thomistic finiteness was challenged irrevocably.

Similarly, in our own time we are not renewing some sort of legendary past. We are creating a new culture. That culture cannot fully emerge while we do not know exactly what makes it different from its immediate past. When politicians and business and labour leaders speak of "industrial strategies", they are too frequently trying to retrieve bygone days when our massive industrial power could be harnessed for national efforts such as World War II.

In Marshall McLuhan's terms, a time of era shift is a time of right-brained emphasis. The right side of the brain controls synthesis, intuition, analogy, pattern recognition, non-linear thought (tangential thinking), simultaneity, and holism.

The left-brain favours literary information, specialization, logic, linearity, sequence mathematics, and analysis. So in other words, we would expect the world of the Industrial Age to be a left-brain time with specialization of

---

If you were a sentient being on another planet with an inquiring mind and the resources to watch and interpret whatever it is that's going on here on Earth, what would you be seeing?

If you have been watching since that Mathematical Congress in 1900, you have seen the most momentous and unpredictable change rate that had ever happened on this planet. You, being a curious and intellectually alert alien, might be trying to diagram what we are calling an era shift.

What metaphorical terms would jump out at you? One might be that the event you were observing looked like a mutation or perhaps even the way that cancer cells expand to take over their host by metastasizing. It might even occur to our voyeur from wherever to think that there was a unity of purpose at some level.

Maybe our unseen observer sees a single system and experiences deep frustration that we down here can't seem to understand it. On one hand we understand how to build and use a computer and envision strategies to build computers of even vaster powers. On the other hand, we are faced with problems that we cannot leave unsolved — such as virus-based diseases and illnesses caused by prions — or we

trade unionism and the focussing of management, with accompanying narrowness, blinkered targeting, and general tunnel-vision.

Our problems do not differ qualitatively from those of the people of the Western European Renaissance. Our quantum jump in the guiding level of abstraction is probably not subjectively more dramatic than that of our cultural ancestors. In the Renaissance there were frequent disagreements about open (free) trade or protectionism and a number of governments rose and fell over the issue. Today we see the same struggle re-enacted over information.

We, too, face challenges to our moral doctrines as our economic and cultural institutions collapse around us. The ability to control conception and the Malthusian pressures on our food production resources places our conventional sexual mores under stress. Our language, buffeted by new technologies and hastened social adaptations, evolves while we scramble to catch up to new words and definitions from diverse sources.

Our political commentators righteously say a lot these days about how "democracy and market reform" will perform some sort of metaphysical redemptive process on the souls of the inhabitants of the former East Bloc nations. It might be useful to apply these standards to NAFTA, the E.U., or any other regional trade bloc. Certainly, the CEO of United Technologies had no reservations about this New World Order when he was reported saying of the trading blocs, "it helps create a worldwide business environment that's unfettered by government interference."

---

are toast. There seems to be no end of entities we know even less about than viruses, perhaps because we lack the alien's unified insight.

We have made great progress in understanding those four "letters," A, T, C and G. Presumptuously, we celebrate that we have solved the code of DNA — just permutation after permutation of those four "letters." But a bit of humility might be in order. Those four "letters" that make up DNA are all that the Lords of the Universe need to write instruction sets controlling all variability we see in the cells of all living things. It makes all the hype about programming languages like C++ sound a bit redundant.

We know from history that the artificial constructs we call superstition frequently take on a life of their own and act as agents to suppress understanding of greater unities. Where is the dividing line between a mammal and a flower, or a coral reef and a zebra? Are those divisions real, or are they arbitrary markers of our own limits of comprehension? If there is even a possibility they aren't real, the Information Age has arrived just in time.

AMERICA'S MILITARY INDUSTRIAL SIMPLEX

On March 8, 1992, *The New York Times* revealed Pentagon plans to implement the president's wishes that no rival superpower would be allowed to emerge in Western Europe, Asia, or the territories of the former Soviet Union. The 46-page pre-release document included a mission statement, which said that part of the military responsibility would be "to convince potential competitors that they need not pursue a more aggressive posture to protect their legitimate interests."

The draft Pentagon document was being circulated to senior officials under the title of the "Defense Planning Guidance", which is usually issued every two years. It was the first such Guidance released since the Cold War's end. The paper argued for a world in which one superpower's longevity can be perpetuated by constructive behavior and sufficient military might to deter any nation or group of nations from challenging its status. The document's greatest break with earlier U.S. foreign policy was, perhaps, its rejection of collective internationalism.

The policy makers saw the U.S. role in very expensive terms: "We will retain the pre-eminent responsibility for addressing selectively those wrongs which threaten not only our interests but those of our allies or friends, or which could seriously unsettle international relations."

One other point is that tucked away in the document is a recommendation that what is really needed is a global anti-missile system. Of particular concern in this area are the "rogue states." On the top of the list of rogue states is North Korea, followed by everyone's perennial favourite, Libya, and Saddam's Iraq. Is this SDI all over again?

The Pentagon document stated that the first strategic objective is to "prevent the re-emergence of a new rival, either on the territory of the

---

The latest iteration of America's Strategic Defence Initiative, better known as Star Wars, has a name and a price tag. The name is Global Protection Against Limited Strikes, usually referred to as GPALS. When an American Pentagon official briefed Canadian reporters, he said Washington wants other countries to ante up $46 billion for GPALS and expects Canada to pick up a share of this action. GPALS technology, it is claimed, can already hit incoming targets with "bullets" weighing only seven kilograms. (In 1984 the interception units were about the size of a Volkswagen and weighed a tonne.)

GPALS Phase I is expected to come in at $25 billion and will deliver four U.S. continental launch positions, plus one in Hawaii and one in Alaska. Phase I has a space-based sensor system called "Brilliant Eye." Phase II involves what the Pentagon calls a "theatre missile system," which can be moved to any place in the world. It operates on land or aboard U.S. naval vessels. Phase II is scheduled to

former Soviet Union or elsewhere, that poses a threat on the order of that posed formerly by the Soviet Union. This is a dominant consideration underlying the new regional defense strategy, and requires that *we* endeavor to prevent any hostile power from dominating a region whose resources would, under consolidated control, be sufficient to generate global power. These regions include Western Europe, East Asia, the territories of the former Soviet Union and Southwest Asia." While the U.S. anticipates acting through the United Nations, it reserves the right to act unilaterally, as befits the only superpower.

The United States is, according to this theory, going to be the only superpower and, as such, will maintain garrisons worldwide. These garrisons will be deployed as a global police force constantly on the watch for bad guys who might upset the New World Order. In other words, the U.S. is claiming the sole right to global sovereignty. One might fear that there are people out there who might think the president just a wee bit pretentious and presumptuous.

Who is going to pay for this new global cop game? As the historian Paul Kennedy argued in his book *The Rise And Fall of the Great Powers*, most empires collapse when they get the bills for those legions out on the far-flung reaches of the empire. Kennedy's latest work, *Preparing for the Twenty-First Century*, was written after the success of *Rise and Fall* and Clinton's electoral victory. It puts him firmly in the camp of those who tag along with that 18th-century depression fan, Thomas Malthus. Kennedy has come down firmly on the side of the Thurow argument. He is less than sanguine about the North American future because he uses an extrapolative model to support his thesis that America is destined to follow Britain in

---

cost $10 billion. Phase III of GPALS is a space-based interception system called "Brilliant Pebbles," which will cost $11 billion.

The U.S. government is urgently looking to its partners to share the GPALS bill. The Canadian journalists didn't buy the argument and seem to have cast Cooper in the roll of a pre-Boesky stock salesman reselling the insiders' stock among those who weren't on the inside, namely America's defence allies.

Pentagon officials use the "rogue states" analysis as the principal argument in favour of this $46 billion defense against peace and tranquility. As for getting the usually compliant defense partners to share the cost of the progressive space-war toys, the likelihood is pretty bleak.

Some cynical international political observers have meanly suggested that it's all part of a plot by North Korea to bankrupt the U.S. in the same way America bankrupted the Soviet Union.

being slowly but steadily eclipsed. He sees Africa, the old Soviet Union, India, and China as disasters.

The Thurow-Kennedy thesis only works when you reject the argument of this book that the profundity of the change shift will not permit solutions which do not accommodate Planck, Einstein, Heisenberg, Schrödinger, and Dirac.

In this book, the argument is that the Thurows and Kennedys of this world are not notably different from the Scholastics of the 15th and 16th centuries, who rejected Erasmus's Humanism and could not understand Pacioli and Bruno. Because they rejected Erasmus, history condemned them to irrelevance, and because they couldn't comprehend Pacioli and Bruno, they lost out on becoming part of a new era. Their lives were pointless except for being the requisite token losers in the struggle for the Renaissance. Being a token loser is not in the category of definitions for "the good life."

IS CONTEMPORARY MANAGEMENT A VIRUS?

The instabilities of the Western world's economies are obvious as we shift from the late Industrial Age to the cyberspace era. Companies whose executives were adaptation-challenged by daily events sink into the oblivion provided by bankruptcy trustees, or disappear in mergers.

Their long-term employees, who believed the human resources managers' and union leaders' promises that the corporate world offered a homeostatic buffer from socio-economic shifts, are cast adrift like 18th-century masterless Japanese ronin or 14th-century European mercenaries of the White Company. Many whine that they put their faith in the big shooters, who had their guns taken away and were left with their sheltered retirement packages.

The mistake of the big shooters was to try to carry ridiculous amounts of intellectual, emotional, and physical baggage in their assumptions about how the world was being reorganized.

In the end-days of the Industrial Age, short-term goal-seeking behavior became rationalized into the economy. When there is an incremental rate of technological and social change, focussing on historic goals to which you have ascribed a value of timeless verity comes close to embracing a death wish.

The corporate world's answer to the recession of the early 1990s was to trash the company's human resources (a.k.a. downsizing), treat R&D as if the CEO were an embryonic Atilla the Hun (an idea advanced by a management book), and rip off the investors.

Now the reality is setting in. A number of academic studies — and even *Fortune* magazine — now show good evidence that while downsizing received big kudos from Wall Street, the City of London, and similar big thinkers, the effects were usually destructive to everyone except the termination consultants who counselled the newly mobile and outwardly bound in résumé writing and contacting five potential employers daily from an "office" established solely for the purpose of keeping the casualties from hanging around the home.

What this slash-and-burn strategy *did* accomplish was to ensure that those left behind were principally the politically adept, those who had never made a mistake because they had never taken a risk. The upper reaches of management found nothing strange in the idea that a pension-fund manager who had never made/created/sold anything in his life was the obvious person to call the shots as captain of the lifeboat.

What has become apparent is that the "business cycle" of the past few years has behaved like no other in documented *economic* history. That's because it is so much like the early days of the collapse of the Medieval Roman Catholic Church and the Holy Roman Empire. The solutions to a recessionary cycle require an open mind, an assignment of old mental baggage to a proper historical perspective, and a willingness to explore the opportunities that become available as the new era unfolds. That doesn't mean that, if the stakeholders are going to take a bath, you pay the senior management seven- or eight-digit salaries. What you do is search out new opportunities and reward those who actually find something.

Many of the big downsizers have managed to throw out all of the kids except for the one or two who actually needed a bath in the first place. They abandoned their corporate wisdom and instituted an environment of fear and terror, all because neither the managers nor the institutional investors understood the fundamental nature of the changing world.

The alternative is to abandon that baggage, including the mind-set of focussing to exclude anything not linearly related to your immediate job and believing that all history began 20 years ago.

As an old era collapses into the caresses of its fatal flaws, a sense of psychopathy takes on the character of conventional wisdom among the leader class.

If you work in short enough time spans, extrapolation works. The corporate world was completely aware of the environmental havoc it was wreaking. As the time-frames of extrapolative predictions became shorter, the willingness to dismiss the consequences of polluting became increasingly common in executive suites. This was particularly true of operations located in the Third World. *Voilà* psychopathy (no longer an acceptable term, according to the diagnostic terminology manual provided by the American Psychiatric Association).

Throughout this book we have concentrated on the human dimensions of the change-rate that we all experience. There is another aspect of this period-shift, fueled by discoveries in science and resultant technologies. The development of these technologies was far more capital intensive than governments or economists anticipated. This capital-intensiveness resulted in highly coercive competition for capital. Commercialization of these new technologies frequently resulted in elongated customer learning curves, which placed further pressure on the globally available capital pools.

This is a long way of saying that there isn't going to be much money around for the next few decades, unless you are involved in implementing the era shift. It also means that the bimodal income distribution pattern becomes accelerated as more and more members of society are excluded from meaningful participation. In other words, you get exponential expansion of Brazilification.

In the previous chapter we introduced the idea that a useful model in an era shift is to think of the revenue generated in one time cycle as having been generated by that period. For example, the growth of retailing and the raising of consumer's expectations in the 19th century came from the machinery of the Industrial Age, which mass-produced goods that were identical in every way. Cloth spun in the steam-driven knitting mills of England had none of the periodic flaws that were normal in hand-spun cloth. The industrialization of the manufacturing processes allowed retailers to *guarantee* the quality of goods.

This changed the level of abstraction of the money which represented either Mercantile Age outputs or Industrial Age products. We also saw the difficulty that investors faced in converting surplus funds (savings, profits, et cetera) from the currency of one period to another.

The choices such an investor faces are not easy and are similar to the choices each one of us faces today. We could, it was suggested, speak of Industrial, Mercantile or Agricultural Age dollars compared to Information Age or digital dollars. It was pointed out that Industrial Age dollars would have little buying power in an Information Age environment.

This happens because once an age becomes stabilized and non-expansive, there is little chance that there will be significant growth in such stable settings. There are few who would be willing to invest in an automobile company to compete with the big three *and* the global imports.

During an era shift, wise and prudent investors will move their capital into investments that are congruent with the new level of abstraction that heralds the emerging era. They do this because it is unlikely they can anticipate real growth if they leave their capital invested in producers of goods and services based on the level of abstraction of a prior age.

The great problem in swapping your investments in smokestack industries for holdings in data jack-based companies is that there are few trustworthy rules. This is true enough when you are moving from the Industrial Age to the Digital Age, but when you add the complication of a new era, you are facing an exponential risk factor.

The new era is not merely affecting one part of the community, as do most ages. The generalized impact of a new era or age is usually increased prosperity, as the society rushes to create goods to support the core events of the age.

New eras in cultures with broadly available information systems relentlessly force reconsideration of all the assumptions the society holds. In the case of our own new era, we have the Information Age pursuing a parallel course — which assures that the new products are distributed globally.

TECHNOLOGY TRANSFERS AND OTHER HORRORS

The new era is not without its challenges. In January 1993, Reuters reported that a new technique had been developed which allowed scientists involved in bovine reproductive research to separate X and Y chromosomes in bull sperm, using a fractionation procedure. This means that a farmer can predetermine the sex of a calf by impregnating the mother cow with sperm that produces a calf of the desired gender.

The first *in vitro* fertilization in humans was accomplished after the technique was perfected with data from successful bovine reproductive research. It isn't a big job to transfer this technology from the bovine species to humans. Moreover, on a planet where a number of cultures practice female infanticide and various forms of genital mutilation, this technology has big growth potential.

Cultures that practise female infanticide have discernibly higher rates of warfare. Their crime rates are so much higher that their penal systems are skewed to non-rehabilitative administration and a normative incidence of enforcement brutality.

It doesn't involve a great leap of intellect to imagine the leader of an authoritarian state recognizing that, regardless of his commitment to ethnic cleansing and institutionalized rape, the day may come when the nation is not producing enough males to fill future military drafts. Such a great leader might be tempted to institutionalize an increase in the ratio of male to female births.

You doubt this is true? Anywhere in India you may find advertisements saying "Healthy Boy or Girl?" The word "healthy" is usually in the smallest type the printer has, so the message, at first glance, appears to read "Boy or Girl?" These ads appear in pamphlets, newspapers, and posters, and are issued by thousands of sex determination clinics offering ultrasound and amniocentesis. Some are even more up-front. They add to the sex determination message "Pay 500 rupees now, or 5,000 rupees later."

The 500 rupees in this offer is the cost of the ultrasound or amniocentesis procedures plus the cost of abortion should the fetus prove to be female. The 5,000 rupees refers to the cost of a future dowry if the female fetus is allowed to be born. The whole message compares the cost of an abortion versus the future costs of raising the female child until the time when it becomes necessary to pay someone to take her off the parent's hands.

Without a serious amount of tangential thinking, there are no solutions to this kind of technological application. The arguments posed by the corporate world's managers and tame economists, with their institutionalized, focussed thinking and their touching faith in the regulatory capacity of market forces, do not seem to hold water in matters of public policy, such as determining the gender of a fetus.

Mature technology is inexpensive. From 1982 to 1987 the number of sex determination clinics in Bombay rose from 10 to 248.

An even less expensive testing strategy than ultrasound or amniocentesis is the alpha test. It is a simple blood test that will tell whether a fetus is at risk from Down's Syndrome (the leading cause of retardation in North America), Spina Bifida (when the bony casing around the spinal cord fails to close), Anencephaly (some parts of the brain and skull are missing), and Trisomy 18 (a frequently fatal genetic condition that leaves children who survive developmentally handicapped). The inexpensive alpha test will also identify the sex of the fetus.

The alpha test comes well-recommended. In May 1993, the Ontario (Canada) ministry of health announced that it believed the test could save $3 million to $4 million annually over the cost of more conventional testing. The province has one of the most sophisticated and successful health insur-

---

In North America, the ratio of women to men is 1,017 women for every 1,000 men. In India the ratio is 929 women for every 1,000 men. In the Punjab, one of India's wealthiest states, the gender ratio is 879 females to 1,000 males. The Punjab is one of the largest suppliers of men to India's armed forces.

A UNICEF report on child mortality found that, of 12 million girls born in India each year, 3 million will die before they reach the age of 15. In the West, men live shorter lives than women. In a single day in India, the total number of deaths due to complications in pregnancy and childbirth is more than that recorded for a month in the entire developed world.

UNICEF also estimates that 75 percent of Indian females are illiterate, with fewer girls enrolled in schools than boys. Girls are given less food than boys, resulting in higher mortality rates. They are frequently sold into slavery (in labour-intensive industries), prostitution, or marriage to elderly men.

The hopelessness of these female children is difficult to comprehend.

ance schemes in the world. With such an endorsement, it will not be long before the test travels to the Third World, where the goals of such testing differ from those in a high-end industrial state.

The technology will migrate globally — as do all products of the new era. It's not the implementation that's expensive. It's what you do with it that can be costly.

Think of sex-selection technology from the position of the governments of Pakistan and India. In India, the government is committed to a strong nationalist policy, which means recovering Kashmir and putting the Pakistanis in their place. The same sort of nationalistic agenda is held by any government in Pakistan.

Rewind. Stop at the Afghanistan War. There are a lot of warriors of God working under various Islamic leaders. These traditional fighters were supplied on the ground by Saudi intelligence officers, who also picked out likely candidates for leadership training in the tactics of fighting the Red Army.

These tactics were developed by the CIA and were effective to the extent of neutralizing the advantages of technology, like helicopters. It was pretty public knowledge that these leadership courses were run by the CIA, using the Pakistani army as a field cadre. The Afghani "freedom fighters" became the Taliban, who control Afghanistan today as a theocratic Islamic state.

The Pakistani training staff included a number of battle intelligence personnel from Pakistan's army. This army has been at war with India since the partition of 1947.

The Hindus of India and the Muslims of Pakistan don't like each other. The partition years resulted in about 17 million deaths, but this dislike has been going on for about a thousand years. All the lessons given to the Afghanis were quickly installed as standard training for Pakistan's army, whose general staff now believe that the odds have been leveled off a bit since 1947. The Long March missiles Pakistan obtained from China make the field even more level.

For much of the Cold War, India was effectively a client state of the U.S.S.R. and made a fetish of giving the United States lectures in international morality. When President Kennedy appointed John Kenneth Galbraith, the Harvard economist, as American ambassador to India, the sum of Galbraith's reports from New Delhi on India's relationship with the Soviets was that they deserved each other. Since 1947, India has managed to get involved in two wars with China and a conflict with the Tamil side of the Sri Lankan independence war. All this may explain why China favours and supplies Pakistan with weaponry, including missiles.

Both India and Pakistan can take out *all* of each other's major cities with about five minutes' warning. With modern sex-selection technology, the cultural assumptions of both countries say they can replace the resulting population and military losses in much the same way that the world's leading cow and swine breeders "retire" 30 percent to 40 percent of their herds annually — and choose the sex of the replacements.

In India or Pakistan, the idea of getting up to 93 percent boy babies is not one that might cause trouble at the polls. It also guarantees that a fresh supply of testosterone-soaked young men will be available in 20 years to fight the next war.

WHO'S IN CHARGE HERE?

Cultures that routinely place one sex or the other in a subordinate category are also likely to practise various overt forms of institutionalized racism. In the new era, if the bimodal revenue curve is stabilized, will public policy sanction the use of sex-determining technology to inhibit the birth of the artificially defined less worthy sex, or those with a skin colour deemed indicative of a lower class?

One issue we might think about is: can you hold the discoverers of basic sciences and the inventors of application technologies responsible for coming up with ways to control abuses of their discoveries and creations? In general, this is not an idea whose time appears to have come. Scientists, as a group, have not demonstrated a strong predilection for anticipating the political or commercial outcomes of their works. Any attempts to limit areas of inquiry have been seen as infringements on their intellectual freedom.

As for inventors, their interest is usually a combination of tinkering and unenlightened self-interest. Most are not uncomfortable with the idea of becoming rich and famous. Entrepreneurs, by and large, have never been held up, by even their greatest admirers, as sources of intellectual probity.

That leaves us with politicians and bureaucrats, if we wish to control the outcomes of science and technology. The frequently fatal malaise of politicians is to be possessed of a particularly damning hubris or pride, for which Dante reserved a notably loathsome circle of hell. Medieval Christianity, which Dante echoed, saw pride as the most deadly of the seven deadly sins. The classical Greek dramatist Aeschylus used a display of hubris as a signal that a character was doomed.

Bureaucrats hate entrepreneuring with a passion. After all, the civil servant is employed as a manager of the power generated by the body politic. They have no mandate for dealing with the future. This was why Machiavelli remained unemployed. He was a cataloguer of the policies of dead Greeks and Romans. It was Machiavelli's fate to be a bureaucrat, unblessed with the slightest iota of intuition about what might be coming.

We have to distrust bureaucrats because, left to their own devices, they will, when confronted with an innovation, try to shoe-horn the new event into existing, historically authorized geometries.

As the corporate world's leaders and their lacklustre political appointees attempt to stabilize the world with an epistemology more suited to the 1890s, we see their strategies bringing about unemployment and general economic conflict.

This is why we need a new epistemology. Epistemologies have "in your face" qualities that stop bureaucrats and managers from forcing new and unfamiliar developments into boxes that neither encompass nor define the new event. An epistemology for today will allow a pellucid view of the world in which we find ourselves.

A new epistemology is frightening to the oligarchical supporters of the New World Order. Epistemologies allow for the design of new learning systems that can unravel the unknown; they do not let tyrannies of the few artificially inhibit new knowledge or set agendas for the discovery process — which the oligarchy claims is stabilizing, but which principally serves to sustain its power base. Similarly, oligarchic institutions oppose cultural change. Challenges to classical forms of culture are repressed because, as the government of the U.S.S.R. discovered too late, popular culture can distribute messages of dissent before the authorities can decrypt them.

All too often, we see books, articles, and TV shows that view the future with some sort of uncritical and nonsensical romantic optimism. This romanticism best serves to warn us that the author has not the slightest idea of what is going on.

Alternatively, there are those self-proclaimed pundits who urge us to put our definitive books, formulae, et cetera into some sort of root cellar, so that we and our heirs can replay the pundits' erroneous ideas of what the Dark Ages were about.

It's not hard to dismiss these doomsayers, who have an intellectual affinity with the science fiction writers who eagerly awaited a nuclear holocaust, to be followed by a dreary recovery fashioned after the pattern of manic-depressive illness in its down-phase.

Dealing with this new era requires first that we understand that it is happening, and second, that we realize we all have a lot of historical baggage in the form of assumptions, which pose an ever-present danger of dragging us down. Third, we have to think much more tangentially. If we follow a path that recognizes these beginning points, we will be on the road to a new epistemology.

Multiple-choice tests and examinations are one source of learning to think tangentially. Unfortunately they seldom teach you to tie a correct answer to other questions on other tests. But that's just irresponsible and topologically improvident test construction.

It's also useful to recognize that our leaders are human and are open to the same pressures we all share. The problem with these leaders is that their capacity to cause havoc increases proportionally to the power they hold, the extent to which their information comes from dubious sources, and the degree to which they have become enthralled by their private hubris.

Effectively, we can only judge leaders — political, economic, military, or social — by whether their analyses were right and whether their judgments, based on their actions, were reasonable. Applying the "reasonable person" test to political leadership is something there is no precedent for. After all, why would any "reasonable person" enter politics in the first place?

BEWARE THE OLIGARCHS

We cannot emphasize enough that the trend toward economic bimodality is truly dangerous. It takes a large part of the population and makes them first marginal and then underclass. The balance of the population becomes an oligarchy with a requisite aristocracy (for sycophantic purposes if no other) having no interest in supporting mobility for the marginal and underclass.

A citizenry composed of the marginal and the underclass looks to the leadership for immediate and short-term solutions, and has a marked indifference as to whether the solutions are in any way real. Of course, the product of this bimodal society is to separate us into aristocracy and proles. As human beings with access to our own history, we know that such a society doesn't work. We also know that those who espouse the New World Order paradigm are trying to make it work yet again.

This system has been known under a host of names, including Roman citizenship; the manorial economy and its feudal society; China's mandarins; the Japanese shogunate; the class system of the British Empire; and hundreds more. The names change each time out of the gate, because whoever announces themselves as the promulgator of the latest new world order invariably leaves behind such odium that the purveyors of the next attempt search out a name that hasn't been used.

The good news is that Japan seems to have the same problems that we in the West have, only their cultural inhibitions are, if possible, even more pervasive.

The government-backed "Fifth Generation" project, which was going to bury the West's computer industry, has collapsed completely. It didn't have much of a chance in the semi-feudal corporate world of Japan's industrial base. A bigger disappointment for the civil servants should be, but probably isn't, that the Japanese hackers, known as the otaku, haven't filled the Fifth Generation project gap with an underground discovery path of heroic dimensions. The otaku are even more institutionally alienated than are the North American hackers.

One of our popular literary devices is that of the romantic and mythic aristocratic figure being hung from the nearest lamppost when the revolution happens. Writers of this style are really authoring a polemic for a return to classical values. They ask us to weep for the tragic figure, to whom the writer usually ascribes all the virtues of purity and beauty.

The Scarlet Pimpernel is a typical example of this category. The body of work dedicated to the search for survivors of the Russian royal family also falls into this genre. The pathetic claimants to the title of Princess Anastasia, who was undoubtedly killed by the Bolsheviks after the Russian revolution, are another example of this myth.

This romantic view of the victims of revolution is not a useful myth. Generally, those who get lampposted deserved it. When you marginalize 90 or more percent of the population, you have failed to recognize any values beyond brute force.

Anyone who uses the emergent, ahistorical phase of this new era to create a new aristocracy is just another fool in search of a lamppost. Revolutions are not directed against classes, they are directed against ways of thinking, which, in the chaotic rough justice of the immediate post-revolutionary period, are usually shoe-horned into a class context.

What these symbolic "enemies of the people" get lampposted for is being stupid and failing to learn. Should you find yourself on the losing side of a revolution, just remember — no radical succession in history has ever run short of lampposts.

OUR CENTRES DO NOT HOLD

Earlier we looked at how our society has become increasingly pluralistic. This pluralism has many superficially attractive appearances. But it is self-indulgent. Pluralistic societies have a fatal flaw. They divide themselves and, as a result, are easily conquered. The jurors of history, at later inquests, frequently ask why a culture, society, nation, et cetera was so willing to abandon a position of preference to become incrementally pluralistic.

The pluralistic society is one where special interest groups are willing to enter into alliances with anyone who will support their narrow agendas. The consequence of this *quid pro quo* is indifference to the inhabitants of other pluralistic sectors — as long as their own goals are achieved. The result is usually a breakdown of the political process because politicians find it impossible to lead the society into a degree of consensus and so lose their capacity to govern.

Without that consensus, politicians resort to the always close-at-hand options of corruption, bribery, short-term answers, bread and circuses, and *après moi le deluge*. In other words, the politicians settle for personal power and self-aggrandizement.

At that point, society is at a crossroads. If it takes one road, it falls into those excesses and corruptions which are the lot of societies that have developed a taste for the *circus* with its attendant jading cruelties. Citizens become indifferent as they find a theatrical quality in crucifixions and judge them to be neither cruel, nor all that unusual. The society's resources go to giving the plebs food and entertainment.

Meaningful work is reserved for trustworthy slaves under the supervision of an ignorant, unlettered aristocracy. All of this is carried out under the political guidance of the oligarchy. The economic infrastructure becomes increasingly bimodal as the nobility loots the substance and capital of the society. The lower end of the aristocracy becomes employed supervising an enforcement appendage of men-at-arms acting as a domestic police, protecting the society from the disenfranchised. Shortly thereafter, the society, nation, or empire collapses.

Alternatively, some societies have searched out a means of redemption. In place of corrupt and incompetent civil administration, the people often are willing to go through a bloody revolution led by a tyrant promising clean government. Life in the puritan commonwealth aftermath is all about recovering a public sense of purpose. Salutary executions become the order of the day. Sometimes it works, and the society finally overthrows the puritans and regains its sense of resolve after amending its epistemology.

Religious fundamentalism, with its accompanying puritanism, happens fairly early in a new era. Every major religion — Judaism, Protestantism and Catholicism, Islam, and Buddhism — has its share of fundamentalist resources, which are a reaction to the adjustments in traditional values that are part of an era shift. As the new era moves into place, much of what was considered unknown and unknowable becomes part of the explainable universe. As the formulations of traditional values lose their potency, hyper-orthodoxy in religion is asserted by those searching for security in values to which a timeless quality can be ascribed.

But fundamentalist and puritanical periods are usually destroyed by their own mechanisms, and everyone breathes a sigh of (hopefully chastened) relief.

WE NEED A NEW WAY OF THINKING

We need a new way of thinking that is not deterministic, or requiring simple cause-and-effect explanations. We need a new epistemology that is congruent with the level of abstraction driving this period. We also have to find ways of selecting and dumping historical baggage that slows us down.

Because we have intensified and raised the density of our information resources, we need to discriminate between freedom of information, freedom of thought, and licence. This is principally a matter of civility. No one of taste aspires to a level of jadedness which makes "snuff" films rollicking good fun for a night at the movies. But how do we popularize good taste or civility? To most of us, who are conscious of the need to keep the censors at bay, this task alone seems insoluble. The Roman Catholic Church attempted this one with the Index, and after a few hundred years trying to make it work and a few thousand souls burned at the stake, gave it up because it was unworkable a few years ago. The contradictions became too apparent for even the Curia.

This is not an attempt to end on a Jeremiah note. North America need not collapse or go through a reign of puritanism, but to avoid these extremes we have to address the issues raised by being on the ground floor of a new era. The new era of cyberspace started here.

It is in the beginning of a new era that the quality is inserted. Later, when the new era is clearly established, the society makes compromises to reach out to and include domestic loyalists of the *ancien régime*, allies picked up along the way, trading partners, conquered nations, and other peoples who are playing catch-up.

It is these compromises that eventually cause the cracks to appear as the *next* new era breaks through. (We don't have worry about that one without some hefty breakthroughs in lengthening our life spans.)

We are, however, fortunate. It is we who will build the underpinnings of the next epoch. This is the time that inspires the mythic tales of succeeding generations. This is where the rules that govern the rest of the era get set down. A longer view is essential, because extrapolative analysis is no longer effective. To extend your vision, you have to learn to be comfortable in cyberspace.

Akio Morita, the founder of Sony Corportion, was for years critical of the values brought to high-technology companies by financial managers. At the World Economic Forum held in Davos, Switzerland, in January 1993, he criticized the management practices of Western companies, in which poor economic performance led to fiscal managers' opinions being given disproportionate weight.

Morita recounted a visit he had made to a Wall Street bank's trading rooms. He described bright young executives trading huge amounts of money on a global basis. "How far ahead do you normally look?" he asked one of the dealers. The dealer replied, "10 minutes."

The answer stunned the Sony chief. He pointed out that when he committed to a research or development position, he was usually locked in for a decade or more of project obligation, and his analysis of the costs and pay-out had better be good.

If your investments are being run by accountants and lawyers, people whose whole being is divorced from the ultimate production of goods, the number crunchers will want to invest your capital in office towers, lever-aged buyouts, junk bonds, and all the other accoutrements of the lawyering and accounting trades. These tradesmen, lawyers, and accountants, operating as deal hustlers, abound in the North American business culture and con-stitute one of our most burdensome loads of historical baggage.

What Akio Morita was saying is not new. Countries that produce noth-ing end up pushing paper which can too often be found to be of dubious merit. To make productivity plans for manufacturing in a cyberspace world requires that your forecasts respect the assumptions of the topography of hyperspace. Simple linear guesses are unlikely to be strong enough to get to the production stage.

Another load of burdensome baggage carried by North Americans is that the size of our domestic markets meant that we didn't need a long-range perspective. Because we were so rich, we didn't have to learn how to build a sustained view. Until we do, we will make some real blunders.

We all have to learn to work with unfamiliar events as new historical forces emerge. Trying to force new events into historically safe pigeon-holes will merely distort our view of reality. Out there in the void some-where is a historian waiting to be born and tell our story to eternity. Historians need heroic figures and villains. If you are alive at this time you get to choose which one you'll be.

Your choice is determined by the people you decide to follow and those with whom you decide to associate, the battles you win and lose, the inven-tions you make, and the values you espouse. How you position yourself in relation to the new era will determine how that historian will see you.

One of the major differences between the Renaissance and our time is that we have an awareness that carries with it a measure of volition. The documentation — institutional, artistic, and historical — gives us a good idea of the profundity of what is going on. After reviewing the problems of the Renaissance, we can look at what is new to our own period.

In this second time around, the process of commercialization reminds us to look at the fundamental discoveries which underlie more prosaic tech-shifts. What is really unique is that, as we move the real discoveries into accessible technologies, we begin to expand and democratize the *new meaning of the world*. Recognizing this is the first step in creating our new epistemology.

In the Renaissance, no one, except for established orders, thought much about an expanding or expanded universe. The old order thought about the consequences of an expanding universe only to deny or suppress them. Today, the old order doesn't seek to suppress and certainly not to deny. Instead, it attempts to co-opt and usurp.

The difference between ourselves and the people of Renaissance is only in the level of abstraction we are learning to manage. If Lysenko had understood modern evolutionary theory, he would have known that evolution doesn't care which ideology wins; it just rewards winners. And that byte of information defines "free will" in the cyberspace age.

To be only half-conscious of the events that drive our time is bad enough, but can be forgiven and is probably the fate of all of us now alive. To live at the time when a new era breaks forth and be unconscious of it, as you tenaciously grip a dead past, is unlikely to be forgiven by the Lords of the Universe, your progeny, and — most of all — yourself.

The problems facing us are worthy of the best efforts humanity has been required to deliver. As we see in the field of viral and genetic research, the leap from the biology of the past to microbiology is so daunting that it almost seems to call for a new alchemy to decode the secrets of these new dimensions. But problems like HIV remain problems thoroughly in the context of our time. We could also use the example of schizophrenia, where the biochemical base is similarly opaque. The complexities of these illnesses are, in many ways, like the aetiology of the economies of nations; biological scientists, central bankers and leading economists confess to being baffled by the loss of their ability to predict outcomes of their actions.

The reason that alchemy appears to be a comfortable metaphor as we search for solutions is that the issues appear so daunting that we lack adequate descriptors. From our viewpoint, some form of transmutation seems to be the only way we can address the things we see rushing toward us. The alchemists of the Medieval and Renaissance worlds understood that the transmutation of lead into gold was a metaphor for acquiring a heightened understanding of the nature of the universe.

Where we differ from the alchemists and their clients is that we have heightened conceptual and linguistic resources to address the problem of a quantum jump in the level of abstraction.

But the new era will not wait. Its time has come.

A long time ago, according to paleontologists, a fish they call Euthenopteron found itself impelled, maybe by the Lords of the Universe, to move onto land. Euthenopteron started a whole new trend — breathing air and walking around. Initially Euthenopteron felt like a fish out of water, but it worked out okay...

EPILOGUE

The Philosopher's Stone: How John Dee turned Britain into gold

This is the final, final chapter. In it, we return to a period that is useful for understanding our own time. We look at Dr. John Dee, a citizen of Elizabethan England who invented the British Empire and inadvertently built a new epistemology that became central to the conclusive stabilization of the Renaissance.

Dee would have understood the problems we face better than most managers of our own institutions. Dee's influence was such that he not only revolutionized his own time, but continues to make a difference to the world we live in.

One of the major differences between our own time and the Renaissance is that they have left us some useful notes. The historical sources they inherited, from the classical records of Greece and Rome and their archives of the Medieval world, were less than high in predictive value. This is why the Europeans of the 15th and 16th centuries needed Humanism as a framework for the Renaissance.

The most useful historical documents they left us describe their attempts to amend strongly held assumptions that had ordered the Middle Ages — whose old epistemology had to be abandoned whatever the cost. Few had any idea that they were addressing posterity because the documents most useful to us are their actual working papers, and they were too concerned with day-to-day survival to think about us. These working papers allow us to judge the necessity — and difficulty — of building a new epistemology.

The Renaissance was a time when people were asking "Why?" and having to work out their own answers, since the conventional wisdom of their authorities didn't even acknowledge the existence of the questions. Of course, the pitfalls that Western Europeans fell into and the occasional sign they had found a small piece of the real goods are a lot clearer from our vantage point. For them, without any experience or accessible history, the risks were immense. The "real goods" were frequently found inadvertently, while looking for something entirely different.

The concept of creating an epistemology may be still a little dim, yet most of us spend a fair amount of our lives working out personal epistemologies. W.H. Auden said it best in a letter to a young poet (quoted by Nicholas Jennings in *The New Yorker*, April 1, 1996):

"Ask yourself constantly and remorselessly 'What am I really interested in?' 'What do I know for myself?' 'What, in fact, are my experiences?' "

The answers to those questions are a personal epistemology.

JOHN DEE, THE RENAISSANCE MAN

One of the best guides to building a new world-view comes to us from Dr. John Dee. He was born in London in 1527 and died in 1608 or 1609. He has been described in many ways, most of them true.

The only mind of the early Renaissance that could play at the same table with John Dee's was Giordano Bruno's. You'll recall that Bruno was busted by the Inquisition for his only epistemological book, *Shadows of Ideas*. Dee was more than familiar with Bruno. It was from Dee's library that most of our knowledge of Bruno has come.

The Inquisition had been established in the 13th century in France and Germany to stamp out heresy. In 1478, Pope Sextus IV expanded the Inquisition to Spain and subcontracted the operational details to the Dominican order. In addition to the usual problems with heretics, this Inquisition was charged with investigating the threat to orthodoxy posed by cultural minorities. By 1492, the main trouble-makers had been identified: the Jews. So 1492 was not only the year Columbus became a poster child for ocean-blue sailing; it was the year the idea of ethnic cleansing was given intellectual authority. In 1502, Muslims were added to the list.

Contemporary records (which aren't all that great) suggest that in its first decade, the Spanish Inquisition burned 2,000 and "punished" another 15,000 people who had bad posture. We can only guess what the "punishments" were. The religious leaders of those days, when confronted by heathens and heretics, weren't the kind of people to shrug and say "sin happens."

We know that many of the Jews who were permitted to move to North Africa were penniless on arrival. Dee records, in his manuscript volume *Of Famous and Rich Discoveries* (1577), that a visitor to his house — a Ninevite, Mr. Alexander Simon — had suffered at the inquisitor's hands. Mr. Simon had been born in Mosul, in the Tigris valley, and had traveled in Orientall [sic] India, where he had managed to make some money — which he later lost due to "the rigour of the Religious Inquisition in Portugal." The Inquisition was a bureaucracy on the march, with a clear understanding of its place in the economic order.

In the case of Bruno, the inquisitor had only to hear a few ideas before making a decision. Doubt about the incarnation of Christ? Doubt about a finite universe? Doubt about whether Church fathers could possess authority? A new epistemology? No decent, fair minded, humble inquisitor had to go any further. It was all too awful. Toast him!

But John Dee could get away with having *everything* Bruno ever wrote in his library — as long as England remained Protestant. He learned from the fate of Bruno. Dee knew that if you were going to create the forms for a new epistemology, a lot of hand-holding would be required. He was also aware that there had to be something in it for everyone, because everyone would have their lives radically changed.

Dee was a true polymath. He was England's greatest alchemist and was so acknowledged by leading alchemists throughout Europe. He was also the first head of Elizabeth I's intelligence service. His signal, in all secret communications with Elizabeth I, was two zeros and a seven with the top crossbar of the seven extending to cover both of the zeros. Yes, John Dee was the original Agent 007.

Dee was educated in London at Chelmsford School; went on to St. John's College, Cambridge; and then became a founding fellow of Trinity College. While at Cambridge he became interested in magic, alchemy, astronomy, astrology, and medicine. He received a doctorate in theology. A tad tangential, you say? This spectrum of interests gave him access, formal and informal, to the best minds in Europe, who were trying to fill in the holes in a new way of thinking — Humanism. He was a Protestant and was drawn to the Reformation because it was more compliant with his own views of Humanism.

As a young man, he became involved with some Protestant plotters who wished ill on Mary Queen of Scots, daughter and successor of Henry VIII, founder of the Church of England. She was a Catholic queen of England, widow of François II of France and, when she ascended the throne, she was the wife of Philip II of Spain. Dee, already a skilled alchemist, was alleged to have counselled his plotter friends on potions which would solve the problems of having a Catholic queen. After being sentenced to death for treason, he looked for a more salubrious climate and found it in Prague. There he became a court astrologer and supplemented his income by practising as a magus. He was also active as a cartographer, an astronomer, and a highly sought-after physician.

After Mary was ousted from the English throne, Dee was invited home by Elizabeth I to name the most astrologically propitious day for her coronation. Once she was crowned, he became her court astrologer and spent most of his life advising the Privy Council of England. He would have, had he lived today, been a "policy consultant" to senior levels of government, or a project leader at a think-tank like Rand Corporation.

Years later, when Elizabeth lay dying, it was Dee for whom she sent. (She wanted more potions, one suspects.) Dr. Dee was, if nothing else, eminently practical. He advised his royal mistress to move out of Whitehall, a drafty place, and into Richmond Palace "as a warm winter box to shelter her old age."

The reason Dee is so important to us is his polymathic character and the integrity with which he went about his many coincident careers. He was a military analyst of international repute, and his understanding of economics was similarly respected. His explorations and rationale for expanding the realm into imperial Britain were assisted by his skill as a cartographer. He planned the retrofit of the British navy and reorganized the tax system so efficiently that teachers of economic history have documented his efforts as a case study for students of that depressing topic. He was a lawyer, having "studied the law" at the prestigious Louvain University.

He was frequently called on as a political analyst, but he was considered a gifted theologian. That was important when he came to consider practical issues about expanding the evolving Humanist epistemology. He understood that, in order to transfer and expand the new knowledge of the Humanists, it was necessary to know the classics better than did the classicists and not to be sucked into some apparently easy hermetic solution to knotty political or economic questions.

He had the greatest private library in England and he was generous in granting access to it, constantly loaning his unique items to leading scholars, merchants, and people in government. His concern with educating the whole country for the future was such that he continually lobbied government and business leaders to set up regional public libraries.

Dee's thorough knowledge of the classics, combined with the solid intuitive sense that came bundled with Humanism, allowed him a greater access to the finest minds of Europe on both sides of the Humanist-classical controversy than probably anyone else.

It is fortunate for us that among John Dee's wide-ranging involvements was an interest in transferring the knowledge of Humanism to as wide an audience as possible. He understood the need to make the Humanist view of the world accessible to English society. He understood the economic benefits that would fall to the first nation state that adopted the massification (or, in the currently popular term, democratization) of Humanism.

His sense of synthesis allowed him to successfully blend true classical knowledge with the new intellectual strategies that were the hallmark of the mature post-Erasmus Humanism. This homogenization was built on a strategy of using an astrological grammar to port the best of the classical world into the Humanist environment.

THE INCLUSION OPTION

For we who live in another Renaissance, the appearance of indeterminacy and the incremental process of commercialization of the quantum universe remind us to follow Dee's example and look for congruence among the fundamental discoveries that underlie more prosaic techno-shifts.

What is really important in our time is that, as the real discoveries turn into accessible technologies, we must begin to expand and *democratize* the meaning of the world we are in the process of discovering. This was the reason for the expressions of contempt earlier expressed toward economic illiterates who urge censorship.

In the Medieval world, sacred literature and art were far more influential than profane forms. But the Renaissance had a greater need for secular literature, particularly in the new sciences. The Renaissance had printing, which distributed new ideas on cheap paper, unfiltered by Church authorities and confusion about what constituted heresy.

The Medieval world did not see thrift as a virtue. Manorial wealth was used to maintain a network of friends and allies. When children reached the age of reason, boys were sent out on their own to bolster the territorial state,

---

Try comparing Dee to someone in our own time who, as a young man in the 1960s, hung out for two or three years with his peers. For those years he devoted a lot of time to smoking pot, imbibing LSD, nibbling mushrooms, contemplating the works of Herman Hesse, and having a lot of free sex at anti-war rallies while listening to rock 'n' roll. Sometimes these events occurred simultaneously.

He might easily become fascinated with computers in such a milieu and manage to get a job with a computer company because he passed the industry's psychological tests for differential problem-solving. Our former hippie would have been fascinated that the tests were so easy and fun.

He quit his job in the early 1970s when he saw that the most optimistic marketing projections were normally 500 percent to 600 percent below actual sales — and that those substandard projections were actually the highest figures that bankers considered realistic. He went on to found, perhaps with friends, a computer, computer-related, or software company and then discovered he no longer had the time to spend eight hours a day in the cosmic consciousness. Besides, his job was more fun than being stoned.

Now he has many millions of dollars and his banker speaks of him reverently. We would not see our young millionaire as being all that unique. If someone were to criticize him for his youthful indolence and drug use, such words would not come from an investment banker. There are, as the reader is aware, literally thousands out there who, to varying degrees, fit this description.

and girls were married off to allies or potential friends. Wars and pandemics resulted in periodic labour shortages that brought about anti-mobility laws just at a time when social and geographic mobility was essential for economic development. In this climate, the old order — the manorial economy — pushed for laws requiring rural labour to remain in villeinage or serfdom. These laws were unenforceable and when they were rigorously applied became arbitrary and effectively placed the legal system itself in disrepute.

Thrift may have not been a virtue in the finite manorial economy, but it certainly appealed to the new middle class, whose visions always exceeded its purse. The Protestant message of frugality and prudence was couched in religious terms that showed these were the very characteristics God had in mind when the topic of salvation came up. So Protestantism was the moral high ground they were looking for. (In our own times, some political lunatic will always try to call this "class warfare.")

This was the world faced by the Privy Council of England, the elite group that advised the Queen and essentially ran the country. The institutions of the Middle Ages were in disarray or teetering on the brink. England was surrounded by enemies and chronically broke. Most of the Privy Council had been classically educated and now faced a world profoundly changed from the one they had been educated for. They needed someone who understood the new era and could take a long look at policy goals.

The council was doing a good job of recruiting wealthy leaders from the new middle class. Among them was Sir Edward Dyer, whose family fortune had come from the cloth trade. John Dee was known to Dyer and trusted by Elizabeth. Dee had the best library in England, and everyone in the Renaissance was a bibliomaniac. Sir Edward was a graduate of Balliol College, Oxford. It is unlikely that any member of his family had recently been dropping bolts of cloth into steaming vats of pungent dye or mixing pigments. (Dyers could be readily identified in the streets of Medieval and Renaissance Europe because of the many hues that adhered to their skin in a period when bathing had not received the attentions of modern marketing.)

Dyer became Dee's lifelong patron and, more importantly for England, gave him a role as an advisor to the council. (In 1576, Dyer became the godfather of Dee's only son, Arthur.) Along with Dyer, Lord Burghley (the Treasurer), and Sir Francis Walsingham (the Secretary of State) were probably Dee's main government contacts.

Dee believed the country would never be safe from its enemies until its financial fortunes were reversed and stabilized. Throughout his life, whatever Dee did, in whatever of his myriad interests, you can be sure that at the kernel of each activity was one part that connected to all of Dee's other undertakings. That was to secure England from continental threats. The best way to assure England's sovereignty was to make England wealthy. In the case of England's immediate impoverishment, Dee solved it, for the short term, by using the cloth trade as a new tax base. This choice of a new stable revenue stream for the government was so successful that within 50 years, the term "woolsack" had become a metaphor, appearing in almost every European language, to denote the quality and power of England's economy.

Dee himself was much too busy to become rich. As a result, like most major Renaissance thinkers, he was constantly in search of patrons who would enable the magus to buy books and feed his family. Dee was good at making others rich; the other side of that coin is that the hermetic tradition said the magus could not use his powers to enrich himself. He could mix up a love potion for a patron but never seemed to get laid himself. Throughout the hermetic literature, there is a wistful overlay in which the immature magus wishes he could have a normal life.

Let's look at how John Dee established the groundwork for a new epistemology for the Renaissance. Dee understood that when an era is changing, successful societies take some of their more robust institutions with them. As a master of the classics, besides being well-versed in hermetic philosophy, Dee could select institutional values that were worth the trouble of taking along.

Dee discovered that taking institutional values through the transition gates between eras was a luxury easily discarded when the price became too high. One of the institutions that Dee believed was worth protecting and bringing along was the monotheism of Christianity — in this case a Protestant Christianity. It rejected the fatalism that would leave the Islamic world with some unfashionable baggage. Christianity had already made it through two era shifts and had demonstrated not necessarily a willingness to change, but certainly an ability for adaptation and durability.

Another institution that had the appearance of mobility was the parliamentary system of England. Ever since the Magna Carta days, it had managed to bring in and absorb the new middle class and make taxpayers out of them.

After a few minor jobs for the Privy Council, Dee's first major move was to suggest that what Elizabeth needed was an empire. This was pretty radical for the time, and divided the business community. There were those who suggested the books could be balanced nicely by raiding the ports of the Spanish Main. Another school of macroeconomic thought was that the Queen could issue a few more letters of marque and finance a few new slaving expeditions. The proponents hoped to trade with the Spanish colonies without doing any of the work of actually running the mines.

In 1570, Dee published a book which has been long overlooked by many otherwise informed Renaissance historians. Its full title is *Brytannicae Reipub[licae] Synopsis: libris explicata tribus. Synopseos* ~~*Politicae*~~ *Adumbratio. à*

Joanne Dee. L[ondinensis]. Designata: A⁰. 1570. You will usually find it referred to simply as the *Synopsis*. The recipient was most likely Sir Edward Dyer.

Dee left us a pile of manuscripts written, usually, at the behest of the Privy Council. The conventional view of Renaissance historians (the smoking gun lies at the door of Frances Yates) is that there were a few Dee manuscripts and they didn't really matter because they were passed hand-to-hand and had no visible influence. But too many Dee manuscripts have surfaced in too many tangentially related files. There's also the not inconsiderable matter of the mores of the times. Elizabethan England's movers and shakers weren't very contrite, humble, polite, or understanding when an outsider criticized the way the realm was being managed. When Dee wrote something that was sure to be upsetting, all that happened was the Privy Council asked for more.

In the *Synopsis*, Dee's views of political essentials were pretty clear. In one section he vehemently came down against expedience. The chapter entitled "Welth" [sic] is subtitled with the Latin epigram *Nihil est utile, quod non sit Honestum* (Nothing is expedient which is not honest).

In this section Dee presented an analysis of the economy in a tabular or point form (a form of instruction popular with the Humanists, called the divisive or dichotomous method).

- The cloth industry had lost its vitality and ability to significantly contribute to revenue generation.

- There was entirely too much debasement of the M1, and coin-clipping was rampant. (As we saw earlier, that problem wouldn't be solved until another Trinity old-boy, Isaac Newton, took it in hand.)

- There was little work being created for the poor, and they were laying about being idle. Dee was not being mean-spirited: he was worried about national morale and believed that everyone should be gainfully employed.

Reading this kind of history is fun, but you have to be careful how you follow the trails. For example, some British historians, like Frances Yates, have suggested that Dee fell into disfavour after 1589. This supposition is based on a quality of mystery assigned to a trip Dee took to the Continent that year. What mystery? Dee was famous throughout Europe.

In 1590, when Dee's daughter Madinia was born, her godparents were Ursula, the Lady Walsingham; Sir George Cary; and Anne, Lady Cobban. Five years later, Dee had another daughter, Margarite, and at her christening the godparents were Lord Keeper Puckering, the Countess of Cumberland, and the Countess of Essex.

True to the divisive style, once Dee had catalogued the sin side of the ledger, he moved to the other side, where things showed some hope.

* Exports were doing well and being carried abroad on England's ships.

Dee was concerned that as the economy improved, the results should be reflected in every purse in the land. He was ambitious about what we call the balance of trade and recommended that imports should never rise to more than one-fifth to one-quarter of the value of exports.

If we look at this in a linear way, we've managed to get near the end of the 16th century and the British seem to be adapting to the violent social shifts of the Renaissance. We should take a look at how the rest of Europe was coping — or, rather, failing to cope.

If they had had polling systems back in the last quarter of the 16th century, pollsters apparently would have found that most of the English were pretty secular and indifferent to what the state religion was. What they didn't like were Spaniards. Thousands of young Englishmen would fight the Spanish in the Netherlands wars of independence with the full support of their government.

The English had been busily absorbing the new middle class into the community. We've seen that English institutions were surprisingly open to the new artisans and others, like the middle-class merchants and lawyers. Elizabeth's Privy Council had six or seven members who were not of the traditional nobility.

Henry VIII had turned England into a Protestant Country, but his eldest daughter, Mary, was a devout Catholic. Her husband, Philip II of Spain, told her to return England to Catholicism. Mary tried, but was deposed and subsequently executed by her sister Elizabeth. Any talk of England being Catholic again was treason as far as Elizabeth and the Privy Council were concerned.

(Dee was 68 when Margarite was born. Maybe we should rethink his adherence to that rule against recreational self-medication for a magus.)

Dee in disgrace? Not with those kind of folks — a privy councillor, a VIP court official, wives of privy councillors of the most influential kind, and two countesses of the realm — showing up at the church to guarantee to protect the souls of Dee's daughters in times of need. These people were Elizabethan survivors who could smell political risk from great distances. Dee was still influential. He met and ate regularly with the establishment. He wrote to the Queen frequently. He spent too much on books. There was revenue there.

A large part of Mary's problem was that Philip kept telling anyone who would listen that England was a province of *his*, just like the Netherlands. The consensus among historians is that England might have been willing to be Catholic again, but the idea of becoming part of Imperial Spain did not sit well in London. Not even the remaining English Catholics supported that one.

IMPERIAL SPAIN DOESN'T FLY

In 1588, Philip II sent an Armada of 130 ships, 20,000 soldiers, and about 8,500 sailors to invade England. They had a skirmish with an English fleet commanded by two former farm boys, Francis Drake and John Hawkins.

The reason for Philip's invasion was first to put a stop to English support for the Protestant rebellion in the Netherlands and, second, to punish the English for executing Philip's wife, Mary. After briefly running into the English gentlemen, the Armada hit a storm that drove it around Northern Scotland, where many ships were wrecked, and on to Ireland, where the rest of the fleet foundered. That was the beginning of the end for Philip and family.

Having the head office of the Inquisition in Spain was not the coup it had seemed in the mid-16th century. After burning a lot of Jews and taking all the money from those Jews it allowed to emigrate to North Africa, the Inquisition started in on the Muslims — Spain's best trading partners. Oh well, not to worry. The Spaniards had a rich new empire.

But paying for a navy that would keep Drake and other like-minded Englishmen away from Spain's galleons became a drain on the petty cash. Then the Protestant English, under pressure from their own Protestant hard-liners, recognized that the Dutch Protestant freedom-fighters in the Netherlands were engaged in a just cause and deserved help from the British. Hence the Armada. In 100 years, Spain would be under new management with Philip V, from the cadet line of the French Bourbons.

THE ITALIANS DEVELOP GEOGRAPHY TROUBLE

Italy was doing very well except for problems relating to the papacy's inclination to wear two hats. As if the papal headgear wasn't heavy enough, there was the hat of being secular ruler of a confusing collection of territorial states. The northern Italian city states were vulnerable because they were right on the invasion route when the likes of Charles V, Holy Roman Emperor and king of Spain, wanted to unite Italy and win the right to elect his own popes.

From an invader's point of view, infiltrating Italy via the north had a number of benefits that can be summed up in one word: booty. Those wealthy city states that had spawned the Renaissance could be captured, producing pillage and all the other good things an army enjoys when it takes a foreign city. An invader could pay for his army simply by invading from the north, where the cities usually offered bribes to keep the invader's army out of town, plus food and weapons to get on with whatever bigger goals the invaders had in mind.

The Protestant movement didn't do very well in Italy. Instead there was the idea, much favoured by various northern city state leaders, to quit being uncouth, déclassé, two-fisted merchants and bankers. The heirs of the Sforzas, the Medici, and Borgias decided that, even though they could buy a pope from time to time, their status would get a definite upgrade if they joined the nobility. This self-promotion was usually a matter of an appropriate marriage or a simple title purchase.

At first glance, the idea of authenticating the descendents of the Northern Italian Renaissance by absorbing them into the European aristocratic gene pool might have had some attractions, but it certainly had some downsides. The northern Italians had been invaded so often that they had made an art form out of looting their latest conquerors. This helped make Italian politics, up to the present, a theatre where the main feature is gratuitous violence based on a uniquely opaque form of political pluralism.

WHY ARE THE FRENCH SO DIFFERENT AND SO AWFUL?

At first, France seemed well on its way to becoming a Renaissance success story. From the middle of the 15th century until later in the 17th century, France had hundreds of representative local assemblies. The central government was tricameral, composed of the King, the bishops, and a representative body, the *Estates General*, which drew equal representation from the nobility, the clergy, and the bourgeoisie.

Kings like François I, who established the French nation state, seemed to have dragged themselves out of those disgusting, impulsive barbarian traits that were the hallmark of Medieval rulers. François was, by all accounts, a pleasant enough person. A scion of the Valois family, he married the daughter of Louis XII, but inherited the throne at a time when there was a strong rivalry with the Austrian Hapsburgs.

The first and only battle François ever won was with the Swiss, which made him the proprietor of Milan. That should tell us a lot about the end the Lombards had found for themselves. He was nominated to succeed Maximilian, the Holy Roman Emperor, but lost the election to a Hapsburg, Charles V. François didn't have the toughness of mind or body the electors were looking for. They were offered a choice between a wimp and a thug, and even the best-intentioned elector needed only look to out his window to realize that the times did not call for a wimp.

Charles V started rampaging over Lombardy, completing the destruction of the Northern Italian Renaissance that the city states' various corruptions hadn't already gotten to. Charles's flaw was that he had access to the Lombards but couldn't read the runes. He financed his invasion with a spreadsheet that assumed just-in-time looting, raping, and pillaging.

François I entered into a pact with Henry VIII of England, Venice, and the pope to oppose Charles V. It wasn't great diplomacy. The deal was that if the armies of Charles needed to be fought, François would do it while the pope, the Venetians, and Henry cheered for him. He began an intermittent war with the Emperor, but was captured and spent a year in a Madrid prison. It cost about half his territory to win his release.

François was a strong supporter of learning and the arts. There was a Humanist idea floating around that the unification of all knowledge would be a good idea, and about 100 years after the discovery and description of perspective, a professor at the University of Bologna, Delminio Giulio Camillo, figured out a system to do just that. He called it the Theatre of Memory. Delminio's idea involved a special theatre in which a speaker would talk on the world's knowledge. Topics would be cued with various art objects suspended on risers, each moving into view to coincide with the speaker's presentation. Delminio's scheme sounds like a living database, much like those chess games in which castle courtyards were paved with coloured squares and living people played the part of the pieces. (Historian Frances Yates' *The Art of Memory* describes Delminio's work more fully.)

François built the Theatre of Memory for Delminio, who had spent 25 years shopping the project. François also provided aid and sustenance to Erasmus and other Humanist scholars in Paris when no other patrons were in sight. On the other hand, François was the first to persecute the Protestants. He also authorized a massacre of peasants in the course of a mild serf revolt.

François tried to combine the romantic chivalry of the Medieval world with a genuine desire to foster learning, exploration, and culture, in keeping with his acute sense of intuition about the importance of the arts that Humanism offered via the Renaissance. He built one of France's better tourist attractions, the palace at Fontainbleu. François I had good instincts about Renaissance values, but he wasn't tough enough to be a Renaissance leader. (Imagine trusting the solemn word of the Doge of Venice, Henry VIII, and the pope. Nice, but stupid.) He somehow left the throne intact to his son, Henri II, but the cash box was empty.

Henri solved the cash crunch by marrying 14-year-old Catherine de'Medici in 1533. With the money problem resolved, he amused himself with mistresses and wars, retaking Calais from England. When he came home, his mistress, an enthusiastic daughter of the Church, urged him to get into activities of a more stable nature.

On her advice he started to pillage the Protestant Huguenot communities — which was pretty stupid because, as elsewhere, they were the new middle and artisan classes and the only ones earning and thus creating money. More importantly, his anti-Huguenot games eventually led to the wars of religion. His sons let their hair grow long and started a rebellion against him; that romantic feudal gene was spilled all over when Henri died from wounds he received in a joust. Three of his sons would become kings of France.

Henri II's son, François II, had been betrothed to Mary Queen Of Scots when she was six, but he was a sickly child and died in 1560, a year after inheriting the throne. Mary went on to marry Philip II of Spain, while François II's brother, Charles IX, inherited the French throne. The best thing that can be said for Charles was that he did love his mother. He made a place for her in the inner councils of the government so that the poor widow would feel useful.

Catherine was a Medici and the Medicis had a gene that drove them to power, mediated by the Medici definition of duty. The tendency was powerful, and girls inherited it just as easily as boys. Catherine was no exception. She advised her son that it would be a good thing to wipe out the remaining Huguenots and purify France. His younger brother, later Henri III, also loved their mother and ordered the well-run massacre of Parisian Protestants on St. Bartholomew's Day, 1572. After Henri's decisive handling of the Huguenots, his mother decided he should upgrade his executive experience, and she arranged for him to be elected King of Poland. The gig in Poland didn't go too well. Henri had to get back to Paris on family business and had barely left Warsaw when he was deposed. On his returned to Paris it turned out to be all for the best because his brother, Charles IX, died, and Henri had another coronation in 1574 as king of France.

During the Dee period in England, Germany was a collection of jealous, feuding principalities that lacked any possibility of cooperation. Few consultative bodies ever established a sense of continuity or amassed a cultural convention of beneficial consultation and/or a legislative body. One key component in the land-mass that would become Germany was that over the course of the 16th century, more than 30 German princes, dukes counts, et cetera (plus one Holy Roman Emperor) were sufficiently clinically insane to be isolated from affairs of state. The German culture has always had a problem with what to do when the beloved leader is wacko.

H.C. Midlefort's Mad Princes of Renaissance Germany deals with this topic in far more detail than anyone could imagine necessary.

The religious wars continued with increased ferocity. Even Henri and his mother noticed that the rental properties were underperforming and began to speak well of bringing peace to France, eventually naming Henri of Navarre — a Protestant — as Henri's successor in 1584. The Catholic League, fearing that the king had become soft on the cause, organized a rebellion in Paris and authorized the assassinations of Henri and Catherine for supporting heretical movements. Henri, in turn, had the head of the league assassinated and joined with Henri of Navarre to retake Paris from the Catholic League in 1589 but was himself murdered by a monk, terminating the Valois gene pool, except for a catalog of the usual bar-sinister claimants. On his deathbed he confirmed Henri of Navarre his successor.

Henri of Navarre was the first Bourbon and also a Protestant. He inherited a kingdom that was economically and geographically in ruins after 50 years of religious civil war. Unfortunately, his mother was Catherine de'Medici's equal in terms of taking a determined and impetuous approach to a religious cause. In the case of Henri IV the adjectives are the same — just substitute Calvinist for Catholic.

Henri had been leader of the Protestant forces since 1569. In 1572, he became king of Navarre and married Marguerite de Valois; the bride wore white, while he — more the traditionalist — wore pistols, a sword, and a knife. He managed to avoid the worst of the ensuing St. Bartholomew's Day massacre by experiencing a timely conversion to Catholicism. Even as a new believer, he was imprisoned at the French court, but he escaped after three years and recanted, claiming that the massacre option had impaired his ability to conduct due diligence on the conversion.

Henri of Navarre defeated the forces of Henri III at Coutras in 1587 but later came to Henri III's aid against the Catholic League's revolt. He defeated the remaining League forces and their Spanish allies by 1590, though he didn't enter Paris until 1594 — after giving up Protestantism again, reputedly remarking "Paris is well worth a Mass." Henri dictated the Edict of Nantes, which guaranteed full rights for the Huguenot minority.

There were no little Bourbons from his union with Marguerite de Valois, so he divorced her in 1600 and married another Italian import, Marie de'Medici. All that Protestant schooling paid off when he handed the job of rationalizing the state's finances to the Duke of Sully, who would have thought Newt Gingrich a wimp. Sully restored the nation to a non-credit watch position while Henri conducted a foreign policy that won plaudits from his contemporaries, who regarded him as a great conciliator. Henri was also known for the slogan "a chicken in every peasant's pot every Sunday."

When war seemed imminent with Spain again, Henri had Marie formally crowned because she was to be regent in his absence. The next day, Henri was assassinated, allegedly by some fanatical Catholic sore loser.

(One lone killer? It could have been the Protestants — he did treat the Catholics fairly and took advice from some Jesuits. It could have been some other band of Catholic activists playing out an internal power struggle. It could have been Philip II of Spain fearing the effect on Spanish dissidents of the accolades the Bourbons were getting for good government. It could have been the Spanish army, seldom noted for being combat-ready, fearing Henry's undivided military power. It could even have been the House of Medici — after all, who needed Henri IV when Marie had the royal seal?)

In Europe prior to 1560 (except Italy), almost every kingdom was governed by a implicit understanding of close and sympathetic consultation between a small group of civil servants who served the king, and various local representatives. It was these groups who implemented political policies involving fiscal intervention in the economy, military policies, and affairs with other countries. The Europeans were learning how to run a nation state.

France led the rest of Europe in this process until, bereft of the Huguenots — who would have brought to the table an understanding of the relationship between the Renaissance and the Reformation — the French leadership decided to go for an absolute monarchy.

Across the channel, the English were assembling an exercise in constitutional evolution, making a virtue of not locking themselves into a formal, written constitution. But the French were falling apart.

France had a vibrant, representative, inclusive system in which the infrastructure of the monarchy assumed the cooperation of all other spheres, since everyone recognized that the system depended on harmony. There were effective municipal councils and very functional provincial assemblies. It was working — and the French threw it away. After 1614, the *Estates General* would not meet again until the revolution of 1789. A working assembly could have provided a forum for building a new epistemology step by step, with everyone effectively consulting with everyone else before making any precipitous moves. But the inability of the nobility, the powerful clergy, and an increasingly wealthy bourgeoisie to resolve their competing world-views led to disaster.

ABSOLUTISM'S ABSOLUTE FAILURE

Louis XIII, son of Henri IV and Marie de'Medici, was only nine when his father was assassinated. At 16 he overthrew his mother and went into the Bourbon king business. He turned to a tried and true formula of national disunity, counselled by the wise and helpful Cardinal Richelieu. He nullified the Edict of Nantes and attempted to suppress the Huguenots, with limited success. More and more French Protestants were emigrating to England and Switzerland, where a Calvinist tradition had become established, if some mob didn't get them first. Almost as if in the grip of a national death wish, France drove out its indigenous source of the benefits that came with the Renaissance and Reformation.

The wars of religion so devastated France's economy and social structure that the *Estates* had supported a temporary takeover by Henri IV. Louis wanted nothing to do with any kind of consultative legacy. He believed, even as the forces of the Renaissance progressed through Europe, that Bourbon absolutism would keep France secure. Richelieu's idea was to make France Europe's sole superpower, absolutely ruled by the king and absolutely run by him.

Then, in 1643, came Louis XIV, who made the big retrograde step and gave the Bourbons the bad name they retain to this day. By the time he became king, the fractious representatives of the three *Estates* couldn't agree on a room in which to have a meeting.

Louis XIV inherited as his *éminence grise* Jules Mazarin, an Italian-born layman with a keen eye for running countries, who had been fast-tracked to the rank of cardinal by Richelieu. Louis, whom no one has ever accused of having the brains needed to paint road dividers on a residential street, was just smart enough to recognize a power vacuum. Louis liked being an absolute monarch, and the constituent parts of the *Estates General* breathed a sigh of relief — they thought they were off the hook. There was some-one in charge!

The nobles were able to get away with recalcitrance occasionally, but only when they combined with the Huguenots or artisans. Mazarin was as much a religious political player as his mentor, Richelieu, and the religious estate wasn't likely to make deals with the nobility, let alone the bour-geoisie, while Mazarin was around. By the middle of Louis XIV's reign, Mazarin had put together a revenue-generating tax base and an army that was firmly in the hands of the king. But the revenue stream was not suffi-cient to support a standing army of any use.

Jean Baptiste Colbert succeeded Mazarin as Louis XIV's first minister. In 10 years he reorganized the colonies and the treasury, made the king the patron of a national scientific institute (similar to the British Royal Society), and supported technological innovation. Colbert was the general France used to oppose the structure England's John Dee had set up. Colbert organized a new maritime ministry, but Dee's reorganization of the British navy was sufficiently advanced that Colbert could not catch up.

Colbert's new colonial administration gave the state a large share of the revenues produced by the colonies. He did not neglect the *Estates General*. He effectively bribed the nobility with patronage and pressured the Huguenots to either die or leave. He made sure the largest burden of the reorganized tax system fell on the peasants. All of this emphasized the severance between the *Estates*. The classes represented in the *Estates General* were closed out of the loop of power.

This closing of the loop barred urban artisans and rural peasants from the social mobility that was so essential to converting the Renaissance from chaos to a middle-class revenue-production machine that believed in the possibility of further upward mobility. To use a military metaphor, Colbert was constantly fighting a rear-guard defensive action while on the march, dividing his forces to prop up the absolute monarchy while competing commercially against the long-term offensive strategy of Dee's British imperialism. Ask any military strategist: a fighting retreat is about the most unlikely road to success there is. Colbert also failed to consider the outcome of this manoeuvre on his domestic tax base.

It was Louis XIV and Colbert who arranged the guarantee that Louis XVI and his wife, Marie Antoinette, would lose their heads. In two reigns, France whittled away the best representative government in the world and traded it in for an absolute monarchy. History is not very forgiving of that

---

Today, France's political commentators use the term "Colbertism" to describe the many benefits of a government that is deeply centralized. France has one tiny elitist school that refurbishes the civil service each year and supplies France's top 200 businesses with their managerial class. It is called the Ecole Nationale d'Administration, and there is no better place in the whole world to get imbued with a devout sense of Colbertism.

In November 1996, the French opposition media began to suggest that the ENA curriculum committee had become lax in its course in chauvinisme. This is the course that requires the student's most diligent attention, because in these studies the student demonstrates the "right stuff" and justifies the selection committee's faith in the original admission.

With 1997 leading into an election, the ENA's graduates showed a startling commitment to Colbertism. Observers particularly enjoyed the sight of a corporate, bureaucratic, and political elite running around trying to flog Thomson, the flagship of France's defence and electronic industries, at an unjustifiably low price, under the table, to a French conglomerate called Lagardere.

Then Lagardere was caught by the E.U.'s privatization commission offloading Thomson's multimedia division to Daewoo, one of the solvent Korean conglomerates. The gnomes of Brussels, in a fit of pique, slapped the wrists of the French and rudely suggested that anyone who was privatizing anything had to give the deal to the highest bidder, who would, hopefully, be European. Foul rumours persisted that the whistle-blowers in this matter were those Dutch Huguenot-related enemies of French greatness at the Philips Electronics group.

kind of blunder. (J. Russell Major, a Johns Hopkins University historian, gives a clear picture in his 1996 book *From Renaissance Monarchy to Absolutist Monarchy* of the decline of France from great power to whining Eurospoiler.)

Earlier, it was argued that some kind of democratic process was essential to surviving an era transition. It would appear that the real purpose of making sure all the stakeholders are involved in the era shift is not some abstract political theory. Rather, democratic systems, as crude as they are, are meant to guarantee that everyone who wishes to be involved is included in a forum exploring amendments to the governing epistemology when it starts to break down.

You don't call it an "epistemology" — that would discourage participation. But when you discourage people from investing in your economy, when you treat fundamental discoveries frivolously, or when you censor ideas, you are losing out. When your political system attracts only self-serving bureaucrats and politicians whose egos challenge those in the theatrical industry and who have no understanding of power management, you are on a slippery slope. That's really being burdened with unwieldy baggage, and attempts to capture the new era from such a position have always — like the Bourbons — been doomed.

In 1789, the misery of France's urban and rural poor led to a revolution that finally terminated the ruling class. The absolute monarchy that began with Louis XIV had lost the consultative resources that come with an elected assembly; Louis XVI didn't miss the consultations an assembly might have provided because he had never used the day-to-day skills of dealing with disagreement while holding the respect of all parties. The French Revolution destroyed any institutions that might have helped ease a catch-up period. French intellectuals rushed to co-opt various revolutionary governments that kept devouring each other until Napoleon brought in the Corsican élan necessary to make everyone to settle down.

We have seen how France was so ready to succeed the Lombards that the daughters of the Medici were set up to marry any French king who came along needing a wife and money. The Medici were in total agreement with the French nobility that consultative authority was not a good thing. This made it impossible to deal with the Protestant Reformation except by all-consuming civil wars. The Bourbons managed to take over Spain and it, too, fell victim to an inability to deal with the Reformation. Spain lost control of the Netherlands and was unable to defend its fleet or colonial ports.

The absolutist states were never able to take advantage of a mobilized middle class. They also missed all the benefits that the merchant class bestowed on England and Holland, where the Protestant middle class expanded and flourished while fattening its economic and political franchise.

The next time you hear a French politician whining that the Internet is an affront to France's honour and status as a great power because it works in ASCII (which can't handle all the accents needed to write French), remember that the French gave away the structure before anyone had ever seen a computer.

DEE DESIGNS AN EMPIRE

Dee's skills as a cartographer led him to consider empire as the route to English security. He was in correspondence with geographers like Gerardus Mercator, Gema Frisius, and John Harpsfield. The mental pictures all those maps gave him were not merely routes for a ship to travel, they outlined an empire that would be secure from the chaos he anticipated on the continent.

Some narrative historians suggest that ships' captains like Sir John Hawkins, Sir Walter Raleigh, and Sir Francis Drake were the founders of the British Empire. They were important, but their crucial function was to carry out the plans of Dee. (Dee made a mistake in his dealings with Drake. He claimed he had rediscovered the formula for Greek Fire, the mythical fireballs hurled by the Athenian navy at their enemies. Dee claimed he had recovered the "secret" and given it to Drake who, Dee wrote, "had become a pyromaniac" and spent his time searching out Spanish galleons loaded with gold and silver.)

Beginning in 1570, Dee wrote a number of monographs, reports, and other documents setting out the evidence for Elizabeth's lawful right to occupy and hold a wide range of lands. Elizabeth was a Tudor, and the Tudors, having had problems with clear title to anything, were meticulous about their documentary evidence. (That snag about their regal legitimacy was always being brought up by the fortunately diminishing Plantagenet loyalists over that Bosworth Field battle that brought Henry VII to the throne.)

Dee's sources were not all that pristine, but it was always nice to find that in the past someone had said something in your favour that no one else had contradicted. Dee's purpose was to give the Queen and her Privy Council justification for the English imperial designs that Dee was putting forward. In these documents (known among historians as the maritime writings) Dee sets out to prove that there were precedents, from both classical sources and more recent medieval commentaries, for the existence of the "British Empire as it hath bene; Yea as it, yet, is or, rather, as it may & (of right) ought to be..." That sample of Elizabethan English was turned up by William Sherman in his excellent recent work, *John Dee*. Here's another that comes from Charles Merbury in 1581 — it gives an idea of the impact of Dee's proposals:

it is no small comforte vnto an English Gentleman, finding him selfe in a farre countrey, when he may boldly shew his face, and his forehead vnto any forren Nation: sit side by side with the proudest Spagniard: Cheek by cheeke with the stoutest Germane: set foote to foote with the forwardest Frenchman: knowing that this most Royall Prince (her Majesties highnesse) is no whitte subiecte, not inferiour vnto any of theirs. But that shee may also (if shee plaise) chalenge the superiorite both ouer some of them and ouer many other kinges and Princes more. As maister Dee hath very lernedly of late (in sundry tables [i.e. maps] by him collected out of sundry auncient and approved writers) shewed vnto her Majestie, that shee may justly call her selfe LADY and EMPERES of all the Northe Ilandes.

This is a merchant of Elizabethan England who has wholeheartedly accepted the Scholastic argument that Dee constructed to justify the British Empire.

In his *Brytanici Imperii Limites* (quoted here from Sherman), Dee writes:

Nowe (at length) ame I come to my chiefe purpose, of some Recordes settinge down; which will be found sufficient, for to stire vpp yor Ma^{tis} most noble hart, and to directe you^r Godlie consciense, to vundertake this Brytish discovery and recovery Enterprize, in yor owne Royall Intereste: for the great good service of God, for yor highnes immortal fame, and the marvailous Wealth Publick of yor Brytish Impire.

We should at this point make something clear. When an advisor employed by a government pumps out a major shift in national policy, it is addressed to someone and was commissioned by someone. In this case, Dee had been devoting most of his time to maritime issues, a specialty of Sir Edward Dyer, Dee's patron. Lord Burghley, as the de facto treasurer of England, would have regarded the maritime portfolio as the golden goose of the realm. In contemporary terms, maritime policy was a cornerstone of defense, the treasury, and industry and trade.

While the *Brytanici Imperii Limites* was addressed to the Queen, Burghley or possibly Dyer would have first secured her permission to so address the document. When Dee says in the quote above "... the marvailous Wealth Publick of yor *Brytish Impire*" (italics added) our eyes should brighten. This means the policy had already been sold, to a degree. Elizabeth had agreed to receive the *Brytanici Imperii* and the sponsor(s) would have lobbied the rest of the Privy Council. Other interested parties would have been made aware of what was going on. If the Privy Council were to approve and the Queen were to sign and seal enabling legislation, piracy would be out, and Empire, with lots of colonies, would be in. If you were in the establishment and disliked the scheme, this was the time to find a councillor who would oppose it.

Dee's "British Impire" was an all-out break with the past. Previous empires had been based on the aspirations of a specific ruler. The Spanish Empire of Dee's day was known to contemporaries as Philip's Empire. The French Empire was seen as the king's property. We know from his other writings that Dee's theory of empire assumed that the nation could outlive any ruler. But he politely alluded to Elizabeth's Empire in public documents — had he exposed his full theory to Dyer or any other member of the Privy Council, they would have been less supportive. They were concerned with day-to-day survival of the country and their persons. The road to the tower was short, as many of their peers discovered.

We know that the arguments of the *Synopsis* and the *Brytanici Imperii Limites* were so compelling that they were adopted without dissent. People like Charles Merbury started to say "Why not?", and the Privy Council decided that Imperial Spain would lose its status if Spaniards couldn't protect their galleons at sea or their colonial ports. Elizabeth issued more letters of marque and exclusive trading rights to buy the time England and the Privy Council needed if Dee's plan, which would take years, were to be implemented.

INVENTING INVESTMENT

The invention of the means to institutionalize investment was one of the significant developments of the mid-16th century. Institutionalizing ownership is a complex idea, but it is essential if you want a strong economy. It is a powerful abstraction, because it allows people who share a similar vision, much larger than any one of them could realistically aspire to or afford to pursue individually, to carry out that vision.

In other words, just like a perspective-based painting, the joint venture company empowered individuals to expand their visions. It gave the new nation states a means to harness the creativity of individuals and to create a legal notional entity (a legal fiction) to pursue economic goals. Identity is a curiously human phenomena. We draw our self-definitions from resources *external to ourselves*. This allows us to differentiate our interests and values from those held by others. It also means that we have no trouble treating other parts of the environment as "otherness." When trade ventures reached a size or risk-level that required multiple partners, it was an acceptable idea to treat the partnership as a legal entity in itself.

Dee had come into possession of some rutters that provided navigation access to the whole Baltic Sea. That meant an experienced ship's captain-navigator could get to one of the land terminuses of the road to China. Dee's Privy Council friends were not the slow-witted types who needed a lot of explanation of the benefits of direct access to Cathay. No one knew where Cathay was, exactly, but no one wanted to admit that, so it went through the Privy Council like a hot knife through pig lard.

English-Asian trade and the problem of all the middle-men who were grabbing a piece of the action was a regular item on the council's agenda. What was needed, considering the risk-factor and the investor shortage, was a royal charter that would grant *exclusive* trading rights into Muscovy.

They didn't use the words "investor," "insider," "bondholder," "stake-holder," "stockholder," or "sucker" in those days. The term they used for investors in these companies was "adventurer", and among the original list of applicants for the royal charter for a trading company of "Adventurers Trading into Moscovia" in 1554 is the name John Dee. The rest of the list reads like a Who's Who of the leaders of the mercantile class, ship captains, the aristocracy, and the Privy Council. That solved the problem of those disgusting, avarice-driven middle-men. Once the charter was granted, if someone other than the Adventurers tried to trade with Russia, they were legally pirates.

The Tsarist government remained absolutist until 1917, avoiding the messiness of the Renaissance completely. The Russian Orthodox Church had an absolute monopoly on education and siphoned off any serf who was bright. As a result, the Reformation had no impact in Russia. The Byzantine power-sharing relationship between church and state did not break down, as Lenin never tired of pointing out. Stalin, having been educated by the church, was somewhat more direct in his dealings with them.

Russia never developed a middle class, because of the enormous percentage of the population who were serfs. A serf-based society, in its heart of hearts, knows that the maintenance of serfdom is really good for keeping the lid on. Factories? Not on your life. Labour-intensive rural lifestyles meant that there was no sense of community beyond an individual's village. There was no motivation to become middle class; social mobility for the masses is not part of any absolutist ruler's agenda.

When Stalin came to power, another absolutist regime was quickly installed. "Unions" for painters and writers guaranteed that Russians would not be exposed to experimenters like Duchamp. Russian writers have been isolated from the inter-change of ideas the West has wrestled with for 75 years. We, on the other hand, have freely imported their ideas. Russia may be locked into absolutism for anoth-er era. That's worse than losing.

The Privy Councillors among the Adventurers handled their jobs well and in 1568, the English ambassador was able to convince another absolutist ruler, Tsar Ivan IV (the Terrible), really a lovely person according to the company records, to authorize the company to trade with the Orient using the Volga River. More atrocious middle-men gone.

Does all this suggest that Elizabethan law had no conflict-of-interest legislation? Not at all — it was called treason. The records of the Muscovy Company go on interminably about the sole interest of the Adventurers being the economic welfare of Her Majesty (who had a nice share in her regal capacity). Besides, the conflict-of-interest problem, if it existed at all, was so minuscule that Francis Walsingham never saw any need to divert any of his slim resources from catching papist spies and traitors to set up a Serious Fraud Office. In the English Renaissance, many key events were tied in some way to the Reformation, or were even parallel with it. Because the Mercantile Age was so much a part of the English Renaissance, and social mobility was its hallmark, individuals saw their own interests as having a commonality with the nation's.

In its first year, the Muscovy Company's return on investment was over 500 percent. When you think about those returns, the approval of people like Charles Merbury does not seem out of place.

This patriotic venture was eventually closed down in 1649, when political intrigues in Tsar Alexei Mikhailovich's court reached a level of complexity that would curl your eyebrows. These machinations resulted in the company's agents and factors being expelled from Russia. Given the nature of Alexei and his minions' willingness to deal expeditiously with hints of trouble, they were probably quite happy with a simple expulsion order.

The company had lasted nearly 100 years. When you consider the risk factors for any enterprise during the mid-16th to 17th centuries, then add the risks of sailing in the Baltic and working in Russia using Dee's maps and stolen rutters, the company's century of survival borders on the miraculous.

ALL ABOARD

Dee was also responsible for something else that is important in our own time. He was deeply concerned that England educate the entire population in Humanistic doctrine. Dee knew that if the Humanist revolution was to work, in the long run it would have to make the new knowledge accessible to larger portion of the population then anyone had ever considered educating before.

Education meant democratizing England. Dee knew it, and the Privy Council knew it. That's why all those English public (private) schools were started around then. The new merchant class and the established orders who had the wit to invest their spare cash in successful ventures of the new middle class wanted their kids to have a modern, Humanistic education, not the anachronistic classical training of their parents.

The plan was certainly grandiose. Remember, only about 8 percent of the population of England could read by the 1580s. (Out of that 8 percent, there was one who wasn't getting a very well-rounded education — no astrology and no alchemy. Thank heaven he was out in rural Stratford-on-Avon and wouldn't be getting in the way.)

Across the channel, the one thing Richelieu, Mazarin, Colbert, et al., never considered was easing the means of social mobility for everyone, from the nobility to the unspeakable bourgeoisie, the urban artisans, and even the labourers and rural peasants.

Frederick the Great of Prussia (1712-1786) once was asked how the average person might respond to one of his campaigns. He said: "Why should war be a matter of concern to some merchant or peasant? War is the business of soldiers and rulers. The merchants and peasants should only go about their business." By Frederick's time, Dee's British Empire was showing a growth curve that made the Muscovy Company's returns look like a pilot project. The new British middle-class were swarming through the corridors of power, and the power-brokers were eagerly consulting them.

The invention of the British Empire was not an ideological response by Dee, or the Privy Council, or Elizabeth I. It was, in Dee's mind, a logical response to the quantum jump in abstraction brought about by the discovery of perspective. The bill of exchange and double-entry bookkeeping meant that trade became a means of producing greater national wealth. The discovery of the telescope and other tools of navigation gave merchants effective instruments of commerce and exploration, if they could get rid of enough Medieval baggage to understand what Dee was saying.

An empire meant a mercantile country had a powerful instrument to distribute surplus trade goods and services. (Elsewhere, governments managed these systems.) If you have a territorial state in a finite universe, there is no means to grow except by war with your neighbours or military alliances. But a mercantile nation state can grow via the sale of goods and services. You just need individuals who understand exploration and trade.

John Dee's prescient, information-packed mind set up the infrastructure that effectively gave Britain a series of empires with room for all of the stakeholder classes Britain was turning out.

One empire in the Caribbean and North America was principally based on settlement and commerce. That meant second, third, and fourth sons had some options other than the navy, the army, and then the church.

Another empire was in Asia. It was based on conquest in India and market-controlling trading centres like Hong Kong and Singapore. Settlement of Australia and New Zealand bound them to the British Empire. Parts of

Africa were an economic empire based on extraction of raw materials and the sale of commercial goods. The Middle East, which initially controlled routes to Asia, later turned out to have oil, which would dominate the global economy.

Just as had the cloth trade of John Dee's time, Imperial Gilts absorbed the accumulated wealth from industry and commerce that gave the City of London world leadership in financial management.

The shift of the values and institutions of the Medieval world to the world of the Renaissance was extraordinary. Our own transition appears much more daunting. We are moving into a quantumized world, where the anchors of the nation state are more fragile than were identifications with the territorial state. The bulwarking institutions of our national identities are apparently more corrupted than the Medieval world could dream of.

If you plan to encourage the continuation of your gene pool, you cannot allow your schools to run an educational system that won't demand that children learn their language, doesn't demand understanding of math and sciences, and treats history as a bad narrative in which heroic figures are role models for the current ideology. That kind of educational system is what you get when you lack a working epistemology.

ANOTHER DAMN ABSTRACT IDEA — THRIFT!

In the Middle Ages, a noble family provided housing, food, a winter cloak, footwear, and a bolt of cloth to their retainers. The shortage of currency meant that, were the lord seen to be inequitably sharing the resources of his territorial state, his political legitimacy would be at risk. If the appearances of equity were absent because the feudal lord was intent on the accumulation of non land-based wealth, it would provide the retainers with a feeling that the lord was not treating his feudal obligations seriously.

Were these inequities to continue, the retainers would believe the feudal system of interactive obligations was being breached. Breach of feudal responsibilities was the one thing that allowed disloyalty as an option, and the lord could wake up to find that his knights and estate infrastructure had just taken an oath to serve a neighbour who had come to call with siege machinery.

One of the key reasons that Medieval historians treat Henry VII of England — the first Tudor monarch — so sympathetically, and the reason he could secure the necessary support from friends and allies to defeat the Plantagenets, was his high reputation for feudal stewardship.

As the Renaissance rolled in, the economy shifted, and the need for larger capital investment pools became apparent. The idea of the feudal leader assuring equity of distribution of the territory's goods and services collapsed, as did feudal loyalties.

In the Renaissance, the Humanist ethic elevated thrift as a necessary tool of financial management. The rewards society offered went to those whose skills involved a sense of inquiry and some knowledge of applied mathematics. If those applied mathematics included a sense of thrift, you could become rich.

"Thrift" was even more abstract than the bill of exchange. The Protestant theological shift to treating thrift as a religious virtue amazed Catholic thinkers. They were sure that this treatment of fiscal management ran so much against established values that the heretical Protestants had done themselves in. (Some argued that God was causing the Protestants to destroy themselves with the meanness of their frugality. The Church fathers also noted another danger of thrift — the falling off of bequests and beneficences.) Instead, the Protestants invested their money and came to control the West's economy.

The Medieval world's emphasis on a finite universe was so strong that it found economic growth a difficult idea to grasp. But once a nation threw off finitism it became prosperous. Such nations also provided their citizens with meaningful work. Economic growth was principally an urban phenomenon, and the proceeds of that meaningful work *belonged* to the citizen. The citizen's life, in turn, was no longer circumscribed by the local castle and village. Rather, it was related to the wider community of the nation state, which encouraged social and geographic mobility.

Nations that clung to the Medieval epistemology, in which thrift had no meaning, chose to recover the classical world's idea of conquest through a revival of the romantic values of chivalry. By excluding thrift, this strategy isolated most of the population, who remained immobile and locked into forms of serfdom. It is little wonder that nations who chose the absolute

---

The word 'meme' serves as a pretty good summary statement for this book. The late Timothy Leary recognized the importance of the word; net surfers and the editors of Wired and Mondo 2000 use it almost promiscuously, as do most science fiction editors.

It was coined by Richard Dawkins, the eminent Oxford evolutionary theorist, in his classic 1976 book, The Selfish Gene. Dawkins has worked on the idea through various publications, including his other major book, The Blind Watchmaker. By and large, other biologists were too busy digesting or vomiting the selfish gene concept to latch onto the meme idea. By the mid-1980s the evolutionary biologists began to realize that Dawkins's meme might be more important.

Simply put, a meme is a cultural tool that makes human adaptation and evolutionary progress more effective. Among nature's creatures, humans are unique for their invention of cultural artefacts as tools of adaptation.

monarchy route discovered themselves foundering in a confusion of feudal loyalties competing with economic opportunities embargoed by religious and royal taboos.

It was John Dee who worked out the idea of an empire as a vehicle to drive an economic system. He also made sure that the benefits of the empire were widely distributed and that social mobility was built into the system. He saw quite early that the new middle class could be defined in educational terms, and devised a way to keep this route open.

His plan unintentionally assured that the crown would remain as a stabilizing national force, but that the monarchy would be a constitutional one. The "official opposition" to the pirates were the first wave of an establishment middle class: the Puritans. They became offended at the lack of commitment of the wealthy risk-takers who, like most entrepreneurs, were unlikely to put the cash that went through their hands into a retirement fund.

The Puritans, on the other hand, took thrift as a serious theological issue and eventually became the government.

In our time, we assume thrift is a good thing. There is an entire industry based on it. Retail bankers, home mortgage lenders, pension funds, and insurance programs are a key component of our daily lives. Our governments even deduct an amount from our salaries to assure minimal resources are there for our old age. Our assumptions about thrift are so pervasive, we find it difficult to imagine a time when it was not part of the normative epistemology.

When Protestant theologians made thrift a religious imperative, they did so with full awareness that their constituency, the new artisans and other middle classes, was already there. These were the people who invest-

---

The meme idea was picked up as a useful notion, particularly by computer and other high-tech explainers, as the high-tech gurus found themselves defending their technologies from accusations of wrecking the family, destroying jobs and whole industries, and giving the FBI the tools to spy on everyone.

For these defenders of cyberspace and beyond, a meme is like a virus (benign or fatal) of idea(s) which sweeps across human (gestation too short for adequate DNA-based development) populations via advanced communications tech, and results in cultural mutation(s). Rock 'n' roll music is a meme. An absolutist ruler is a meme — a deadly one. The semi-conductor chip is a meme. A video game is a meme. The term "the pill" is a meme for reproductive technology.

A meme is a cultural artefact that becomes widely adopted when it is useful, or acts as a warning device when the survivors see the casualties.

ed in shops, mercantile ventures, and the invention and manufacture of new tools. They had a clear idea that savings made them wealthier, and they separated their personal funds from the monies assigned to business ventures. Profits reinvested meant not only an improvement in their substance, but a visible sign that they were pleasing God.

Like our Renaissance forebears, we are faced with an expanding universe that offers us a rich but challenging future. It is easy to marvel at the wonders of lasers, the DNA molecule, and the all-pervasive computer chip, and it is easier to believe that these are only the start of a shift in the assumptions about how we will work in this new world. The laser, the chip, and molecular management all work. They have all been constructed on quantum theory.

It is comforting to know that Richard Feynman, certainly one of the five most important physicists of the 20th century, said frequently, "Nobody understands quantum mechanics."

Just as the Renaissance required the concept of "thrift" to build a workable epistemology, we must invent similar building blocks for our epistemology. If you thought that some international congress of philosophers was going to gather over spring break and give us the answer, forget it. The philosophers won't come in until it's all there in bits and pieces, and then they'll argue about what fits where.

As a beginning, you might take a look at the word "meme." It has the feel of a term that wants to be part of a new epistemology. Then again, maybe it's just another buzz word.

In chapter 21, you heard about a dead fish whose evolutionary offspring at one point branched into a strain, some of which were successful, called placental mammals. It seems only fair to end this book with further recognition that the most significant science being done today comes from evolutionary biologists. This work is going to radically affect any epistemology we cook up.

POSTING ODDS: WINNERS AND LOSERS IN THE RENAISSANCE

Dee rethought the whole concept of an empire in non-classical, non-ideological, non-territorial state terms and he shifted the role of empire from aggrandizing a single leader to a new historical perspective that emphasized stewardship.

But how did England, an island nation of 3.5 million people, become the big winner in the race to capitalize on the Renaissance? If we were running a bookmaking operation, what odds would we have given that the English would win?

Certainly, the Lombards had a head start on everyone else. Unfortunately for those northern Italians, failing to recognize how much of a threat they posed to the established order assured their own collapse. Their failure to distinguish how much their key discoveries meant in the longer term assured that they would not be the ultimate profit takers. Their *nouveau riche* leaders focused on becoming territorial state princes — this inability to move beyond managing city states, surrounded by hostile, insolvent territorial states, was their downfall. In their heart of hearts the Lombard leaders all wanted to be noble, not déclassé bankers and traders.

The Lombard leaders opted for bribing enemies and friends alike, and hiring mercenaries when they had to fight. They failed to recognized that the nobility was a meme for a collapsing social and economic system. Their city state governments were volatile and subject to frequent coups. Citizenry was reserved for an elite few.

They knew the Church was corrupt and thought that was a good thing. It meant they could buy religious support. The Church's attitude toward deviation from the finite Medieval world-view, enforced by a church-state alliance of the Inquisition, Holy Roman Empire, and the local territorial state, should have been enough of a warning.

It is noteworthy that there is a record of only one cardinal who actively resisted the Inquisition's assaults on the presses of the Tuscan plain cities in 1539. This was the Venetian nobleman Pietro Bembo (1470-1547), later Cardinal Bembo of Florence. Bembo was a true scholar and an authority on Renaissance prose and poetry in both Latin and Italian.

In 1539, Pope Paul III, who had made Bembo Cardinal, issued the results of an inquiry that found, among other things, that a number of profane, secular, popular writers (including Chaucer, Dante, and Boccaccio) had offended the Church by characterizing priests in lewd and lascivious positions in their work. Pope Paul asked the Inquisition to search out the offending works in various cities, and the Inquisition accepted.

The inquisitor assigned to Florence went to a printer's shop, where he expected to find some of the offending books. He found, however, that the printer had published Bembo's own works, and the establishment had the cardinal's seal upon the door. The inquisitor went to Bembo's house, where he advised the cardinal that he would have to remove his seal, since the inquisitor had to search the premises for offensive books and manuscripts.

Cardinal Bembo responded in an admirable way, which make him the first person to resist modern censorship. He said: "Get thee from this city hence, e'er I order my men to illuminate thy rectum with a red hot poker." (In those days anyone of quality kept a staff of loyal retainers to handle hot poker work.) We know about this event because the inquisitor wrote about it to Pope Leo from Naples, which is just about as hence as you can get from Florence. That's standing up to censors.

But back to our problem — Why England? Why not the French? Their absolute monarchy was an attempt to deliver the sureties of the Medieval world. If we are going to pursue our career as bookies, we can make money on suckers who bet on the French. The French looked good as quarter-milers, but more than a mile and their supporters had better have cab fare home.

The Germans were never in the running. The Iberian world had a Dominican-compatible culture that wasn't even up to the level the French had attained in understanding that the world was changing.

But these also-rans don't explain: Why the English? The Western world could have collapsed as the feudal-manorial world aborted under the weight of its own inertia.

The English had been extremely fortunate in their governments. To get the throne, the Tudors had to create alliances; it was a process of consensus building. After all, that is what modern democracy is all about. Those Tudor allies made it clear that they would not be all that reliable unless Henry VII could demonstrate that he had a good idea of what stewardship meant to the longevity of a ruler. The none-too-stable consensus partners had the Magna Carta on their side. Henry recognized that England was an island and needed a merchant navy to survive. Because he had trouble getting money, he used naval funds to arm and support this mercantile fleet, which created the infrastructure for a trading power.

Henry VII also did the best he could for an orderly succession by assuring that Henry VIII had the best education of any prince in Europe. (Bacon and Erasmus were among the royal tutors.) And as luck would have it, Henry VIII was a bright student.

Henry VIII was certainly the best diplomat of any European prince. He was politically astute and courageous. He managed to maintain an army at home, in the form of a militia that was domestically popular and would have been more than a match for any invader's combination of professionals and mercenaries. He recognized that a national church would allow him more manoeuvring room than he got from a distant and expensive papacy.

His daughter Mary allowed herself to become a tool of English papal supporters after the Protestants had established a national church that was surprisingly compatible with the culture of the country. The Protestants were also the majority of the population. They seem to have taken a hatred of the Spaniards into the national myth, and Spain became the straw-man that put England firmly in a mercantile, wealthy middle-class Protestant camp. Obviously, this majority got rid of Mary and brought Elizabeth I to the throne.

Elizabeth's government — the Privy Council — was *very good* as governments go. They brought on board the newly rich merchant-traders and middle-class lawyers. These lawyers were a new breed. They weren't trained as canon lawyers, civil law was their metier and the new commercial classes were their constituency. After all, as a dispute settlement device, canon law is a little incongruous when you have a Magna Carta. Even the King is subject to the law! They brought in John Dee, who was well known for his diverse abilities, to advise them on maritime events, cartography, taxation, and reorganization of the armed forces. That was over and beyond his Royal astrological duties and counter-espionage activities.

There is one thing missing from the English scene. Every European government of the early Renaissance tried to enshrine itself with some form of a written constitution. We don't know whether the idea of avoiding a written constitution was intentional, but the idea of a written constitution doesn't come up in England until the latter days of Charles I and is part of the process leading up to the Commonwealth. Instead the Brits enshrined "custom" in their "Common Law" — common law meant everyone.

Earlier, it was argued that anyone who wants to write a constitution at this time in history is either a lunatic, French, or an underpaid academic who wants to be a TV talking-head. (Jeremy Bentham made his living writing constitutions for newly industrializing European states, but that was in the mid-19th century, and a comparison of an 1850s map of Europe with a current map makes Bentham's career as a political entrepreneur suspect.)

Either by luck or foresight, the Brits managed not to saddle themselves with a written constitution, kept a common law that drew heavily on custom, and only changed the law when it was obviously flawed. It also gave them the flexibility to respond to unforeseeable events, quickly when they had to, while assuring continuity with reference to custom.

By binding everyone to a common law and bringing emerging classes into the main stream, usually via offspring who were admitted to the new colleges of Oxford and Cambridge, the English were able to take full advantage of the Renaissance. By the time Charles I tried to turn the clock back, the House of Commons was able to win a small revolution and play with a constitution. Cromwell chose the title of Lord Protector of England but failed to demonstrate he could spell "stewardship," which cost him his head.

From our vantage point, it seems impossible to write a constitution at this stage of an era shift. We certainly know now that the quantum era has just begun and our lives will be in turmoil for as long as the author or any reader will be alive. In the U.S., supporters of the ERA amendment might be moved to suggest that the odds on remedying social shifts are not very good either.

Canada has shown the world the folly of attempting to write a constitution. It's swell fun for politicians and otherwise unemployable lawyers, but no one else seems to care. U.S. President Richard Nixon was well known for his dislike of Canadian Prime Minister Pierre Trudeau. Nixon should have had advisors who could explain to him how vulnerable Trudeau was as a person. Trudeau's single agenda was to write a constitution that would legitimate the French fact in Canada. The people who gerrymandered that eventual piece of paper didn't have the slightest idea that within a decade satellites would make national borders trivial.

Earlier, we saw how Dee insisted that it was essential to bring as many people along as possible. Dee recognized that the nation's resources had to be fully mobilized. The stream of visitors to his house shows that Dee himself was indifferent to the station of a guest. His only interest was in the knowledge they brought. He assumed anyone would want to learn.

While Dee showed us that an era shift could be accommodated, his divisive tutelage reminds us that there is a sombre warning. We have better history than he had. We know what happened to those countries that chose to suppress the new knowledge, those countries that opted for censorship, and the leaders who decided they would entrench their absolute power. Even with our technology, there's no way to dig trenches that deep. The countries that decided against social mobility didn't come to a pretty end.

INDEX